# The
# ATLANTIC
# CROSSING
# GUIDE

## *Also by the RCC Pilotage Foundation*

### *Published by Adlard Coles Nautical*

*The Pacific Crossing Guide:* ISBN 0 7136 4442 7
(USA: Sheridan House Inc)

*South Biscay Pilot:* ISBN 0 7136 3698 X

### *Published by Adlard Coles Nautical*

*Atlantic Islands:* ISBN 0 85288 267 X

*Atlantic Spain and Portugal:* ISBN 0 85288 298 X

*North Biscay:* ISBN 0 85288 245 9

*North Brittany:* ISBN 0 85288 162 2

*Faeroe, Iceland, Greenland:* ISBN 0 85288 268 8

*North Africa:* ISBN 0 85288 155 X

*The Baltic Sea:* ISBN 0 85288 175 4

*Islas Baleares:* ISBN 0 85288 389 7

*The Channel Islands:* ISBN 0 85288 389 7

### *Published by the RCC Pilotage Foundation*

*A Cruising Guide to West Africa:* ISBN 0 95277 712 6

*South Atlantic South America:* ISBN 0 05277 710 X

*Falkland Island Shores* (and supplement): ISBN 0 95277 711 8

## *Other titles of interest from Adlard Coles Nautical / International Marine*

*Atlantic Pilot Atlas,* James Clarke:
ISBN 0 7136 3640 8 (UK), 0 07 011921 X (USA)

*Ocean Cruising on a Budget,* Anne Hammick:
ISBN 0 7136 4069 3 (UK), 0 07 158012 3 (USA)

*World Cruising Handbook,* Jimmy Cornell:
ISBN 0 7136 4419 2 (UK), 0 07 013396 4 (USA)

*World Cruising Routes,* Jimmy Cornell:
ISBN 0 7136 4838 4 (UK), 0 07 013406 5 (USA)

# The ATLANTIC CROSSING GUIDE

Fourth Edition

RCC Pilotage Foundation

Edited by Anne Hammick and Gavin McLaren

INTERNATIONAL MARINE
Camden Maine

ADLARD COLES NAUTICAL
London

Published by Adlard Coles Nautical 1998
an imprint of A & C Black (Publishers) Ltd
35 Bedford Row, London WC1R 4JH

First edition published in Great Britain by
Adlard Coles 1983
Reprinted with amendments 1984, 1985
Second edition 1988
Revised reprint 1989
Third edition published by Adlard Coles Nautical, 1992
Reprinted with amendments 1994
Reprinted 1996
Fourth edition published by Adlard Coles Nautical 1998

ISBN 0-7136-48392

Published in USA by International Marine
a division of The McGraw-Hill Companies
PO Box 220
Camden, ME 04843

ISBN 0-07-026032-X

A CIP catalogue record for this book is available in the UK from
the British Library and in the USA from the Library of Congress.

Typeset in Garamond, by Falcon Oast Graphic Art,
East Hoathly
Printed and bound in Great Britain by
St Edmundsbury Press, Bury St Edmunds, Suffolk

**Caution**

Every effort has been made to ensure the accuracy of this book. It contains selected information and thus is not definitive and does not include all known information on the subject in hand; this is particularly relevant to the plans which should not be used for navigation. The Pilotage Foundation believes that its selection is a useful aid to prudent navigation but the safety of a vessel depends ultimately on the judgement of the navigator who should assess all available information, published or unpublished.

**Charts and diagrams**

Where indicated, plans and diagrams were based with permission on British Admiralty Charts and Publications and where foreign information was used, permission was sought from the Hydrographic Services of France, Spain, Portugal, the USA and Canada.

## THE RCC PILOTAGE FOUNDATION

In 1976 an American member of the Royal Cruising Club, Dr Fred Ellis, indicated that he wished to make a gift to the Club in memory of his father, the late Robert E Ellis; of his friends Peter Pye and John Ives; and as a mark of esteem for Roger Pinckney. An independent charity known as the RCC Pilotage Foundation was formed and Dr Ellis added his house to his already generous gift of money to form the Foundation's permanent endowment. The Foundation's charitable object is 'to advance the education of the public in the science and practice of navigation'. This it does by publishing and revising pilot books.

The Foundation is extremely grateful and privileged to have been given the copyrights to pilots written by a number of distinguished authors and yachtsmen including the late Adlard Coles, Robin Brandon and Malcolm Robson; charged with the willingly accepted task of keeping the original books up-to-date. Present guides and pilots range from the Baltic to the West Indies and from Greenland to the Rio Grande.

The first entirely new work undertaken by the Foundation was the production of *The Atlantic Crossing Guide*, edited by Philip Allen and first published in 1983. The usefulness of such a guide was earlier pointed out by another member of the Club, Colin McMullen, who made available his extensive knowledge of the subject, and Philip Allen went on to do a magnificent job, most ably supported by his wife and fellow sailor, Plat, assembling a mass of information both personal to himself and obtained from a range of contacts with wide experience of the Atlantic and of ocean cruising in general. Since then techniques, gear, navigational aids, hazards, port facilities and a host of other factors have changed greatly, so that no less than four editions have been needed to keep *The Atlantic Crossing Guide* up-to-date. This latest edition has been edited on behalf of the Pilotage Foundation by Anne Hammick and Gavin McLaren, who between them have made fourteen transatlantic passages by a variety of routes and in many different yachts.

W H Batten
Chairman and Director
RCC Pilotage Foundation

## PHILIP ALLEN – AN APPRECIATION

Phil Allen was a man of talent and, though shy and hampered by a stammer, his charm immediately made itself felt. The talents most easily perceived by a stranger were his skill with watercolours and in gardening, if only because his house was full of the one and surrounded by the other. Sooner or later it might emerge that he was also a joiner, a technical draughtsman and a good seaman. Yet it would still be possible to miss the fact that he both designed and helped build his last yacht, *Tallulah*.

After retiring from a successful business career, Philip was able to take *Tallulah* to the Atlantic which he did most happily with his wife Plat, whom he met whilst studying art shortly after leaving school. *Tallulah* was one of the early yachts to cruise in the West Indies. When the Foundation started work on *The Atlantic Crossing Guide* money was short, and an editor had to be found who would give the very considerable amount of time required for no rewards other than the satisfaction of doing the job and being of service to cruising people. Philip's character and experience clearly made him the candidate for the job.

Though not a professional writer he had a shrewd idea of the work involved and only took on the task after considerable hesitation. In a roundabout way his stammer helped him hone his skill in writing. He devoted himself to the book. As an artist he was utterly ruthless in demanding the very highest standards from himself and from others. Based on his extensive experience of the Atlantic and through exhaustive correspondence, he produced a manuscript which others might have delivered to the publishers with relief as their final word. Not so Philip; being the self-effacing man he was, he insisted on circulating it chapter by chapter to his critical friends. And then, to incorporate all their suggestions, he started all over again.

The success of the original edition lay in Philip's insistence on perfection. The Pilotage Foundation is confident that this latest revision by Anne Hammick and Gavin McLaren will maintain the standard set by Philip Allen, who sadly died in 1990 at the age of 79.

O H Robinson
RCC Pilotage Foundation
Director 1986–96

# CONTENTS

## Part III - Port Information     115

Harbours selected as being suitable for landfall or departure and, where possible, having above-average facilities by the standards of the area.

## Appendices

# INTRODUCTION TO THE FIRST EDITION

I can think of few things more exciting (or at times more worrying) than preparing for the first ocean voyage, knowing as we do that anything forgotten, overlooked, omitted, or badly done may prove to be a matter of some consequence, and that, perhaps for the first time in our lives, we will be dependent entirely on our own resources for everything; when we get to sea there will be little chance of assistance, even if it occurs to us to seek it, should some disaster befall. As the months slip quickly by and the weeks then shrink to days, it seems as though those long lists of requirements which we have prepared with such care, have ticked off, added to, revised and redrafted again and again, will never be completed by the set sailing date. And the questions we ask ourselves (and others): Will the eggs really keep if smeared with Vaseline? Does the roll of new charts, clean and smelling enticingly of good paper and printer's ink, cover our requirements, with harbour plans of likely ports of arrival such as Crosshaven, Falmouth, Cherbourg in the east; or Barbados, mangrove hedged English Harbour, Newport and St John's in the west? Is there a spanner aboard to fit that awkward little nut on the bilge pump, or to service the roller reefing gear and alternator? Have we sufficient sail needles and twine, shackles, screws, rope, Primus prickers? And, above all, are we carrying enough water (suppose it does not rain) and food so as to be independent of the land for at least twice as long as we expect the passage to take? Do we have all we need for navigation, and the ability to use it with confidence when, for weeks on end, our only trustworthy guides will be the sun, moon and stars?

Then there is the broad overall plan to consider: which way to go, where to put in, how long will it take, and what will the weather be like? In earlier days, and I am thinking back more than twenty-five years to my first Atlantic crossing, information about these important matters certainly was available, but we had to search for it. For a start we read as many as possible of the accounts written by earlier small boat voyagers, a fascinating occupation which in the rush of today is often omitted, for not only did it reveal much of the character of each seaman/author, but told us which places he had found most suitable and enjoyable, which to avoid, and in general what kind of conditions he experienced. The big volume *Ocean Passages for the World*, first printed in 1923, was available with its lists of routes which experience had shown to be most beneficial to sailing vessels, and its pocket at the back bulging with route, current and rather sketchy wind diagrams. Most important of all there was that remarkable dogged collation of weather information provided by hundreds of thousands of ships . . . the US *Pilot Charts*, one for each month of the year for the north Atlantic.

To select the most advantageous route twenty-five years ago indeed took time and patience; but now, with the publication of this book, planning for an Atlantic crossing in either direction will be much quicker and simpler than it was in the day of Nutting, Long and Robinson, Mulhauser, O'Brien and Worth, for thanks to Philip Allen and his fellow members of the Royal Cruising Club, assisted by many others, including members of the Cruising Club of America, it will no longer be essential to do so much time consuming research. In this one volume will be found most of the required information simply presented and enriched with a wealth of individual knowledge and experience, together with much good advice on preparing the vessel, on stores, navigation and radio. It has a certain something, difficult to define: a love, I think, of small vessels and the people who sail them, an aura of confidence, and – this is the essence of the deep water community – a desire to assist.

How very much easier it would have been for Susan, my wife, and I and others of our day if such a comprehensive book had been available when we were preparing, a little apprehensively, to set out on our first Atlantic crossing.

Eric Hiscock, 1983

# PREFACE TO THE FOURTH EDITION

There is a strong element of responsibility in writing any book on which other people may depend. Updating an established and successful work such as this, which already contains the pooled knowledge and experience of some of ocean cruising's most respected figures' only adds to the feeling.

The third edition of *The Atlantic Crossing Guide* represented a major restructuring and reorganisation of the book as well as an update of the information it contained. On this occasion we have decided to leave that structure and organisation largely unchanged. The book remains, therefore, in three sections, each one dealing with a specific aspect of the preparation for and execution of a transatlantic passage. Minor changes have been made to the Appendices and some, which now seem unnecessary, have been deleted whilst a new one containing information on regional weather forecasts has been added.

Although the structure of the book has altered little, the content has undergone extensive revision. In the six years since the last edition some major changes have taken place in ocean cruising, in particular the almost universal adoption of GPS and the growing appearance of computers aboard, used both in sophisticated communication systems and for navigation. There is also a widespread, and growing, tendency to fit what might be termed 'domestic conveniences', ranging from fridges, now seen aboard more commonly than not, through watermakers, televisions and VCRs to microwaves and washing machines. These last two are still rarities, but less so with every passing month.

As well as, and partly because of, these changes the number of yachts crossing the Atlantic has soared, and their average size has increased as well. The pressure on space and resources in many traditional cruising ports is severe. However, this is not entirely the retrograde step it may initially seem – increased demand has led to greatly enhanced facilities and to new cruising grounds being opened up, while competition has often improved efficiency.

We have updated the *Atlantic Crossing Guide* to reflect these new circumstances. As might be expected, **Part 1 – Preparations** has seen the most obvious changes, but there have also been many in **Part III – Port Information**, with a few less useful ports deleted and others added. We originally envisaged that **Part II – Passages and Landfalls** would need little alteration, but even here quite significant amendments have been needed to reflect the increased capabilities of many voyaging yachts.

A transatlantic passage in a small boat is a major undertaking, and it is quite impossible to cover all its aspects comprehensively in a single volume. Even if every topic could be mentioned it would hardly be feasible to give each one the detail it deserves. We cannot even be certain that all the advice given is the very best possible, though we have made great efforts to ensure that it is. What we can say with certainty is that what is contained in this book is based on practical experience. It works. We have never sailed together, or even in company, but between the two of us we have covered most of the routes described, skippering yachts ranging from a 31 ft cruiser to a 55 ft ocean racer. Over the years one or other of us has visited all but two of the harbours described and used practically all of the equipment mentioned. But lest we appear immodest, we must both admit to our share of misfortunes too – and there are few cruising grounds in the north Atlantic where the imprint of one or other of our keels cannot be found somewhere.

Ocean cruising should be a pleasure rather than an ordeal and we hope that this book will help to make it so. We also hope that all those who put its advice into practice gain as much enjoyment, forge as many good friendships and suffer as few real dramas and emergencies as we both have in the last twenty-two years of transatlantic voyaging.

Anne Hammick, *Wrestler of Leigh*
Gavin McLaren, *Margaret Wroughton*
Falmouth, 1998

## ACKNOWLEDGEMENTS FOR THE FOURTH EDITION

Many voyaging yachtsmen and yachtswomen have given generously of their knowledge and time to assist with the production of this book. For this edition particular thanks are due to Bill Kellett (*Islay*), who organised and co-ordinated information from many of the Americans; to Hugh and Susan Cownie (*Keelson II*), who did the same for Chaguaramas Bay, Trinidad, a new port in this edition, and to John Melchner, who together with Erica Lowery enabled Annapolis, Maryland, to be included for the first time. Valuable contributions were received from many other people including: Peter Adam, UK Hydrographic Office; Harry H Anderson (*Annie B*); Sam and Maggie Bayliss (*Brilleau*); Ron Barr and staff at the Armchair Sailor Bookstore, Newport, RI; Jeremy and Ann Bradshaw-Smith (*Thetis of Tamar*); John Brooks; Warren A Brown, OCC Port Officer Bermuda; Amy Bull, Norfolk, VA; Calor Gas Ltd; David Caukill; Brian Dalton, OCC Port Officer Rockport, ME; Peter Deeth, Antigua; Tor Erling (*Godbonden*); Falmouth Coastguard; Paul Fay (*Faiz III*); Hugh and Angela Farrant (*Spring Gold II*); Edwin G Fischer; Colin and Marylyn Ford (*Nandisa*); Bill Fowler, OCC Port Officer Antigua; Ann Fraser (*Gollywobbler II*); Steve Grant, OCC Port Officer Halifax, NS; Jeremy Grindle (*Bowfin*); Mike Grubb (*Tilos*); Kitty Hampton and Simon von Hagen (*Duet*); Pete and Annie Hill (*Badger*); Glenn and Margaret Honey (*Juliet*); Alan Hooper, OCC Port Officer Grenada; Mo Jenkins (*Lucia*); Adrian and Barbara Kelly (*Kelly's Eye of Hamble*); Harold La Borde, OCC Port Officer Trinidad;

Ted Laurentius, OCC Port Officer Newfoundland; David Lumby, Viana do Castelo, Portugal; Ken Maisler, New York Nautical Instrument & Service Corporation; Allan Hopton, Marine Instruments, Falmouth; John and Sally Melling (*Duran*); Donal McClement, OCC Port Officers Norfolk, VA; Mrs Pat Miller, Millers Maritime Bookshop, Falmouth; Berni Mitchell; Graham and Margaret Morfey (*Flight of Time*); Guy and Mary Morgan (*Mor-ula*); Gary Naigle and Greta Gustavson, OCC Port Officers Norfolk, VA; Tim Norman-Walker, General Secretary, Royal Naval Sailing Association; Malcolm Page (*Tainan of Barkley*); Niki Perryman and Jamie Morrison (*Siandra*); Ben Pester (*Marelle*); Pat and Mike Pocock, OCC Cruising Information Service; Alistair Pratt (*Border Raider*); Kaye Price; Pat and Pippa Purdy (*Ganilly Rose*); Liz and Mark Scott (*Lone Rival*); D Scott-Bayfield (*Physalian*); Robin Sellwood (*Golden Chance*); Anna Stratton (*Mary Bryant*); Jon Trumble, Harbor Master Rockland, ME; David Whitten (*White Trillium II*).

Thanks are also due to all those who responded to letters, faxes and phone calls requesting information about their marinas and other businesses.

Even with the help of so many fellow yachtsmen, this edition of the *Atlantic Crossing Guide* would not have seen the light of day without the encouragement of Janet Murphy, Director of A&C Black; the firm but gentle chivvying of Carole Edwards, production editor; the meticulous work of Linda Crosby, copy editor; and Jennifer Johnson, creator of the new harbour plans as well as many of the older ones. The willingness of our RCC Pilotage Foundation 'boss' Scrap Batten to let us get on with the job in our own way has been much appreciated. We hope that his agreement for this edition to be a collaborative effort has proved to be justified. Finally, thanks are due to Georgie McLaren for her forbearance, encouragement and support.

## Photographs

Many of the photographs in this edition are new, and a colour section is included for the first time. A number were taken by the authors, and for the others we would like to thank: Michael Beaumont; The Bowman Group; Ann Bradshaw-Smith; Di Bralsford; Tom Doe; Falmouth Harbour Commissioners; Mike and Libby Grubb; Liz Hammick; Margaret Honey; Georgie McLaren; John Melling; Malcolm Page; Mark Scott; Anna Stratton; Jill Vasey; David Wallace.

*This book is dedicated to the memory of*

### GEOFF PACK

*voyager, writer, friend*

# PART I - PREPARATIONS

## 1   THE PHILOSOPHY OF OCEAN CRUISING

The most important quality in the ocean cruising skipper and his or her vessel is self-sufficiency. To some extent this may be said of anyone who ventures beyond the harbour mouth, but the coastal cruise will normally be planned around convenient harbours where water, fuel, provisions and, if necessary, repairs are available. Regular and accurate weather forecasts are also available when cruising within the home waters of most countries. Awareness of the need to become self-sufficient begins when, with growing experience, one ventures further afield only to run short of some necessity in a place where it is simply not available.

Self-sufficiency implies many things. First, that the yacht herself is sound and seaworthy; second, that she has a crew capable of sailing and maintaining her and who can make all normal repairs, both in port and at sea; and third, that she is equipped and provisioned sufficiently to avoid running short of any essential item before a replacement can be found.

The sound and seaworthy ocean cruiser must be more than just a strongly built hull that does not leak, with an efficient rig and good gear. Of course these things are essential, not only to avoid catastrophe but also to inspire those aboard with a reasonable degree of confidence in the yacht's abilities. But she must also be seakindly and must have an interior in which it is possible for her crew to live in reasonable comfort for extended periods. Whilst the average yacht spends most of her time at a mooring or in a marina, the ocean cruiser will spend weeks on end at sea and those aboard cannot exist for that length of time on snacks and the odd hot drink. Neither can they be expected to catnap in insecure sea berths. The most limited resource aboard the ocean cruising yacht is the energy of her crew, and without regular food and sufficient sleep this cannot be maintained.

Self-sufficiency is of course a relative term, and a small community, such as the crew of a yacht, cannot survive for ever without calling on outside help. The newcomer to ocean cruising tends to overstock in the anxiety not to run short in far-off places. With growing experience it becomes apparent that some things can be replaced easily, others with difficulty, and a few only at home. One learns, too, that a place that is good for one thing may be unexpectedly bad for others, that water does not always come conveniently piped, and that when something which is bound to be needed later is available it had better be bought while the going's good.

The ocean skipper must also have a certain determination, a resolve that once a task has been started it will be carried through to its conclusion despite the difficulties which will arise. Whilst most long distance cruising is pleasant and enjoyable, this will not always be the case. Some destinations may not be the paradise envisaged before departure – obstructive officialdom may cause frustrating delays or the anchorage may turn out to be overcrowded or untenable due to wind or swell. On passage, there will sometimes be bad weather to endure and inevitably there will be the occasional gear failure and breakdown to be dealt with. Such problems may seem overwhelming at the time, but they are seldom insurmountable and determination on the part of the skipper will overcome them. In retrospect they will usually seem insignificant in the context of the cruise as a whole.

A yacht capable of crossing oceans is a complicated and diverse piece of equipment, and those aboard must possess the skills to keep at least the more important aspects functioning. The idea that 'I'm just the skipper, he's the engineer, she's the cook' is long dead aboard cruising yachts, and every ocean skipper must be resourceful enough to look after all the vital equipment on board, aided when appropriate by a manufacturer's handbook or well illustrated manual. On a coastal cruise repairs to a torn sail, a slipping winch or a flooded engine can be left until the next harbour is reached, where expert help will probably be available. On an ocean passage these things will have to be dealt with by those on board – often by the skipper – usually in less than ideal circumstances and sometimes using improvised equipment and parts. He will have to be sufficiently resourceful to make at least temporary repairs.

A self-sufficient, determined and resourceful skipper will certainly be able to make successful Atlantic crossings, but he must also decide what type of ocean cruising suits him. His boat can be very large or very small, or of any size in between. She may be fitted with a vast array of the latest, high technology, mechanical, electrical and communications gear to make sailing effortless and to give all the comforts of home; at the other extreme she may have nothing more complex than a Primus stove aboard. For some owners it will be essential that she is fast and can make swift passages, but for others this is quite irrelevant. In some boats, the sailing is all important, with time spent in harbour tolerated only to prepare for the next trip. For other yachts the passages are chiefly a means to reach a new cruising ground. Some cruisers never spend more than a couple of nights in one harbour and visit as many parts of a particular area as possible, whilst others prefer to linger and get to know fewer spots more thoroughly. Some are sociable and seek out the popular places; others are happy with their own company.

Most prospective ocean cruisers will have little choice in some of these matters. The size of boat and budget and the time available may be constrained. On other aspects, you may already have strong views. But where you are uncertain – and have the choice – you should adopt a middle course. Choose a boat which is not too big, but not too small either. One that is not uncomfortably fast but not unbearably slow; that is not brand new, but not excessively old. Have some mechanical and electrical gear for comfort and convenience but not too much, lest it take over. Plan to visit a selection of harbours in a cruising ground, not just one, but not all of them either. Experiment with traditional techniques, such as astro navigation, but don't reject the modern alternatives.

This middle course will not be perfect. After experiencing a spell of ocean cruising, individuals will be able to improve upon it. By then they will have a clear idea of their likes, dislikes and priorities, of what they feel is essential and what can be dispensed with. But until that experience has been gained, the middle course is likely to be the best. At the very least, it will not be disastrously unsatisfactory.

To live aboard a well found boat and cruise in her over long distances is to experience a sense of independence and freedom that is almost beyond description. The petty annoyances of the land fall away, you live by the look of the sky, the feel of the wind and the run of the sea. As time goes on and experience is gained, both you and your craft become increasingly efficient, able to deal with any eventuality, and that sense of affection and empathy felt by nearly all long distance sailors towards their vessels begins to make itself felt. Putting to sea, while still a busy time full of anticipation, loses some of its overtones of anxiety and the prospect of an ocean passage is no longer quite as daunting as it once was. However, to reach this happy state you must observe the rules, which are simple but exacting: careful planning, good seamanship and vigilance.

In many of the Atlantic's cruising ports it is traditional for a yacht to leave a record of her visit. *Photo: Gavin McLaren*

There is no ideal type of ocean cruiser. Comparatively few yachts are designed specifically for ocean passage making, despite the claims made by some manufacturers. The majority of people who make long voyages do so in the boats that they happen to own at the time. Successful Atlantic passages have been made in yachts of almost every type and it is likely that a boat which has been cruised successfully in home waters for several seasons will be quite suitable. She will have the advantage that her owner will be familiar with her, and will trust her. The modifications she will need before an ocean voyage will vary according to her design; a yacht built purely with cruising in mind will need fewer changes than a cruiser-racer.

Similarly, a yacht's age is unlikely to affect her suitability. The majority of ocean going yachts are well past the first flush of youth and, providing they are structurally sound, yachts of almost any age should be quite capable of crossing the Atlantic. It is likely, however, that the older the yacht, the more work she will require before an ocean passage.

## The hull

Although the vast majority of yachts are built of fibreglass, other materials are equally satisfactory for long distance cruising. Steel is often quoted as the ideal hull construction material, and it is certainly strong. But steel boats under 12 m (39 ft) are likely to be heavy and the maintenance of a steel hull will be more time consuming than that of a fibreglass one. It is worth remembering that corrosion occurs more rapidly in warm water, and a steel (or aluminium) boat will need considerably more looking after in the tropics than she will in northern climes. Similarly, the owner of a wooden boat must be prepared to spend a good deal of time on basic hull maintenance.

Of whatever material it is constructed, it is vital that the hull is sound. This implies that a steel or aluminium boat has not become dangerously corroded, that fibreglass has not succumbed to serious osmosis, and that wood has no worm, rot or sick fastenings. If a boat has not had a survey for several years, then get one done at the start of the preparation process. Tell the surveyor your plans and ask him to look at the boat as a potential ocean (as opposed

Although the design is nearly twenty-five years old, the Rival 41 makes an ideal centre cockpit ocean cruiser, large enough for comfort but easily handled by a couple. *Photo: Di Bralsford*

to coastal) cruiser. Even if his inspection reveals no significant problems, the reassurance will more than justify the cost. It is more likely however that the unbiased eye of the surveyor will find some defects that have escaped the owner's attention. It will be far easier to rectify these before departure than to deal with them along the way.

Protection against worm is particularly important for wooden boats. Although attack by marine borers is possible in temperate waters, it is much more likely in the tropics and damage can be rapid and severe. Antifouling paint must be in perfect condition and will need to be renewed regularly. The underside of the keel is particularly difficult to paint, and it will be rubbed off by even the most minor grounding. Consider having this vulnerable area sheathed with copper or fibreglass.

### Skin fittings

Every hole in the hull should be protected by a seacock; below the waterline this is essential. Seacocks should preferably be of the bronze cone type, although ball valves are adequate if they are made of suitable materials. (In the interests of reducing costs some builders fit ball valves more suitable to domestic water systems than the marine environment. Although these may outwardly appear the same as the proper fitting, and may last a good while in northern waters, they corrode rapidly in the tropics.) Gate valves, which are operated by turning a handwheel, are sometimes seen. Although cheap, they are unreliable, and if they must be used at all it should only be above the waterline. Unlike a proper seacock, it is impossible to tell by looking at them whether they are open or shut, they are particularly vulnerable to corrosion, and almost invariably leak a little.

Whatever type of skin fitting is used it must be in good condition. Each one should be stripped, examined and renewed if suspect. All seacocks should be dismantled, cleaned and greased regularly – a good rule of thumb is to do this every time the boat is antifouled.

Hoses connected to seacocks need periodic replacement and if reinforced plastic hose has hardened it should be changed. Double hose or jubilee clips of good quality stainless steel should be used to secure hoses to skin fittings, and softwood bungs in a range of sizes to fit every through hull aperture kept handy. Ideally, each fitting should have its own plug attached on a lanyard, ready for immediate use in an emergency.

### The stern gland

The stern gland is one of the most frequent sources of leakage, partly because access is often poor and adjustment difficult. If it is of the traditional type, the packing should be replaced before departure to ensure plenty of scope for further adjustment, but if on inspection the propeller shaft is significantly worn, no adjustment of the gland will prevent leakage and the shaft will have to be repaired or renewed. Spare packing of the appropriate size should be carried. The stern greaser needs to be turned regularly while the boat is motoring so it must be installed in an accessible position; it should be large enough to limit refilling to an occasional chore.

The more modern design of stern gland relies on two perfectly smooth discs – usually of ceramic or carbon materials – pressing against each other to maintain a seal. One disc revolves with the shaft whilst the other, con-nected to the hull, remains stationary. These seals are maintenance free, and, if correctly installed, are completely drip free. Eventually the discs become worn and the complete unit must be replaced, an operation which requires partial withdrawal of the propeller shaft. There is little warning before failure occurs. The manufacturer should be able to give an approximate life of the seal (in terms of engine hours) and if it seems likely that this will be approached during an extended cruise, the seal should be replaced before departure. A spare seal should be carried.

Most engines are flexibly mounted and the stern gland must accommodate the movement of the shaft that results. Normally this is achieved by connecting the gland to the hull using a short length of heavy rubber hose, secured with double hose clips. Failure of this hose will cause severe leakage and it cannot be replaced without withdrawing the shaft. Unless its condition is beyond doubt, it should be replaced before departure.

### Decks and hatches

Once certain that water cannot enter the hull from below, the possibility of it doing so from above must be considered. A watertight deck, cockpit, coachroof and hatches are essential for safety – and for comfort too. Few things can spoil the enjoyment of an extended cruise so fast as continuous wetness below decks.

The deck must be leak free. This may seem obvious, but there are a huge number of potential places where water can enter. Fastenings through the deck and topsides secure headsail tracks, stanchions, winches, hatches, chain plates and a host of other fittings. Their watertightness is dependent on the sealing method and material used. Sealants have a finite life and all will eventually need replacement.

Wooden decks need more looking after than do other types, particularly in the tropics. They should be protected from the sun as much as possible and never allowed to become really dry – a sluice down with salt water morning and evening should be the rule. The seams will need attention from time to time; however, a complete recaulk is a major job, and if it is likely to be necessary it should be done before leaving. Teak laid over fibreglass, metal or plywood makes an attractive deck, comfortable to walk on and initially watertight. But when leaks do occur in such decks, it may be hard to identify their source. Water can travel between the teak and the base material for some distance, emerging into the accommodation far away from the fitting whose faulty seal admitted it.

Although it is rare for the cockpit to be completely filled during heavy weather it is a possibility that must be considered. In such conditions it is likely that the motion will rapidly throw a good deal of the water back out, but much will remain and the cockpit drains must be adequate. Look at the size of the cockpit in relation to that of the boat as a whole – a larger boat is better able to cope with the weight of water in a big cockpit than is her smaller sister. Cockpit lockers are notorious as a source of leakage in heavy weather and a lot of water can get below through them. They must have stout lids, good seals and strong hinges and clasps to secure them in bad weather.

A bridgedeck between cockpit and companionway is a great source of structural strength, but even if there is no bridgedeck the companionway opening should not

A simple bar to protect the propeller will come into its own in New England waters, where lobster traps abound.
*Photo: Gavin McLaren*

extend right down to the cockpit sole. If possible, there should be a permanent barrier up to cockpit seat level. If this is not the case then consider temporarily sealing in the lower washboards when on passage. Washboards must be strong, and those that drop into slots should be capable of being secured or released from both the cockpit and below, with lanyards so that they cannot be lost. There should be at least one strong exterior attachment point for harness lines within reach of the companionway.

Hatches must be so well secured that there is no possibility of a hatchcover being ripped off by a powerful sea, and they must not leak. Frequently it is not the hatch itself that leaks so much as its fitting on the deck, in which case removal and rebedding may do the trick. Opening hatches and portlights depend on rubber seals, which also need periodic renewal.

### Bilge pumps

Inevitably, a little water will occasionally find its way below, and at least two manual, high-capacity bilge pumps are essential. One should be operable from the cockpit (without the need to keep a locker open), preferably within reach of the helmsman, and the other from below. If an electric pump is fitted, it should be additional to, not instead of, these two pumps. Spare parts for all pumps should be carried.

No manual or electric bilge pump will be able to cope with the flow from even a minor below-water leak for very long – a fit man can pump about 90 litres (20 gallons) of water a minute, but he will soon tire. A large yacht or

one with a weak crew should consider fitting a large-capacity pump driven directly from the engine via a clutch; this is the only type of pump that has the slightest chance of coping with the water from significant underwater damage for any length of time.

## The rig

Just as there is no perfect hull material for a transatlantic cruiser, neither is there an ideal rig. Although the majority of today's boats are bermudan sloops or cutters, many schooners, ketches and yawls have made highly successful crossings. Gaff rig has its proponents and it may be better downwind. Modern materials have produced the unstayed mast and wishbone rig adopted by the Freedom class, whilst junk rig enthusiasts point out its simple, low-technology advantages; both these types regularly cross the Atlantic. One thing, however, is certain. Whatever its type, the ocean cruiser's rig must be well designed, regularly inspected and conscientiously maintained.

### Masts and spars

Both keel and deck stepped masts have their own advantages and drawbacks, and both have been well proven at sea. A keel stepped mast has at least some in-built support, and should it break will probably do so high enough to furnish at least the beginnings of a jury-rig. However, it is difficult to prevent leaks where it passes through deck or coachroof, and an older aluminium mast may suffer from corrosion at its heel. A mast stepped on deck is utterly dependent on the rigging for its support, and any failure there is likely to be catastrophic. While both types require considerable reinforcement below to prevent the hull distorting, usually a main bulkhead, a deck stepped mast should also have a kingpost to transfer its loading to the hull.

Aluminium spars should be checked for corrosion around every fitting, particularly those of stainless steel. It is quite possible for the aluminium to degrade unnoticed, until either the fitting pulls out under strain or the spar simply tears and folds. Mast steps are a great convenience, but do add to the weight and windage aloft and may snag halyards, although some designs are less prone to this than others. As a preventative, a lanyard is often run from each step out to the nearest shroud; an alternative is to run a vertical light line down each side joining the outermost extremities of the steps.

### Standing rigging

It is imperative to ensure that all standing rigging is above reproach as failure on an ocean passage may lead to disaster. The life of stainless steel wire is generally considered to be about ten years, although regular surveys may enable replacement to be delayed for a year or two. Failures most commonly occur where the wire enters a terminal and these points should be examined frequently. The fracture of a single strand indicates that something is seriously wrong and the shroud or stay should be replaced as soon as possible.

Either swaged or swageless terminals are fitted to the ends of the standing rigging. Swaging involves applying great pressure to the terminal in a special machine so that the metal is forced into the construction of the wire. Providing a conscientious operator using the proper machine has made them, swaged terminals are strong, but it is hard to tell a good swage from a bad one, as the defects are likely to be inside the fitting. Warning signs are ridging on the outside of the swage itself, or a swage that appears bent. Both are symptoms of a poor joint. Although the legendary 'banana swage' is seldom seen, any fitting showing even the slightest trace of a bend should be replaced.

Because the condition of swaged joints is so hard to assess, swageless terminals (Norseman or Sta-lock) are preferable. Although initially considerably more expensive, these terminals can usually be reused when the wire has reached the end of its life. Other advantages of this type of terminal are that it may be fitted in a few minutes with no special tools and can be dismantled periodically to inspect the condition of the wire inside. Even if swaged terminals are used, it is wise to carry a selection of swageless ones and some spare wire for use in an emergency.

Stainless steel is vulnerable to repeated bending stresses and it is essential that the load is straight along the axis of the wire and fitting. All masts move a little in relation to the hull and toggles accommodate this movement. These should be fitted between the bottlescrew and chain

Despite the preponderance of Bermudan boats, other rigs also make excellent ocean cruisers. Since her launch in 1980, the gaff schooner Mary Bryant has already made four successful Atlantic crossings. *Photo: Anna Stratton*

plate of all shrouds and stays and must allow complete freedom of movement. Stays upon which sails are set are subject to extra bending forces, as a glance up the luff of a headsail will show. It is essential that these wires be fitted with toggles at the mast end as well.

The fittings to which the rigging is fastened are as important as the rigging itself. The points of attachment of all standing and running rigging should be examined – chain plates (including those for forestay and backstays), sheet tracks and eyebolts. Satisfy yourself that they are strong enough in themselves, and that their anchorage to the hull or deck, and the way in which the loads are spread, is adequate. The fittings aloft are equally important and should be periodically dismantled and carefully examined. The modern 'ball and socket' mast fitting, in which a hook shaped terminal with a ball at its end is slotted into the spar, has failed so often that it is surprising to see it still used. It might be adequate for round-the-buoys racing, where the reduced windage it involves is advantageous, but has no place on an ocean passagemaker.

Any terminal, mast tang, chain plate or other rigging component which has ever sustained damage must immediately be suspect – even if returned into apparently perfect shape it may have invisible faults which will weaken it seriously. Short of testing to destruction, it is difficult to check the state of older stainless steel fittings, although some new electronic techniques appear promising, and a surveyor specialising in the subject should be fully up-to-date. At the moment, however, the advice must be to inspect rigging regularly and to replace it periodically.

Do not necessarily heed the old advice that the rigging of a yacht bound across the ocean must be increased in size. This may have been true with galvanised wire, where increase in diameter gives a greater margin against corrosion. But the designer of a modern yacht will have specified the stainless rigging as part of a complete system. Increasing the wire size will disrupt that system; for example, the compression on the mast may be increased beyond the safe limits for the particular aluminium section used. Moreover, it is pointless to increase the strength of a single component of the rigging 'chain' without considering the rig as a whole. To be worthwhile, heavier wires and bottlescrews probably need heavier chain plates and mast tangs, and larger bolts to fasten them with – perhaps even reinforcement to the hull. If the rig for your chosen ocean passagemaker seems inadequate, get an expert to advise you on the changes needed.

### Running rigging

The strength and durability of modern synthetic ropes has made wire halyards unnecessary on all but the largest cruising yachts. Troublesome wire to fibre splices are eliminated and so are the jagged 'fish hooks' which are liable to injure fingers and clothes. To avoid chafe it is essential that the sheaves over which the halyards pass are large enough for the rope used, and that they are in good condition. Going aloft at sea is unpleasant, and in rough conditions may be impossible, so it is important to ensure that there are sufficient spare halyards to make a trip up the mast unnecessary should a halyard be lost aloft or damaged. An oversize topping lift will suffice for the main or mizzen and a spinnaker halyard for a genoa. The fittings at the masthead must be sufficiently strong for these secondary purposes and the ropes must lead fairly without chafe. This is much more important on an ocean passage, where a spare halyard may be in use for days, than it is for coastal cruising where the original halyard can be retrieved or replaced at the next port within a short time.

The modern tendency is for running rigging to be led aft from the mast to the cockpit. This has the advantage of reducing the number of times that it is necessary to go forward and, by using a set of jammers, a winch each side of the companionway under the sprayhood can serve almost all sail control purposes. To work efficiently it is essential that the turning blocks used be of the best quality, that lines run fairly through them, and that these are regularly inspected for chafe. Such convenience has a price however, and the drawbacks should be considered. Even with the best hardware, friction will be increased and ropes will be subject to additional wear. The forward end of the cockpit is liable to become cluttered with lines, and winches and jammers fill the useful space under the sprayhood. With half a dozen jammers lying side by side, it is easy for the wrong one to be cast off inadvertently, particularly at night. Probably the most significant disadvantage of the 'lead everything aft' approach is that the deck outside the cockpit becomes unfamiliar territory, and so when it is necessary to go forward, probably in response to some emergency, the positions of handholds, obstacles, clipping-on points and so forth will have to be thought about. For a crew who routinely go forward such things are second nature, and so they are better placed to concentrate on the job in hand.

## Below decks

Arrangements below decks will of necessity be a compromise between the requirements of extended periods at sea on passage and those of life aboard in harbour. A centre cockpit is probably only worthwhile if the aft cabin can be reached without a trip through the cockpit and this generally limits this arrangement to yachts over about 11 m (36 ft). Above that size, the advantages of a completely separate sleeping cabin, away from the saloon, become increasingly attractive.

### Ventilation

If a yacht from cooler climes is to be taken to the tropics, the problems of ventilation should be studied with great care. The ideal is to have at least one good-sized hatch in each cabin, preferably of the type with reversible hinges, thus allowing it to be opened either forward or aft. A smaller hatch or opening port in the heads will also be appreciated. Opening ports in the living quarters are a great advantage in warm weather, but they must be of good quality otherwise they will leak. Lightweight aluminium frames have a tendency to corrode over time and then they will never seal properly.

Dorade type ventilators should have two holes in the top of the box, one over the watertrap and the other immediately over the deck inlet. In port, the vent can be put directly over the inlet with a cover on the other opening. The reverse position is used at sea. There should also be an emergency cover for the deck inlet in case the box is smashed.

Comfort below is greatly improved by proper insulation, which may also prove beneficial on the return to colder areas. In a steel or fibreglass boat the whole of the area under the deck and coachroof should, if accessible, be covered with expanded polyurethane, the thicker the better. This should not be done in a wooden boat where it might promote rot, but in any case timber provides relatively good insulation.

### *The galley*

No crew will be at their best unless properly fed, making the galley one of the most important areas below. The general layout will probably not lend itself to major alterations, but even so certain improvements can be made. Whereas the average boat's galley is mostly used in port, the ocean cruiser's must continue to work efficiently at sea. The stove must be able to swing freely on its gimbals to at least 35 degrees in either direction, while a high surrounding rail and efficient pot-clamps are essential. So is a protective 'crash bar' in front, both to protect the cook from possible injury and to decrease the likelihood of gas taps being turned on or off by accident. Some people also like a strap to lean against while cooking, in which case one should be provided.

Even if bulk food stores are stowed elsewhere, the many items used regularly must be handy to the galley. This means safe stowage for a variety of containers – often bins or shelves with high fronts are more secure than lockers, which may dump their entire contents when the door is opened – and somewhere to put implements or open containers while in use. Work surfaces should have high fiddles, and should not be too large. Most galleys

work well when the yacht is on one tack or the other, when everything naturally gravitates to, and remains, in the 'downhill' areas. It is much more difficult to arrange things to cope with constant rolling, but it is important to do so, as this is the motion most likely to be experienced during the crossing.

A deep sink is essential and it should drain on either tack. As well as its normal use for washing up, the sink will often be the best place to stow things temporarily during cooking operations. It is advantageous if there is a salt-water supply at the sink so that, even in harbour, the initial washing up can be done in salt water.

An important feature of the galley layout, and one which can sometimes be improved with a little thought, is that of ensuring that the cook can work without interfering with (or being hampered by) those who need to get past. If the cabin sole is varnished, some form of nonslip surfacing should be used in the galley area. Provision must be made for rubbish – preferably two containers, one for biodegradable rubbish which can be disposed of at sea, and one for plastic and items to be taken ashore. On passage, where they will remain on board for a lengthy period, these items should be thoroughly rinsed in seawater.

### *Cooking fuel*

For most cruisers, the cooking fuel of choice is LPG (liquefied petroleum gas). Paraffin (kerosene) is still used by some who consider it safer, but supplies are increasingly difficult to obtain as LPG is now widely used in even the remotest places. The quality of any paraffin available is

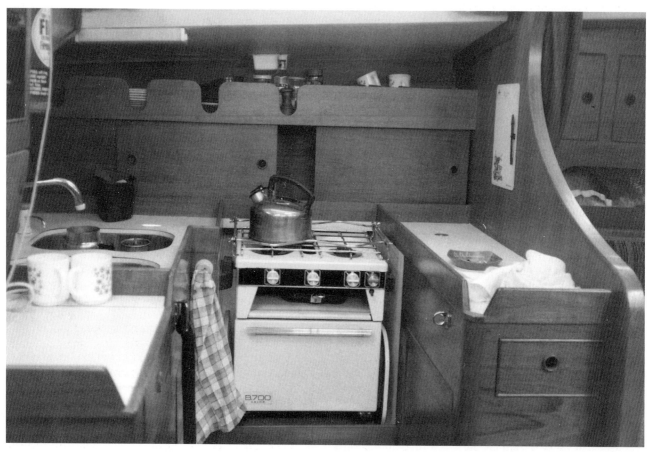

A well thought out U shape galley, with everything to hand. Although there is a belt to support the cook, a crashbar is needed to prevent him being thrown against the stove. *Photo: Georgie McLaren*

often poor. If a paraffin cooker is fitted then provision should be made to store fuel for about three months and it should be filtered. A good supply of spares for a paraffin stove must be carried as their availability has declined along with the use of the fuel.

LPG is relatively cheap but is unfortunately produced in different forms and pressures (propane and butane) and is supplied in a variety of different, non-interchangeable, bottles. There is a danger of explosion through carelessness or faulty installation; to some extent this can be guarded against by fitting a gas detector, but such a device is no substitute for regular inspection of the gas system and safe procedures when using the stove.

As mentioned, LPG comes in more than one variety. Broadly speaking, propane is supplied for boats in North America, Bermuda, the Caribbean and Scandinavia, while butane is more usual throughout the rest of Europe. The primary difference is one of pressure, propane being stored at considerably higher pressure than butane and needing a different regulator. Propane cylinders incorporate a pressure release valve whereas some butane cylinders do not. Although in many places butane cylinders will be filled with propane without comment or objection, this is a highly dangerous practice – do not assume that just because the supplier agrees to do so it is safe. Most gas appliances will run off either fuel, provided that it is supplied through the correct regulator.

Throughout Europe the normal practice is for LPG bottles – be they propane or butane – to be leased. For practical purposes this amounts to much the same as purchase, but the bottles remain the property of the supplying company, who are responsible for their testing and maintenance. Subsequently, empty bottles are exchanged for full ones, with only the gas being charged for. Most yacht chandlers and many hardware shops carry a stock of full bottles in the popular sizes. The supplying company refills empty bottles at a regional depot. Outside Europe, it is normal for individuals to purchase their own bottles outright and have them refilled when necessary. In the USA, refilling facilities are available at many petrol stations and some marinas; most Atlantic and Caribbean islands have a single central refilling plant that will deal with bottles of almost all types.

Each European country has its own LPG supplying companies and bottles are not exchangeable between them. Companies *may* refill bottles from another supplier or country, but normally only if they are satisfied that the bottles are suitable and are in date for test. A visit to the nearest refilling plant will be necessary and there is no guarantee that it will have the necessary thread adapters to fill bottles other than its own. The only pan-European bottles are those from Camping Gaz, which may be exchanged in nearly all European ports and in most of the Atlantic and Caribbean islands. Unfortunately the bottles are small, the gas expensive, and only butane is available. Camping Gaz bottles are not fitted with safety valves and should *never* be filled with propane.

The best gas system to fit for an Atlantic cruise will depend upon the route to be taken; however, the following guidance is given:

1 A British yacht should be fitted with a Calor Gas system. If it is certain that the USA will not be visited then an existing Calor butane system will suffice, but it would be preferable to fit a propane regulator and exchange butane for propane bottles before departure, as propane will be available throughout the voyage. Only in France, Spain and Portugal will it be difficult to get propane bottles refilled, but it will be possible. If retaining a butane system then one or more Camping Gaz bottles (with the necessary adapter) may be useful in areas where they are readily exchangeable. If planning to visit the USA then the change to propane should be made before departure. Calor propane bottles can be refilled using the standard US fittings (but see note below).

2 An American yacht will find her propane system quite adequate until she reaches Europe. There it may be possible to get her cylinders refilled, provided that there is the documentation to prove that they are suitable for the purpose and in test date, but it may be a time consuming process. If planning to remain in a single European country for a length of time it will be preferable to lease local propane cylinders, and to fit the necessary adapters to connect them to the yacht's propane regulator. If the intention is to visit several European countries over an extended period then it will be more convenient for the yacht to be converted to a butane system using Camping Gaz cylinders. The exception to this is in the Scandinavian countries where only propane may be available.

All yachts should ensure that their bottles are in good condition before departure, and that they will remain in test date throughout the cruise. Bottles that are dented or have become rusty are unlikely to be acceptable for refill, so it is worth looking after them. Bottles should be marked with their tare weight and never overfilled. Cylinders could become hydraulically full (and burst) through expansion of the LPG with increase in temperature, so never overfill cylinders. In hotter – tropical or semi-tropical – regions, cylinders must only be filled to 70 per cent of their capacity to allow for this expansion.

*Note*: Although American and Calor propane connectors appear identical they are not absolutely so. An American propane connector can be attached to the female fitting on a Calor bottle and a gastight seal can be made. However, it is physically impossible to get a UK Calor connector into an American female bottle fitting.

A great deal of useful information on gas systems is contained in the leaflet LPG (Bottled Gas) for Marine Use, published by Calor Gas Ltd and available free from showrooms or direct from the Boating Industry Liaison Officer at the company, telephone (UK) 01345 661111.

Gas is potentially dangerous and basic safety procedures must be laid down and then stringently observed. The ideal is to turn the gas off at the bottle as soon as it is no longer required. If, as is usually the case, this means going out into the cockpit and opening a locker, a shut-off valve for routine use should be fitted where the piping enters the cabin. But it must be far enough from the stove to be accessible in the event of fire. Newer gas stoves and other gas appliances are likely to be fitted with some form of flame failure device. However, this will not prevent leaks from defective piping.

Stove and gas system spares should be carried. If burners rust out or a regulator fails, replacements will be almost impossible to find. It is worth carrying a simple alternative method of heating food, either a single-burner Primus with some paraffin and priming alcohol, or a miniature camping stove with a supply of solid fuel tablets. On an ocean passage a diet of uncooked food palls quickly.

## *Refrigeration*

Although not absolutely essential, some method of keeping food and drink cool in the tropics should be high on the agenda, the choice being between an insulated icebox and a refrigeration system. An icebox has the advantage of simplicity and reliability, but is dependent on ice from ashore; with the increased use of refrigerators, block ice is becoming harder to find. An icebox is of limited use on longer passages, although with really good insulation a block of ice will last a surprisingly long time.

Refrigeration systems fall broadly into two categories, those that are directly driven from the yacht's engine (or auxiliary generator), and those that run from the DC electrical system. The former are usually considerably more powerful, enabling a larger volume to be cooled and ice to be made, but will require the engine to be run at least once, and often twice, every single day. Running a diesel on such a comparatively light load in harbour will do it no good and, in crowded anchorages or when alongside, may be antisocial.

In the tropics, a DC-powered refrigeration system will be the largest consumer of electricity on board. Indeed, its requirements will probably exceed those of all the other electrical equipment combined. Whatever type is fitted, in tropical waters it will use at least twice the number of amp-hours that it would in temperate conditions and this energy will have to be put back into the battery. A DC-driven fridge should therefore be considered in the context of the boat's overall electrical and charging systems. All fridges should use water to cool the refrigerant; air cooled systems are hopelessly inefficient in hot climates. Fridge systems contain an unhealthy mix of metals, so ensure that sacrificial zincs are fitted in the cooling circuit.

The amount of energy a fridge consumes, or the amount of ice an icebox requires, is directly proportional to the efficiency of the insulation of the box, and a system designed for northern waters will almost certainly need extra insulation. A minimum of 4 in (10 cm) of modern insulation, preferably closed cell polyurethane foam, is needed; 6 in (15 cm) is preferable, and is the minimum for any part of the fridge/icebox that is against an engine compartment bulkhead. The insulation should incorporate a vapour barrier, and a reflective layer to reduce radiated heat transmission. A tightly fitting lid, with efficient neoprene seals, is essential and a drain (with a swan-neck to prevent cold air escaping) should also be provided.

## *Water tankage*

In many boats, it will be necessary to increase fresh water capacity before undertaking an ocean voyage. About 2.5 litres (just over half an imperial gallon or nearly three-quarters of a US gallon) per person per day should be sufficient in cooler areas, but is barely enough in the tropics and allows nothing for personal washing or laundry.

Allowance must also be made for a longer than anticipated passage time. The calculation for the Canaries/Barbados passage aboard a yacht with a crew of three might be:

2.5 litres x 3 people x 24 days = 180 litres
50% reserve = 90 litres
Total required = 270 litres (about 60 imperial gallons or 75 US gallons)

It should be stressed that this is the absolute minimum consistent with safety and 400 litres (100 gallons) or more would be preferable. At least 45 litres (10 gallons) of this should be carried in plastic containers, reasonably accessible in case of emergency; as fresh water is lighter than salt the containers will float.

The water supply should be split between at least two tanks, and preferably these should not interconnect. The best arrangement is to have three tanks; the suction from each should be from the top via a standpipe so that a fracture in the pipework will not allow the tank to drain away. The suctions should be connected to the water distribution system via a set of valves so that an individual tank can be selected for use.

On passage, water consumption must be monitored and the skipper must always have a good idea of the amount remaining in each tank. It is prudent to check the actual capacity of each tank by filling it from a container of known volume rather than relying on the figure provided by the manufacturer. Most tank gauges are notoriously unreliable and a better method of keeping track of consumption at sea is to use a 1 or 2-gallon plastic can as a service tank, all water used coming from this can. Each time it is refilled, the fact is recorded, and so the amount of water used is always known. It is often said that the contents of one water tank should be left unused until near the end of the passage to allow for an unexpected emergency, but this is not good advice. Each tank should be used for a day or two in turn throughout the passage, so that the quantities in each remain roughly the same. In that way, the consequences of the loss of one tank's contents will be minimised.

Whilst at sea a pressure water pump should invariably be switched off when not actually in use, and it may be better to disconnect the pump when on an ocean passage and to rely on the hand pump which will in any case be needed as a back-up. Having to work for it deters most people from being careless with fresh water.

The plastic containers mentioned above in which reserve water should be carried will also be invaluable in those places where it is not possible to fill the tanks by hose. It may sometimes be necessary to carry water several hundred yards before transporting it out in the dinghy, and for this reason 5 or 10-litre cans (1 or 2 gallons) will be preferable to the unwieldy 22-litre (5-gallon) variety. They are also easier to stow, and should one can split at sea only a small part of the reserve will be lost.

Reverse osmosis watermakers, which produce fresh water from seawater, are increasingly popular – and though still costly, their price has fallen considerably in recent years. They may be driven by the ship's electrical system, or directly from the engine or generator – the latter arrangement is preferable if useful quantities of water are to be produced. Manually operated models are

Most voyaging yachts need extra storage space. Here a bunk has been converted into a shelf with cupboards.
*Photo: Gavin McLaren*

also available, but these are only suitable for use in survival situations. As long as it continues to work, a watermaker will allow more water to be used at sea, but such a complicated device cannot be completely relied on, and there must always be sufficient water remaining in the tanks to enable a port to be reached, even if only under strict water rationing. The watermaker should therefore be run frequently in the early part of an ocean passage to keep the tanks fully topped up.

In harbour a watermaker will eliminate the need to go alongside for fresh water, or to carry it in cans, and will allow the profligate use of water for laundry and cleaning. Some may consider that these advantages hardly warrant the complication or expense, but it is significant that those long distance cruisers who have fitted a watermaker usually maintain that it is the last mechanical device that they would forgo.

## Berths

Along with regular food, adequate and relaxing sleep will do much to keep those aboard not only functioning but reasonably cheerful through the worst conditions. It is desirable for there to be as many good sea berths as there will be people aboard for the passages; it is just acceptable for there to be one fewer, but this will mean hot bunking and should be avoided if at all possible. In harbour, berths that would be untenable at sea, perhaps those in a forward cabin, can be used. A good sea berth is one in which it is possible to sleep in any weather and on any point of sailing. Ideally it should be as close to the centre of the boat

as possible, to reduce the motion, should be parallel to the fore and aft line, should be located so that normal watch-keeping and ship's activities do not disturb the sleeper and should not need to be unrigged when not in use. Few sea berths achieve these ideals but they are worth striving for.

In practice, quarter berths, the saloon settees and possibly pilot berths rigged above them will probably have to suffice. In a centre cockpit yacht the aft cabin may be used. Wherever the berths, it is absolutely essential that the sleeper cannot be thrown out however extreme the conditions. High leecloths or bunkboards will be needed and they must be strong, as must their attachment points. In many pilot berths, the canvas base is supported by a full-length bar that slips into bulkhead sockets at the head and foot of the berth. This bar must be positively fastened into the sockets and not rely merely on the weight of the sleeper to keep it in place.

Berths must not be so wide as to allow the occupant to slide from side to side as the yacht rolls, which she is likely to do for most of a tradewind crossing. Nor must they be so narrow as to prevent one from turning over. Leecloths of smooth plastic fabrics should be avoided; in the tropics the minimum of bedding, if any, will be needed, and such materials adhere to the skin. Acrylic canvas is very much more comfortable.

Every effort should be made to avoid the crew having to sleep in the saloon when the yacht is in harbour, although it may be necessary for occasional guests to do so. A permanent harbour-sleeping cabin will make life in port very much more civilised. Having to make up bunks each evening and stow them each morning may be acceptable for a few weeks' holiday but is tedious for long term living aboard.

### Stowage

The ocean cruising boat will need more space devoted to stowage than will her coasting counterpart. Much of this will be devoted to food stores, but extra sails, clothes, spares, tools and all kinds of other paraphernalia must also be accommodated. The modern production boat tends to be lacking in storage space. Fortunately she is also likely to have more berths than are good for her and one or more of these will probably have to be converted into storage space by building in lockers, partitioning into bins or whatever method is most suitable. If extra crew are taken on for the ocean passages it is important that they are allocated a locker for their clothes and possessions.

Lockers – whatever they are to hold – should be lined so that water cannot spoil their contents. This is easy to do in a wooden hull where battens or hardboard can be fixed over the timbers but may be less easy with steel or fibreglass. Never allow a locker shelf, or the cabin sole, to be fitted right up flush with the hull. If this is done, any water trickling down will collect on the shelf, soaking the contents and probably causing rot in the longer term.

It is better to have many small lockers than a few large ones – the larger a stowage the more likely it is to have 'everything on top and nothing to hand'. In a modern fibreglass yacht with modular joinery there are often many inaccessible spaces behind the joinery work or under the sole. These can often be opened up, lined and then fitted with a door or hatch to provide extra stowage. Space under the sole is particularly suitable for heavy items, provided that they are protected against the water that will find its way there from time to time.

## The engine and electrical system

The engine and electrical system should be in first class condition before departure. More extended cruises are delayed, curtailed or abandoned due to mechanical or electrical failure than for any other reason. Engine problems are usually caused by lack of maintenance or poor installation. The electrical system usually fails because it is inadequate to meet the extra requirements placed upon it.

### The engine

The engineless cruising yacht is now so rare as to be almost extinct. As anchorages become more crowded so manoeuvring under sail alone has become increasingly nerve-wracking. A few harbours and most marinas are impossible to enter except under power. The increased electrical demands of modern yachts mean that an efficient and powerful battery charging system is needed, which the engine can provide. Finally, engines themselves have become lighter, more reliable and relatively cheaper over the years.

On most Atlantic cruises an engine is needed less for propulsion at sea than for battery charging and harbour work. Only if the range under power is several hundred miles will an engine be much use for propulsion on passage, although sometimes it may be profitable to motor a shorter distance to find the wind, or to speed the last lap to the destination.

The engine should be thoroughly checked before leaving home waters. It will be far easier to have major work done at this stage, even if it is not yet absolutely necessary, than along the way. Engine mounts should be examined, as should all flexible hoses – those whose condition is not first class must be renewed. If the engine is past the first flush of youth it may be wise to have the alternator and starter motor overhauled and to renew the thermostat. If it seems likely that they may be dirty, fuel tanks should be opened up and cleaned; injectors and fuel pumps will benefit from being serviced before departure. The exhaust system should be thoroughly checked and any suspect components renewed – corrosion in this system is particularly common. There must be some method of closing the exhaust overboard discharge – water flooding back through the exhaust system in heavy weather has destroyed countless engines. Fresh and saltwater cooling systems need descaling periodically. A fresh water cooling system should contain the correct proportion of antifreeze; icing is unlikely to be a problem but antifreeze is also an effective anti-corrosive. The engine compartment should be thoroughly clean.

Comprehensive engine spares should be carried. Most engine manufacturers can supply a kit of long-range spares, or at least a list of recommendations. Plenty of fuel filters are essential. If routine – or not so routine – maintenance requires any specialised tools, these should also be carried. Diesel mechanics are to be found almost everywhere and, even if more used to fishing boats or tractor engines, will be able to carry out work on a yacht's diesel provided the correct spares and tools are available.

Having set off with an engine in good condition it is relatively easy to ensure that it remains so. The manufacturer's service schedule should be meticulously followed. Modern, lightweight diesel engines are particularly hard on their lubricating oil. This must be changed and a replacement filter element fitted at the correct intervals. If the engine is regularly run on light load – to power a fridge or to charge the battery for example – then the oil and filter should be changed more frequently. Fuel filters should also be changed regularly. Working on the engine is much easier if it, and its compartment, are kept clean – which will also enable minor leaks to be identified and rectified early.

### The electrical system

The demands placed on yachts' electrical systems have increased dramatically in recent years. Unfortunately the systems themselves have often not developed at the same pace. This may not be significant for the average cruiser, limited to weekend sailing and the occasional two or three-week cruise. That pattern of use is likely to involve a proportionally much greater use of the engine, and therefore the alternator, than an extended voyage. During a home waters cruise it is likely that at least the occasional night will be spent connected to shore power, when the battery can get a good charge. But the ocean voyager must be completely independent of the shore during the passages, and even when in harbour is much more likely to be at anchor than alongside. His electrical demands must therefore be met entirely from onboard resources.

The design of the electrical system is a complex matter

and if in doubt expert advice should be sought. There are also some excellent books on the subject. It is not possible in this book to duplicate these sources of information but the following points are worth considering.

It may seem obvious, but is an often overlooked fact, that every amp-hour taken out of the battery must be replaced by an amp-hour put back in. (In reality, because of the characteristics of batteries, every amp-hour taken out must be replaced by more than that – usually about one and a quarter amp-hours.) However big the battery, however powerful the alternator or efficient the auxiliary charging devices, however smart the regulator or accurate the battery metering instruments, there is no avoiding this principle. Generally speaking, the bigger the battery bank, the longer can be the interval before the amp-hours used have to be replaced; the bigger the alternator, the more rapidly can the recharging be done. 'Smart' (modern electronic) regulators enable the full potential of a powerful alternator to be used without damaging the battery.

The rate at which the amp-hours used can be put back in varies not only with the power of the alternator, but also with the capacity of the battery – the bigger it is, the more rapidly it can accept a given number of amp-hours; 50 amp-hours can be returned to a 300 amp-hour battery much more quickly than they can be to a 100 amp-hour one. It is generally damaging to a battery for it to be regularly discharged below about 45 per cent of its capacity; it is time consuming to recharge it above about 85 per cent, although for long battery life this should be done periodically.

Given these simplified facts some general guidance for an ocean cruising yacht's electrical systems can be given. The amp-hours used each day in harbour and at sea must be estimated. When doing so, allowance should be made for the longer nights of the tropics and for the very much greater load that any electric powered fridge will take in a warm climate – the daily consumption of such a fridge is likely to be at least twice that of temperate conditions. It is wise to overestimate the total daily amp-hourage rather than to underestimate it. Domestic battery capacity in amp-hours should be not less than three time the larger of the sea and harbour estimate. If space and weight considerations allow, a greater capacity should be fitted. Rated continuous alternator output in amps should be around a third of the battery capacity in amp-hours. Again, a larger alternator will do no harm, though to gain full benefit a 'smart' electronic regulator should be fitted. These are general guidelines for a system that can be maintained with less than two hours of engine running each day. A system that falls significantly outside these parameters will need longer and/or more frequent periods of charging. Alternative means of charging are considered in Chapter 3, but (apart from a large yacht's dedicated diesel generator) they should in general be considered as additions to, rather than substitutes for, the engine charging system.

Unless it can be started by hand, the engine should have its own dedicated battery, kept fully charged. The electrical system should be designed so that this battery cannot inadvertently be used to power the domestic system, whilst at the same time provision should be made for the domestic batteries to be used to start the engine should its own battery fail. This is usually achieved either by manual switches or blocking diodes. A battery state indicator is also useful, and should be installed in such a way that it can indicate the state of each battery individually.

### Corrosion

Any water-cooled engine is liable to be affected by galvanic or electrolytic action. A salt-water cooled installation should have sacrificial zincs somewhere in the water jacket and these will need regular inspection and replacement. Even when fresh water cooling is used, the heat exchanger is exposed to the corrosive action of hot salt water and an anode may be needed for its protection. Galvanic corrosion is rapid in tropical waters and must be guarded against. Most boats will need at least one external hull anode correctly bonded to the metal fittings. This is a complex subject, and unless you are an expert, get a surveyor who specialises in this field to check your system during your preparations. Anodes should be in good condition before departure and at least one spare carried.

## Routine maintenance

Keeping up with routine maintenance is essential to the smooth running of the long distance cruising yacht. Part of it will be cosmetic – brightwork in particular deteriorates rapidly in the tropical sun – but more is related to safety at sea. Regular inspection on the 'stitch in time' basis will often avoid more serious damage. Checking sails for worn stitching, running rigging for chafe, shackles and other metal fittings for rust, corrosion or abrasion – all may avert failure at a critical moment. Mechanical equipment (including the winches) will need periodic servicing, halyards should occasionally be 'end for ended' to even out the wear, the outboard motor will benefit from a fresh water flush from time to time, and once in a while the sprayhood and dodgers will need cleaning. These tasks, and a myriad similar ones, are part of the routine aboard a long distance cruiser, and most owners find it satisfying to keep their yachts in good shape.

One advantage of the ever increasing number of yachts based in the Caribbean is the dramatic improvement in facilities, including those for hauling out, over the past two decades. However, most slipways and travel lifts are in regular use and you may have to book well in advance. If you have a full set of plans for the boat it can do no harm to carry them with you, though photographs to show sling positions, hull shape and keel length may be more practical. In tropical waters much routine work on the hull can, if necessary, be done with the boat afloat. With snorkel and mask it is easy to keep the hull clean and inspect the rudder fittings, propeller and anode regularly.

Before going to sea, make a comprehensive list of items to be checked and mark each item off as you complete it. Examine the rigging meticulously – an inspection aloft should be made regularly and certainly before each ocean passage. Ensure that rigging screws are properly secured, that every shackle is moused (small plastic cable ties are good for this), and that all masthead sheaves are running freely. Check the engine is in good shape, and that the batteries are topped up if necessary and are well charged. Navigation lights should be checked individually, a task often best done several nights before departure.

The spares and tools most likely to be required will naturally vary from boat to boat, but some suggestions will be found in Chapter 3.

Much of the equipment discussed in this chapter may already be on board, particularly if the yacht has already cruised extensively in home waters, but its importance is such that it deserves further mention.

## Ground tackle

For most people, one of the greatest differences between cruising in home waters and cruising long distance will be anchoring. Away from northern Europe and the major American yachting centres it is normal to spend time in port at anchor. Often this is because alongside berths are simply not available, but even when there is a marina, considerations of privacy and security often make the anchorage preferable. Other advantages in the tropics are that there will be less trouble from insects, the breeze will keep the yacht cooler, and her crew will be able to swim from her.

The ground tackle must be able to cope with bad weather too. On hearing a gale warning at home, most people think in terms of finding a secure mooring or sheltered marina berth (not least because these now occupy so many of the best former anchorages). On an ocean cruise there will be many occasions when there is no alternative to riding out bad weather at anchor, sometimes in indifferent holding or poor shelter and possibly with rocks or coral heads astern. At these times the safety of the yacht, and her crew, will totally depend on her ground tackle and the skill with which it is deployed.

### Anchors

Most cruising yachts use a CQR, Danforth or Bruce as their main anchor. All three have imitators, which are unlikely to be manufactured to the same exacting standards. The CQR is probably the favourite general use anchor and can often be stowed permanently on the bow roller; the Danforth may be superior in very soft ground, but is notoriously difficult to handle. The Bruce claims to overcome this problem but may have difficulty in digging into very hard bottoms. A relative newcomer to the anchoring scene is the Delta anchor. This appears superficially similar to the CQR, and is made by the same company, but it is a one-piece anchor. Amongst the claims made for it are ease of stowage, strength and very high holding power in a variety of bottoms. Those who have used it are impressed.

Every cruising yacht should carry at least three

The Rustler 31, though designed as a cruiser/racer over thirty years ago, remains a good example of the smaller voyaging yacht. Here *Wrestler of Leigh*, veteran of four transatlantic passages, lies at anchor in Vigie Cove, St Lucia. *Photo: Anne Hammick*

anchors, preferably not all of the same type. Anchor manufacturers and cruising reference books provide tables giving recommended weights for various types of anchor and the skipper should study these. For his own peace of mind he would be wise to choose anchors somewhat heavier than those recommended, and one (not necessarily the one in daily use) should be considerably heavier for use in extreme conditions. A windlass becomes worth its weight aboard a yacht of over about 9 m (30 ft). Above 11 m (36 ft) a power operated windlass becomes increasingly attractive, particularly for a short-handed crew. Although the current it draws will be high, it will only be used for brief periods and so overall power consumption will not be particularly great. On many of the occasions that it is used the engine will be running. Amongst the advantages of a power windlass are readiness to anchor in deeper – and therefore probably less crowded – water, a willingness to move and reanchor if the first attempt is not in exactly the right place, and readiness to lay out plenty of cable without concern for the labour of recovering it. This last factor is a considerable safety advance, as chain that is still in the chain locker is not much use.

### Anchor cable or rode

The main anchor cable or rode may be of chain or of rope. Rope has few advantages except in a very small yacht where it may be impossible to stow a sufficient weight of chain. Rope is particularly liable to chafe on unseen rock or coral and provides no natural catenary to ensure a horizontal pull at the anchor. To help overcome this, if rope must be used, then a length of chain should be inserted between the rope and the anchor; this may also help to overcome some of the chafe. Rope cable will not self-stow, and compared to chain has a relatively short life. A yacht lying to rope will also require considerably more room in the anchorage – typically a seven to one scope is needed. Finally, rope is much more liable to be snagged by passing yachts or dinghies.

Chain increases holding power to such an extent, both through its own weight and by forcing the anchor to lie flat and dig in, that a scope of three to one is sufficient in normal conditions. Increasing the scope is a powerful weapon if the wind increases. This, together with its long life and invulnerability to chafe, makes it the unhesitating choice of at least 90 per cent of experienced cruising yachtsmen. Additionally, except in really windy conditions in shallow water, chain will drop almost sheer from the bow, and thus be next to impossible for others to snag. Chain is far easier to handle and stow, particularly if a windlass is fitted. Self-stowing will be improved if the chain falls straight down from the chain gypsy (wildcat) into a deep locker.

There are few anchorages along the normal Atlantic route with depths much in excess of 15 m (50 ft), and provided chain is to be used then 60 m (200 ft) should be sufficient. In a larger yacht 90 m (300 ft) would be preferable; a third of this might be a separate length stowed in the bilge to be used with a second anchor in extreme conditions. Even if chain is routinely used, a mixed cable – 15 m (50 ft) of chain plus 75 m (250 ft) of three-strand or multiplait nylon – will be needed for those occasions when a second or third anchor must be taken out by dinghy, a task which is difficult with chain. This line will also be invaluable in those steeply shelving Caribbean

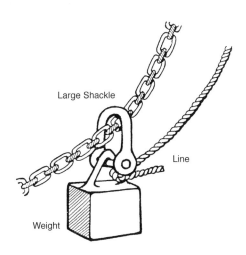

*Fig 1* The 'Chum' helps to prevent snubbing the anchor-rode in a hard blow. Suitable for use with chain cable, but would chafe a nylon line.

anchorages where one drops a bower anchor and takes a stern line ashore, and so it should therefore not be permanently attached to the chain.

It is seldom a steady pull that breaks out an anchor. Far more often snatching and jerking are to blame. An anchor weight (Fig 1) is one way of preventing this, but the weight needs to be at least 20 kg (45 lb) to do much good. An alternative is to use a nylon spring. Here, after the anchor has been set, one end of a length of elastic nylon rope is attached to the chain and the other secured to a cleat in the bow. Chain is then veered until the nylon takes the weight, and the chain hangs in a bight beneath it. (The chain should then be made fast in case the nylon parts.) Some 3–4 m (10–13 ft) of nylon is adequate, and it should not be too heavy otherwise it will not be sufficiently elastic. Routine use of a spring has the additional advantage of reducing the noise transmitted up the chain as it moves around on the bottom and of taking the strain of the windlass.

## Automatic steering

Unless there will always be a crew of at least three aboard, some form of automatic steering device will be more than a luxury. Even with a larger crew it will make life considerably easier. 'Autopilots' use electronic systems to steer the yacht, 'vane gears' use the wind to do the same. Both devices have their advantages – and disadvantages – and many ocean cruising boats are fitted with both.

### Vane gears

The principal advantage of a vane gear is that it requires no electrical power, and being a purely mechanical device should be reliable. This alone is enough to outweigh any disadvantages and to make it the choice of many skippers. Vane gears are easily understood and, with luck and a few spares, maintenance and minor repairs can be carried out by the crew. A good gear will steer a yacht however heavy the weather. The disadvantages are cost, weight – this is particularly important in a very small yacht as the weight of the gear is in just the wrong place – and vulnerability to damage in harbour. (The better gears can be easily removed to circumvent this.) Major repairs, particularly to the aluminium models, may be beyond local resources in all but the major yachting centres. Vane gears will not normally steer the yacht under power, and many are not particularly efficient in very light downwind conditions. They can be time-consuming to rig and set up after leaving port.

There are three types of system. They steer relative to the apparent wind and when that changes the yacht's course will change too. All have a vertical wind vane, normally made of plywood, arranged so that when the yacht is on course the vane faces into the apparent wind. When the yacht veers off course the vane turns or tilts on its axis and this motion causes the gear to bring the yacht back on to the correct heading.

In the oldest type, a linkage connects the wind vane directly to the yacht's rudder (or to a trim tab on its trailing edge). The Haslar gear is a typical make. It is the simplest gear, and the only one that the average owner is likely to be able to build himself, but as it generally lacks power is suitable only for smaller yachts. It is now seldom seen.

The second type of gear is completely self contained and uses an auxiliary rudder. The wind vane turns this rudder, or a trim tab attached to it, when the yacht is off course. The boat's main rudder is either left free to trail or, more commonly, set in the position that makes the vane gear's work easiest. This type of gear avoids complicated connections to the wheel or tiller, and has the considerable advantage of providing the yacht with an auxiliary rudder, should the main one be lost or damaged. However, the steering forces are directly transmitted from the auxiliary rudder to the hull – normally to the transom. This may not have been designed or built with these sideways forces in mind and, before fitting this type of vane gear, the designer or builder may need to be consulted. The Hydrovane is the most common example of this system.

The third type of vane gear is the servo pendulum. The Monitor and Aries gears are the most prolific makes but there are many other manufacturers. In these gears, movement of the wind vane rotates a blade in the water. This blade, or servo-oar, is free to swing from side to side (hence the name servo 'pendulum') and, once it has been rotated out of the fore-and-aft line, the water flowing past it causes it to do so. This swinging movement is used to turn the yacht's rudder via a system of steering lines connected to the wheel or tiller. Servo pendulum gears are powerful and, as the power comes from the flow of water past the servo blade, the faster the yacht is travelling the more powerful they become. The steering forces act on the yacht's rudder and its fittings; the forces on the gear itself are only those required to move the helm. Although this is the most complex, and therefore the most expensive, type of vane gear it is the choice of most experienced voyagers and the variety most commonly seen.

Whatever type is fitted, for a vane gear to work well the sails need to be trimmed to balance the yacht. The system must be arranged so that it can be disconnected instantly in an emergency, as it will be impossible for a helmsman to overcome the movement of the gear by brute force. It takes time to learn how to get the best out of a vane gear

and to discover the most efficient way to arrange tiller or wheel lines. It is advisable therefore, if at all possible, to fit the chosen gear and experiment with it for at least one season of local cruising before using it to cross the Atlantic.

A typical servo pendulum self-steering gear. This Aries has steered for about 40,000 miles and is still going strong.
*Photo: Gavin McLaren*

### Autopilots

An autopilot uses a compass sensor, an electronic control system and an electric power unit to steer the yacht. In smaller sizes these three components may be combined into a single unit and models are available for either wheel or tiller steering. Larger units for wheel steered yachts may either be mounted in the cockpit and turn the wheel via a belt and wheel drum, or may be mounted below decks and connected into the steering system there. This is the better arrangement as the power unit will be out of the weather and less vulnerable to accidental damage, or to theft. The electronic control systems vary in sophistication, with the most advanced models incorporating circuits that automatically adjust the autopilot for weather helm, sea state and steering load; these are said to reduce the power the autopilot will use. Most models can be fitted with a small wind direction sensor, so that the course may be set relative to the apparent wind. It is sometimes possible to use the masthead wind direction sensor for this purpose. Some autopilots can be connected to GPS receivers so that the yacht is automatically kept on track and steered to the chosen waypoint. This is a dangerous practice – particularly in a sailing vessel – and should be avoided.

The principal advantage of an autopilot is that it is

cheap, at least in the smaller and medium sizes, it is light, and it is simple to use. It will steer in the lightest winds and when under power. It avoids clutter on the stern and if lost or damaged is relatively easy to replace. Its main disadvantage is lack of reliability. Electronics and salt water are uneasy companions. (The built-in units are considerably more dependable for this reason than the cockpit mounted ones.) It is rare to meet a voyaging yacht that has been cruising for any length of time that has not had an autopilot problem. Experienced cruisers who rely on them for ocean passages carry at least one complete spare system.

The other significant drawback is that autopilots are completely dependent upon electric power and, in most cases, plenty of it. Running an engine or generator regularly will almost certainly be necessary to meet the demand. Should the engine fail, then the autopilot will fail shortly afterwards. Of the alternative charging devices mentioned later in this chapter, only the towing generator is likely to provide enough power, and then only when the yacht is moving fast. Finally, it is impossible for most owners to make any sort of repair to an autopilot and so problems will have to be dealt with by a specialist, who may have to order components for a particular model.

Without doubt, the ideal is for the ocean cruising yacht to fit both a vane gear and an autopilot. The drawbacks of each are largely compensated for by the advantages of the other. The vane gear will be the main helmsman on an ocean passage. The autopilot will come into its own in very light weather, when under power and for short coastal sails. The reassurance of having two independent systems, each able to do the bulk of the steering during the crossing, is overwhelming – particularly for the short-handed crew.

## Sails

If ordering new sails give careful thought to their weight and design. It is a fallacy to think that cruising sails need to be heavier than racing sails, and unless those already on board are showing signs of wear and tear there may be no need for new sails in any case. If the boat has done much racing she may well have more sails than will be needed on an ocean cruise, when she might carry the following:

- Mainsail
- Two or three headsails (whether or not roller furling is fitted)
- Storm jib
- Trysail
- Mizzen and mizzen staysail if a ketch or yawl
- Spinnaker or cruising chute if already aboard

A major enemy of sails is sunlight and their casualty rate will be high unless care is taken to protect them. Covers for main or mizzen are essential, roller-furling headsails must either have a cover or protective strips on the leech or foot. Sails that have to stay on deck when in harbour must be bagged. For preference, these bags should be of a heavy acrylic material as light nylon gives little protection from ultraviolet rays. Triple stitching is advantageous and it is helpful if the thread can be of a contrasting colour so that damage can more easily be spotted; one's sailmaker should be consulted about this, however, as some coloured thread is less resistant to sunlight than white is. Careful

attention should be paid at all times to avoiding chafe – the most likely place for this to occur is where a mainsail touches the lower shrouds when running downwind.

### Mainsails

Few yachts today carry mainsails cut specifically for ocean cruising, and a well made sail suitable for coastal sailing will be quite satisfactory. It should have a minimum of two – and if a trysail is not to be carried, three – reefs, and there is some advantage in having these arranged so that the boom end will be raised a little as each reef is pulled down. This will reduce the risk of dipping the boom into the water when rolling. There should be a jam cleat on the leech for the leech line at each reef position but these will not usually be accessible without sheeting in the sail. Consider running the leech line over a sheave on the headboard and down to corresponding jam cleats on the luff of the sail. The method used to secure slides to the sail should be beyond reproach and some spare slides should be carried. The clew of the sail carries a very considerable vertical strain; if the foot is fitted directly into a groove in the boom (without slides) a lashing through the clew cringle around the boom will help to prevent the sail gradually pulling out. Fully battened mainsails are now common. Such sails set well, and are easy to hoist and lower, but some have batten cars that are less than satisfactory. A fully battened main is very vulnerable to chafe where the battens press against the shrouds and some extra protection will be needed here.

In-mast reefing mainsails are increasingly popular and those who have used them speak highly of them. A well-made gear is quite up to the demands of ocean passagemaking, but it must, however, be absolutely impossible for the system to jam. Should it do so in a rising wind there may be no alternative to going aloft and cutting the sail away. The clew of the sail is normally outside the mast when the sail is furled and therefore particularly vulnerable to sunlight, so some form of small cover may need to be devised for it. With this gear a separate trysail should certainly be carried.

### Trysails

Opinion about the need for a trysail is divided and some long-distance cruising skippers do not carry one, preferring to rely instead on a very deep third reef on the mainsail. This may be adequate on a small yacht but a trysail is preferable and should certainly be carried aboard a vessel over about 11 m (36 ft). Ideally the trysail should have its own separate track, which will make it very much easier to rig and hoist in storm conditions. A major advantage of the trysail is that it is set loose-footed and so can be used if the main boom is damaged – a bermudan mainsail set without a boom is seldom much use, even if deeply reefed. The trysail will also come into its own on an ocean passage if the main is damaged beyond repair. These two uses alone justify carrying one, quite apart from heavy weather considerations. The trysail may also be useful as a roll damper when running downwind under twin headsails.

### Headsails

Roller furling and reefing headsails are now the norm rather than the exception, although many cutters retain a hanked on staysail. There appears to be little doubt that if a reputable gear is chosen, and correctly fitted, the likelihood of problems is extremely low. It will need to be well maintained; in particular the system should be dismantled periodically so that the condition of the forestay can be checked. The sail must be protected from sunlight, and although strips on the leech and foot are effective to some extent, it may be better to remove the sail and stow it below during a long stay in port. This should certainly be done if strong winds are expected.

If using a roller headsail it may become necessary to deal with a jammed gear at sea. If the jam occurs with the sail reefed it will not be possible to lower it. The best way to furl the sail in this situation will be to motor in circles, passing the sheets around the sail, something best practised for the first time on a windless evening in harbour, preferably without an audience. At least one reserve headsail of No 2 genoa or working jib size should also be carried and the means of setting this - a spare stay, halyard and sheet leads - should be provided. Whatever other headsails are aboard it is essential to carry a small, heavy storm jib, set on a wire luff and fitted with shackles to pass around the stay at head and foot for extra security. If using roller furling, either a permanent or temporary inner forestay will be needed on which to hoist it. This forestay may need extra support, either from running backstays or additional lower shrouds swept well aft, and the deck fittings must be substantial.

### *Downwind rig*

The principal transatlantic yacht routes are downwind, particularly the trade wind east to west crossing. Unfortunately the bermudan rig is not particularly efficient on this point of sailing - this is an area where gaff rig has a distinct advantage. An ocean cruiser needs to organise his boat so that she can be sailed downwind safely, efficiently and comfortably for prolonged periods. There are three methods for achieving this.

One way is to rely on a spinnaker. For a large, experienced crew this is the simplest and fastest downwind rig. Little needs to be said about it here as the arrangements for coastal cruising under spinnaker will be quite satisfactory. Chafe can be a problem where sheets and guys cross the guard rails and at the pole end. Unless the halyard block is perfectly fair chafe at the masthead can occur unnoticed and the nip should be freshened regularly. If complete reliance is to be placed on this rig, spinnakers of various sizes will be needed for differing wind strengths. Few skippers are happy with a vane gear or autopilot when under spinnaker, although in strong winds a servo pendulum gear should be adequate. For the majority of ocean cruisers a spinnaker, if used at all, will only be set under settled daytime conditions. At other times she will revert to one of the other two common downwind rigs, twin headsails, or main and poled out genoa.

A twin headsail rig, with twin poles stowed up and down the mast, was for many years the hallmark of the ocean cruiser. The rig evolved not so much for its efficiency as for its self-steering attributes. Before the advent of reliable vane gears, twin headsail rig was the only way that most yachts could be persuaded to steer themselves before the wind. For this reason it remains the easiest rig on the helmsman, whether human or mechanical. Other advantages are that it is remarkably free from chafe, wear and tear on the mainsail is avoided, and there is no danger of an accidental gybe. Drawbacks are that with no fore

and aft canvas to steady her the yacht is likely to roll heavily, and that once the gear is rigged, manoeuvrability is considerably reduced. Setting the trysail and sheeting it hard amidships may ease the rolling. It will gybe repeatedly, but will come to no harm. Twin headsails need at least one pole and preferably two. If only one is available the main boom will serve as the other, with a foreguy holding it as far forward as the shrouds will allow. The headsail sheet is run through a block at the boom end. Poles proper, attached to a mast track, need to be controlled by a topping lift, a guy led to the quarter and a foreguy led to the foredeck. This will ensure that should the sail have to be got in in a hurry, the pole will remain safely stationary to be dealt with later. The foreguy will also prevent the pole being driven aft into the shrouds should the end dip into a sea.

Nowadays the twin headsails themselves are unlikely to be special sails, kept for this purpose alone, and they do not need to be of equal size. The usual arrangement is for one sail to be the normal roller furling genoa, and for the other to be a spare headsail hanked to a temporary stay. An alternative is to have two identical or similar sails, each set in one of the twin grooves of the roller gear. These sails can be furled and unfurled together as the wind strength varies. Those who have used this arrangement are enthusiastic about it, describing the headsail furling line as 'the throttle'. But the loads on the furling gear will be larger than normal so it must be man enough for the job.

The simplest downwind rig is mainsail and boomed-out genoa. The main - reefed as necessary - will be set to leeward, and the roller genoa poled out to windward, the pole being secured as described previously with topping lift, guy and foreguy. The roller genoa is reefed and unreefed as the wind strength varies. The advantages of this rig are that no special gear or sails are needed and that the yacht is likely to roll less than under the twin headsail rig. More significantly, she is much more manoeuvrable; the headsail can be sheeted to leeward and the yacht brought on to the wind quickly without touching the pole at all. The drawbacks are that there will be more wear and tear on the mainsail and it is vulnerable to chafe. This can be minimised by using a tightly set up foreguy, and if necessary a block and tackle between the boom and the lee rail, to prevent the boom, and therefore the sail, moving up and down against the lee rigging.

## Power generation

Many cruising yachts rely solely on their main engine for the generation of electricity, particularly those whose power requirements are low. However, the amount and importance of electrical equipment aboard cruising boats has steadily increased over recent years. Additional methods of power generation are regularly fitted to ensure that this electrical equipment remains available. It should be appreciated, however, that 'alternative' energy sources - solar or wind power - are unlikely to completely meet the needs of an electric fridge or autopilot. Such devices will, however, reduce the frequency and length of time for which the main engine must be run.

### *Wind generators*

These are commonly found aboard long distance cruisers and fall into two main types, 'turbines' and 'propellers'.

Turbines are more commonly available in Europe. They usually have six blades and revolve at high speeds. Blade tip velocity limits the size that these generators can be made and maximum power output is likely to be around 100 watts, but average output will be much less. Such generators may be mounted on a permanent pole rigged on the stern, or on a mizzen mast. Some are designed to be hoisted in the rigging when the yacht is at anchor, and stowed below at other times. At least one of these types can be fitted with a towed rotator to generate power when the yacht is at sea and is reported to produce sufficient power in this mode to meet the needs of a fridge and autopilot. The Ampair and the Aerogen are typical examples of turbine wind generators.

'Propeller' types of generator have two or three blades. They are much larger than turbine generators, but rotate more slowly. They can produce more significant amounts of power, possibly as much as 300–400 watts. They are considerably more complex and may have to incorporate devices to prevent them overspeeding in strong winds, and they must be permanently mounted. The American Windbugger is typical of this type of generator.

All wind generators are noisy, some more so than others, and it is worth listening to a selection in strong winds before making a purchase. It is absolutely imperative that whether permanently or temporarily rigged, they are well above head height. The blades of even a small generator can inflict fatal injuries.

### Solar panels

Solar panel technology has improved markedly in recent years and modern panels are considerably more efficient than older ones. Their power output is still severely limited, however, and even a large array will only produce worthwhile amounts in the tropics. The manufacturer's figures should be treated with considerable scepticism. A '100 watt' panel is highly unlikely ever to produce 100 watts in practice. For an hour either side of noon, in high summer, in the tropics it might produce 80, but only if it is completely free from even the slightest shadow, is connected to the battery through perfect wiring and is held at right angles to the sun. Such conditions are highly unlikely to be achieved in practice. For 12 hours of the day solar panels will produce no power at all, and for at least a couple of hours either side of sunrise and sunset, output will be milliamps. Unless a very large array can be fitted, solar panels should be considered more as a way of keeping the batteries charged when the boat is unused, than as a serious power supply.

### Auxiliary generators

These are increasingly carried as they provide the only means of keeping the batteries of most boats charged without frequent recourse to the main engine. Either an inbuilt diesel generator or a portable petrol driven one may be used. The diesel has the advantage of being permanently available, of producing several kilowatts of power (which may be useful for other purposes than battery charging), and of using the same fuel as the main engine. Sadly, most small single diesel generators are unreliable; in an anchorage it is common to find as many yachts with defective ones as with working ones. As generator size increases, so does reliability. For a yacht over about 14 m (45 ft) a built-in diesel is probably ideal, but it must have a first class installation and be conscientiously maintained.

For most yachts a portable petrol generator is probably a better choice. Such units are highly reliable, surprisingly quiet, and relatively cheap. A four-stroke model is much to be preferred to a two-stroke one. Although larger sizes are available, one kilowatt is about the maximum size that can realistically be considered portable, but running through a good battery charger, such a generator should enable the batteries to be charged at about 30 amps and a couple of hours' running a day in harbour will probably be sufficient. In light weather it can be run at sea. Compared to any other auxiliary charging device portable petrol generators are far and away the most cost effective. Prices vary, but a one kilowatt model is likely to cost about the same as a small wind generator or a couple of modest-sized solar panels. It will probably be less than a quarter of the price of the smallest inboard diesel generator.

### Shore power

The voltages and frequencies used around the Atlantic vary from 50 Hz to 60 Hz and from 110 to 240 volts. It is difficult to devise a simple shore power system or battery charger that can cope with all the possible permutations. Rather than attempt to do so, the best scheme is to set the boat up for the power supply of the home country. If time is spent connected to shore power of a different voltage (frequency is normally less critical), the appropriate transformer can be obtained. It can probably be passed on to a new arrival on departure.

## Awnings and forced ventilation

Most Atlantic cruises involve a spell in the tropics and a yacht that is cool in a hot climate will be pleasant to live aboard. Minimising exposure to the sun is important not only for comfort, but also for health reasons. Therefore it is worthwhile paying particular attention to awnings and ventilation during preparations for the crossing.

### Sailing awnings (biminis)

A permanent awning over the helmsman's position will improve comfort at sea in the tropics, and many people feel that they are essential. The rigid bimini top is more commonly seen aboard American boats than European ones, where a fabric sea awning is more common. Whatever type is chosen, it must not interfere with the working of the sails, and preferably should not obstruct the helmsman's view of the masthead. This is not easy to arrange, particularly in a centre cockpit yacht. It is worth studying a variety of biminis before designing one's own. Whatever the type, it must be removable in heavy weather.

### Harbour awnings

For only a single season in the tropics a bimini alone might be adequate, but even for such a short time a proper awning is infinitely preferable. Traditionally, the ideal awning covered the whole deck, and certainly reached from mast to backstay. This had more to do with keeping a wooden deck cool than protecting the crew from the sun, and aboard a modern well insulated yacht, with adequate opening ports and hatches, such a large awning may not be necessary. It is essential, however, that the cockpit, where the crew will spend most of their time in a warm climate, is fully shaded.

The simpler an awning the better. A complicated design will take too long to rig and unrig, and therefore will not often be used. The awning may go over or under the boom; for preference it should not be so high as to need sidescreens, nor be so low as to make movement around the deck awkward. The smaller the yacht the more likely it is that sidescreens will be necessary. Spreaders will probably be needed to extend the awning athwartships at each end, and a halyard in the middle may prevent it from sagging.

A secondary use for an awning is to collect rainwater in areas where shore water is hard to come by or is of doubtful quality. An awning will collect a surprisingly large amount of water in a tropical downpour. Plastic pipes can be attached using small plastic through-hull fittings, and should ideally be long enough to reach the tank filler. It may be best before fitting them to set up the awning and experiment with a hose to discover the natural 'low points' where the pipes should be placed.

Awnings should be made from a fairly heavy synthetic material – the acrylic used for many sprayhoods is ideal. Light nylon is not satisfactory – sunlight rots it and much ultraviolet light will in any case pass straight through. Because of its light weight, it will rattle in any breeze.

### Forced ventilation

The simplest method of forced ventilation when in harbour is by means of windscoops – lightweight nylon triangles, shaped rather like miniature spinnakers, set above each hatch to direct the breeze below. In the Caribbean, during the usual cruising season, there will nearly always be enough breeze for a windscoop to be effective.

In less breezy areas or during the Caribbean summer one or more electric fans will make life more pleasant, particularly in the galley. Power consumption may limit running time, however, and this should be checked on purchase. Small solar-powered ventilators are available that will get round this problem, but while useful in the heads, or for a boat left closed up and unattended, they cannot be expected to cool the interior significantly.

### Mosquito netting

There are very few places in the Lesser Antilles where mosquito nets will be required, particularly aboard a boat that anchors off. However if visiting central America, Venezuela, Maine or the Canadian coasts, nets will be needed. There are also plenty of mosquitoes and midges on the west coast of Scotland. A light wooden frame can be made to fit the washboard area, with nets for hatches set on elastic or Velcro. Anti-mosquito coils are obtainable in the places where mosquitoes are found, but some people find they irritate the eyes and throat. The best defence against mosquitoes is to anchor out.

## Dinghies and outboards

Because she will spend so much time at anchor, a good dinghy is essential to the long distance cruising yacht. Either an inflatable or a rigid dinghy may be chosen, and many owners will already have strong feelings on the subject. Much depends on the size of yacht and the number and agility of those aboard. Each type has its advantages and disadvantages.

Rigid tenders are generally easy to row, have a long life, and are unlikely to be stolen. However, hoisting aboard must be simple, particularly as this may be desirable every

The dinghy will often be used to ferry water out to the yacht at anchor. *Photo: Georgie McLaren*

night in a few harbours. A wooden or fibreglass dinghy is comparatively easy to repair if damaged, and will put up with a good deal of abuse. Deck stowage is likely to be the limiting factor with a solid dinghy. The normal places for it are forward of the mast, an impossibility for most cutters, or amidships on the coachroof, a location only possible in larger yachts. For many, therefore, a rubber dinghy is the only possibility.

The inflatable's main advantage is that, deflated, it takes up little deck room and when on passage it can often be stowed below. It is lighter and easier to hoist aboard at night; this is just as well as an inflatable is particularly vulnerable to theft. If fitted with a solid transom and inflatable keel, an outboard of sufficient power to make the dinghy plane may be used. An inflatable is easier to board from the water than most rigid dinghies and therefore more suitable for snorkelling or diving expeditions.

The inflatable's drawbacks are that it lacks durability – coral or sharp rocks can rapidly damage any inflatable – and it is difficult to make lasting repairs to. Few inflatables row well, and for reasonable comfort bottom boards are needed. These can be a struggle to fit. Because of the theft risk (due to the ease with which they can be deflated and hidden) inflatables should be padlocked to a strong point when left unattended.

A relative newcomer to the dinghy scene, at least in sizes suitable for yachts, is the rigid inflatable boat, or RIB. These dinghies have a solid fibreglass bottom and transom, with inflatable tubes forming the sides and providing the buoyancy. The main advantages of a RIB are that a powerful outboard can be fitted, it is easy to board from the water, and it is much less likely to be damaged by coral or rock than an inflatable. Its principal drawback is that it is as hard to stow on deck as a solid dinghy. For enthusiastic divers and snorkellers the RIB is probably the ideal dinghy provided deck space can be found for it.

Whether or not an outboard is carried will depend as much on the type of dinghy used as on personal preference. It should be borne in mind that as anchorages become more crowded so it becomes necessary to anchor further out and in the Caribbean in particular there will often be a fresh offshore wind blowing. Almost all cruising yachts do carry an outboard, and for those with an inflatable dinghy it can be considered almost essential. As fishermen everywhere use outboard motors it will usually be possible to get one serviced or repaired in even the remotest places, provided that parts for the particular model are available. It is wise to padlock an outboard to the dinghy in some anchorages, and even if the dinghy is left in the water, to stow it aboard at night. If at all possible an outboard should be stowed below during passages. If it must be left on a bracket on the transom, then a waterproof cover is essential.

It is usually an insurance requirement that a dinghy be marked with the parent yacht's name. Whilst this may make recovery easier if the dinghy is lost or stolen, when the dinghy is tied up ashore it does advertise which yachts are probably unattended. A solution is to mark the name on the underside of the dinghy.

## Spares and replacements

It is hard to strike the right balance between carrying too few and too many spares. It is obvious that the lack of a simple part can delay a yacht for days or weeks. It is less apparent that overstocking with unnecessary spares will increase weight and lead to slower passages. A plethora of spares will also make it more difficult to locate the items needed in a hurry, and space that could be put to better use will be wasted. The newcomer to ocean sailing is likely to err on the side of caution and carry too much.

Those who have always done their own fitting out will have a better idea of what to take than will those who have relied entirely on a boatyard. The number of items to be carried can be limited to an extent if some standardisation is adopted. Many boats have, for example, six or eight different sizes of shackle in various locations. With a little thought this number might be reduced to three. The same reasoning can be applied to everything from running rigging to bilge pumps. That way, many spares will be interchangeable, with cannibalisation of less important equipment a possible last resort.

All things mechanical are certain to need servicing, and possibly replacing, during the course of a long cruise. Pumps will need new valves and gaskets; engines will need new fuel and oil filters, and alternators will need new brushes and belts. Hard working winches will need to be stripped down for cleaning and oiling from time to time and, in this case, spares should include not only internal parts but also at least one spare handle.

Diesel injector pumps are costly, and can only be repaired by experts, so if embarking on a very long cruise it might be wise to carry a spare. A complete set of the moulded rubber hoses that fit the engine is essential, as if they fail there is no substitute. It should not be assumed that the engine maker's recommended list of spares and tools will necessarily include everything needed; it will, however, be a good starting point.

Many ocean cruising yachtsmen do much of their routine work themselves, both for convenience and their own satisfaction. Workshop or users' manuals will be found useful in servicing less familiar equipment and may also be requested by a professional – an electronics engineer will probably need a circuit diagram. Facilities for getting reliable work done throughout the north Atlantic have improved dramatically over the last decade and there are few places where it is not possible to find a diesel mechanic or electrician. If the necessary spares are carried it will generally be possible to get them fitted, but obtaining the same items locally may be impossible.

Synthetic sheets and halyards will last for years if not allowed to chafe but a few hours of careless use may destroy the strength of an important line. A replacement length should be carried for each diameter in use. To suggest carrying enough stainless steel wire to replace any part of the rigging en route would perhaps be a counsel of perfection, but some provision must be made for possible rigging problems. At the very minimum, several one metre lengths of wire, together with a plentiful supply of bulldog grips (wire rope clamps), should be carried so that a temporary repair can be made to a damaged wire. It would be preferable to carry (in addition) a length of wire suitable for replacing the longest shroud or stay. One or two extra rigging screws and a selection of swageless terminals should also be aboard.

Sail repairs will be routine when ocean sailing, even if the sails are new at the start of the voyage. Palm, needles, beeswax, twine and sailcloth in the weight of each sail

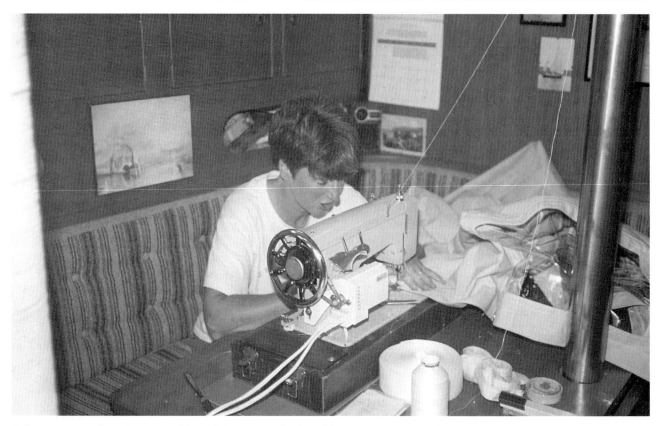

Sail repairs are a fact of voyaging life, and if space can be found for one, a sewing machine will be invaluable.
*Photo: Gavin McLaren*

will be needed. Store needles in a tin containing plenty of grease. If space can be found for one, a sewing machine will save many hours of stitching and should be high on the priority list of the larger yacht. It need not be a sail-maker's model, although one of those is ideal – a simple hand machine will suffice for temporary repairs.

When deciding what to take and what not to take consider what it might be reasonable to find in any moderately sized town and what is likely to only be available in a major city or yachting centre. Ordinary paint, for instance, can be bought in most towns and it is not worth carrying a large supply, whereas anti-fouling will not be nearly so readily available. Dry cells for torches will be readily available/easy to find but the special batteries needed for some cameras may be almost unobtainable.

Thought must be given to the problems of metric sizes too. In the USA and much of the Caribbean few items are available in metric sizes, whereas in Europe metrication is almost universal. The difference may be critical for parts for gas and fuel systems and for rigging items. Although the difference may not be obvious, a $^3/_8$ in swageless wire terminal may be disastrously inappropriate to 9 mm wire, and 6 mm compression fittings may not make leakproof joints to $^1/_4$ in copper pipe.

Having decided what to take and what not to take and accumulated all the items needed, stowage must be carefully arranged and recorded. It is not enough to know that an essential spare or tool is aboard 'somewhere' – the more urgently it may be needed the more accessible it must be. A few minutes could mean the difference between catching a problem before it can escalate, and being faced with a whole chain of damage and disaster.

## The toolbox

Tools must be appropriate to the jobs they will be expected to do, and may need to be bought specially – vane gears, for example, often require hex keys of particular sizes. Almost without exception good quality tools are easier to use than inferior ones and, with reasonable care, will last a lifetime. On a yacht, salt water is the principal enemy of good tools and it is worth going to considerable lengths to protect them from it.

The loss of an important tool or part could prove serious, and neither tools nor pieces of dismantled equipment should be left lying about on deck where there is a risk of them going overboard. Aloft, wrist lanyards to prevent tools being dropped are essential. If working on a vital piece of equipment outboard – for example a vane gear – the dinghy secured beneath it will save the items that will inevitably be dropped. If this cannot be arranged, then some other catch-all should be devised. A sun umbrella, rigged upside-down, is ideal.

Tools are often needed in an emergency and should therefore be readily accessible and in known locations. Few yachts under about 12 m (40 ft) boast a complete workbench, but well sited and organised tool stowage is nevertheless essential. In smaller yachts this may consist of several boxes, each one devoted to tools of a different type – mechanical, electrical or woodwork, etc. It is a sound idea to have a small selection of the tools most often used in a particularly handy stowage. This 'first aid' toolkit might include mole grips, pliers, an adjustable spanner and a couple of screwdrivers.

For the transatlantic yacht, the most significant change that has taken place over the last decade has been the advent of the Global Positioning System (GPS). As little as ten years ago, the vast majority of yachts making the crossing relied exclusively, once away from the land, on navigation by the sun and stars, and if the sky was overcast the position became increasingly uncertain. The electronic aids available then – Satnav, Loran and Omega – were expensive, bulky, frequently inaccurate and required considerable skill to use successfully. Most sets took a lot of power and their reliability left much to be desired.

Today the situation has altered beyond recognition. At the touch of a GPS button, the navigator can read his position, accurate to within a few tens of metres, day or night, rain or shine. If he wishes, the same set will instantly give him his course and speed made good, together with the bearing and distance of his destination; many other features may be available. All this in an easy to use package not much bigger than a paperback book (and possibly much smaller), whose power requirements are measured in milliamps and which probably cost less than a week's berthing in most marinas. It is hardly surprising that the yacht without at least one GPS set is considerably rarer than the yacht without an engine.

There is more to navigation, however, than simply knowing the yacht's position. Other instruments will be needed, as will charts and pilot books. The capabilities and limitations of the GPS set itself must be understood. Although it is still quite possible to cross the Atlantic relying on traditional means alone, this book assumes that a GPS set is carried. The situation in case of GPS failure is considered at the end of this chapter.

## The chart table

The most practical chart table in heavy weather is one facing either fore or aft. Ideally, it should be close to the companionway, but not so close that there is a significant risk of it getting wet. There should be a chart table light; the type on a flexible stalk will enable an area of the chart to be brightly illuminated without disturbing nearby sleepers. There should be some book stowage within reach, together with a place where navigational instruments – pencil, rubber, dividers and parallel rulers – and spectacles (if needed) can be safely stowed, and an accurate timepiece must be visible. Nearly as important as the table itself is a secure seat where the navigator can sit safely with all necessary equipment within reach. Using it should not entail evicting another person from their bunk. It will often be necessary to use both hands when navigating and a strap to keep the navigator in his seat may be useful on one or other tack, or when the boat is rolling heavily.

Charts must be stored flat as few things are as irritating as a chart perpetually trying to roll itself up while in use. There must be some stowage for charts handy to the table itself; the 'school desk' type of table with a lifting work surface and stowage within is not ideal, but will serve. A depth of 2 in (5 cm) will take a hundred British Admiralty charts folded once, ie as the majority of them are supplied.

The dimensions of chart tables aboard British yachts have traditionally been dictated by the size of a standard Admiralty chart. Currently this is 28 in deep by 42 in wide (71 cm x 107 cm) and a chart table this size has been the ideal, although often impossible to accommodate. Admiralty charts are set to increase in size – in line with European standards – to about 33 in x 47 in (84 cm x 119 cm) and this should be considered if building or modifying a chart table. A size of 33 in x 23.5 in (84 cm x 59.5 cm) will allow most American or Admiralty charts to be used folded.

It should not be thought that the chart table will be wasted space when the yacht is in harbour. Some area apart from the saloon table is invaluable for letter writing

The Bowman 42 is an almost ideal example of the modern ocean voyaging yacht – fast, spacious and comfortable, but still within the handling capabilities of an experienced couple. *Photo: The Bowman Group*

and other paperwork and the chart table will double as a desk, a workbench (for clean jobs) and even a temporary bar.

## The log book

An accurate and up-to-date log is no less important than it was in pre-GPS days. Apart from its navigational uses, the log is also a legal document and possible evidence in case of a collision or insurance claim. Whether you use a purpose-designed ship's log or a ruled exercise book is immaterial, but in either case allow enough room to devote a separate page to each day at sea.

It is the responsibility of the person on watch to write up the log; in larger crews where formal watches are not kept during the day, the task may perhaps be allocated to a younger or less active crew member. Two-hourly is the usual interval for regular entries and, as a minimum, the following should be recorded:

1 Time
2 Compass course steered since the last entry
3 Log reading
4 GPS position
5 Wind strength and direction
6 Barometric pressure

The same information should be noted whenever any non-routine entries are made. Which other events are to be recorded should be laid down by the skipper, and a note of them made inside the front cover of the log. As a minimum, the list should include: all changes of course; significant changes in the wind or weather; the running of the engine; any sail changes or reefs taken in or shaken out. Other useful, interesting or memorable events can also be mentioned, and the odd remark about dolphins or a triumph of cordon bleu cookery will not detract from the log's basic purpose as the official record.

Although not strictly a navigational matter, many skippers use the log each evening to write a brief summary of the day. As well as recording a general impression of the previous 24 hours, this is a good time to note the distance covered and the amounts of fuel and fresh water used and remaining. Such a summary need not be a literary masterpiece but, long after an ocean passage is over, reading it will evoke many memories.

## The compass

A reliable, good quality steering compass is essential, and it should be checked and corrected for deviation before leaving home waters. Do not fall for the fallacy of believing that GPS has rendered this unnecessary. A hand-bearing compass should also be carried, and this can be used to check that the deviation of the steering compass has not altered noticeably. Deviation can change at sea but this is normally a very gradual process and is not significant during an Atlantic crossing, although on a very long cruise the compass may need to be reswung. However, a lightning strike, or even a near miss, can cause major changes. Fortunately, deviation can be determined at sea by taking a compass bearing of the sun as it rises or sets. This is compared with the true bearing, which can easily be calculated, or obtained from a simple table. A full description of the procedure is given by Eric Hiscock in *Cruising Under Sail* and is also included in most textbooks on astro navigation, but it must be appreciated that the method only gives the deviation *for the course being steered at the time*.

Ferro cement and steel boats, particularly those with steel decks, pose special problems of deviation. Their compasses should be professionally checked and adjusted before departure and at regular intervals during a cruise. Once a year should be the minimum and for new boats, whose deviation may take many months to settle, more frequently than that.

## Barometers and thermometers

An aneroid barometer should be fitted and checked and adjusted before each ocean passage. A barograph is an attractive and useful instrument, but is bulky and may not, in any case, work well on a small yacht due to the motion. If a barograph is not carried then the barometer reading must be regularly recorded. In some areas of the Atlantic a thermometer will be useful for checking water as well as air temperature, particularly on the fringes of the Gulf Stream.

## GPS receivers

GPS sets calculate position by using signals transmitted from geostationary satellites operated by the United States Department of Defense. A description of the GPS system is found in the manuals provided with most sets. It is sufficient to say here that position is available at all times, worldwide, and to a nominal accuracy of about a hundred metres. The system is capable of much greater accuracy, but this is denied to civilian users by deliberately inserting errors into the signals the satellites transmit. This downgrading – which is referred to as 'Selective Availability', or 'SA' – may be reduced or discontinued during the lifetime of this book and full system accuracy, around 10 m, will be available to all. This is a political decision, and in any case is only of academic interest to most yachts.

There are many makes of set and the handbook should be consulted for details of installation and use. Power may come from the yacht's 12-volt system, or from dry cell batteries, or from either. Some are described as waterproof and a few certainly are. If a set is to be used in the cockpit, however, the manufacturer's specification should be carefully checked as definitions of 'waterproof' vary. All sets will give position in latitude and longitude on the GPS datum, which is WGS 84 – most have the option of selecting other datums. Most sets allow waypoints to be entered and also give a readout of course and speed over the ground, but in cheaper sets this is likely to be a fairly crude estimate. Almost all sets can give a highly accurate reading of UT – Universal Time, formerly known as GMT. Many can be connected to other electronic instruments, log, compass, wind speed and direction sensors etc to give a variety of sophisticated readouts.

Occasionally sets are seen which have what may be described as a 'DR mode', although individual makes will name this mode differently. When it is in operation, the receiver takes no data from the satellites, but instead calculates positions based on the last course and speed made good. It is imperative that if this feature is in use there is a conspicuous indication of the fact. Often, it is automatically selected if satellite signals are lost, which will happen if the aerial or its wiring are damaged. Not realising that this has happened, and that the apparently precise positions displayed are nothing more than electronic guesswork, has caused many groundings.

The ocean passagemaker should select a GPS set that is simple, robust and easy to use. A good sized screen which can be read in all lights, large clear figures, substantial buttons set far enough apart and operating procedures that are logical, count for more than the ability to store a thousand waypoints or remember a hundred routes.

## Charts, pilots and other publications

### Charts

There is no basic difference between the charts required for an Atlantic cruise and those needed for home waters, except perhaps their quantity. Charts can sometimes be bought along the way but, except in major ports, only local stock will be available. For reasons of space and weight (not to mention cost), few yachts carry complete cover for a transatlantic cruise and a selection has to be made. Before departure, study a copy of NP 131, the worldwide *Catalogue of Admiralty Charts*, or its US equivalent, the *Defense Mapping Agency Public Sale Nautical Charts and Publications Catalogs*, of which Regions 1 to 5 will be relevant to an Atlantic cruise. The Armchair Sailor Bookstore in Newport, Rhode Island (see Appendix D) produces a useful *Atlantic Crossing Checklist* of relevant charts and other publications kept in stock, including the above.

Deciding which charts to order can be difficult, particularly if they cannot be inspected before purchase. Once the route has been chosen, small scale passage charts can be selected, with larger scales for the landfalls and inshore work. Very large scale plans of commercial harbours are generally unnecessary, since these areas are likely to be well buoyed and lit. Charts relevant to areas in Parts II and III of this book are listed in the text.

Some plotting sheets will be needed for working up the DR in the open ocean, where the chart is likely to be on too small a scale for accurate work. Various types are available from chart agents – some cover only a single band of latitude, others are universal and the user constructs the longitude scale appropriate to the latitude he is in, following the instructions on the sheet. This type is preferable. British Admiralty plotting sheet D6018 is recommended as it has clear instructions, will fit easily on a yacht's chart table, and is supplied in pads of 25 sheets.

In the major cruising 'crossroads', yachts with charts for sale are often found, or it may be possible to borrow charts. In such places, if a full plan copier is available, charts are often copied. With American charts, and those of some other countries, this may be done freely, but British Admiralty charts and publications are protected by copyright and may not be reproduced without permission. Working with a copied chart is less satisfactory than with an original and the copying process may well introduce inaccuracies.

### Chart datums

The great accuracy of GPS means that the horizontal datum of a chart and positional accuracy of the charted features, something that until now the yachtsman has taken for granted, must now be considered. GPS operates on WGS 84 datum, but charts may be on a completely different datum, which can differ by several hundred yards. Where possible, new editions of charts use WGS 84 and this fact is noted. If a different datum is used, a correction to be applied to GPS positions may be given. If the datum is not specified on the chart, caution should be exercised.

It must be remembered that many areas of the world, including parts of the Caribbean, were surveyed before the advent of electronic aids or radio time signals. Latitude and longitude in these areas could only be determined by astronomical means, often using a chronometer that had not been independently checked for months. These surveys are remarkably accurate, but there are sometimes errors, more usually in longitude than in latitude, and these can be as much as half a mile. When making a landfall on a Caribbean island, the date of the survey given on the chart should be checked and the cautionary notes read with care. Although your GPS may be certain where it is, the land you are approaching may not be so sure!

### Pilot books and yachtsmen s guides

Ideally, pilots or guides should also be obtained before departure. A careful study of them will help in selecting the route, and if they contain clear plans, it may be possible to dispense with some charts.

The 'official' publications, the *Sailing Directions* produced by the British Admiralty and the US Defense Mapping Agency, are highly accurate and updated by regular supplements. They are, however, mainly slanted towards commercial and naval vessels and this means that many of the harbours and anchorages most suitable for yachts are only briefly mentioned. These books are bulky and expensive, but they do contain a wealth of general information, particularly about climate, currents and tidal streams which gives a useful background to a cruising area. Not many yachts carry them, but consider borrowing them for study before departure.

Yachtsmen's guides vary both in quality and up-to-dateness. It will be worth enquiring amongst people who know an area well for recommendations both as to the best guide available and the extent to which it should be trusted. Such guides are protected by copyright, and although photocopies are sometimes made (and occasionally offered for sale) this is illegal. Pilot books and guides relevant to areas in Parts II and III of this book are listed in the text and in Appendix B.

### Annual publications

Opinion differs amongst experienced yachtsmen as to how many annual publications need be carried aboard the yacht equipped with a good set of reasonably up-to-date charts. Tide tables and tidal stream atlases are obviously a necessity in areas where the tidal influences are great, but are less important for the Atlantic and Caribbean islands. In northern Europe, the Caribbean and North America a commercial almanac will usually contain the information contained in several official volumes – *Light List*, *Tide Tables* and *Tidal Stream Atlases*. To some extent, the books needed depend on the equipment carried; a yacht with weatherfax and HF transceiver will need the appropriate volumes of the *List of Radio Signals*.

In the English Channel and its approaches, the tidal range is great and the streams strong. It is essential that a yacht has the necessary tidal information on board for the area before making a landfall in these waters. The same is true, but to a lesser extent, for those bound for the American coast north of the Chesapeake.

### Notices to Mariners

Charts, pilot books and lists of lights start going out-of-date even before they have left the printer. Ideally, all should be amended using weekly *Notices to Mariners*. In Britain these can be consulted at any Customs House, or obtained on a regular basis from chart agents. In the USA, *Notices to Mariners* are available from the Defense Mapping Agency.

In practice, hardly any yachtsmen do keep their charts and pilot books up-to-date in this way. To what extent older charts and publications can be relied upon is a matter of judgement. The older the information, the greater the caution that must be exercised before relying on it. It should be remembered that the rocks, reefs and islands generally alter only slowly, but that the works of man, including lights, buoys and other navigational marks, can change overnight.

### *Gnomonic charts and great circle sailing*

The shortest distance between two points on the globe is a great circle. A rhumb line, the straight line on a Mercator chart, goes by a longer route. In practical terms, the difference is negligible except in high latitudes and the only transatlantic passages where it may be relevant are those between the northern part of the USA and northern Europe. Only in these high latitudes is the saving of distance made by keeping to the great circle route likely to outweigh considerations of finding favourable winds and currents. To plot a great circle, a chart drawn on the gnomonic projection is needed. Details of the procedure can be found in navigational textbooks. GPS receivers usually display course to the destination waypoint as a great circle bearing, although on many sets the rhumb line option can be selected.

## Ocean navigation in practice

There is more to ocean navigation than merely switching on the GPS, entering the destination as a waypoint, and then following the set's directions. Although such an approach may work, it offers no protection against mistakes. It would be all too easy, for example, to inadvertently enter 12° 42' instead of 14° 22', and not discover the error until land fails to materialise.

The yacht's position must be plotted on the passage chart at regular intervals. In the open ocean this will usually be once each day but, when approaching land or near the Gulf Stream, may need to be done more frequently. In this way, the navigational picture can be seen at once and mistakes are likely to be spotted quickly. Successive daily positions should be heading for the intended spot, be it landfall or turning point, and the distance to go taken from the chart should be the same - within the limits of measurable accuracy - as that calculated by the GPS. If there are discrepancies, then something is wrong and the

Although over fifty years old, the 30 ft cutter *Viking*, seen here in the British Virgin Islands, has cruised extensively in Europe, the Caribbean and the USA. *Photo: Georgie McLaren*

navigator should double check to find out what it is.

As well as this regular plot, the daily run, as recorded by the GPS, should be compared with the DR worked up from the information in the log. The passage chart will be on too small a scale to do this and a plotting sheet must be used. The two runs, GPS and DR, are unlikely to be the same, the difference being due to either error in the log and/or compass or to the influence of current. If discrepancies are consistently in one direction and of roughly the same size, suspect the former, but before checking the compass ensure that the DR and GPS computations are both using magnetic or true courses. It matters little which, but they must be the same.

As the land is approached the position should be plotted more often and a larger scale chart used as soon as the yacht lies within its limits. The DR should be worked up frequently and the current regularly assessed. With GPS, one ought to be certain of the landfall, but it is still possible to be set a long way off the intended track by a wayward current, and currents frequently change significantly near the land. Once the landfall has been made, the normal techniques of coastal navigation take over, and GPS becomes just one of the tools used in the process. Hand-bearing compass, echo-sounder and the navigator's eyes will be more important. For the reasons mentioned in the section on chart datums, GPS must not be relied on when entering a strange harbour.

The end of an Atlantic crossing is always exciting, even for the most experienced ocean passagemaker. In the euphoria, it should not be forgotten that the period after land has been sighted is likely to be the most navigationally hazardous part of the entire passage and demands the utmost care. Celebrations must wait until the yacht is safely berthed.

## Equipment failure

All man made items are fallible and some consideration must be given to the situation should GPS fail. This might happen for two reasons: the system itself could break down or the yacht's equipment could become defective.

The first reason, system failure, whilst theoretically possible, is so unlikely as to be inconceivable. The GPS system was designed to be highly resistant to deliberate attack, let alone accidental failure. All the critical components are duplicated, often several times. There are, for instance, spare satellites in orbit, ready to be switched on should an in-use satellite fail, with others available for launching. GPS was designed to be highly resistant to radio interference and to be unaffected by sunspot activity. It is possible that the system might be deliberately turned off, but the huge, and growing, number of civilian users, for many of whom it is literally vital, makes this possibility remote in the extreme.

The likelihood of onboard equipment failure, whether of the GPS set or of the yacht's power supplies, is far higher. Installing good quality equipment, maintaining the electrical system conscientiously, and keeping the batteries well charged will do much to reduce this possibility, but it is still a real one and provision must be made for it.

The traditional fallback is astro navigation. This is not the black art that some would make it out to be, but, rather like riding a bicycle, it is a skill that must be acquired by practice rather than just by theory. Equally, it is a skill that, once acquired, is never completely lost. If astro navigation is to be the fallback, then a sextant and various books of tables will be required, together with an accurate timepiece. Courses in the subject are available and there are many textbooks, some of which are listed in Appendix A.

The alternative to astro navigation is to rely on back-up electronics. In practical terms this means one, or more, waterproof, hand-held, battery powered GPS receivers, with the necessary converters to enable them to be run from the ship's power system. With such a set, failure of the main GPS receiver will be little more than an inconvenience. If it is the electrical system that has failed, a hand-held GPS can be switched on once or twice a day to give a position. Used in this way a set of batteries will last for the duration of the crossing. If this option is chosen, the spare set should be treated like any other piece of emergency equipment, serviced when necessary, tested before departure, and kept in a dry and secure stowage. Plenty of batteries should be carried (in case the set is inadvertently left switched on), reserved exclusively for the GPS; they will need periodic replacement, whether used or not.

Astro navigation has the advantage that it is well proven and that it is independent of any outside agency. Its drawbacks are that the equipment is costly – a good sextant will cost at least twice as much as a hand-held GPS – and that the techniques take time to learn and need to be practised at sea before they can be relied upon. In heavy weather it is difficult to achieve accurate results, particularly for the novice. It is not available when the sky is cloudy, a point often overlooked by astro enthusiasts, and on the northern and middle latitude crossings it may be cloudy for many days at a time. Relying on a back-up GPS has the advantages of simplicity, accuracy and indifference to weather conditions. Its drawbacks are that it relies on an outside agency and that, should the yacht be struck by lightning, the back-up set could be destroyed along with all the other electrical and electronic equipment on board (including the astro navigator's digital watch).

The choice between these two options must rest with the individual. It is a subject on which strong views are often held, not always well thought out ones. The following suggestion is made with some trepidation. Those who have experience of using astro navigation at sea may depend on it as their only back-up system. Those who do not have that experience should carry a reserve GPS set. They may wish to take a sextant and tables and learn astro navigation techniques along the way, but they should not count on being able to do so unaided, however many textbooks are carried or courses have been done.

# 5  ELECTRONICS AND COMMUNICATIONS

Both electronics and communications are highly specialised subjects and ones in which change is taking place at almost breakneck speed. It is only possible here to give more than an overview of the current (1998) situation and to mention some of the general points to consider before installing any electronic equipment. There are excellent books available – many aimed at the less technically minded – covering specific topics and giving comprehensive advice on the choice of equipment, its installation and operation. However, when fitting complicated or interconnected systems, professional help will often prove worthwhile.

Most transatlantic cruisers now fit more, and increasingly complex, electronic equipment than a few years ago. Today, gear that used to be confined to the largest yachts is now commonplace. Much of this gear makes long distance cruising more comfortable and convenient, but hardly any of it is essential. Each owner must decide for himself what level of comfort and convenience he feels is necessary – this is an individual matter and what seems an opulent luxury to one yacht may be an absolute essential to another. It should not be forgotten, however, that each piece of equipment must not only be purchased and installed, but must also be maintained, kept dry, and provided with the necessary power. Although modern electronics are remarkably reliable, there will inevitably be periodic breakdowns, and getting electronics repaired in faraway places can be frustrating, time consuming and costly. The most successful ocean voyagers are those who have limited the equipment fitted to that which is necessary (to them) for an acceptable, as opposed to the highest possible, standard of cruising life.

The borderline between electrics and electronics has become increasingly blurred. Many items that would in the past have been thought of as part of the electrical system, now contain quite complex electronics – for example, alternators, regulators and battery chargers. Fridge systems will probably contain an electronic controller and some engine instruments may too. Although the electrical system has been discussed in Chapter 2, the yacht's electrical and electronic systems must be considered together; if a lot of electronics are to be fitted then the basic electrical installation may need modification.

It is obvious that all electronics take power and that at some point this power will have to be put back into the batteries. What is not so often appreciated is that much electronic equipment needs a comparatively stable supply voltage to run reliably, and this may not be easy to provide. A yacht's battery voltage might vary from 14.2 volts when being charged by a 'smart' alternator, down to 11.5 volts when a heavy load is being taken from it by, for example, a fridge or autopilot. The bigger the battery, the less will its voltage vary under a given load; a big battery acts as a kind of voltage 'shock absorber' smoothing out the variations. So when fitting electronic items, a larger battery bank may be needed, not only to provide the power but also to steady the voltage.

The voltage at the battery is one thing, but the voltage at the equipment is quite another. Every time electricity is squeezed down a wire or through a connection some voltage is lost, and the longer or thinner the wire, or the poorer the connection, the greater that loss will be. It is important, therefore, that sufficiently heavy wiring is used throughout and that all the joints in it are meticulously made. Electricity can leak away to earth through dirt and damp, causing further voltage drop, so the batteries, switchboard and cabling must be kept clean. If electronic equipment fails to work, or only works intermittently, check that the voltage *at the equipment* is within the manufacturer's specification. Generally, better quality devices have a greater tolerance of voltage fluctuations.

Damp, salt laden air and electronics do not mix well. Not only is salt water a conductor, which causes damaging internal short circuits, it is also corrosive. Salt crystals can attack the circuitry on printed circuit boards with disastrous results. Well made units, designed for the marine environment, should have cases that fit properly with efficient seals to keep the damp out; cheaper gear is less likely to. Even so, below decks electronics should be installed where they are unlikely to get wet. Cockpit instruments should be genuinely waterproof. It is worth checking exactly what the manufacturer means by that word, and that the instruments really will keep the water out when repeatedly drenched, day after day.

Electronics need less maintenance than many items on board, but they do need some. Connections in cabling and aerial runs should be checked periodically to ensure that corrosion has not set in; log and echo sounder transducers and radio earth plates will need occasional cleaning; log impellers must be renewed at intervals; masthead instruments may need replacement bearings every few years. Many electronic devices contain small internal batteries to retain information in the memory when the equipment is switched off. Although their life may be several years, these batteries do not last for ever and they can normally only be replaced by an expert. So before leaving home waters have older electronic equipment checked and serviced by a professional. Often this will mean removing it so that it can be tested in a workshop with the right specialist facilities. This gives a good opportunity to ensure that the onboard installation cabling and connectors, normally hidden away out of sight, are in good condition.

## Instruments

### Echo-sounder

This is probably the most useful electronic device aboard. The ocean going yacht actually spends most of her time within soundings, very often in unfamiliar waters, and a reliable echo-sounder is a necessity. A shallow water alarm that can be set to go off when a selected depth is reached is a boon for the short-handed crew, as long as it is dependable.

For the majority, who have never cruised without one,

doing without an echo-sounder is nerve-wracking. A lead and line makes a very unsatisfactory substitute, even for those with the skill to use it. For this reason, the echo-sounder is one of the few items of electronics for which it is worth carrying a spare. A simple rotating neon (Seafarer) sounder is cheap and reliable and can run from the ship's supply or an internal dry battery. Its transducer can be fitted before departure and the set itself stowed away in the depths of a locker. It will enable the cruise to continue should the main set fail.

### Logs

Some sort of log is essential for accurate dead reckoning. Although many voyagers carry a mechanical towed log as a back-up, the electronic through hull type has significant advantages. If properly calibrated it is more accurate, will measure speed as well as distance run, and may incorporate a trip mechanism. Various types are available. The impeller can be a paddlewheel or a rotator; some logs use sonic or electromagnetic arrangements to measure the water flow and this has the advantage of eliminating fouling problems. If static for any length of time in the tropics it is worth withdrawing the log to keep it clean. Some transducers also measure water temperature, and when near the Gulf Stream this is of more than academic interest. A final advantage of the through hull log, as opposed to the towed type, is that it will co-exist with a fishing line.

### Wind speed and direction

Masthead sensors to measure the apparent wind speed and direction are frequently seen. Provided there is a repeater visible from the helm, the direction indicator may enable a better course to windward to be steered and help to prevent an accidental gybe when running downwind. The speed indicator can be informative, but it should be remembered that the wind speed at the masthead is considerably higher than that felt at sea level. Some form of variable damping control is desirable as, particularly in light winds, the movement of the masthead will significantly influence both direction and speed readings. Wind speed indicators are seldom very accurate and it is common for two adjacent boats in an anchorage to report wildly different readings.

### Integrated systems

These consist of a small, dedicated, computer unit into which information from various sensors is fed. A variety of complex outputs can be calculated and displayed, the range depending on the sophistication of the system. At a minimum, log, wind speed and wind direction data is combined to give true wind angle and true wind speed. If a heading sensor is added (usually a fluxgate compass), then course and magnetic wind direction can be given and this information may be supplied to an autopilot. Connecting a GPS receiver will enable - in theory - leeway and tidal stream or current vectors to be computed. Multiple digital readouts and analogue displays can be provided, both at the helm and at the chart table, and alarms can usually be set for wind speed, heading and other functions. The capacity and complexity of an integrated system is limited only by the owner's inclination - and the depth of his pocket.

The major drawback is that the failure of a single component can bring the whole edifice crashing down. For example, should an electronic wind direction indicator fail on passage it is unlikely to be more than an inconvenience. But if that failure leads to the loss of all the instrumentation, including the log, echo-sounder, autopilot and GPS, then the situation might be serious. For this reason, many very experienced ocean voyagers prefer to have individual, stand-alone, electronic instruments rather than such complex systems.

## Navigation aids

### Position fixing systems

The almost universal adoption of GPS by commercial shipping and aircraft has led to the demise of most other electronic position fixing systems and, in the long term, only LORAN is likely to remain. This hyperbolic system uses radio signals transmitted from shore stations to compute the receiver's position. Most of the North Atlantic is, or will shortly be, covered. Other than independence from the US Department of Defense, LORAN has no advantages over GPS for the yachtsman.

The current situation regarding other systems is as follows. The TRANSIT satellite navigation system and the OMEGA worldwide land based system have been discontinued. Parts of the European DECCA medium range hyperbolic network remain, but it is intended that DECCA operation will cease by the year 2005 at the latest. The extensive network of coastal DF beacons has been largely dismantled, although many aeronautical beacons remain.

### Radar

Radar sets are increasingly seen aboard cruising yachts. Radar has obvious uses as an aid to collision avoidance in poor visibility or at night and, during the trade wind Atlantic crossing, it will help to spot approaching squalls. It may be of assistance when making a landfall and, in the hands of a skilled user, can enable some unlit harbours to be entered at night. In the North Atlantic, radar comes into its own for those boats planning to cruise in Maine and Nova Scotia where fog is common. It will also be valuable, for the same reason, on the north European coast, particularly in the western approaches to the English Channel. However, yachtsmen should be aware that, under the Collision Regulations, vessels fitted with radar are obliged to use it, and use it properly, when visibility is poor; failure to do so might result in an insurance claim being rejected.

### Chart systems

The information on charts can be stored electronically, and many charts, including those from the British Admiralty, are available this way. The chart, or a selection of charts, are usually supplied on a Compact Disc (CD) and can be displayed on board using either a special display unit or, more commonly for yachts, a personal computer. The output from a GPS may also be input to the computer, and the yacht's position is thus continuously displayed on the screen in relation to her surroundings. Many advantages are claimed for electronic charts and, for those who like computers, they are certainly fun to use. In the future they are likely to become the norm, certainly for ships. At present, however, the yachtsman should view them as an adjunct to, and not a substitute for, paper charts.

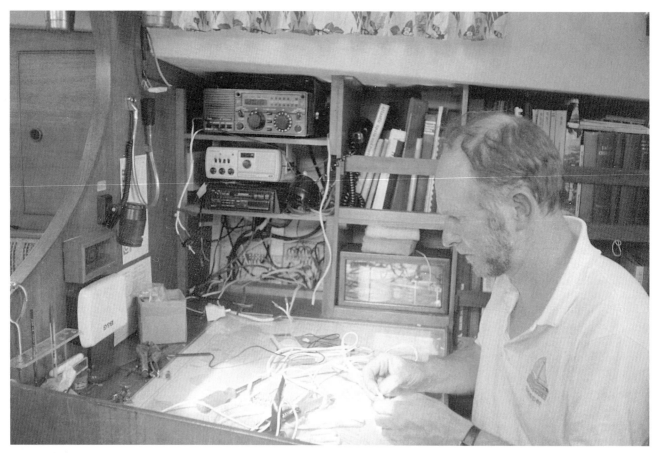

Electrical systems are increasingly complex and need to be well installed. As equipment is added they will need modifications.
*Photo: Georgie McLaren*

## Personal computers

A personal portable computer (PC) is now commonly seen aboard voyaging yachts. With a printer, it has largely replaced the typewriter for correspondence. Many skippers keep records of stores, spares and charts in the computer, reference books are increasingly available on CD, and it is only a matter of time before equipment manuals are supplied that way too. With the right software, astro navigation calculations can be performed with ease and tides predicted. A PC can be taken ashore and connected into the telephone system to give access to the Internet and e-mail and, increasingly, connected to a radio set to provide a wide range of facilities.

Computers are seldom designed with yachts in mind and are more vulnerable to the effects of life afloat than most electronics. If choosing one specifically for the yacht, physical robustness should be a high priority. It is a considerable advantage if both it and the printer can either be run, or have their batteries recharged, directly from the yacht's electrical system rather than via an inverter, but the manufacturer should be consulted about the risk from voltage fluctuations. A secure, dry stowage will be needed and every effort made to protect the PC from damp.

It will generally be impossible to get a PC or printer repaired en route. Probably the best chance of dealing with problems will be to find a fellow yachtsman who is a computer expert (there are a surprisingly large number in the voyaging community). To give him any chance of assisting, the most comprehensive manual available should be carried, as should the necessary CDs or floppy discs to enable essential software to be reinstalled. Afloat, it is even more important to make back-up copies of valuable data than it is ashore, as a PC aboard a yacht is much more prone to failure. Computer consumables will be available in very few places, so a supply of printer ribbons or cartridges, floppy discs etc should be carried.

## Communications

The ocean going yachtsman needs a radio receiver to obtain weather forecasts. Most also listen to news and other broadcasts and many yachtsmen wish to be able to communicate with other yachts, with ships, or with those ashore. They may use VHF, HF/MF or satellite radio to do some or all of these things.

## Receivers

Whatever other radio equipment is carried it is worth investing in a good quality, stand-alone receiver with frequency coverage from 150 to 30,000 kHz. It should be capable of receiving both ordinary public broadcasts, such as those transmitted by national and commercial radio stations, and single sideband (SSB) transmissions on both the upper and lower sideband (USB/LSB); SSB is generally used for long range communications. The set should be capable of running from either dry batteries or the ship's supply, and several sets of batteries should be carried.

Such a receiver can be connected via a suitable modem to a PC to enable Weatherfax and Navtex broadcasts to be received. If this is to be done then a digitally tuned set – one where an exact frequency can be entered via a keypad – should be chosen.

### Navtex

Much of the information broadcast by Navtex stations is of interest to the yachtsman, in particular weather messages, navigation warnings and distress and safety messages, but the range is limited to within about 400 miles of the transmitting station. Coverage around the North Atlantic is patchy, being better in Europe than America, and at present little of the Caribbean is covered. A dedicated Navtex receiver, which is relatively inexpensive, is preferable to using a PC as it will receive all relevant messages automatically. Messages, which consist of words rather than pictures, may be displayed on a screen or printed on special paper, depending on the set chosen. Navtex forms part of the Global Maritime Distress and Safety System (GMDSS) mentioned later.

### Weatherfax

Once the preserve of large racing yachts, Weatherfax, by which synoptic charts, pictorial forecasts and satellite pictures can be received, is now widely used by cruising sailors. Dedicated Weatherfax receivers are available that print out charts on special paper. These are expensive, however, and many yachts use a PC and printer to achieve the same result. The drawback is that unattended operation is often impracticable. Various software and hardware packages are available and it is worth viewing a selection before choosing a specific one. Weatherfax is generally transmitted on HF and it can be received at long range with virtually worldwide coverage. There are many transmitting stations and some are listed in Appendix G. For comprehensive information a specialist publication such as the British *Admiralty List of Radio Signals, Volume 3* must be consulted.

## Transmitters

Yachts may have VHF, HF/MF or satellite transmitters, as well as Emergency Position Indicating Radio Beacons. These latter are for use solely in distress, but the others allow the voyager to make routine communications with ships and shore stations. They too may be useful in an emergency, but no one should embark on a transatlantic passage in the expectation that help can be summoned should things go wrong. Quite apart from any other considerations, in many disasters – fire, hull damage or dismasting – radio transmitters are quite likely to be damaged beyond use.

Whilst receivers may be fitted and operated without restriction, all radio transmitters fitted in yachts (other than those operated by a licensed Radio Amateur) must be of an approved type and the operator must be licensed. The yacht will require a ship station licence as well. Requirements for type approval and ship and operators' licences vary from country to country. Operators need to pass an examination on radio procedures, with the complexity of the exam depending on the equipment to be used. Most sets on the market will meet the technical requirements, but a secondhand set may not.

## VHF

This is widely fitted and will be familiar to most yachtsmen. It is limited to line of sight communications between ships or with shore stations. Transatlantic voyagers should be aware that the frequencies of some channels (5, 7, 18, 19, 21, 22, 23, 65, 66, 78, 79, 80, 83 and 88) are different in the USA and its environs from the rest of the world. Internationally these channels are duplex, with transmission and reception by ship and shore station on different frequencies. In the USA, they are simplex, with both transmission and reception taking place on the international ship transmitting frequency. They should be referred to with the designator A after the channel number, eg '65 alpha' (except for channels 21, 22, 23 and 83 which use the designator CG for Coast Guard), but in practice in US waters the number alone is usually used – this results in plenty of confusion. Modern VHF sets should have a facility for selecting either the international or US set of frequencies; the latter will also allow reception of the continuous, dedicated US VHF weather transmissions.

Increasingly, VHF sets are fitted with inbuilt Digital Selective Calling (DSC), an electronic device that automatically detects calls made to the particular set, as well as distress and safety calls. A SELCALL number is issued to the yacht by the ship licensing authority. DSC calls are made on VHF channel 70, which is now reserved for this purpose – channel 70 is the digital equivalent of voice channel 16 – and even if an older set allows voice transmission on this channel, this is forbidden as it may interfere with distress traffic. VHF DSC forms part of the GMDSS.

## MF/HF and amateur radio

Strictly speaking, Medium Frequency and High Frequency are separate bands. MF runs from 300 to 3000 kHz, with a maximum range of around 500 miles, whereas the HF band is from 3000 to 30,000 kHz and can achieve worldwide communications. But MF-only sets are seldom seen today and a combined HF/MF set is the norm; for practical purposes MF and HF can be considered together and are generally referred to by yachtsmen as HF, divided into marine HF and amateur or 'ham' radio. It should be noted that in this context amateur equates to 'enthusiast' rather than to 'less competent'.

Marine HF takes place on specific simplex or duplex frequencies within the marine bands. To operate within these bands a set must meet certain agreed specifications; such sets are referred to as 'type approved'. It is often possible to modify such a set to operate on the amateur bands as well and this is frequently done. Such a modification, however, means that the set may no longer be used legally on the marine frequencies. Using marine HF, calls can be made to other ships and to coast radio stations and the telephone network accessed. With the right equipment, normally a PC and a modem, telex and fax messages can be sent and received and it may be possible to use e-mail.

Amateur radio operates throughout the amateur bands and not on particular laid down frequencies. There are no technical specifications for sets and many amateurs build their own. To ensure that they do not interfere with other radio users, amateurs must pass a considerably more complex exam than marine HF operators before being issued with a licence. A reasonable level of technical knowledge on radio theory and practice is required as well as the ability to send and receive Morse code at 12 words per minute, although almost all amateur communications take place using voice. In the UK courses are run (usually as evening classes) lasting about six months, although it is possible to study for the exam by correspondence course. Exams are held twice a year. Only qualified amateurs may transmit on the amateur bands but anyone may listen.

HF sets, whether marine or amateur, must be properly installed to work satisfactorily. They take a good deal of power when transmitting, often up to 25 amps, and are particularly sensitive to a reduction in input voltage – heavy supply cables are essential here. An insulated shroud or backstay will usually form the aerial and is relatively easily arranged, but providing a good earth for the set and aerial tuning unit is equally important and often more difficult. A wood or fibreglass yacht will probably need to fit an external ground plate below the waterline and this must be connected to the installation using copper strip (not braid) at least 4 cm (1$\frac{1}{2}$ in) wide. In a metal yacht, the hull itself will provide an excellent earth.

HF radio requires some knowledge to use. The frequency chosen must be appropriate for the range required and different frequencies used by day and by night. Propagation is also affected by sunspot activity. There are many unlicensed HF users throughout the world, often using indifferent equipment, whose transmissions spill over into adjacent frequencies, and it is common for interference to be so severe that communication is very difficult. Despite these drawbacks, HF –

either in the marine or amateur bands – is at present the most popular way for the transatlantic yachtsman to keep in touch with other yachts and those ashore whilst on passage. HF sets are relatively expensive. A reasonable installation will cost at least seven times as much as the average VHF set, but it is possible to spend very considerably more.

## Satellite communications

Once the exclusive preserve of warships and the largest merchantmen, satellite communications are increasingly available to yachts, using the INMARSAT system. For yachtsmen in the North Atlantic the Phone Mini-M service will give complete cover. The equipment is sufficiently lightweight to be fitted in the smallest ocean cruiser and power requirements are modest. Once fitted, the yacht has what is in effect a conventional telephone aboard – phone and fax calls may be made and received. The system is completely free from interference and for those who wish to make regular contact with the shore this is undoubtedly the best system. Although it is at present the most expensive equipment, costing about twice as much as a reasonable HF installation, prices are expected to fall rapidly.

## EPIRBs

Emergency Position Indicating Radio Beacons are self-contained devices that can be activated in an emergency to alert the rescue authorities. There are three types avail-

Many Moody yachts have made ambitious cruises. As well as three Atlantic crossings, this 36 footer has explored the Hawaiian Islands and Alaska. *Photo: Georgie McLaren*

able. Older and simpler EPIRBs operate on a frequency of 121.5 MHz, the air distress frequency. An aircraft within range may detect the signal, but it is more likely to be received by satellite. There is almost complete coverage of the North Atlantic Ocean, but not of the entire South Atlantic.

Because there are so many 121.5 MHz EPIRBs in existence, and because the frequency is subject to considerable interference, reception from more than one satellite pass is needed before the rescue authorities respond. This may take as long as an hour. For this reason, and because the other two types of beacon are so much superior, it is likely that satellite monitoring of 121.5 MHz will cease within the next few years.

The new type 406 MHz beacons are much superior, but more expensive. They also transmit to satellites. Each beacon sends a unique identification signal and so should be registered individually with the authorities. If this is done, the rescue centre will have the details of the yacht and her position within a few minutes of the beacon being activated. Positional accuracy is considerably better than that of the older type; 406 MHz beacons incorporate a 121.5 MHz beacon to enable rescue aircraft to home in.

The latest type of beacon operates on 1.6 GHz and operates with INMARSAT communications satellites. These beacons, which are also individual and again should be registered, incorporate a GPS receiver and continuously transmit their position as part of the distress message, thus rendering a homing beacon unnecessary. Hitherto these beacons have been bulky and expensive, but a compact version for yachts has recently been produced at a similar price to the 406 MHz beacons. This is the beacon that the rescue authorities recommend; 406 MHz and 1.6 GHz beacons form part of the GMDSS.

Whatever its type, once activated, a radio beacon should be left operating continuously until rescue arrives. If a beacon is switched on inadvertently it should also be left on until shore authorities can be informed that the alarm is false. This should be done as a matter of the utmost priority.

## GMDSS

The Global Maritime Distress and Safety System is currently being introduced. The basic concept of the GMDSS is that onshore Search and Rescue authorities, in addition to shipping in the immediate vicinity of a ship in distress, will rapidly be alerted to the situation so that they can co-ordinate rescue with the minimum delay. The system also allows appropriate safety information, weather forecasts, navigational warnings etc to be disseminated rapidly.

The equipment which must be carried varies, depending upon where the vessel is operating – broadly, the further from land, the more complex the communications gear needed. GMDSS communications are largely initiated by digital means, a much more reliable and rapid method than the voice.

Although yachts are not required to comply with GMDSS, it does affect them. It is mandatory for most ships and fishing vessels, which must carry appropriate equipment and follow GMDSS procedures. As an example of the effect for yachts, from 1999 merchant ships will only be required to monitor VHF channel 70, by digital means. Yachts without a DSC fitted VHF may therefore be unable to contact them. Increasingly, coast radio stations will optimise their operations to GMDSS-fitted customers.

Unfortunately, apart from EPIRBs, there is currently little GMDSS compliant equipment designed specifically with the needs of the voyaging yachtsman in mind, eg low power consumption, water resistance and compactness. What is available at present is expensive. It is anticipated that this state of affairs will improve, and when buying new equipment the current situation should be considered. If possible, GMDSS compatible equipment should be chosen, as it will increasingly be necessary, even for non-emergency communications.

Despite its present relatively high cost it should be remembered that the appropriate GMDSS equipment significantly, and increasingly, improves both the chance of alerting the authorities to an emergency and of subsequently being rescued. If this is a high priority to the transatlantic yachtsman he should comply with the system.

# 6 THE CREW

Most Atlantic crossings take place as part of a longer cruise. The majority of extended cruising is done by couples, sometimes with children. Guests join from time to time; these are normally friends or relatives who can seldom stay for more than a few weeks, so little advice needs to be given about them. But many boats embark crew, who may be neither close friends nor relatives, for the actual ocean passages, and this aspect of an Atlantic voyage needs careful thought. With a happy ship's company consisting of people who know how to live afloat and who enjoy each other's company, a long voyage can be an experience which all will remember with deep and lasting satisfaction. An ocean voyage blighted by friction or argument amongst those aboard will be miserable.

## Recruitment

Crew may either be organised before departure or en route. There is a risk in attempting to do the former too far in advance, as promises are often made by people who are full of enthusiasm until an attempt is made to pin them down to a firm sailing date. Others may genuinely intend to come, but be prevented by changes in circumstances beyond their control. Before approaching anybody it is best to have the cruise planned in broad outline. To avoid misunderstandings the following points should be agreed at the outset:

1 Starting date and likely duration
2 Who pays any travelling expenses to or from the points of embarkation and disembarkation
3 What financial contribution, if any, is expected
4 What liability the owner will accept in the event of accident or injury or for the costs of any changes to, or cancellation of, the arrangements

Once these points have been agreed verbally it will be as well to drop the prospective crew member a note of them in writing. This is not mere pedantry as he or she may not be joining for several months and memories of the exact arrangements made can fade. Even the best of friendships will be strained by an unexpected demand for a considerable sum of money, or a complete change of itinerary after flights have been booked.

In most countries a yacht's skipper is liable for the costs of repatriating any crew member who leaves the vessel, for whatever reason. In most cases the person will be leaving by pre-arrangement and will hold an airline ticket, or may be transferring to another yacht. With relatively unknown crew, however, particularly those who have been 'picked up off the dock', it is a sensible precaution to insist on a deposit to cover the cost of a flight from the furthest point of the cruise to their country of origin. All prospective crew will need valid passports, with visas where necessary, and it is important that these should not expire during the duration of the cruise.

## Selecting crew

Actually deciding whom to invite is a personal matter on which little advice can be given. Provided that the skipper is competent in all aspects of seamanship and navigation he will be entirely free in his choice, be it a young novice crew or experienced older sailors. The important thing is to find people with whom he will get along and who will get along with each other, taking account of character and temperament rather than technical knowledge or skill. Even so, one of the crew will have to be the second in command and they should be competent to replace the skipper in the event of illness or injury; whoever this is must be acceptable to the others without question. The only reliable test as to whether people can sail together in harmony is to go for a short trial cruise.

## Replacements en route

Crew changes during the course of a cruise may be pre-arranged, or may rely on finding a suitable person when and where they are needed. The former should be simple enough – many people cannot take the time off work for an entire cruise, but may be eager to join for a limited period. A reasonably firm cruising schedule will allow flights to be booked well in advance, though it must be accepted on both sides that other things may intervene. Absolutely rigid schedules are not practical and will, in any case, ruin a relaxed cruise. Rather than push the pace to reach a particular rendezvous it is better to have a flexible arrangement. The crew can book their flights to or from a particular international airport, but will leave or join the yacht from wherever she happens to be lying at the time. This is particularly necessary in the Caribbean where, for some reason, schedules seem to be especially hard to maintain! Travelling between islands is easy by local airline or by ferry.

The seaports of the world all have, from time to time, itinerants who go from boat to boat trying to thumb a passage to another place. There may well be good crew among them, but a fair percentage will not be. The really good ones will be snapped up by charter yachts as paid hands, and in most cases only the inexperienced, unknown or unreliable will have to rely on casual berths. All in all, taking on casual crew in this way cannot be recommended. If it must be done as a last resort, take precautions. Screen quayside applicants carefully, always ask for references from previous skippers and, whenever possible, take up these references. Examine passports and visas carefully, and insist on the flight deposit already mentioned. Ensure that the crew joins the yacht several days before departure and assists with the storing and preparations, both to get some idea of what they are really like and to find out if they will pull their weight. It is always possible that an unknown crew member may be carrying drugs, and if these are discovered on arrival the consequences may be serious for the skipper as well as the offender.

## Training

Forging a group of individuals into a team capable of coping in difficult conditions takes time, and in any case it is impossible to simulate ocean sailing except by making an ocean passage. Assuming that the crew has basic sailing skills, all that remains is to give each person the chance to get to know the particular boat. The sensible skipper will encourage feedback and even if he has sailed the yacht for years will probably find that a fresh viewpoint, based on different experience, is valuable and stimulating and will enable him to improve layout, routines or equipment. That being said, it is the skipper's prerogative to say 'I prefer this particular job done like this' and crew who are not prepared to accept this should find another boat.

Every ship has her own routine - 'different ships, different long splices' - and this should be established as early as possible. Some standardisation is essential to safety: which line goes to which cleat, exactly how to belay a sheet or halyard, where each item of gear is kept. These are not just owners' fads - they could mean the difference between life and death on a dark night.

Ground rules regarding standards of tidiness and cleanliness should be established early. There is no need for this to be done formally, but it is easier to nip problems in the bud rather than have to recover the situation when things are getting out of hand. One person's belongings constantly left lying about for example, or a galley habitually left for

In a warm climate the cockpit makes a perfect bathroom for the liveaboard child. *Photo: Liz Hammick*

the next watch to clean up, will lead to discord and resentment. A good skipper will be aware of these and similar problems and will sort them out firmly, but diplomatically.

It would be ridiculous to suggest that the skipper should make a formal daily inspection in a small boat, but he should check over the whole yacht both on deck and below at least once a day. This will give him an opportunity to keep an unobtrusive eye open for any incipient crew problems. Praise is also important and should be given where it is due. Few things are as dispiriting to a hardworking crew as to have their efforts go apparently unnoticed.

### *Division of responsibilities*

The small size of the average ocean cruiser's crew demands that each member should have some particular skill - or preferably several - and for both efficiency and to encourage a sense of involvement, a division of responsibilities is essential. One person, usually the skipper, will be in charge of navigation. The only other area that is usually an individual responsibility is the galley. Even if the actual cooking is shared on a rota basis, one person should oversee the catering and storing. Regular food is fundamental to the efficiency and morale of the whole ship's company, yet there are few more difficult tasks than cooking interesting meals at sea in a small boat. With a large crew there may well be a full time cook who will keep no watches. In a smaller yacht, if one person is prepared to do all, or the majority of, the cooking, the remainder of the crew should count themselves lucky. Certainly any such person should be suitably rewarded - perhaps by exemption from some of the night watches.

## Friction aboard

A happy ship's company is so well worth achieving that no effort should be spared in the attempt. The skipper must not only maintain a good relationship with each person on board, but must also try to prevent disputes arising between crew members. Should these occur he will often be called on to arbitrate, an unenviable task in which it is seldom possible to satisfy all parties.

Crew problems may arise in port as often as at sea, perhaps more so. The common challenge of actively sailing a small yacht will often paper over minor cracks, but when this is removed they reappear. It is also in port that differences in personal habits become most significant - preferred times of rising, eating and turning in, sociability towards fellow yachtsmen, consideration over the use of a dinghy on which others also depend. Regular routine maintenance must be carried out, and if friction is to be avoided it must be made quite clear from the start what the crew are expected to do. One solution is for the mornings to belong to the ship and for work on board to be carried out then, whilst the afternoons are for relaxation.

It is hard to define a happy ship, but it is possible to tell one the moment one steps aboard. Common factors appear to be a sound ship, a competent, fair and considerate skipper, well thought out organisation and good communication - in both directions - between the skipper and the crew and amongst the crew themselves. Above all, there will be willingness by all on board to do just a little more for the yacht and for those around them than they have to.

## The skipper

The role of the skipper depends, to a large extent, on the formation of the crew – a family crew will not view the skipper in the same light as a crew composed of semi-strangers. They, in turn, will have a different attitude to that of friends who have sailed together for years. Some couples, who have cruised together for a very long time and who are both equally experienced and competent, may truly be co-skippers, but they are rare. Normally one person must be in charge and be prepared to shoulder the responsibility not only for the safety of the boat and all those aboard, but also to a large extent for their happiness as well.

The idea of doing an 'apprenticeship' as crew before aspiring to skipper one's own yacht across an ocean no longer prevails, and nowadays most first-time transatlantic skippers have no more experience of the passage than their crews. Only a fool feels no apprehension at the start of an ocean voyage and although, with experience, this reduces it should never vanish entirely. A good crew will understand that the skipper has more on his plate than they do and will allow for it. They will expect him to appear calm and confident, but will be uneasy if this is overdone. Only the most experienced skippers can appear completely relaxed and at ease in all circumstances. For others to attempt to emulate them will not inspire confidence in the crew – in fact, quite the reverse.

It is for the skipper to set the tenor of life aboard, and he can do this more by his example than by any other means. The problem of incompatibility in a small ship's company is often the result of inexperience – living at close quarters is an art that does not come easily to all. For every cruise that has been marred by one selfish individual, there have been many others so rewarding that the experience binds the participants together for the rest of their lives. This will not happen without a good skipper. If things do not go so happily he should remember that 'there are no bad crews, only bad skippers' and learn from his mistakes.

Provisioning for a long Atlantic cruise, which is to include several ocean passages, is less difficult that it was even a decade ago. The range of foods available in most places has increased markedly. Even quite small European villages are likely to have a reasonable food shop, whilst in the larger ports, where major stocking up is likely to be done, there will be a selection of supermarkets. In the Caribbean islands the facilities are not quite so good, but here too the range available is quite adequate and only a yacht with a very large or demanding crew will find provisioning difficult. In North America major storing can be carried out at almost any harbour, although here, because supermarkets are normally out of town, it may be necessary to organise transport.

Whether or not the task of cooking is to be shared among the crew, calculating and buying food stores is best done by one person. They must not only take into account the length of time the boat is expected to be away, but also have some idea of the stowage space available, what can be bought en route, and the limitations of the galley equipment, as well as the individual likes and dislikes of those on board.

## Storing before departure

There is a major difference between storing up at home for an Atlantic cruise, the first leg of which may be only a few days across the Bay of Biscay or out to Bermuda, and storing for a specific passage such as the Atlantic crossing. Before leaving home is the time to lay in those items which are likely to be expensive or simply unavailable elsewhere; instant coffee, tea bags, bread mix and yeast extract fall into this category, as would favourite branded products. This is also the time to stock up on 'national' foods, be it British Branston pickle and tinned steak and kidney pie or American peanut butter and jelly. Within reason, buy as much of these products as can be stowed. However, avoid overstocking staples which can be found almost everywhere – bread, flour, sugar, pasta, rice, canned fish, canned fruit and vegetables and fresh eggs. A couple of weeks' supply of all of these will be ample initially for most boats – perhaps a little more if the first passage is to be a long one.

Provisioning for an ocean crossing is time consuming and allowance must be made for this when planning the trip.
*Photo: Michael Beaumont*

## Storing for a single passage

Calculating the stores needed for a specific passage is more complicated. The first step is to establish how many meals there will be each day, and the type of food to be eaten at each. For example, some crews prefer a cooked breakfast, others are happy with cereals and toast, and yet others eat no breakfast at all, but have a larger and earlier midday meal. If possible the whole crew should be consulted, but if it is very large, the skipper will have to lay down a policy for everyone. Eating habits will almost certainly change at sea, and a generous allowance of nibbles such as biscuits (both sweet and savoury), chocolate bars and sweets will seldom be wasted. Having estimated what might be consumed on any given day it should not be difficult to expand this to cover the entire passage, allowing an extra 50 per cent for unforeseen delays. Some people like to do a dummy run in home waters, laying in and then living off stores for a one-week cruise to check if anything has been forgotten. Much depends on the experience of the person in charge of catering – few people used to running and feeding a household will need this kind of reassurance.

Food can help to provide variety and boost morale during a long passage and it is a good idea for the caterer to lay in some luxury items for notable occasions or celebrations. Unobtrusive enquiries before departure can be made to see if any crew member will celebrate a birthday or other anniversary during the trip so that a surprise special meal can be cooked that day. Some crews like to have a celebratory dinner to mark the halfway point. A good caterer will plan for these and similar events and the ability to produce something out of the ordinary when the occasion demands will be much appreciated.

## Provisioning in different areas

Storing up for a long passage will be easiest if done at a port of some size as the choice will be better and the prices cheaper than in smaller places. The ports listed in Part III are capable of meeting most needs unless stated otherwise. Even so, it may be useful to have a broad indication as to what each area is likely to offer.

The Iberian peninsula is noted for the quality of its fruit and vegetables and is an excellent place to stock up on Mediterranean produce such as pasta and olive oil. Canned fish and seafood of all kinds are another speciality. For British yachts, mainland Portugal has supermarkets stocking a surprisingly large range of English foods. In Porto Santo supplies are adequate for everyday living; it would be possible for a small crew to store there for the crossing but choice is limited. Both Madeira and the Canaries have excellent supermarkets, making stocking up for a long passage a positive pleasure. The local markets are good too, but beware that in the larger ones some of the apparently fresh fruit and vegetables may have been chilled, which harms their keeping qualities. Arrive early in the day and check the items buried deep down in the displays; if these are icy cold, then the produce will not keep well. In the Cape Verde Islands, which are both very dry and very poor, little is available and even the staples mentioned above may be difficult to find. If stopping there before the tradewind passage, arrive with the yacht already stored up.

In the Lesser Antilles, both the quality and variety of food available has improved markedly over recent years, and a mixture of modern supermarkets, smaller stores and the excellent local markets can provide almost every need. Those islands which are mountainous and therefore have plenty of rainfall (Grenada, St Vincent, St Lucia, Martinique, Dominica, etc) produce excellent fruit and vegetables, whilst those which are generally lower and drier (Antigua, St Maarten, the British Virgin Islands, etc) generally do not. In addition to local produce, the French islands are noted for the range and quality of imported foods such as cheese and paté. In the British Virgin Islands, most food is imported and fresh vegetables with good keeping qualities are difficult to find. The American Virgin Islands and the Bahamas can supply most of the products available on the American mainland.

The quality of food available along the eastern seaboard of the USA and Canada is well known, though owing to the wide use of freezers it may be difficult to find canned meats. There is a greater likelihood that fruit and vegetables will have been chilled than in less sophisticated areas, but a little asking around may well lead one to a farmers' market where real fresh produce can be found.

Although supermarkets in Bermuda are well-stocked, nearly all food is imported – making this probably the most expensive place to store up in the North Atlantic, and it is extremely difficult to find produce which has not been chilled. All in all, it is best to avoid a major re-stock in Bermuda.

The Azorean islands vary, with the best provisioning at Horta in Faial, Angra do Heroismo in Terceira and Ponta Delgada in São Miguel, towns which also have good markets. Basics, such as bread, fish and some fruit and vegetables, are available on all the islands but imported foods may not be. Dairy products are widely available and good cheese is made.

## Non-perishables

Aboard the smaller yacht every cubic inch of space available will be pressed into use for the storage of food and other essentials. The purist, and certainly the owner of a very small yacht, will go to great lengths to keep weights as low as possible, but if tins are to be kept in the bilge they should have the contents marked in indelible pen and their labels should be removed. This is to prevent them clogging bilge pump strainers and should be done even in a boat whose bilge is normally bone dry as, if a lot of water comes aboard unexpectedly, her bilge pump will be vital.

The galley itself should include a ready-use locker for coffee, tea, sugar, salt, etc, and many cooks also like to keep a day or two's supply of other food handy in order to avoid scrabbling in lockers after dark or in heavy weather. If, as is usually the case, bulk stores are spread around the boat then some kind of system will be needed. By far the most efficient, and essential if more than one person is doing the cooking, is to have a notebook showing where each item will be found and, in the case of tins and packets, how many are on board. A pencil stub tied to the notebook, reinforced by dire threats from the caterer, should ensure that each individual item is crossed off as it is used.

Some non-perishables will of course be bought in bulk, and it may be possible to negotiate a small discount on

Baking bread, a routine activity at sea. *Photo: Gavin McLaren*

cans bought by the case. However, always test unknown brands before buying in quantity. Avoid the 'giant economy pack'. It may not fit the boat's lockers and once opened, unless its contents can be used quickly, they will probably go bad. Dry stores may be bought in bulk and decanted into smaller airtight containers for use as required. This is also true of margarine, available in large square containers from which a table tub can be refilled. Margarine seems to keep for ever and to retain a semi-solid state even without refrigeration, whereas butter, even in tins, is best avoided unless the boat has refrigeration.

Along with edible non-perishables it may be convenient to include those 'housekeeping' items without which the cruise will not be a happy one. In the galley: kitchen towel, detergent (dish soap) and surface cleaners. Elsewhere, washing powder, bleach or the equivalent, and toilet rolls. Though the last can be bought everywhere, the quality in some countries leaves much to be desired.

## Fresh stores and storage

The length of time that fresh stores will keep depends both on their quality and the care with which they are stored. Sound potatoes, carrots and onions will last for a month-long voyage even in tropical latitudes provided they are picked over regularly and any suspect ones removed. Fresh eggs will also last for a month without treatment, but not if they have been chilled at any time. There are various methods of preserving eggs which have

been chilled, and unless certain otherwise, assume this to be the case. Coating with Vaseline (petroleum jelly) certainly works, and eggs treated in this way will last for at least six weeks. Untreated eggs should be turned twice a week to prevent their shells from drying out and the yolks from settling.

Fruit is less predictable. Green tomatoes will ripen gradually in a warm atmosphere, but do not need daylight. Nearly all citrus fruit will keep for weeks if not months, providing a useful source of vitamin C. Lemons keep well if wrapped in foil. A hand of green bananas will be inedible for several days but will then all ripen at once. Hard green cabbage will last for the crossing, and will form the basis of a reasonable salad or coleslaw. Some voyagers grow sprouting seeds during long passages; this is probably not necessary for health, but it is fun, particularly for children, and easy to do. Fresh green stuff such as mustard and cress or alfalfa will be welcome in the latter part of the crossing, as will crispy bean sprouts.

If faced with unfamiliar local produce in West Indian markets, the local ladies will generally be delighted to advise, and it may also be worth buying a book on Caribbean cookery.

## Fishing

While it would be most unwise to depend on catching fish for food, they can nevertheless provide welcome variety and some yachts fish regularly on passage with great success. Others using similar gear never catch anything. A fishing line will need to be both strong and easy to grip, and heavyweight gloves may be useful. If towing a line for long periods it is common practice to run a few turns anti-clockwise around a winch before making up the inboard end. Any pull on the hook will cause the winch to spin, alerting the crew immediately. Ideas on suitable lures vary – the polished spoon can work well, others prefer to camouflage the hook among strips of coloured polythene cut from carrier bags. Special lures can also be bought. If a large fish has been landed and is thrashing around, a little neat spirit poured into the gills will kill it immediately.

Many cruising areas are nature reserves where fishing is either restricted or banned. Spear fishing is forbidden in the Tobago Cays, parts of Antigua, the Virgin Islands and Bermuda among other places, although local people may be allowed to fish by traditional methods, usually traps or pots. In the Bahamas a fishing permit is needed, and fishing of any sort is prohibited in the Exuma National Park. The local cruising guide should give the details.

Towing a lure on ocean passage is generally safe, but owing to the prevalence of ciguatera poisoning in parts of the West Indies, fishing should not take place there without seeking local advice. Ciguatera only affects predatory fish, which build up dangerous concentrations of the poison in their bodies through years of feeding on the smaller fish. Predatory fish include kingfish, tuna, dorado, dolphin fish and barracuda, all of which are otherwise excellent eating. The first three are of the familiar tuna shape, the dolphin fish (no relation of the mammal) somewhat tall and narrow with iridescent blue colouring, and the barracuda a long, evil-looking beast with a powerful jaw and large teeth. The barracuda is the only one likely to be met when snorkelling, when it can be unnerving though seldom actually dangerous.

In the tropics there may be the bonus of flying fish landing on deck during the night, and displaying a light will tend to attract them. Even so, there are unlikely to be enough to provide a substantial breakfast except perhaps for the singlehander.

## Liquid refreshment

The subject of drinking water and tankage has already been covered in Chapter 2. Choice and quantity of non-alcoholic beverages will, of course, depend on the tastes of the crew. Carbonated drinks are generally available everywhere; the diet or sugar-free varieties are the most thirst quenching. Fruit juice, either in cans or increasingly in cartons, can be found in most places but concentrated fruit squash is much rarer.

A yacht may be allowed to embark bonded stores - duty free alcohol - before leaving for a long voyage. In the UK this procedure is no longer worthwhile unless really large quantities are involved - at least five cases of spirits - as the fixed charges, fees for attendance of customs officers, delivery charges etc, have been increased recently. The procedure is in any event tedious: a special sealed locker must be provided and the stores may not be used until beyond EU waters.

Most yachtsmen prefer to experiment with the local produce as the cruise progresses. Iberia produces wine, port, sherry and brandy (all for sale in the Canaries, which are a duty free zone); 'Madeira' comes in a range from very dry indeed to rich and creamy. In the Caribbean rum is of course the staple and there are many varieties to sample. The French islands (Martinique, Guadeloupe, St Barts and St Martin) are good places to stock up with wine or brandy. In the USA, spirits (liquor) are reasonably priced by European standards and excellent wines are produced. Imported alcohol is more expensive and Scotch whisky particularly dear, although this is true in most places. Bermuda appears to sell everything, at a price, while the Azores offer Portuguese brands in addition to locally made wines. Beer, either in bottles or in cans, is available almost everywhere.

In addition to his responsibility for the boat, her equipment and her crew, the skipper of any small vessel must deal with all her day-to-day affairs, from coping with officialdom to changing the clocks and organising the watch systems. The following is a mixed bag of reminders and suggestions.

## Watchkeeping systems

A happy voyage depends to a great extent on establishing a daily routine. As well as ensuring that all the necessary work gets done, it must also be a routine with which all those on board can live with for weeks at a stretch. This applies as much to singlehanders, who must work out for themselves whatever compromise between sleep and watchkeeping they feel they can live with. Whatever the size of the crew, be it one person aboard a small cruiser or sixteen on a maxi racing machine, the energy and resilience of those aboard is a finite resource which must not be squandered.

Though the watch system must take account not only of the sailing, but also of the daily chores such as navigation, cooking and ongoing maintenance, its prime objective must always be to ensure the safe conduct of the ship. Ideally this entails having enough manpower on deck to deal with whatever needs to be done without calling those below, but as few cruising yachts will have more than one person on watch at a time this may not always be feasible. In bad weather or in extreme cold, one hour on deck steering by hand may be as long as even a strong, fit person can stand. In such conditions the yacht with a crew of three or less will depend heavily on a powerful and reliable self-steering gear, and it is essential that it should be equal to the task.

Many watchkeeping systems have been evolved for small boats. How long the watches should be is a matter of choice. If it is necessary to helm continuously, not many people will manage more than two hours even in good conditions and less would be preferable. If it is possible to leave the helm, even for only a short spell occasionally, perhaps by using the autopilot for five minutes every half-hour, then this period can be considerably extended. The watchkeeper will be able to move around, to visit the head or prepare a snack. In a warm climate, with a good self-steering system, a watch of six hours in the open ocean may be quite acceptable - at least during the day - and for a two-handed crew will give the off watch time for a worthwhile period of rest. If there are more than two aboard, then it should not be necessary for watches to be more than four hours.

The watchkeeping routines that follow have stood the test of time, but they are not the only ones. They will, however, give an idea of some of the factors to consider.

### Watch systems for two people
1 A straightforward system of three- or four-hour watches with extended periods to provide a two-hour overlap twice a day at mealtimes. Convenient where one person does all the cooking and the other all the navigation, as each person is on watch during the same period each day - Figure 2(a).
2 As above, but not considering overlap periods as part of a watch. This allows the times each person is on watch to alternate between one day and the next, providing some variety aboard those boats where both navigation and cooking are shared equally - Figure 2(b).

### Watch systems for three people
1 An adaptation of either (1) or (2) above with watches carried on day and night - Figures 2(c) and 2(d).
2 Formal watches during the hours of darkness only. It will still be necessary for someone to keep a lookout during the day, but this may be on a volunteer rather than a duty basis - Figure 2(e).

### Watch systems for four or more people
1 Again a straight three- or four-hour system, either permanently or just at night. Assuming that only one person is normally on watch at any time, this will effectively mean the crew spending most of the night in their bunks, so sleep during the day is unlikely to be more than the odd nap - Figure 2(f).
2 If one person is doing all the cooking for a larger crew they deserve a suitable reward, possibly exemption from the unpopular 0000–0400 watch or even exemption from watches entirely. This is also feasible if cooking is alternated, a full night's sleep being awarded to the day's cook - Figure 2(g).

In general, the more people there are aboard the easier it will be to organise a system which not only meets the watchkeeping requirements, but also allows time for relaxation, hobbies and some feeling of community amongst the crew - a regular 'happy hour' before supper is often popular. With a very small crew it is possible to barely exchange a word with the others aboard for days at a stretch, apart from a few minutes on handing over the watch and a brief period at mealtimes.

With any crew of more than two it is important to keep the noise at the change of watch as quiet and as brief as possible, particularly at night. Most skippers sleep with half an ear open, and to be regularly disturbed while off watch will do nothing for their alertness in the long term, or probably their temper.

It must be clearly understood who is 'on call' should assistance be needed on deck. On some yachts this will always be the skipper, on others the person due on watch next. Though it must depend ultimately on the capabilities and experience of the crew, the skipper should beware of having his sleep so broken that he has no reserves of energy should a real emergency arise. Bad weather or a sudden crisis can disrupt the watch system with little or no warning, and it will usually be the skipper who will have to bear the greatest load when this happens.

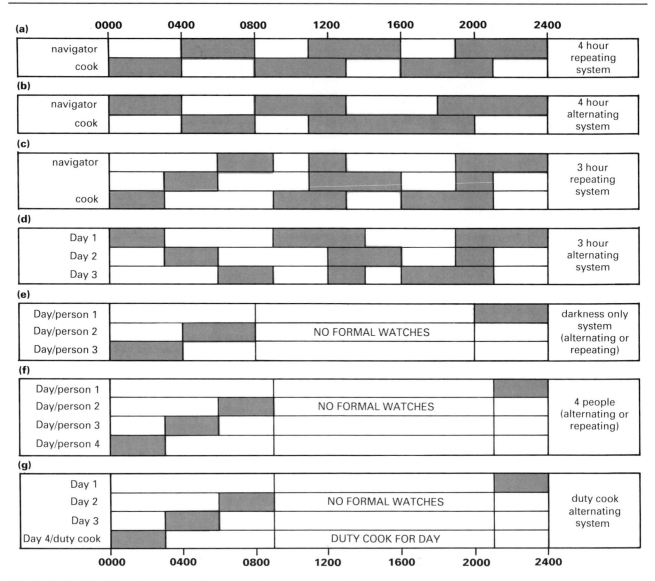

*Fig 2(a)-(g)* Watchkeeping systems for crews of two or more people.

## Ship's time

It is best to alter the ship's clocks periodically during the course of an east/west (or west/east) crossing, both to avoid a major alteration on reaching land and to keep some resemblance of normality on board – it is disconcerting to watch the sun rise at 0200 or to eat the evening meal at 2300. The time change is one hour for every 15° of longitude, the clocks being put back when heading west and forward when heading east. The change need not be made slavishly on crossing an imaginary line in the ocean, but rather when convenient – and should not always be when the same person is on watch!

When writing up the log it must be crystal clear what time zone is being used. To avoid confusion, two columns can be used, one with GMT and one for ship's time.

## Paperwork

### *Documentation*

Requirements vary from country to country and it makes sense to carry anything one might possibly be called upon to produce. In most cases original documents will be needed, although it is useful to have several sets of photocopies on board, with a further set at home in case the originals are lost. Not all the documents listed here will be examined in every country, but items 1–5 will be regularly required.

1 Valid passports for everyone on board, with visas as necessary. If the crew are multi-national it must be remembered that some may need visas for a particular country while others do not. Neither passports nor, if possible, visas should expire during the course of the cruise.
2 Crew list. Normally everyone aboard should be listed as crew rather than passengers, as some countries levy high fees for charter yachts or other passenger-carrying vessels.
3 Certificate of Registry, or (for British yachts) Small Ships Registry Certificate. American yachts should have national, as opposed to state, documentation. For British yachts, both full and small ships registry need to be renewed periodically; if possible, ensure that this will not happen during the cruise.
4 For European yachts, evidence of VAT status – either that

tax has been paid or that the vessel is exempt, most often on grounds of age (yachts launched before 1985). The correct evidence is the Single Administrative Document (SAD), in practice Copy 8 of the multi-part Form C88, which is used throughout the EU in connection with the movement of goods. Although a full Certificate of British Registry gives the date when the vessel was first registered and may be accepted as evidence of age, all European customs officials will recognise the SAD.

5   Clearance papers from the previous port of call. In certain countries, notably Spain and the Canaries, these can be difficult to obtain.
6   Stores list, which should differentiate between opened and unopened items. In practice very few countries are interested in stores other than alcohol, although fresh fruit and vegetables should always be mentioned, as these may have to be destroyed to prevent the spread of pests.
7   Cruising Permit (issued to visiting yachts in the USA, Canada and some Caribbean islands), if applicable.
8   VHF and other radio licences/operator's certificates as applicable.
9   Insurance papers - a few marinas will not allow boats without at least third party insurance to berth.
10  Bill of Sale.
11  World Health Organisation Yellow Card, plus Bills of Health or Pratiques acquired en route. Few countries now demand a Bill of Health, but a sudden epidemic could alter the rules overnight.
12  Charter documents, if applicable.
13  For British yachts, Ensign Warrant, if applicable.

## Preparations for arrival

The last few hours of an ocean voyage may be amongst the most demanding of the entire passage for the skipper, and the practical aspects of making a landfall are covered in Chapter 4. However, while the crew can often relax as soon as the anchor is down or the yacht secured, few officials allow the skipper to do so before dealing with the formalities. For this reason it is worth making a few preparations in advance - ideally the day before the landfall.

Check through the entry procedures for the country to which you are going, not least to ensure that the port for which you are heading is an official port of entry. Check whether it is necessary to report by radio before entering harbour. In most places the skipper should go ashore to report as soon as the yacht is secured, but occasionally he - and the rest of the crew - must remain on board until the officials visit. If unsure, another yacht in the anchorage may be able to advise.

Collect all the documents needed and make out a crew list with full names, dates and places of birth and passport numbers. Some people carry photocopied crew lists but, though this can obviously do no harm, they must be updated to keep track of any crew changes - a computer can be useful here. Different countries demand different information, and many insist that the details should be written on their own printed forms. Make a list of dutiable stores, especially wines and spirits, and ensure it is

Falmouth is the first English port of call for many transatlantic yachtsmen. The Royal Cornwall Yacht Club provides a warm welcome, as it has for over a century. *Photo: Anne Hammick*

correct. If you have medical drugs aboard there should be an accompanying certificate from a doctor, naming the patient and stating the quantity of each drug. Along with the documents, in many places things will go quicker if the skipper remembers to take his own ballpoint, a supply of carbon paper, some blank paper for making notes, and a phrase book if applicable. Some cash is likely to be needed; this should preferably be in the local currency but US dollars are usually acceptable. The more weary the skipper, the greater the chance of something being forgotten and the more irritating the chore of returning for it.

Finally, hoist the national ensign if it has not been worn at sea, and have both the Q flag and a courtesy ensign ready to hoist on entering territorial waters. Not surprisingly, yachts flying an incorrect, tattered or upside down courtesy ensign are unlikely to be welcomed with open arms.

### The ship s stamp and modern equivalents

It was once fashionable to have a ship's stamp – often a small drawing of the boat together with name, home port and perhaps registered number or radio call sign – with which to adorn customs documentation. However, times have changed and officials in nearly all countries are now professionals who will be unimpressed by such things. Keep the rubber stamp for books and letterheads.

A more useful item is a boat's 'business card' with similar information, plus the skipper's or owner's mailing address, and/or small adhesive address stickers. It is also possible to obtain adhesive-backed prints bearing a coloured photo of the boat and her crew together with brief written details. These look well in visitors' books and may even make suitable small gifts for local people.

### Books and miscellaneous paperwork

Bibliographies devoted to various topics will be found among the Appendices. While it is not suggested that every single volume should be carried, there are some which can claim to form the nucleus of every yacht's bookshelf. For lighter reading most yachts carry many paperbacks, especially on long passages, exchanging them either with other yachts or in one of the book-swaps to be found in most of the larger harbours.

Most boats carry some non-nautical reference books. A dictionary and an atlas will be useful, as well as the compact editions of other reference books that would normally be used at home. Tourist guides to the places being visited will enhance the enjoyment of the trip, as will books about the flora and fauna. Comprehensive reference works, including complete encyclopaedias, are now available on computer CDs and some yachts carry these as well.

Letter writing is a favourite occupation with many people, so airmail paper and envelopes (preferably with self-sealing flaps that won't stick until intended) will be needed. Note books, both lined and plain, take up little space and will find a multitude of uses, as will a pad of tracing paper. Plenty of pencils, pens, coloured felt-tips, erasers and adhesive tape complete the stationery locker.

## Money

There is much to be said for obtaining some currency of each country to be visited before arrival. About £50 or US$100 worth will suffice. Dues normally have to be paid on arrival, and although US dollars are acceptable for this purpose, in most places the rate of exchange may be exorbitant. A quantity of the local currency will also be useful for small purchases until a bank can be visited.

The almost universal acceptance of Visa and MasterCard by banks has largely solved the problem of obtaining cash during an extended cruise. Increasingly they can be used in shops as well. Automatic teller machines (ATMs) continue to spread to even the smallest islands. Where one is not available it is safe to say that, if there is a bank, it will be able to issue cash against one or other of these cards. It is sensible to carry a selection of cards of both types and not to keep all of them together, so that the loss or theft of a handbag or wallet will not be completely disastrous.

Obtaining replacement cards abroad is a fraught process. For this reason, some experienced skippers refuse to use ATMs (which can retain cards) at all, but instead use the bank itself and, if following their example, a passport will be needed for identification. Cash can also be obtained with traveller's cheques and some cruisers carry these as a fall-back.

In the USA, Visa or MasterCard is almost essential. Cash is sometimes not welcome and occasionally not accepted. A card will certainly be required to hire a car or book an airline ticket.

Many yachts carry a concealed reserve of cash in the event of an emergency. There is no doubt that this can sometimes be an advantage – an immediate offer of a cash payment might prevent a salvage claim, for example. If deciding to do this, the cash – preferably in US dollars – should be split into reasonably sized amounts and hidden separately. Never tell anyone where this cash is hidden, or even that it is aboard.

## Insurance

### Marine

Whether or not to insure is a personal decision, but if one considers the size of a third party claim which might have to be met in the event of an accident involving others, protection against this risk seems highly desirable and is relatively inexpensive. It is difficult (but not impossible) for yachts sailed by two or even three people to get comprehensive insurance, and the desirability of having insurance may have to be balanced against the undesirability of being forced to carry extra crew.

Companies are much more likely to provide cover if they believe that the proposed cruise has been properly planned and sensibly thought out. This is something that should be discussed with insurers or brokers at an early stage. Evidence of careful preparation, a well found and properly equipped boat, thorough research into the most sensible itinerary and plans to deal with problems gives the best chance of convincing an underwriter that a particular proposal is an acceptable risk. Willingness to accept a high excess (deductible) will demonstrate that trivial claims – which are as administratively expensive as major ones – are not being contemplated. Yet however careful one's preparations, it will still be extremely difficult to obtain insurance cover for the Caribbean during the hurricane season. If insurance can be arranged, it is important to remember that a fundamental principle of all marine insurance is that one should act at all times with the caution that one would if uninsured.

Small boats continue to make Atlantic passages. Despite her diminutive size – she is only 23 ft 6 in long – *Zeewind of Poole* made a very successful singlehanded circuit of the North Atlantic in 1994-5. *Photo: Georgie McLaren*

### *Medical*

A standard medical insurance policy may or may not protect you while cruising, and this should be checked and the cover amended if necessary. Europeans should complete a form E111, which entitles them to free, or reduced-cost, treatment in EU countries. Private medical fees are high in the West Indies and the USA compared with Europe, though many West Indian islands have free health schemes based on the British National Health model, and in some islands reciprocal arrangements for free treatment have been established with Britain and some other EU countries.

## The law

Very few cruising yachtsmen have any dealings with the authorities in foreign countries, other than with customs and immigration officers. Other officials are generally only met when a problem arises – a lost or stolen item, a navigational mishap, or a dispute with a local tradesman. In these circumstances, people are seldom at their coolest or most rational and it is easy for misunderstandings to arise.

By and large, officials of all the countries around the North Atlantic are co-operative, fair and honest. Of course there are exceptions, but they are rare and should they arise the visiting yachtsman can do little but go elsewhere. Before he is too quick to criticise, however, he should remember that he is, to the countries he visits, a tourist. It is hardly surprising that his problems sometimes appear to be less significant to the authorities than those of local

working people. He should also bear in mind that there are some cruisers who behave badly, who ignore regulations, who leave without paying their bills, or who show contempt for local people. He should ensure that he is not one of them.

The golden rules are: abide by the regulations; be meticulous in declaring items which might possibly be restricted or prohibited; infringe as little as possible upon the local community; respect their customs and ideals, even if they do not accord with your own; care for the local environment; treat officials, who have a job to do, honestly and considerately; avoid political discussions. Above all, remember that you are where you are by choice and that you are a visitor. The treatment other visitors receive will depend, in part, on *your* behaviour. Leave a clean wake.

## Clothing

An Atlantic cruise calls for a variety of clothing. Some of the northern routes are in near-arctic temperatures, though for the majority of cruising people the whole object of the exercise is to reach the tropics.

If starting from a northern area waterproof clothing will probably be in daily use at sea. Once the tropics are reached this clothing may be put away for several months, but will be needed again on approaching home waters. Good quality oilskins (foul weather gear) are essential. They need a rinse in fresh water and careful storage when not in regular use – if they are just crammed into a locker and forgotten they will be in poor condition when next needed.

In the tropics clothes will be light and few in number, but they will need frequent washing. It is a pleasant habit to keep a set of clean clothes tucked away for arrival – a freshwater shower will be a much higher priority than getting the laundry done, and one's first trip ashore for several weeks will be more enjoyable in clean clothes. A reasonably clean and tidy crew will also make a better impression on customs or immigration officials than a dirty and dishevelled one.

Almost anything will pass on the beach, but in the Caribbean going topless for women is generally not accepted except in remote areas, or the French islands. It is possible to cause offence by failing to conform to local standards of dress in public places, restaurants or shops. Except in the most informal bars men will be expected to wear a short-sleeved shirt, while women in overly skimpy blouses or shorts may attract undue attention. In any case, looser clothing or a cotton skirt may well be cooler. Only in a very few places will men be expected to wear a collar and tie or jacket when dining ashore.

Protection from the sun is a high priority. Although darker complexions will acclimatise more quickly than fairer skins, it is generally accepted that over-exposure to the tropical sun is harmful. Covering up should be the rule rather than the exception and a wide brimmed hat will do much to help. Guests who fly out to the tropics from the northern winter should take particular care as a bad case of sunburn will ruin what should be an ideal holiday.

Suitable footwear should not be forgotten. Although many people prefer bare feet on deck it is dangerous to walk ashore without shoes – broken glass, sea urchins and the fallen fruit of the manchineel tree (common on Caribbean beaches) can all cause painful injuries. Shoes are considered a part of normal dress in nearly all areas and many restaurants will not serve barefooted customers. Lightweight sandals are both practical and cool. Most voyaging yachtsmen do a lot of their exploring on foot and comfortable walking shoes are important.

### Stowage of clothes

Each person aboard should have some completely private stowage space, much of which is likely to be devoted to their clothes – no one should be expected to live for weeks out of their luggage. In larger lockers, not provided with shelving, generous use of polythene bags, preferably of the self-seal variety, will provide protection from damp and keep some semblance of order. Ideally the only shared locker should be for oilskins, though in many yachts this will also have to double as a hanging locker for whatever tidy clothes are carried. Protect the latter with plastic sacks or purpose-made zipped clothing bags. Unprotected clothing allowed to swing incessantly backwards and forwards in a hanging locker during an ocean passage is likely to emerge with conspicuously threadbare patches where it has chafed against the bulkheads.

## Firearms

Very few experienced voyaging yachtsmen have firearms aboard, not only because they are of little use but also because the inconvenience they cause far outweighs any possible benefits they might conceivably have. In most countries firearms will be impounded on arrival and not returned until departure; this will normally have to be done at the port of arrival and, except in the smallest of countries, will be impracticable.

Apart from their possible use to scare away sharks it is hard to envisage a use for firearms at sea. Pirates or drug smugglers, who might theoretically pose a threat to a yacht, are unlikely to be deterred by the weapons that it would be feasible for her to carry aboard. In those countries where firearms may be retained on board in harbour, the authorities will need to be satisfied that they are secured in a proper stowage and if this is done they will not be readily available. This is just as well as it would be a rare situation aboard a yacht, however unpleasant or frightening, which the use – or threat of use – of firearms would not make worse.

## Pests

These fall into three categories: waterborne, airborne and land-based. Of the waterborne pests, owners of wooden yachts should be concerned about both teredo worm and gribble, and although protection is provided by anti-fouling paint, it needs to be in perfect condition to give complete immunity. Almost every yacht collects a crop of goose barnacles during a tradewind crossing, principally in the splash zone above the waterline on the quarters, but these do no harm and can be removed at the end of the passage.

Airborne pests include flies, mosquitoes and occasionally wasps. The best protection is to anchor well off and ensure good ventilation at all times – see Chapter 3. Experience suggests that the vast majority of mosquito bites are sustained whilst ashore, particularly around dusk.

Anchoring off will also give protection against many land-based pests, other than those unwittingly brought aboard in food or boxes. In some areas, including the Caribbean, rats may make their way on board a yacht with lines ashore and once established are very difficult to get rid of. They can do a phenomenal amount of damage in a short time, chewing through food containers, wiring and plastic hoses, including those attached to open seacocks. Should a rat take up residence aboard resist the temptation to poison it – it is likely to retreat into an inaccessible place, normally under a water tank in the bilge, to die with less than fragrant consequences. Either a trap, or a cat, left aboard the sealed and deserted yacht overnight, is an infinitely preferable solution. The pretty little rope guards sold in some chandlers, or improvised protectors made from plastic funnels, may look impressive but are completely ineffectual. To do any good, a conical rope guard that will defeat a determined rat – and there is no other kind – needs to be made of metal and be a minimum of 2 m (7 ft) in diameter, which is hardly practical for the average cruiser.

Weevils are difficult to avoid, since they are generally brought aboard in the food in which they are later found. However, they are less prevalent than used to be the case, although they are still occasionally found in flour, rice or pasta bought in the islands.

Cockroaches are the most unpleasant of the insect pests if they are allowed to gain a firm hold. Preventatives include avoidance of lying alongside, careful examination of all foods brought aboard, especially fruit and vegetables, and a complete ban on cardboard cartons which frequently harbour eggs. If these must be embarked, then they should be thoroughly sprayed with insecticide, inside and out, before being taken below. Frequent use of one of the sprays available should be routine to catch any stray intruder that may get aboard. If a yacht does become infested the best solution is to use boric acid, a white powder, which can be obtained from chemists on special order. A couple of pounds of this costs little and it is worth laying in a supply before departure. If needed, it should be used 'undiluted' and not mixed with condensed milk or sugar as is sometimes suggested. A generous sprinkling of the powder in all the areas that cockroaches frequent is necessary. Typical places are behind the headlining, around the cooker, in the backs of cupboards and drawers, and behind books. The treatment should be repeated frequently and will take around a month to be fully effective.

## Communications with home

Almost all cruisers need to keep in touch to some extent with friends and relatives in their home country. Most will have some affairs that need to be attended to as well, even if only an arrangement for the credit card bills to be paid and mail to be forwarded.

The telephone system around the North Atlantic is now excellent and it is possible practically everywhere to make direct dialled calls. A telephone credit card from one of the major companies will be almost universally accepted. Alternatively, local phone cards can be bought and this tends, at present, to be a cheaper option. Fax facilities are becoming increasingly widespread and it is worth considering installing a fax machine at the home base. The use of electronic mail is growing. Usually this is accessed by taking a laptop computer ashore and connecting to the local telephone network, but e-mail can be accessed using HF radio. Arrangements for this need to be made with a specialist company and at present it is expensive, but has the advantage that messages can be sent or received at sea.

If cruising in one area for a length of time some people choose to buy or rent a mobile phone to keep in touch with those at home. This can be done in much of the Caribbean and most of northern Europe and North America. As the use of mobile phones in coastal waters increases it is likely that the facility to make link calls via VHF radio will be withdrawn.

For most voyagers mail still remains the principal way of keeping in touch. Mail may be sent *post restante* (general delivery) to post offices in most towns, to be collected on arrival, but the time that it will be retained varies from country to country. Some marinas, yacht clubs and harbour offices will hold mail for visiting yachts. Local pilot books should give details. Mailing addresses for the ports in Part III are given in the text.

Crossing an ocean aboard a seaworthy yacht carries no more inherent risk than coastal sailing – in many ways less. On an ocean passage there is no risk of grounding, heavy weather is much less hazardous in deep water and the chance of collision is much reduced. However, equally, the option to seek shelter at the onset of bad weather is removed, and should something serious go wrong, assistance is unlikely to be available. Even if help can be summoned it will probably take a considerable time to arrive. On an ocean voyage the yacht is on her own and the crew must rely entirely on their own resources in the event of difficulty. It is not the purpose of this book to teach basic seamanship, and before contemplating an Atlantic passage the skipper should be satisfied that he and his crew are equal to most eventualities, that he knows how his boat should be handled, and how she will react in all circumstances.

The chance of meeting bad weather is always present, and must be faced. Fire, collision, man overboard and, to a large extent, gear failures are avoidable, but will have to be dealt with should they occur. The possibility of illness or injury cannot be ignored, and both skipper and crew should be aware of any ailment to which they might be prone. However, a well-prepared boat in the hands of a competent and resourceful crew has no more reason to encounter problems while crossing the Atlantic than while crossing the English Channel or the Florida Straits. In particular, those who have cruised extensively in the unforgiving waters of northern Europe or New England, with their strong tides, heavy traffic and frequently bad visibility, should be well equipped to deal with whatever the open ocean can throw at them.

## The deck: design features

Moving about the deck of a small boat at sea has been likened to trying to walk on a wet, sloping roof in an earthquake. It is surprising how few of us fall off. Good design, the sensible provision of handholds and plenty of points to clip on to are essential. The larger the yacht, the easier will be the motion and the more stable the deck. It should also be drier, and although the risk of being physically washed off the deck of any yacht is only really present in extreme conditions, a wet deck is more slippery than a dry one and a soaked crew member is more likely to make a careless mistake. But, whatever the size of yacht, moving around the deck at sea will always require care. It is as easy, and in some ways easier, to fall overboard in light weather, when one is relaxed and off guard, than it is in heavy weather when the dangers are obvious and every precaution will be taken. The camber of the deck of a good ocean cruiser should not be too extreme; excessive camber may make the weather deck more or less level when the vessel is heeled, but the lee deck will be untenable. It should be possible for crew to move all around the deck in the worst conditions, even if only on hands and knees.

A solid toerail is essential, though deep bulwarks combined with low freeboard, such as Grandfather's boat had, are a mixed blessing, often scooping up water and holding it there. Guard rails also provide some protection, but they must be strong enough to take the weight of a heavy person thrown right across the deck. This is not easy to arrange, particularly in a small yacht where the structure may not be equal to that sort of strain without reinforcement. Stanchion sockets must be securely attached – through bolted to a wooden or fibreglass hull with adequate backing plates, or welded to a metal one.

Plastic covered, stainless steel wire can have hidden defects beneath the surface and it is better to use bare wire even though this is less pleasant to fall against. Pre-stretched polyester line, very little thicker than covered wire, is equally strong and any defect will be obvious, but is very liable to chafe where it passes through the stanchions and for this reason is best avoided. Wire guard rails may be secured either by lashings or by small bottlescrews. The former can be cut quickly, but are subject to chafe and need frequent checking. If bottlescrews are used, then there should be some way of disconnecting the guard rail in a hurry – a properly moused pelican hook will serve.

If dodgers (weather cloths) are fitted there must be a gap of at least 10-15 cm (4-6 in) between them and the deck. Otherwise, should a big sea come aboard they may carry away, possibly taking guard rails and stanchions with them. Dodgers should be secured with elastic cord rather than with rope for the same reason. Some skippers remove them completely at the onset of bad weather, or they may be brailed up to avoid the risk of damage.

Pulpits must be strong beyond all question. A man working at the stemhead must both feel, and be, completely safe. It should be possible to move all over the deck from one handhold to another without ever having to let go with both hands – handrails along the entire length of the coachroof on each side are very desirable. Waist-high stainless steel rails either side of the mast give valuable support to a person working at its foot.

Finally, the deck and coachroof surfaces must provide as good a grip when wet as when dry, for bare feet as for seaboots. GRP decks often have a diamond pattern moulded in, but with an older yacht this may have become worn and ineffective and some form of commercial non-skid deck covering or non-slip paint may be required.

## Heavy weather

Although the prospect causes much apprehension, it is a fact that most people cross the Atlantic, especially by the more southerly routes, without ever experiencing truly severe weather. Gales, with winds of 35 to 45 knots, occur relatively frequently north of about 40°, but storms, with gusts reaching 60 knots, are rare except during the winter months in high latitudes. Even so, the possibility of a deep depression or out of season hurricane is always present and only a fool would set off on an ocean crossing unprepared for heavy weather.

The best tactics to employ in severe conditions depend to a large extent on the yacht herself and on the number, strength and skill of those aboard. Few people will deliberately seek out a gale before departure in order to test out their theories and, in any case, ocean seas are very different, and far easier to deal with, than those in confined waters. However, if the opportunity arises, experimenting with using the trysail, heaving-to, lying a-hull and running under bare poles, with or without warps, even in force 6 to 7 (25 to 30 knots) will give a good idea of how the boat will behave in stronger winds.

There are many excellent books on the subject of coping with bad weather at sea, notably *Heavy Weather Sailing* by K Adlard Coles, revised by Peter Bruce, the standard reference work on the subject. Accounts by less experienced yachtsmen facing heavy weather are also worth reading, as they will describe the situation from the perspective of those experiencing a gale for the first time.

While it is impossible to prevent solid water coming aboard any yacht, steps must be taken to ensure that it will disappear again as quickly as possible, and that it does not find its way below. A cockpit filled with seawater can seriously affect a boat's trim and stability, making her much more susceptible to the next wave. Large drains are essential and, if fitted with strainers, these must be cleared regularly. In practice, the violent movement generated by seas likely to come aboard will often throw much of the water out the same way it came in.

The importance of a solid bridgedeck and strong washboards has already been mentioned in Chapter 2, along with the need to be able to secure locker lids. Doghouse and coachroof windows are a source of weakness aboard some yachts, and should be provided with plywood covers for temporary repairs in the event of breakage. GRP yachts with small, aluminium framed windows of toughened glass are less likely to be at risk. It is essential that the glass is secured by more than just the rubber seal, which should only be there for watertightness. Whilst aesthetically unpleasing, the transparent slabs bolted to the outside of a coachroof as windows are probably stronger than the structure itself, provided that they are not too large. They are, however, prone to leak unless bedded on generous amounts of good quality sealant.

The hazards of a knockdown, and particularly the danger posed to the crew by heavy, unsecured fittings flying about below, are well known. Few yachts these days carry inside ballast, but if there is some it must be immovable. Batteries must be secured so that, even if the boat is rolled right over, they cannot move either. The gimbals for the stove must be of the closed variety, preferably backed up by bolts. Make sure that lockers containing heavy tools, cutlery or glassware cannot empty their contents. This is hard to achieve and if knocked down you will certainly wonder how on earth some of the items managed to get where they did.

Many knock-downs occur after the worst of the weather has passed, when the seas are still big but the wind has begun to moderate. This is particularly true if a front has gone through and the wind direction changed significantly. If the boat is undercanvassed she will be more at the mercy of rogue waves than if she has the power to answer the helm quickly. Increasing sail early runs counter to the natural inclination of a tired crew to take life a little bit easy for a while and ensure the worst really *is* over, but it is a point worth remembering.

An ocean gale is an awe-inspiring spectacle but it is much less dangerous than one in confined waters. It is sensible to have one's first brush with bad weather in deep water, with plenty of sea room and as far from a lee shore as possible. This is not quite as silly as it sounds. Although the weather for a landfall must, by and large, be taken as it comes, the departure time, and therefore the weather, can be selected. Leaving with a favourable forecast gives the opportunity to get well clear of the land, and preferably off the continental shelf, before bad weather can reach you. Both boat and crew will have had a chance to settle down and from then onwards they will be able to take bad weather in their stride.

Although never pleasant, heavy weather is much worse in anticipation than in actuality and until one has had a brush with it the prospect is particularly alarming. Once experienced, the terrors it holds will be much reduced. Until then it is worth remembering that for every account of disaster in bad weather there are literally hundreds of small yachts, often with quite inexperienced crews, who have come through similar weather unscathed, but with heightened confidence in themselves and in their yachts.

### Lightning

One facet of bad weather which worries many people, more for the damage it causes than any immediate threat, is being struck by lightning. Although comparatively rare, it does occur from time to time and little can be done to prevent it. Some yachts have lightning conductors fitted, usually in the form of heavy copper strapping from the masthead straight down through deck and kingpost to the keel, terminating in a large grounding plate. If considering fitting one then professional advice should be taken.

The effects of a lightning strike are likely to be severe. There is a distinct possibility of structural damage – aluminium mastheads can be melted or split, and if the charge leaves through a skin fitting it may be destroyed. If it exits via an encapsulated keel, then a section of the GRP can be blown off. It is likely that most of the electronic equipment aboard will be destroyed, whether powered by the ship's supply or by batteries, and whether in use at the time or isolated. The damage may be obvious – in some cases instruments will virtually explode, or be blown from their mountings – or it may not be apparent until the equipment is tested. Alternators and their regulators are not immune to damage, but it seems that starter motors are less vulnerable. The main electrical system will also probably suffer and many yachts need complete rewiring following a strike. Even if the wiring is undamaged individual light bulbs are likely to blow, either immediately or within the next few days. Fluorescent light fittings are almost certain to be destroyed. Surprisingly, injuries to the crew are rare.

There may be less obvious damage as well. Very high currents may affect rigging terminals and insulators, and current passing along the propeller shaft has occasionally damaged internal gearbox components. A large compass error will probably be induced. A yacht that has been struck should have a thorough survey as soon as possible.

On an ocean passage the consequences for a yacht dependent on electronics for navigation will be serious, as

It is vital that a thorough check is made aloft before each ocean passage. *Photo: Gavin McLaren*

hand-held GPS carried as a back-up is quite likely to be destroyed along with the main set. In theory, objects completely enclosed in a metal container are protected from lightning by the Faraday Cage effect, but the authors know of no case where this has been demonstrated at sea. At least one highly experienced voyager, a doctor of physics to boot, puts his back-up GPS in the oven if there is lightning around, but he has fortunately not had his caution put to the test. Such a measure might prevent damage to a GPS set and can do no harm – provided that the oven is not lit!

## Gear failure

Prevention is better than cure. Routine inspection for chafe should be made every day, and careful checks made before, during and after each passage to ensure that both standing and running rigging are in good order. All seacocks and pumps should be worked periodically and all machinery given regular tests to make certain that it will function when needed. See Chapter 2.

### Emergency steering

Any wheel-steered yacht should carry an emergency tiller for use should the linkage to the wheel fail, and a tiller-steered boat should carry a spare tiller (unless the fitted one is so strong as to make breakage impossible). Often,

the point of attachment of a tiller to the rudder is a weak link, particularly if a large amount of material has been cut away from the rudder stock to accommodate the tiller, and if this is the case then some reinforcing plates may be needed. Other forms of steering – a sweep over the stern, towing buckets or warps, or simply balancing the sails – should be experimented with.

## Collision

Some 95 per cent of collision avoidance depends on three things: a good lookout, bright navigation lights, and an efficient radar reflector. The other 5 per cent is down to sheer luck. Yachts do occasionally hit semi-submerged debris that the most conscientious lookout could not hope to spot. However, hitting debris is not necessarily very serious, particularly to a relatively slow-moving boat, and many ocean cruisers have received a loud and unexpected thump without any real harm to the hull beyond a few scratches or chipped gelcoat.

Collision with a ship would be another matter, and there is little doubt that from time to time yachts are lost in this way. The risk factor is, in reality, extremely low when well offshore and away from fishing grounds, but it does exist. The continental margins are much busier, which adds to the potential problems inherent in any landfall. Wherever the yacht is, a good lookout is the best defence, with white flares ready to hand at night. If fitted, radar is a powerful protection and some sets will sound an alarm if a contact reaches a pre-set range.

Although the risk of being run down is ever present and vigilance should never be relaxed, electronic aids may help. Warning devices that sound an alarm if a radar signal is detected are useful. Radar reflectors of the octahedral type should be hoisted in the catch-rain position, but the majority of experienced cruising skippers prefer the cylindrical reflectors, often permanently mounted on a mast bracket. There are newer reflectors available using the Fresnel lens principle. The different types vary in their efficiency (a favourite topic with sailing magazines) and, before fitting one, some research should be undertaken into the different makes available. A radar transponder, which detects an incoming radar signal and transmits a response to enhance the echo on the screen, requires continuous power to operate and is expensive, but virtually guarantees that a yacht will be detected. It should be remembered that none of these devices is the slightest use against a ship that is not operating radar, and in the open ocean some ships do not do so, at least by day.

### Oil rigs

At present, there appear to be fewer exploratory oil rigs stationed in the western approaches to the British Isles than was the case in the past, but the occasional fixed rig may still be encountered. They may also be found off the coasts of Nova Scotia and Cape Cod (see Chapter 19), or may occasionally be met under tow. Fixed rigs should be shown on up-to-date charts while newly established ones are listed in *Notices to Mariners*.

In fact, it would be extremely difficult to collide with an oil rig unless no watch at all was being kept. They present a confusing sight at night – a mass of lights visible from far off in clear weather, either alone or in groups, with the chief hazard being the many unlit buoys marking the ends of mooring cables. Rigs on the move are attended by several tugs, whose long towlines will be largely submerged and therefore invisible. Night or day, fixed or moving, oil rigs should be given a very wide berth. International regulations require all vessels to keep 500 m (1640 ft) away from rigs, but at least a mile would be preferable.

### Whales

There have been a number of well-publicised accounts of yachts having close encounters with whales, and most ocean cruisers see whales at some stage. However, in very few cases does a collision or any direct contact take place. The very rare attacks that do occur are usually by a frightened or injured creature. Otherwise the danger is of running into a whale dozing on the surface, usually at night and, as with floating debris, the faster the yacht is going the greater the likelihood of serious damage to yacht and injury to the whale.

Whales are curious and, like dolphins, may approach a boat for no apparent reason; they are only likely to react violently if startled. If there are whales in the vicinity and you suspect they may not be aware of your presence, start the engine but keep the revolutions low.

## Fire

Serious fires aboard cruising yachts are very uncommon, but the consequences of a major fire on an ocean passage might be disastrous and adequate precautions must be taken.

### Galley fires

The most common cause of fire in the galley is attempting to light a paraffin pressure stove without adequate priming. Fuel spillage, either of paraffin or alcohol, is another possible cause and, though neither of these fuels is volatile, wood or fabric soaked in either of them will burn vigorously. It is not enough just to mop up any spillage – the area should be washed with detergent to emulsify paraffin or to dilute and render alcohol harmless. Carelessness with bottled gas is more likely to cause an explosion than a fire. Careful installation and maintenance together with safe operating procedures are the best way to guard against this risk (see Chapter 2). Galley fires have also been started by the ignition of hot fat or cooking oil – deep fat frying should never be risked at sea and is unwise even in harbour.

### Engine fires

Engine compartment fires are particularly dangerous as they can take hold unnoticed and become well established before anyone is aware of them. Although the engine itself is unlikely to burn, most engine compartments contain a good deal of inflammable material including the fuel coming in to the engine. It is essential that the engine space is kept clean and, in particular, that any sound insulation material is not allowed to become saturated with oil or fuel. This can happen gradually over a long period and such insulation will probably need eventual replacement. Fire in the engine compartment is most likely to be started by an electrical short circuit, a ruptured fuel line or inflammable material touching an unlagged section of an exhaust pipe.

An engine fire will almost certainly flare up, possibly explosively, if the engine hatch is opened thereby admitting oxygen. The ideal way to combat such a fire is with a permanently installed extinguisher within the compartment, operated either automatically or manually by remote control. Since the operator will not be near the fire, a chemical (BCF) or $CO_2$ extinguisher may be chosen. An alternative is a hole in the casing, normally closed with a flap or plug, through which a hand-held extinguisher may be discharged. There must be a means of shutting off the fuel supply without opening the engine compartment covers.

### Electrical fires

The chances of an electrical fire are greatest on boats where additional loads have been added to the system without the wiring being upgraded. Overloading may result in overheating, and poor connections can cause heat and possibly sparks, either at the switchboard or elsewhere. Starter motors, alternators and electric anchor windlasses consume or generate very high loads and therefore call for wiring and circuitry of the highest standard. Fuses or breakers of the correct rating must always be used – keep a list of the values and never replace a fuse with one of a higher rating. Batteries generate explosive gases when being charged and therefore must have adequate ventilation.

### Smoking

Careless smoking can be a fire hazard and is banned below decks on many yachts, although this is usually for aesthetic, rather than safety, reasons. If smoking is allowed in the cockpit, care must be taken that a lighted end does not fall into an open locker or get flipped into the dinghy (a particularly common failing amongst non-sailing guests). Smoking in one's bunk is as foolish and dangerous afloat as it is ashore.

## Firefighting equipment

An adequate number of fire extinguishers should be carried – the minimum is three but more are preferable. There are various types, but dry powder extinguishers are the best choice. Although they make a lot of mess, so does a fire. They should be shaken regularly to prevent the contents of the extinguisher from settling. $CO_2$ is very effective in confined spaces because it denies the fire oxygen, but is dangerous to the operator for the same reason. Halon (BCF) smothers the fire with foam. It will not damage electrical wiring or connections and is easier to clean up than dry powder, but gives off dangerous fumes in confined areas. Water is a very effective extinguisher, is available in large quantities, and can be used on most fires. The exceptions to this are fat or fuel-based fires or those involving mains voltage electricity which may be present if an inverter or HF radio is involved. A fire blanket is effective for smothering a small fire and is particularly appropriate in the galley. It must be accessible without having to reach over the stove itself.

### Siting of extinguishers

This is important. There must be extinguishers on both sides of any point at which a fire might start so that, wherever the crew may be, it will be possible to tackle the fire with the right equipment. There should be an extinguisher adjacent to each hatch, one immediately available to the cook, and one close to the engine compartment. One should not be parsimonious with fire extinguishers. If a fire does happen, no one will complain that there are too many of them.

Finally, it should always be remembered that a big fire is simply a little fire that nobody put out. The golden rule is to tackle any fire, however small, instantly, using all the means available.

## Lifesaving equipment

### Liferaft

A conventional liferaft will need servicing by an approved centre before departure and at intervals throughout a longer cruise. It is well worth watching the raft being inflated and getting to know how it works and what equipment it contains. Most service centres are happy for owners to do this. Do not be tempted to pull the cord at home. Not only is the canister or valise likely to be badly damaged, but the valve will probably freeze as the pressurised $CO_2$ expands (if used at sea the water dissipates the chill). At the testing centre the sealing gasket is first removed and the raft then inflated by air pump.

Some cruising yachtsmen prefer a sailing tender as a liferaft and the 'Tinker' range from JM Henshaw (Marine) Ltd are available with $CO_2$ bottles and an inflatable canopy for this purpose. Except in a very small yacht, such a liferaft should be in addition to, rather than combined with, the dinghy in everyday use. It is not reasonable to expect such a vital piece of equipment as the liferaft to put up with the hard use that a yacht's tender gets.

Among the dedicated rafts various options are available, including different types of container, single or double floors and more or less comprehensive emergency packs. The ocean-going yacht will obviously require the full pack. When the raft is serviced, extra gear can (within reason) be added to the pack. Items to consider include: any vital medications; reading glasses if needed; a hand-held watermaker; an extra EPIRB; a hand-held VHF radio. If there is room, extra water should also be included. In addition to this pack, an emergency 'grab bag' should be assembled and kept accessible. Suitable contents include: extra water; foil survival blankets; flares; heliograph; fishing gear; sunscreen; additional anti-seasickness pills; glucose tablets. Some skippers also like to include ship's papers, passports, some cash and credit cards for the duration of each passage.

### Lifebuoys

Two fluorescent lifebuoys, both equipped with automatic lights and one attached to a danbuoy, should be within reach of the helmsman and ready for throwing overboard. The danbuoy pole will need a brightly coloured flag on top and a counterweight to keep it upright. The whole assembly must be carefully stowed so that danbuoy, lifebuoy, light and connecting line can be deployed instantly without fouling.

Danbuoy, lifebuoys, harnesses and lifejackets all benefit from having reflective tape stuck on them for location in the dark. Some materials do not hold their reflective quality indefinitely, so make sure that those in use at the start of the voyage are in good order and replaced as necessary.

### Flares

It makes sense to carry plenty of flares, particularly of the parachute type – it is said that the first draws attention, the second confirms it wasn't an illusion, and the third provides the opportunity to take a bearing. An ocean cruising yacht should carry at least a dozen, together with orange smoke markers, hand-held red flares and hand-held white anti-collision flares. A supply of white parachute rockets will greatly help the search for a man overboard at night. Rockets should never, however, be used to warn of an impending collision situation at night, despite the advice given in at least one chandler's catalogue. They will simply serve to surprise and distract the bridge crew of the approaching ship who are unlikely to realise that they were launched from a yacht close ahead.

## Personal safety gear

### Harnesses

Losing a person overboard is one of every skipper's worst nightmares, and rules must be established as to when harnesses are worn. The skipper must lay down whether a harness is mandatory whenever one person is on watch alone, or only at night, or only if leaving the cockpit or only in bad weather. Whatever the rules, they must be adhered to. Wearing a harness without getting snarled up takes a little practice, and an inexperienced crew would be wise to accustom himself to working in a harness before needing to do so in anger.

Most harnesses are manufactured to nationally approved standards, and each person should be responsible for adjusting and stowing their own. The safety line is as important as the harness itself. It should be about 2 m (6 ft) long, with a clip at each end and preferably one in the middle also. In cooler climates there is much to be said for the harness being built into an oilskin jacket, but during a tradewind passage, or in the Caribbean, one may sometimes need to wear a harness without wanting the additional warmth and weight such a jacket provides.

A harness is no stronger than its point of attachment. Several through-bolted eyes will be needed in the cockpit, with one for the helmsman and another within reach from inside the companionway, together with webbing jackstays running along the sidedecks. (Although webbing has a shorter life than wire it is safer as it provides a stable surface if trodden on.) The crew must know what points can be used to clip on to when working forward or at the mast. Shrouds should never be used as, in the event of a knockdown, a person clipped to them may find himself at the spreaders.

### Lifejackets

Very few adults routinely wear lifejackets, but every cruising yacht should carry enough for the maximum number who may ever sail aboard. A lifejacket should support a heavy person with their head out of the water, and turn them face up even if unconscious. It should be equipped with a whistle and possibly an automatic light which will activate when immersed.

Regulations in some countries require lifejackets to be carried in the dinghy when going ashore (leaving the problem of what to do with them once landed), and non-swimming guests should always be given the opportunity to put one on.

### Personal lights and flares packs

There are some excellent personal strobe lights available, operating from a single dry cell and fully waterproof. They may be kept in a pocket or worn around the upper arm. When switched on they give a very bright intermittent flash that would be hard to miss even at some distance and would certainly help to locate a man overboard. Several types of miniature flares are also small enough to fit in the pocket, and could prove invaluable at night or in high seas. Personal locator beacons also exist, but they require special gear aboard the parent craft to track them and are generally only suited to large, fully crewed yachts.

## Man overboard

Every boat should have a drill to recover a person in the water, and this must reflect both the boat's handling characteristics and the capabilities and physical strength of the crew left aboard. The situation on an ocean passage will be identical to that when sailing close to the coast except for two factors. The first is that there will probably be a large swell, which will make spotting the man in the water much more difficult. The second is that the boat may be under downwind rig at the time, and consequently more difficult to manoeuvre quickly.

Not much can be done about the swell except to ensure that the danbuoy is launched as quickly as possible. The downwind rig problem can be overcome, but a well thought out routine will be needed and it must have been rehearsed beforehand to have any chance of success. For the shorthanded crew the engine will be used and, despite the urgency, it is vital to check that there are no lines in the water before starting it. In the haste to lower or furl sails, it is likely that there will be. When the boat is turned she will probably pitch and roll heavily and solid water may come aboard, washing loose ropes overboard; they must be secured as well. It is far quicker to jettison a towing log rotator than to recover it.

Once the man has been located he will have to be got back on board, possibly a bigger problem than finding him. The routine used in coastal waters will serve equally well in the ocean but it must have been practised.

The overriding principle for all man overboard situations is that they should not be allowed to occur in the first place. A properly planned cockpit and deck incorporating non-skid surfacing and plenty of handholds, together with sensible rules on when harnesses are to be worn, are the best way of keeping the crew on board where they belong. Everyone should be aware that should they go overboard, particularly at night or when running in strong winds, their chances of survival are poor.

## Illness and injury

Cruising is a remarkably healthy way of life and serious illness or injury is rare. By far the commonest ailment, which affects most people at some time or other, is seasickness. Fortunately, this is usually a passing phase and after a couple of days most people recover and become immune for the rest of the voyage. Of the various remedies on the market, Stugeron (cinnarizine) seems to be the most effective of the pills. Patches worn behind the ear and from which the drug is absorbed through the skin are also highly spoken of.

Medical and dental check-ups before departure are an obvious precaution, and while a chronic condition should not necessarily prevent anyone from crossing the Atlantic, it is only fair for the rest of the crew to know the details. A good supply of medication or drugs will be needed, and these should be accompanied by a doctor's certificate to show to customs officials. Many years ago there was a fashion for ocean sailors to have their appendix removed, but unless it has already given trouble this seems over cautious. It is worth remembering that during the typical Atlantic cruise a yacht will only be out of reach of help for a very small proportion of the time.

Accidents are much more likely to happen ashore than in the familiar environment on board, particularly if sensible precautions are taken against burns and scalds while cooking in heavy weather, and against accidental gybes. However the risk is there, and everybody should have a knowledge of first aid. There should also be a good book on the subject on board (see Appendix A).

### The first aid kit

A really comprehensive first aid kit should be carried. As well as plenty of remedies for common ailments, cuts and bruises, sunburn and minor aches and pains, it will need to have sufficient gear to cope with serious emergencies at sea. It should include strong painkillers, several types of antibiotics (necessary as some strains of infection respond better to one kind than another), plenty of wound dressings, sutures or steristrips and adequate burn dressings. Treatments for eye or ear infections or injuries should not be forgotten. One's own doctor or other medical professional will be able to give more comprehensive advice, and in any case many items in the first aid kit will have to be obtained on prescription. There should also be included a basic dental kit, sufficient to apply a temporary replacement filling or to deal with a broken tooth.

If the cruise will take in any areas where malaria is present then the appropriate prophylactic drugs will be needed. Parts of central and northern South America may be affected and up-to-date information should be obtained. The normal courses of inoculations for travellers should be organised well before departure, as some of them will need a booster dose some time after the initial injections.

### Blood transfusions

With the increasing spread of the HIV virus (AIDS) in some parts of the world, the possible need for a blood transfusion – or even the stitching of a relatively minor injury – is a growing worry. The best way of approaching the latter problem is to carry a traveller's pack of sterile equipment including needles and syringes available from larger chemists.

Blood transfusions pose more difficulty. It is not possible to carry an emergency supply of blood or plasma aboard because of the controlled storage conditions necessary. If speed is not of the essence, British subjects abroad can usually be supplied with blood from the UK. Another possibility might be for one member of the crew – or indeed a volunteer from another yacht – to donate blood for the immediate use of the patient. It will be far preferable for him or her to be transferred, if at all possible, to an area where adequate precautions against the virus are taken. Blood Transfusion Centres will be able to offer more detailed advice and identify the countries where the risk of infection during medical or dental treatment is high.

## Security

Although the subject of security when sailing in foreign waters is often brought up by those who have not done so, it is not generally amongst the primary concerns of those who have. Accounts of crews being injured, or even murdered, aboard their yachts receive a great deal of publicity, not least because such incidents are so rare. The stories are often embellished in the retelling and it is not uncommon for a minor scuffle with a petty thief to develop within a few weeks into a tale of piracy, kidnapping and murder. It is very hard to sort out the fact from the fiction and even what is reported in the media is often incorrect.

What is certain is that very little violent crime against yachtsmen actually takes place around the North Atlantic. Of course there are areas where the risk is greater – any major city or seaport will have areas where a stranger will be vulnerable. But in the yachting harbours assaults are extremely rare, and the risks for the average cruiser are considerably less than they would be if he stayed at home.

Some theft, however, occurs pretty well everywhere, at home as well as abroad, and in both cases there are two kinds of thief. The serious one will steal valuables, for which there is always a ready market, whilst the petty thief picks up any trifle left within reach. The first kind will take outboard engines and rubber dinghies, and has even been known to unscrew winches and vane gears from yachts left unattended. The second variety will take the oars or rowlocks from a dinghy on the beach, or a coil of rope left on deck. Neither sort of thief is likely to resort to physical violence unless extremely frightened. Sensible precautions include never leaving the boat unlocked, stowing valuables below and, in some areas, chaining up both dinghy and outboard when ashore and hoisting them aboard at night. It is regrettable, but a fact, that other yachtsmen rather than local people are responsible for much of the theft from yachts.

Piracy at sea is also another favourite topic for discussion before departure. In fact, piracy in Atlantic waters is almost unheard of; what little there is being totally confined to those areas in which drug smuggling is rife – and which are best avoided. There have been no cases in the Lesser Antilles for decades.

## 10 THE NORTH ATLANTIC – BACKGROUND

### Routes, seasons and timing

Among the many things that go to make a successful ocean cruise, two are essential. One is to be in the right place at the right time, the other to move in the right direction. It is an over simplification, but a useful one, to think of the North Atlantic as a giant roundabout always turning clockwise. The ocean currents revolve in a clockwise direction and the weather systems (though not always the local winds) do too. Both have their centre south-west of the Azores. By keeping within the limits of a favourable wind and current system, a yacht may cover extra miles, but the sailing will be far more pleasant. She will probably reach her destination more quickly than those who take what appears, at first glance, to be a more direct route.

No matter where you begin your Atlantic cruise, hop on to the roundabout and let it help you on your way. From America or Canada, head east during the summer; from northern Europe, head south in summer or early autumn; from Madeira or the Canary Islands, wait until mid-November or December and make for the trade wind zone (perhaps with a stop in the Cape Verde Islands) before heading west. From the West Indies, go north or north-west in the late spring. Figure 3 shows, in simplified form, the best times and seasons for each cruising area or ocean passage. Detailed information will be found in the relevant chapters.

### Winds and weather

Winds and weather in the North Atlantic are dominated by the permanent high pressure in mid-ocean and by the relatively low pressures surrounding it. Winds tend to blow clockwise and slightly outwards from the high. This is true for the eastern side of the ocean to around 45°N, and for

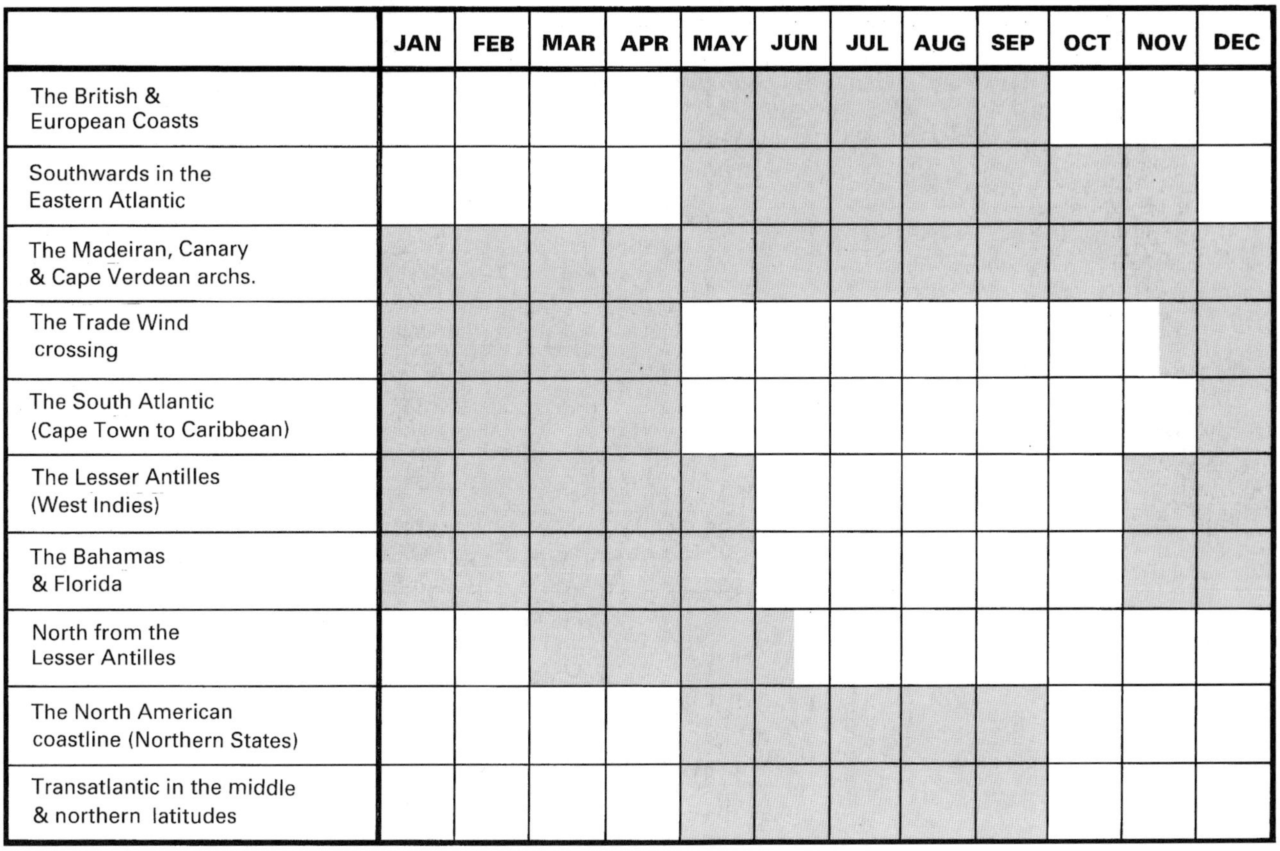

|  | JAN | FEB | MAR | APR | MAY | JUN | JUL | AUG | SEP | OCT | NOV | DEC |
|---|---|---|---|---|---|---|---|---|---|---|---|---|
| The British & European Coasts |  |  |  |  | ▓ | ▓ | ▓ | ▓ | ▓ |  |  |  |
| Southwards in the Eastern Atlantic |  |  |  |  |  |  | ▓ | ▓ | ▓ | ▓ |  |  |
| The Madeiran, Canary & Cape Verdean archs. | ▓ | ▓ | ▓ | ▓ | ▓ | ▓ | ▓ | ▓ | ▓ | ▓ | ▓ | ▓ |
| The Trade Wind crossing | ▓ | ▓ |  |  |  |  |  |  |  |  | ▓ | ▓ |
| The South Atlantic (Cape Town to Caribbean) | ▓ | ▓ | ▓ |  |  |  |  |  |  |  | ▓ | ▓ |
| The Lesser Antilles (West Indies) | ▓ | ▓ | ▓ | ▓ | ▓ |  |  |  |  |  | ▓ | ▓ |
| The Bahamas & Florida | ▓ | ▓ | ▓ | ▓ | ▓ |  |  |  |  |  | ▓ | ▓ |
| North from the Lesser Antilles |  |  | ▓ | ▓ | ▓ | ▓ |  |  |  |  |  |  |
| The North American coastline (Northern States) |  |  |  |  |  | ▓ | ▓ | ▓ | ▓ |  |  |  |
| Transatlantic in the middle & northern latitudes |  |  |  |  |  | ▓ | ▓ | ▓ | ▓ |  |  |  |

*Fig 3*  Where to be and when. Shaded areas indicate best times for cruising or passage-making.

the trade wind latitudes north of about 10°N and on towards the Bahamas and Florida. There are modifications elsewhere, for the land mass of North America, the warm Gulf Stream and its confluence with the cold Labrador Current result in unstable conditions in that region. These give rise to the typical weather patterns of the British Isles – a succession of lows which form over the western North Atlantic and are then propelled east or north-east towards Europe. Each of these depressions creates its own wind system in its immediate locality – anticlockwise around the low. In spite of this, the whole area from west to east, in the forties and fifties of latitude, is known as 'the Westerlies', indicating that the wind blows from that quarter more often than not. Gales are frequent in this area, though they are generally less common and less severe in summer. Details of some regional weather forecast transmissions will be found in Appendix G.

## Hurricanes

Tropical revolving storms, or hurricanes, occur on the western side of the North Atlantic, chiefly during the summer months. As the old rhyme has it:

> June, too soon
> July, stand by
> August, come she must
> September, remember
> October, all over

But this is not entirely accurate and Figure 4 gives the average number of hurricanes per month. These are only average figures, however, and from year to year there may be considerable variations.

Although each individual one is small in area, perhaps as little as 100 miles across, hurricanes are amongst the most destructive forces of nature, on a par with earthquakes and volcanic eruptions in terms of the devastation they cause. Sustained winds can reach 135 knots, with gusts far in excess of that, and the seas will be huge; if the storm passes very close, the wind direction will shift rapidly and a lethally confused wave pattern will result. When a hurricane reaches land, the surge associated with it may temporarily raise the sea level by as much as 3–4 m (10–13 ft). Even large commercial ships encountering such storms are often damaged and sometimes lost. Yachts, whether at sea or in the snuggest harbours, will be

fortunate to survive the direct passage of a hurricane. Therefore, one of the most important considerations in planning an Atlantic passage or cruise is to avoid the hurricane area during the season. If this cannot be achieved then time spent in the risk area should be during the months when storms are least likely.

The advent of weather and oceanographic satellites means that much more is now known about tropical storms. They form both east and west of the Lesser Antilles. Those that form to the east usually have their origins hundreds, or even thousands, of miles out into the Atlantic. Occasionally, in mid-season, a hurricane will form much closer, sometimes even between Barbados and the main island chain, and there is likely to be very little warning of such a storm. Hurricanes that form in the Caribbean basin do not usually affect the Windward or Leeward Islands but may track over Florida and the Bahamas. The energy that generates and sustains a hurricane is drawn from the sea water beneath it; a very broad generalisation is that the warmer the sea in any year the more frequent and more severe hurricanes are likely to be. Very small temperature changes – as little as 1° or 2°C – are significant, and it is likely that even minimal global warming will affect the frequency and severity of tropical storms.

Hurricanes are closely monitored and tracked and their movements forecast. These forecasts may not be entirely accurate and will certainly not be accurate enough for a yacht to move from one island to another in time to avoid the centre of the system. Fast moving storms tend to behave more predictably than slow moving ones.

Some characteristics of hurricanes in the North Atlantic will help with passage planning and cruise timing. Storms hardly ever pass south of Grenada; only very occasionally (once in five to ten years) do they affect the east coast of the USA north of Cape Hatteras, and by then they are losing their tropical characteristics and are usually more akin to a normal (but nonetheless severe) winter storm system. However, even a distant brush with a hurricane by a yacht in the Gulf Stream may prove disastrous due to the enormous and steep seas that may form where the current runs against the wind.

In general, the following advice will minimise the chances of experiencing a hurricane:

1 Bound for the Caribbean, do not leave the Canaries or Cape Verdes before the middle of November.
2 If remaining in the Caribbean for the summer, be south of Grenada by the beginning of June.
3 If sailing directly to Europe leave the Caribbean by mid-May; if going via Bermuda leave earlier to allow for the time to be spent there. Whether bound for Europe or for the north-eastern USA, leave Bermuda by early June.
4 If transiting the Bahamas and the US Intracoastal Waterway northwards, be north of Cape Hatteras by the beginning of June.
5 Monitor the forecasts regularly when on passage between late May and November. (See later in this chapter.)

## Hurricane holes and harbours

Many Caribbean islands have harbours known locally as hurricane holes. These traditional refuges for shipping, unlike many West Indian anchorages which are often wide open to the west, are sheltered from all directions. Over

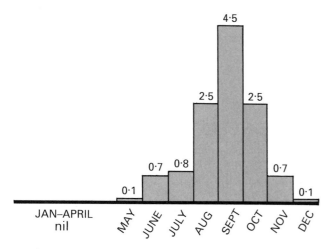

*Fig 4*  Hurricane months in the Caribbean.

Yachts piled up on the beach in the lagoon at St Maarten following Hurricane *Luis*. *Photo: Malcolm Page*

the years many, but not all, ships using them have ridden out hurricanes.

Recently, however, the belief has grown that yachts too can safely remain in the Caribbean during the summer provided that they stay in one of these so-called 'safe' harbours. Island governments, anxious for the economic benefits that visitors bring, have encouraged this idea; yachtsmen, eager to remain in the Caribbean for more than one season, are only too ready to believe it. Unfortunately, it is a myth. In even the most secure hurricane hole a well prepared yacht, with several heavy anchors out and with plenty of space around her, or moored amongst the mangroves, may simply be overwhelmed and destroyed by the forces generated in a hurricane.

Lately the situation has become worse, due to the vast numbers of yachts in the Caribbean. During a storm alert, hurricane holes become impossibly crowded. Often these are large charter fleets, hastily and inadequately anchored and then abandoned. Once a few of these start to drag, fouling other yachts, the situation becomes hopeless. For those berthed in marinas things are little better. Often the storm surge floats pontoons, complete with boats attached to them, off their securing piles.

Despite the initial appearance from the chart, most of the US Intracoastal Waterway is not a safe place in which to weather a hurricane either, as much of the land area it runs through is only a few feet above sea level. The marinas are particularly vulnerable to the surge already mentioned. To make matters worse, the lifting bridges which cross the waterway will cease operating well before a storm arrives so as to allow residents to evacuate the areas at risk. Yachts will therefore be unable to move away from the dangerous zone.

Before deciding to stay in the Caribbean during the summer, the risks and consequences of a hurricane should be calmly and carefully considered. Of some one thousand yachts in the lagoon at St Maarten - long considered one of the safest of hurricane holes - over 800 were sunk or wrecked during Hurricane *Luis* in 1995. Not all of their crews survived. The strength of the wind was over four

times greater than in the 'hurricane' which devastated southern Britain in 1987. In the face of such forces, the yachtsman is completely powerless to influence events.

It should be noted that most insurance companies now exclude cover for loss or damage to yachts that remain in the Caribbean during the hurricane season. Those considering doing so should check the specific details of their policies.

### Fog

When a south or south-west wind takes warm moist air over the cold Labrador Current, fog becomes widespread on the coast of Maine and in the region of the Grand Banks. It is most prevalent in spring and summer, and can be expected on about ten days in every month. All of the coastal areas on the eastern side of the North Atlantic, from Norway southward, are subject to fog.

British and European yachtsmen who tend to associate fog with light winds or calms should be aware that this is often not the case in the western Atlantic, where fog may be accompanied by steady winds of 25 knots or more.

### Ice

North Atlantic icebergs form by 'calving' from Greenland's glaciers, and are then carried south by wind and currents. They are almost totally confined to an area north of 40°N and west of 40°W, though bergs have occasionally been found south or east of this; they are most widespread between March and July. The International Ice Patrol locates the position of bergs and gives radio reports.

## Ocean currents

There is a close but complex relationship between prevailing winds and ocean currents. That currents will be set up wherever the surface water is continually blown in one direction is fairly obvious, but that this should in turn give rise to coastal currents may be less so. Basically, the mass of moving water must go somewhere on reaching the continental margins, and is generally deflected towards the 'intake' area of the next major wind-driven current.

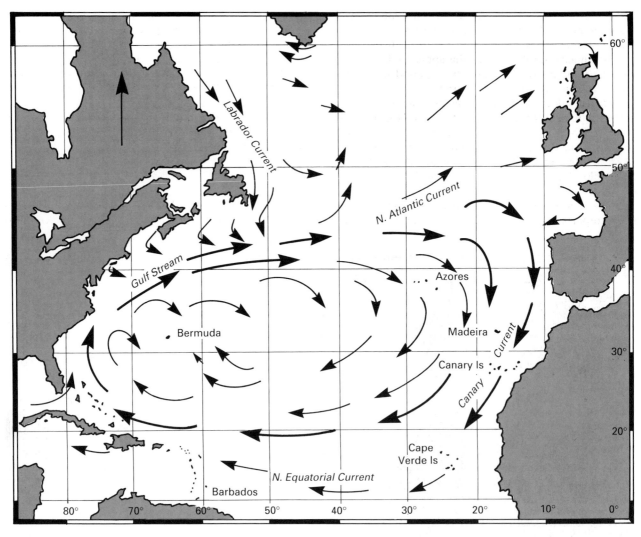

*Chart 1*    General direction of current flow in the North Atlantic.

Thus the north-east trade wind gives rises to the North Equatorial Current, flowing east to west across the Atlantic between about 10° and 25°N. This creates a head of water in the Gulf of Mexico and the Caribbean Sea, which emerges through the Strait of Florida and, named the Gulf Stream, flows in a north-easterly direction until it meets the Labrador Current flowing south around New-foundland and Nova Scotia. This causes the Labrador Current to divide, one part forcing a passage down between the Gulf Stream and the American coast and the other turning eastward and combining with the Gulf Stream to form the North Atlantic Current.

The North Atlantic Current, urged on by the prevailing westerly winds, eventually meets the obstruction of the continent of Europe. Again it divides, one stream going north of Scotland and the other being deflected south-east and then south to form the Azores Current, the Portuguese Current and finally the Canaries Current. This in turn feeds the embryo North Equatorial Current to complete the giant circle. In addition there are local features, such as the currents flowing into the English Channel, the Bay of Biscay and the Mediterranean, but these have little importance beyond their own margins.

When a current flows past a continental coastline its course tends to be orderly, but in mid-ocean, or on

encountering islands in its path, its track may split or become very ragged at the edges. In some places there are well-documented changes of course, due to land masses, and there are areas in which eddies or counter-currents occur predictably. The study of these can be important because parallel courses only a few miles apart may be in waters moving in opposite directions. When this happens, the choice of the right track can make a significant difference to the day's run.

The Gulf Stream is carefully monitored by the US Coast Guard, and their 1600 and 2200 UTC weather forecasts from NMN in Portsmouth, Virginia (see end of this chapter) give the co-ordinates of the West or Cold Wall (the line of demarcation between the Gulf Stream and the Labrador Current flowing along the US coast), the speed and position of the middle of the Gulf Stream at various latitudes and the position of major established eddies. That this service is considered to be necessary emphasises that the stream cannot be accurately predicted – it has to be observed and reported.

## Sources of information

Until fairly recently there was no single volume of route planning information specifically for yachts. When the classic *Ocean Passages for the World* talks about sailing vessels it means 'those able to stand up to, and take advantage of, the heavy weather to be found on many of the recommended routes'. Although this applies to few cruising yachts, the book contains good background information on the weather systems of the world.

Detailed information regarding prevailing winds and currents, percentage frequency of gales and calms, wave and swell heights, hurricane tracks, icebergs and fog is presented on the Admiralty *Routeing Charts* (BA Chart 5124, monthly (numbers 1–12) and the US *Pilot Charts* DMA Pilot Chart 16, produced quarterly, three months in each).

These charts, which are similar in form, are compiled using reports from merchant vessels, naval units and weather ships collected over a long period. While they can only show the average, they give an excellent basis for timing and route planning.

Much the same information, presented visually on monthly charts with explanatory text, but in a more handy size and format for the yacht with a small chart table, is to be found in the *Atlantic Pilot Atlas* compiled by James Clarke. This covers the North Atlantic and Caribbean in considerable detail and the South Atlantic and Mediterranean in more condensed form.

*World Cruising Routes* by Jimmy Cornell adopts a similar approach to *Ocean Passages for the World*, but is aimed specifically at cruising yachts and describes each passage individually. In addition, the regional weather and currents for each ocean and cruising area are discussed,

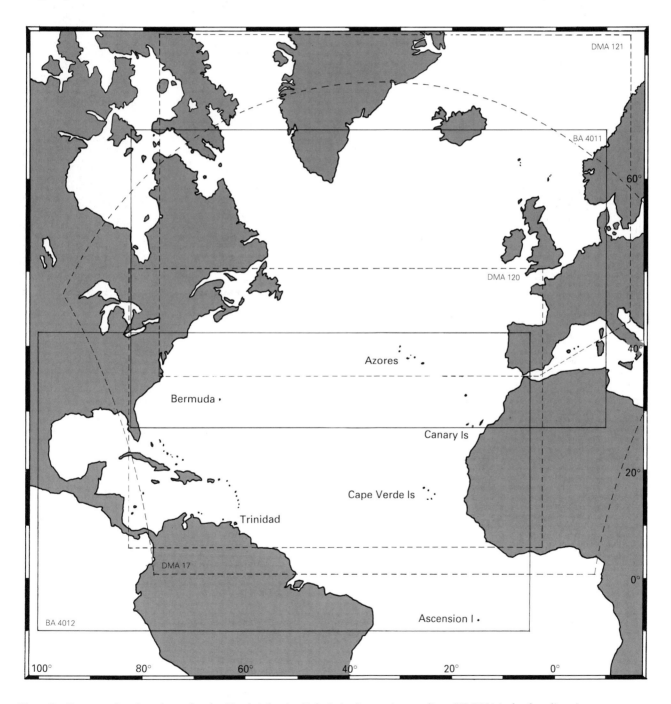

*Chart 2*   Passage planning charts for the North Atlantic. (Admiralty in continuous lines, US DMA in broken lines.)

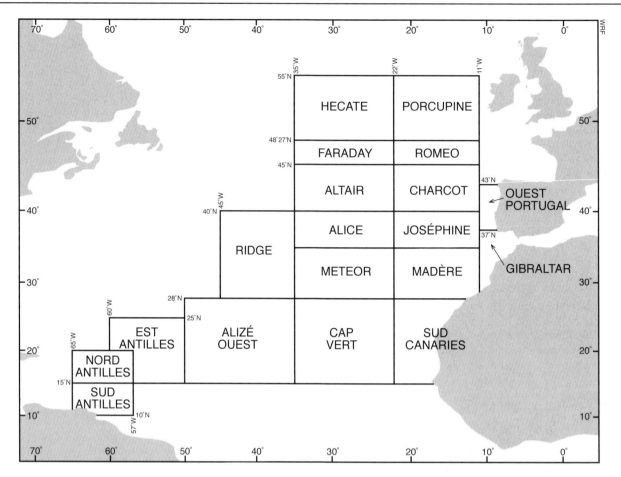

*Chart 3* Radio France Internationale weather forecast areas. Based on information from *Admiralty List of Radio Signals*.

together with tactics to be adopted should a tropical storm be met at sea.

## Charts

Charts will need to be bought over a period of time. Basic ocean passage charts (see Chart 2) will be found useful for reference in the early stages of planning and again later for plotting daily positions at sea. As each section of the intended route is studied, the relevant passage planning charts will be found useful – lists are included in each chapter. These small scale charts carry little detail, and it will not matter if they are months or a few years out of date by the time the cruise starts.

No attempt has been made to provide a comprehensive list of all charts available for each area. Far too many are published, and in any case needs will vary according to the route chosen. First plan the itinerary – where you intend to stop, where coastal passages will be made, which are the possible ports of refuge in the event of bad weather or emergency. Only then should a current chart catalogue be consulted and an order placed. Plenty of time should be allowed for the order to be filled, but large scale charts should not be collected until shortly before departure. This is particularly important in the UK where charts should be corrected up to the date of sale, less so in the United States where uncorrected latest editions will normally be supplied. Although there are chart agents throughout the world, many of them only carry local stock.

### Ocean passage charts

| Coverage | Admiralty | US |
| --- | --- | --- |
| Northern | | |
| N Atlantic | 4011 (1:10,000,000) | 121 (1:5,870,000) |
| Southern | | |
| N Atlantic | 4012 (1:10,000,000) | 120 (1:6,331,100) |
| Gnomonic | | |
| (great circle) | 5095 (1:13,500,000) | 17 (Variable scale) |

## Pilots, guides and sailing directions

Pilots and guides fall into two distinct types – official publications intended primarily for use by naval and commercial shipping, and those written purely with the yachtsman in mind.

Chief amongst the former are the *Sailing Directions* published by the British Admiralty, the US Defense Mapping Agency and the Canadian Hydrographic Service. Each volume of these comprehensive books covers a specific area and contains a wealth of detailed information on the climate, the coast and the harbours. Every danger to shipping is described and every harbour detail is covered, but only those relevant to big ships. Little information specifically for the yachtsman is included. They are kept reasonably up to date by periodic supplements. However, they are expensive and it is probably not worth any but the largest yachts carrying them.

Much more useful to yachts are the pilots and guides written specifically for them. The margins of the North Atlantic are particularly well covered by such books and a list will be found in Appendix B. However, it should be remembered that these privately researched guides vary dramatically in their content and accuracy. Only the better books are updated by supplements from the publishers, and many of them continue to be sold long after time has rendered them inaccurate.

Pilots applicable to each area are listed at the end of the relevant chapter.

## Weather forecast transmissions

Weather forecasts for the coastal regions of the North Atlantic are comprehensive. Almost every country broadcasts forecasts for shipping in some form. General details of the more useful ones appear in Appendix G. The remainder of this section gives brief information on ocean forecasts, which are much less readily available.

The only voice forecast that covers the complete trade wind crossing from Europe is that broadcast by Radio France Internationale at 1145 UTC daily on the following

AM (A3E) frequencies:

6175, **11700**, 11845, 15300, **15530**, and **17575** kHz

Those frequencies in bold type broadcast the forecast for all the areas on Chart 3. The remainder broadcast a selection relevant to the frequency reception area. The forecast is read clearly in French; it may be advantageous for non French speakers to record it for translation. It will be seen that this transmission also covers much of the area crossed by mid-latitude passage makers. The remainder, on the west side of the ocean, is covered by the American High Seas forecast. This is broadcast from several stations – probably the most easily received is that transmitted by the US Coast Guard Portsmouth, Virginia (Callsign NMN). Frequencies and times are as follows:

| *Frequency kHz,* USB (J3E) | *Time, UTC* |
|---|---|
| 4426 | 0400,0530,1000 |
| 6501 | 0400,0530,1000,1130,1600,2200,2330 |
| 8764 | 0400,0530,1000,1130,1600,1730, 2200,2330 |
| 13089 | 1130,1600,1730,2200,2330 |
| 17314 | 1730 |

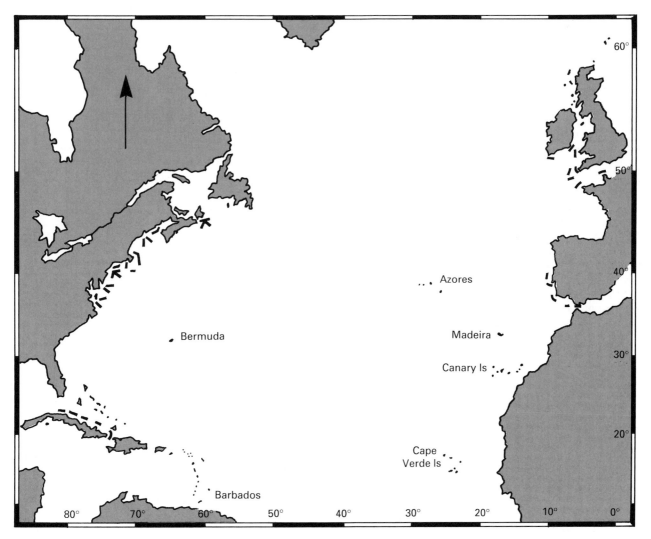

*Chart 4*  Traffic Separation Schemes in the North Atlantic. Based on information from the International Maritime Organisation. Consult large scale charts for individual details.

The area covered is the Atlantic north of 3°N and west of 35°W, together with the Gulf of Mexico and the Caribbean Sea. Any hurricane warnings will be transmitted before the forecast. In addition the 1600 and 2200 broadcasts include a Gulf Stream analysis. This forecast is read by a computer generated voice synthesiser, which takes some getting accustomed to. Again, a tape recorder will be useful.

Station WWV in Colorado broadcasts storm warnings for the North Atlantic, Caribbean and Gulf of Mexico at 8 and 9 minutes past each hour. However, this station primarily transmits time signals and the weather information is squeezed into the time gaps remaining. The information is read very quickly; it is particularly useful to record it if there is a hurricane or tropical storm brewing.

Frequencies, kHz AM (A3E) are:
2500, 5000, 10000, 15000, 20000

Other forecasts are available to yachts fitted with weatherfax. Extremely comprehensive details of all weather forecasts worldwide can be obtained from *Admiralty List of Radio Signals Vol III, Parts 1 and 2*. All transatlantic yacht skippers will find this book well worth carrying; for those with weatherfax or telex facilities it is virtually essential.

## Amateur forecasts

Several amateur or 'ham' nets transmit useful weather information. Only licensed amateur operators may transmit on these nets, but all may listen and useful information can be obtained. Nets come and go, but three are long established. All frequencies are USB (J3E)

**a** The **Transatlantic Maritime Mobile Net**, run by Trudi in Barbados (callsign 8P6QM) broadcasts at 1300 UTC on 21400 kHz. Yachts throughout the Atlantic check in, giving positions and actual weather conditions. If it is available, a translation of the Radio France weather forecast is broadcast at around 1330 UCT. This net is most useful for those crossing west on the trade

wind route. It may not operate for periods during the hurricane season.

**b** The **Caribbean SSB Weather Net** run by David from the yacht *Mistine* (callsign ZHBJ5). The weather is broadcast at 0815 Eastern Caribbean Time (ECT, GMT-4) on 4003 kHz and at 0830 ECT on 8104 kHz. When hurricane warnings are in force there will be a further broadcast on 8107 kHz at 1815 ECT.

**c** **Herb's Net**. Herb Hillgenberg, callsign GX498 (but more commonly known as *Southbound 2*), broadcasts on 12359 kHz starting at 2000 UTC. This gives a detailed forecast to each boat that checks in; those who are only listening will gain much useful information and may well find that a forecast is given for a boat close to their position.

## Traffic Separation Schemes

In many areas where shipping is heavy – particularly around headlands, where a number of major routes converge and in constricted waters – IMCO Traffic Separation Schemes have been set up. Typically they consist of two lanes down which vessels pass port-to-port, a central separation zone, and usually an inshore traffic zone. The rules governing separation schemes are detailed in the International Regulations for Preventing Collisions at Sea, but so far as yachts are concerned the most important points are as follows:

**1** As far as possible avoid crossing traffic lanes, but if obliged to do so cross on a heading as nearly as practicable at right angles to the general direction of traffic flow. (It should be noted that it is the heading rather than the ground track which is to be at right angles to the traffic flow.)

**2** Use inshore traffic zones whenever possible.

**3** Do not impede the safe passage of a power-driven vessel following a traffic lane.

Traffic Separation Schemes are often monitored by coast guards or other official bodies, usually by radar, and yachtsmen have been prosecuted for ignoring the regulations.

# 11 THE BRITISH AND EUROPEAN COASTS

## Regional weather

The Atlantic coast of Europe reaches from 36°N at Gibraltar to the Arctic Circle and beyond, the vast majority of yachts staying south of 60°N. The cruising season around the coasts of Britain and France runs from May until early October, extending later into the year as one progresses south.

From the latitude of northern Spain northwards, winds blow predominantly from between south-west and north-west, although winds from other directions are common. The weather pattern is unstable and yachtsmen used to the more settled summer conditions found off the east coast of America may be startled by how quickly conditions can change. The BBC shipping forecasts covering the area are generally reliable (See Appendix G).

The Bay of Biscay has long had a reputation for particularly unpleasant weather, dating back to the days of the square-riggers and beyond. While this may not be entirely deserved during the summer months, setting off across Biscay too late in the year is unwise. To risk catching a gale without sufficient sea-room and before the crew have settled into their stride is an appalling way to start any long cruise and it is best to plan to reach Spanish waters by the end of August.

A large area of low pressure forms annually over the Iberian Peninsula in early summer, dominating weather patterns until late autumn. The western edge of this depression gives rise to the Portuguese Trades, northerly winds which blow parallel to the coast in a band some one hundred miles wide. These winds are most reliable from July through to September or October, and may be augmented near the coast by strong sea breezes, sometimes giving rise to strong or even gale force winds for a short time in the afternoon.

If making a diversion into Gibraltar, the wind may be more variable in both strength and direction after passing Cape St Vincent and, on reaching the Strait of Gibraltar, be blowing either straight in or straight out. There is a constant flow of current from the Atlantic into the Mediterranean, due to the high rate of evaporation in the confined area of the Mediterranean Sea. The speed of this current is affected partly by the tide, which retards or accelerates it, and partly by the wind. In moderate weather there is no difficulty in beating into Gibraltar, but against the levanter (the local name for a strong easterly wind) it may be impossible for a small yacht to make much progress, due to the steep seas kicked up by wind against current. In that case, shelter may be sought in one of the Spanish ports westward of the Strait. A strong westerly or south-westerly wind, which reinforces the current, can make it difficult for a yacht to get out from Gibraltar and into the Atlantic. Even a very slight easing of the wind strength does, however, make an immediate and remarkable difference and as soon as this happens good progress may be made by hugging the Spanish coast as far as Tarifa, after which the strength of the current falls off rapidly.

Once clear of the coasts of Spain and Portugal, the chances are that a breeze from a northerly quarter may be found to take the yacht towards the Madeiran archipelago or the Canaries.

## Currents

The North Atlantic Current divides in two before reaching the British Isles, one part running up the west coast of Scotland towards Scandinavia and the other deflected south-west and then south past the Iberian Peninsula. Smaller branches enter the English Channel and Irish Sea. The relatively warm water of what was previously the Gulf Stream provides a moderating influence on temperatures in western Europe, which tend to be much less extreme than those inland.

The Portuguese Current, again part of the vast clockwise circulation of water in the North Atlantic, runs in a generally southerly direction from Cape Finisterre to the Canary Islands where it becomes known as the Canary Current. It is reinforced by the constant flow through the Strait of Gibraltar mentioned above.

## Tides and tidal streams

Both tidal range and strength of stream vary a great deal along the Atlantic coast of Europe. Greatest spring range among the relevant ports listed in Part III is the 6.1 m (20 ft) experienced at Brest, while the least is the 1.1 m (3 ft 7 in) found at Gibraltar. However ranges of 12 m (40 ft) may occur in some areas, notably around the Channel Islands and the adjacent French coast and in the Bristol Channel.

These great ranges naturally give rise to strong tidal streams, which are generally much more significant to the yachtsman than is the current. On the coast of the British Isles and France tidal streams regularly reach speeds of three or four knots, while in the famous 'Alderney Race' between the Channel Islands and the Normandy peninsula the flood can exceed ten knots. Tidal streams can be especially strong off headlands, with heavy overfalls. If these are marked on the chart it is particularly important to keep clear of them, but tide rips and overfalls can occur off most headlands and one must always be prepared for this. Strong winds against the stream will aggravate the situation and can create dangerous conditions. Conditions may moderate significantly when the tide turns.

Details of tidal ranges, streams and races will be found in the various local nautical almanacs.

## Approach and landfall

Approaching the European coastline there is always the chance of strong onshore winds and poor visibility. If the yacht's position is uncertain the best action may be to heave-to and await an improvement before closing the coast.

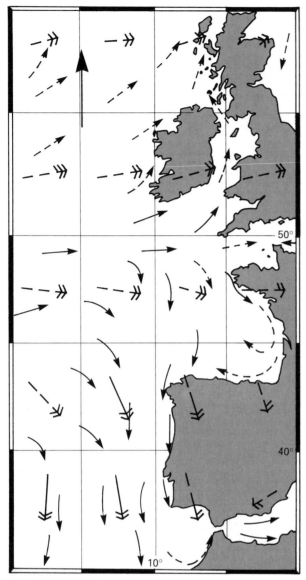

*Chart 5* Prevailing winds and currents off the coast of Europe – August. (Winds in feathered arrows, currents in solid arrows.) Based on information from the *Atlantic Pilot Atlas*.

The network of marine DF beacons has been largely discontinued. Most of those retained have reduced ranges; some broadcast DGPS information. There are many aero DF beacons, but these are not easy to use. Most fog sound signals have also ceased. A landfall in thick weather based on DF information alone should now only be attempted in a real emergency. In general, navigation aids are well maintained and can be relied upon.

### The Scottish coast
Boats making direct for Scandinavia, and passing round the north of Scotland, should have no problems provided they are well clear of Rockall (57°37′N 13°41′W). The St Kilda Island group and the Flannan Islands, 40 miles and 20 miles off the west coast of the Outer Hebrides, should be well clear to starboard, but Sula Sgeir (59°06′N 6°11′W) and North Rona (59°08′N 5°50′W) could be close to the route and are hazards to be avoided in thick weather. Both are now lit.

The passage through the Pentland Firth, between the north Scottish coast and the Orkney Islands, should not be attempted in strong winds or poor visibility. Shelter can be sought in the lee of Lewis by passing round the Butt of Lewis, and Stornoway on the east side is an official entry port.

If the prevailing or forecast conditions make it inadvisable to approach the mainland coast, then seek shelter on the east coast of the Outer Hebrides. Under no circumstances should the Sound of Harris be attempted by a stranger in other than ideal conditions. If approaching the southern end of the islands, pass at least three miles clear of Barra Head to avoid the strong tidal stream and heavy overfalls in the vicinity. The best haven in the vicinity is Loch Boisdale on South Uist. When anchoring in Scottish waters, beware of kelp. A heavy anchor should be used – see page 13.

### The Irish coast
A landfall on the south Irish coast is generally straightforward. If making for Crosshaven in Cork Harbour under deteriorating conditions, shelter can be found at several places on the south and south-west coasts. North of Mizen Head, identifying the coast by eye can be difficult. If approaching Castletown in Bear Haven on the north side of Bantry Bay, ensure that the correct bay is being entered. South of Mizen Head, Crookhaven is safe in almost any weather and anchorage can also be found at Baltimore. The Old Head of Kinsale gives a lee to the entrance to Kinsale Harbour where there is an anchorage and marina.

### The English coast
If making for Falmouth or Plymouth, the Bishop Rock lighthouse marking the south-western extremity of the Scilly Isles is the traditional first landfall in good visibility. There can be strong tidal streams off the Bishop Rock, and overfalls on the Pol Bank, three miles to the south-west. There may also be strong streams off Lizard Point and heavy overfalls extending to the south for three miles or more. Give these points a wide berth, and in strong south-westerlies make no attempt to close the coast until well round the Lizard, when a course for Falmouth can be shaped northwards in the lee of the land.

There is often considerable shipping in the vicinity of the Lizard though there is no longer a formal separation zone off the headland. In addition to traffic up and down the English Channel, vessels may also be altering course for Falmouth or Plymouth. The whole situation can be very confusing, especially at night, with the addition of brilliantly lit fishing vessels, often working in fleets and occasionally in pairs. In heavy or thick weather it is safer to keep well clear to the south until able to turn north towards Falmouth and cross the traffic at right-angles.

### The English Channel
The English Channel has one of the world's highest concentrations of ship traffic, and it is essential to maintain a good lookout and to proceed with great caution if visibility is poor. Most of the traffic is concentrated on two main routes, one on the northern side running from the Scilly Isles and Land's End towards the Dover Strait, and the other on the southern side, rounding Ushant and the Casquets before again heading east to the Dover Strait. Each of these corridors carries two-way traffic. There are

The fishing harbours of north-western Spain are full of interest for the visiting yachtsman. *Photo: Anne Hammick*

also ferries sailing between England and France, and coastal trading vessels, fishing boats and yachts continually on the move. If at any time after entering the English Channel weather conditions or bad visibility make it advisable to seek shelter, it will generally be found safer to close the English coast rather than the French.

### The French coast

The north-west coast of France (the Brittany peninsula) is a particularly dangerous coast to approach in thick or heavy weather because of the many offlying rocks, strong tidal streams and, particularly during summer, the likelihood of encountering fog. There is heavy shipping in the separation lanes off Ushant, a turning point where ships often alter course. The Traffic Separation Scheme extends for a lateral distance of 35–40 miles in a general north-westerly direction from Ushant, and it is essential to study an up-to-date chart before approaching this area.

The many dangers are well marked but it is essential to have adequate visibility, a suitable chart, an awareness of the tidal streams and a reliable and accurate position before closing this coast. If the weather is thick and the marks cannot be identified with certainty, it is far safer to stand well off the land, clear of the strongest tidal streams and shipping lanes, and either await fairer weather or proceed elsewhere.

If making for Cherbourg or further east it is perfectly feasible to proceed up the English Channel in heavy weather if the wind is fair. However, conditions may be uncomfortable as Channel seas tend to be short and steep, particularly when there is a strong tidal stream running against the wind. The streams increase in strength as the

Channel narrows towards the Cherbourg peninsula and can have a marked effect on both progress and sea state. There is a Traffic Separation Scheme off the Casquets.

### The Spanish and Portuguese coasts

The coast of Iberia is in some ways safer than that of northern Europe, with relatively few outlying rocks or tidal races. However, this is balanced by heavy shipping and frequent poor visibility, both prevalent along a narrow band relatively close inshore. Sudden northerly gales are another feature of the area. It may be best to keep well offshore until on the approximate latitude of one's landfall, before crossing the shipping lanes and approaching the coast at right-angles. There is much commercial fishing, often by large seagoing trawlers which may travel at speed to and from the fishing grounds, and are not always known for the efficiency of their lookout.

## Formalities

Both customs and immigration regulations and the formality with which they are applied varies from country to country within Europe. Throughout the UK, France and Portugal the paperwork is taken seriously on both arrival and departure. In Spain the attitude is generally more relaxed. Generally speaking, European officials treat yachtsmen very fairly, a situation which will only be maintained so long as the attitude is mutual.

All those ports listed in Part III are official entry/exit ports. Traditionally, once within the territorial waters of any country the Q flag had to be flown and clearance obtained as soon as possible, but most authorities will accept that, in stress of weather, a vessel may have to shelter in the nearest available haven before moving to an official port of entry. In some places, where smuggling or gun-running are not unknown, a yacht entering a remote harbour or anchorage may be treated with suspicion – to allay these fears always contact the authorities, even if only the local police, by radio, telephone or in person.

Changes within the structure of the European Union have made the situation more complex. In theory, there is complete freedom of movement of goods and people between the member states of the Union, but both Great Britain and the Irish Republic have exemptions to retain immigration controls. Some officials take the view that the freedom of movement applies only to the goods and nationals of EU countries, others take the more liberal view that once cleared into any EU country one is cleared into the Union as a whole. There is little consistency between the interpretation of the rules by different states, and sometimes even by different officials within states. One certainty, however, is that full clearance procedures must be completed at the first EU port visited. After this, non-EU flagged yachts, or those with non-EU citizens aboard, are advised to arrive in each EU country at a reasonable sized port, to fly a Q flag, and to immediately enquire what formalities, if any, should be completed. Neither the Channel Islands, Gibraltar or the Canaries are part of the EU and full formalities must be completed when departing for, or returning from, them.

There is a universal ban on the import of hard drugs, and many countries look carefully at prescribed medicines, which are best accompanied by a letter from the prescribing doctor. Import of fresh meat is forbidden in some European countries as are growing plants and some fresh vegetables. All countries have limits regarding the import of alcohol and tobacco for personal use. All firearms, including any flare guns, must be declared and failure to do so will incur very heavy penalties, particularly in the UK.

There are very strict regulations in the UK and the Irish Republic regarding bringing animals of any kind into the country, and if planning to do so it is essential to contact the authorities at the intended port of arrival well in advance. The anti-rabies laws are taken very seriously indeed and any breach will inevitably lead to the destruction of the animal and a heavy fine for the owner.

## Facilities

Depending on where the boat is lying, facilities may be anything from top class to non-existent. All European harbours detailed in Part III have adequate facilities, with those in the UK, Ireland and France in general more attuned to yachts than those in Iberia. Full details for each harbour will be found in Part III.

## Sailing directions and yachtsmen's guides

In addition to the official publications mentioned in Part I, the following almanacs and yachtsmen's guides, listed by area, are relevant to the Atlantic coast of Europe. See Appendix B, page 217 for recommendations and publishers' details.

*The Cruising Association Handbook*
*Macmillan Nautical Almanac*
*The Simpson-Lawrence Yachtsman's Almanac: North and West*, Michael Balmforth
*The Yachtsman's Pilot to Skye and North West Scotland*, Martin Lawrence
*The Yachtsman's Pilot to the West Coast of Scotland: Crinan to Canna*, Martin Lawrence
*The Yachtsman's Pilot to the West Coast of Scotland: Clyde to Colonsay*, Martin Lawrence
*West Highland Shores*, Maldwin Drummond
*Clyde Cruising Club Sailing Directions*
*East and North Coasts of Ireland Sailing Directions*, Irish Cruising Club
*South and West Coasts of Ireland Sailing Directions*, Irish Cruising Club
*Cruising Guide to Northwest England and Wales*, George Griffiths
*Lundy and Irish Sea Pilot*, David Taylor
*Bristol Channel and Severn Pilot*, Peter Cumberlidge
*Isles of Scilly Pilot*, John & Fay Garey
*West Country Cruising*, Mark Fishwick
*The Simpson-Lawrence Yachtsman's Almanac: South and East*, Michael Balmforth
*The Shell Channel Pilot*, Tom Cunliffe
*North Brittany and Channel Islands Cruising*, Peter Cumberlidge
*Brittany and Channel Islands Cruising Guide*, David Jefferson
*North Brittany*, Nick Heath
*Secret Anchorages of Brittany*, Peter Cumberlidge
*North Biscay*, Nick Heath
*South Biscay Pilot*, Robin Brandon
*Atlantic Spain and Portugal*, Anne Hammick
*Macmillan Nautical Almanac: Iberian Supplement*

## Relevant ports covered in Part III

The trend of the prevailing wind and current systems of the eastern Atlantic is southward, in tune with the wishes of most European yachtsmen. Thus, most cruising yachts leaving Europe head in this direction, by a variety of routes. There is a wide choice of possible departure and landfall points, and while those chosen are both typical and popular, there should be little difficulty in interpolating for other passages.

| Passage | Approx distance | |
| --- | ---: | --- |
| Falmouth to Madeira via the coast of Iberia | 1300 | miles |
| Falmouth to Madeira direct | 1250 | miles |
| Falmouth to the Azores | 1200 | miles |
| Azores to Madeira | 500 | miles |
| Madeira to the Canaries | 240 | miles |
| Canaries to the Cape Verde Islands | 850 | miles |

## Passage planning charts

| Latitudes | Admiralty | US |
| --- | --- | --- |
| 60°20′N to 48°20′N | 4102 (1:3,500,000) | 102 (1:3,500,000) |
| 50°30′N to 34°40′N | 4103 (1:3,500,000) | 103 (1:3,500,000) |
| 38°50′N to 8°20′N | 4104 (1:3,500,000) | 104 (1:3,500,000) |

In addition to the small scale charts listed above, many large scale charts are published by the Portuguese and Spanish Hydrographic Offices as well as the British Admiralty and the US Defense Mapping Agency.

## Falmouth to Madeira via the coasts of Spain and Portugal

This is one of the pleasantest ways to start an Atlantic circuit cruise. It avoids overlong passages in the initial stages, takes in an attractive and interesting cruising area and meshes perfectly with the seasonal weather patterns.

A yacht intending to depart from British shores before mid-August has time in hand to wait for a good forecast to cross the Bay of Biscay and may spend an enjoyable month or six weeks cruising in Spain. Landfall can be made at La Coruña, but it may be wiser to keep well to the west and close the land south of Finisterre to avoid a hard beat along the north-west Spanish coast. Allowing a couple of weeks for the Portuguese coast and a further week or ten days on passage to Madeira or the Canaries, the yacht will arrive there around the end of October with another month to explore the area and get organised for the Atlantic passage. This is so near to the ideal that it is well worth aiming for if at all possible.

If time is limited, two choices are open. The better one is to sail south in the summer and leave the yacht in some safe port for collection later in the year. Lagos or Vilamoura are the most obvious choices, while further east in Spain many new marinas have opened in the last few years. Gibraltar, although further from the route to the Canaries or Madeira, offers advantages to English speakers. There is little chance of finding room to leave a yacht in Funchal or Porto Santo. There are several harbours in the Canaries where an unattended yacht might be left – see Part III or consult *Atlantic Islands*. Early booking will be essential and charges are likely to be high.

The alternative is to leave the English Channel later in the year and run the gauntlet of the autumn weather. This is a poor second choice as the incidence of gales in Biscay increases from an average one day a month in August to nine in November. The detailed long range forecast will dictate departure timing, and consideration should be given to sailing from Falmouth to south-west Ireland to await suitable conditions. This increases the amount of searoom in the Bay if caught out. Leaving Falmouth after the end of September should only be considered by a strongly crewed larger yacht, able to make a fast passage between the depressions and prepared and equipped to approach the Iberian coast in deteriorating conditions.

When crossing the Bay of Biscay fishing vessels are likely to be met, and when approaching the northern coast of Spain there may be some shipping heading to and from such ports as Bordeaux and Brest. If the passage includes a diversion into Gibraltar, a yacht returning westwards will encounter a high concentration of traffic in the Strait. This fans out as soon as the narrowest part is passed, the merchant shipping dividing into three main streams. One goes westward to St Vincent, one coastwise to the south, and one in the general direction of Madeira and the Canaries. There will, in addition, be large numbers of fishing craft. In twenty-four hours most of this will be left behind and little more will then be seen until the main north/south Atlantic shipping lane is crossed, west of the longitude of Cape St Vincent.

The 500-mile passage from the Portuguese coast towards Madeira is usually a pleasant one, often carrying the north-easterly winds to one's destination. The first island to be seen will probably be Porto Santo, and in normal conditions if planning to visit it will be best to do so at this stage and avoid the beat back from Madeira.

## Falmouth to Madeira direct

Although the direct course from the English Channel to Madeira passes close to the Spanish coast, if the passage is to be made direct it will be worth making enough westing to remain a safe distance off this potential lee shore. The greatest concentration of traffic will also be found near the coast, an area known for its poor visibility. By staying fifty to one hundred miles offshore one should escape both of these problems while still receiving the full benefits of the northerly Portuguese Trades and Portuguese Current.

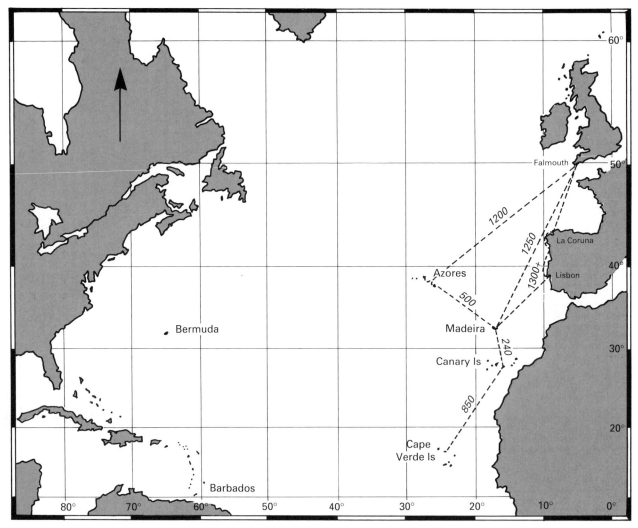

*Chart 6*   Typical routes in the Eastern Atlantic.

## Falmouth to the Azores

This passage might be the first stage of a transatlantic voyage by the middle latitudes, a dog-leg on the way down to Madeira or the Canaries and the trade wind passage, or the outward part of a return cruise from England to the Azores. Timing will probably depend largely on the purpose of the voyage, but any period between late May and early August would be suitable.

Unless it is particularly desired to visit Spain or Portugal en route, in which case headwinds will probably have to be faced on the westward passage to the Azores, it is best to keep as near the rhumb line as conditions permit. The current sets south-east and prevailing winds are likely to be between south-west and north-west. The Azores high will probably be encountered en route and in the early summer may extend as a ridge a considerable distance to the north-east of the islands. As much fuel as possible should be carried.

## Azores to Madeira

A pleasant passage can be anticipated, with winds between north-west and north-east backed by a favourable current. There is generally good visibility and

relatively little shipping. Though there may be a temptation to linger in the Azores, it would be wise to depart before the middle of September.

## Madeira to the Canaries

This passage may be made at any time of the year, but the chances of increased wind and decreased visibility will be greater from November onwards. The south-going current is relatively constant. If intending to cruise the Canary Islands it makes good sense to head for the eastern end of the group; if planning only a brief stop-over before the Atlantic passage, keep further west. The passage from Funchal to Santa Cruz de La Palma lies close to the Ilhas Selvagens or Salvage Islands (see Chapter 13), known for the unreliability of their lights, and unless conditions are perfect, it would be wise to keep well off.

## Canaries to the Cape Verde Islands

It is debatable whether this passage should not be considered as part of the trade wind route, since many yachts pass near the Cape Verde Islands after leaving the Canaries whether they stop or not. For European yachts it may also be their first passage made mainly under downwind rig.

The fine sandy beaches to be found at the Islas Cies, just north of Bayona at the entrance to the Ría de Vigo, give Caribbean-bound yachtsmen a foretaste of pleasures to come. *Photo: Alfredo Lagos*

Both current and winds are likely to be favourable, with the latter becoming more reliable as one progresses south. However, as the wind picks up so visibility will decrease. This is the *harmattan*, a dust laden wind from west Africa, which often reduces visibility to a few miles or less. Even though the sky may be clear and the horizon apparently sharp, the latter may actually be much closer than it appears. Until the advent of satellite based surveys, the positions of the islands were incorrectly charted by as much as three miles. Even the latest charts of this area may be significantly in error and a good lookout is even more important than usual.

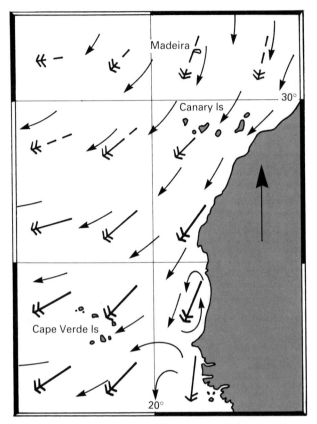

*Chart 7* Prevailing winds and currents of the eastern Atlantic between 10° N and 35° N – November. (Winds in feathered arrows, currents in solid arrows.) Based on information from the *Atlantic Pilot Atlas*.

## Regional weather

Although the Madeiran, Canary and Cape Verdean archipelagos cover a stretch of ocean more than 1000 miles from north to south, prevailing weather conditions are much less varied than would be the case further north. All lie in the path of the north-east trades, the main difference being that whereas Madeira and the Canaries may be influenced by the southern edge of winter depressions, in the latitude of the Cape Verde Islands the north-east trades hold almost total sway with the only real variation being in wind strength. Within the Canary Islands a yacht may encounter sudden and gusty increases in wind, typically around the south-west and south-east coasts of the higher islands. These 'acceleration zones' can be quite distinct and may produce an increase from less than 5 knots to 25 knots or more within a few hundred metres. Mention has already been made of the *harmattan* wind, which blows off the African continent south of about 20°N and can carry dust up to 500 miles offshore – or occasionally right across the Atlantic Ocean to the Caribbean. This is not so much a distinct wind as the visual result of any breeze blowing at 20 knots

or more over a period of several days, and can thus be anticipated with reasonable accuracy. Whether or not visibility appears to be bad, if the wind is above 20 knots *harmattan* conditions should be suspected – clear skies and an apparently firm horizon, out of which islands or other vessels may materialise when only a few miles distant.

## Currents

Madeira and the Canary Islands lie squarely in the path of the south-west setting Canary Current, which swings somewhat further westward by the latitude of the Cape Verde Islands. In summer the influence of the Equatorial Counter Current may set up south or south-east setting eddies between 10°N and 15°N, but by November or December these have retreated south of 10°N. As in all areas, an ocean current averaging one knot or less may, when constricted between islands, run at considerably greater speeds.

## Tides and tidal streams

Tidal rise and fall in the area is relatively slight, the mean spring range decreasing from 2.2 m (7 ft 2 in) at Porto Santo to 0.8 m (2 ft 7 in) in the Cape Verde Islands. Even so, tidal streams in the Cape Verdes can run strongly between the islands, and may reach over three knots when combined with the current.

## Approach and landfall

Landfall will most often be made from northwards and should present no particular hazards. With the exception of one or two of the Cape Verdes all the islands are relatively high, some excessively so, and Tenerife in particular may sometimes be seen from 50 or 60 miles away. The vast majority of yachts making the trade wind passage leave from either Madeira, one of the Canary Islands or the Cape Verdes, and the passages between the groups are covered in the previous chapter. Each area has its advantages and disadvantages, and all offer some interesting cruising in their own right.

### *The Madeira group*

This group comprises Madeira Grande, Porto Santo lying some 30 miles to the north-east, the two Ilhas Desertas, and the isolated and rocky Ilhas Selvagens just over 150 miles south on the course between Funchal and the western Canaries. Only Madeira and Porto Santo are regularly visited by yachts, though both the other groups have fair-weather anchorages.

First sight of the Madeiras is likely to be of the conical peak of Porto Santo. This is a most satisfying landfall, rising as it does in solitary grandeur, visible in daylight at a distance of 40 miles or more. The islands are well lit.

If planning a stop at Porto Santo it is wise to do so first

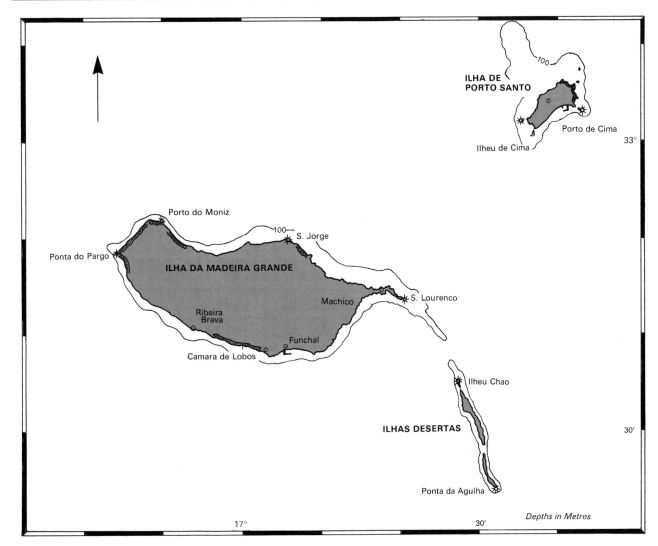

*Chart 8*   The Madeiran archipelago. Based on Admiralty Chart No 1831.

to save beating back. It is an official port of entry. There is a large harbour with room for several dozen yachts to anchor, visitors' moorings (these may be unreliable and should be used with care) and a small marina. Provided the wind stays in the north-east excellent anchorage can be found off the sandy beach between the harbour and the old town pier. (Anchoring west of the pier is now prohibited.) Porto Santo is well worth a visit, and if the marina at Funchal is full – often the case in October and November – then it is preferable to remain at Porto Santo than to use the exposed and uncomfortable anchorage at Funchal.

To most yachtsmen Madeira effectively means Funchal (see page 145), as although there are a number of other possible anchorages none offer remotely comparable facilities. The harbour is well lit and the town quite unmistakable, making it possible to enter at any hour of day or night. It is, however, a busy harbour and in addition to the normal commercial traffic and fishing craft there are often cruise ships on the move.

Many yachts spend a month or more in Funchal, either rafted alongside in the small marina or anchored off (note the caution on page 146), while their crews explore the island. It is arguably the loveliest of any visited on the standard Atlantic circuit and, once outside the tourist area

round Funchal, is remarkably unspoilt. Local buses provide a cheap and entertaining way to travel.

Funchal has several large supermarkets and an impressive fruit and vegetable market, with a fish market next door. It is a reasonable place to store for the transatlantic passage, but prices in the Canary Islands may be cheaper on many items, and the selection better. The international airport on the south-east coast makes crew changes simple, and if conditions are settled, it may be found easiest to anchor off the nearby town of Machico and save on taxi fares.

## The Canary Islands

The Canaries have become popular with yachtsmen over recent years. As well as attracting those en route to the Caribbean the islands have developed as a cruising ground in their own right, with increasing numbers of yachts based locally, together with a rapidly growing charter fleet. Although there are now many more yacht harbours and marinas than previously, some popular small ports have closed to visitors. Pressure on facilities is intense, especially in the autumn. At that time the cruising yachtsman may have difficulty in finding a secure berth or anchorage, particularly in the more popular areas.

Approaching from the north the 3717 m (12,195 ft)

volcanic peak of Tenerife will be seen from a great distance in clear weather, often complete with a scattering of snow despite being less than 300 miles from the tropics. Those yachts only planning to pause briefly in the Canaries should make for the western end of the archipelago; for those intending to cruise the islands it is logical to make a landfall further east, either at Lanzarote or the small island of Graciosa which lies off its north-eastern tip.

The harbours detailed in Part III are all within reach of good places to store up for an Atlantic crossing, but are by no means the only ones. Excellent quality fruit and vegetables are available almost everywhere, and even smaller towns generally have at least one supermarket.

The annual ARC rally currently leaves from Las Palmas de Gran Canaria (see page 149), where there is a large marina, good anchorage and excellent facilities. Whether the mushrooming development of tourist resorts is felt to be a plus or a minus, one by-product is that air communications are particularly good in terms of both frequency and value. The Canaries, technically a province of Spain, are not part of the European Union, and time limitations that may be placed on non-EU yachts remaining in the Union should not apply. The islands are a duty free zone and therefore a particularly good place to embark beer, wine or spirits.

## The Cape Verdean archipelago

Due to poor facilities and lack of available information, the Cape Verde Islands were visited by few cruising yachts until the early 1990s. However, this has changed, and now more yachts enjoy the practical advantage of shortening the transatlantic passage by nearly a third – the distance to Barbados is under 2000 miles, compared with 2700 miles from the Canaries, and as the islands are well within the trade wind belt a direct course can usually be steered on departure.

Yachts are expected to make their landfall at Porto Grande, São Vicente (see page 153), Ilha do Sal (where the international airport is situated) or Porto da Praia on Santiago. Of these Sal ('salt') is potentially the most difficult, being low lying and often lost in the haze until close by, while sand spits extend well offshore. However, it does have the advantage of being furthest to windward, allowing other islands to be visited without unnecessary beating. São Vicente is more easily identified, not least because the mountains of neighbouring Santo Antão generally rise above the low-lying *harmattan* band. The same is true of Santiago further south.

Throughout the Cape Verdes, maintenance of navigation aids is poor and even the major lights cannot be

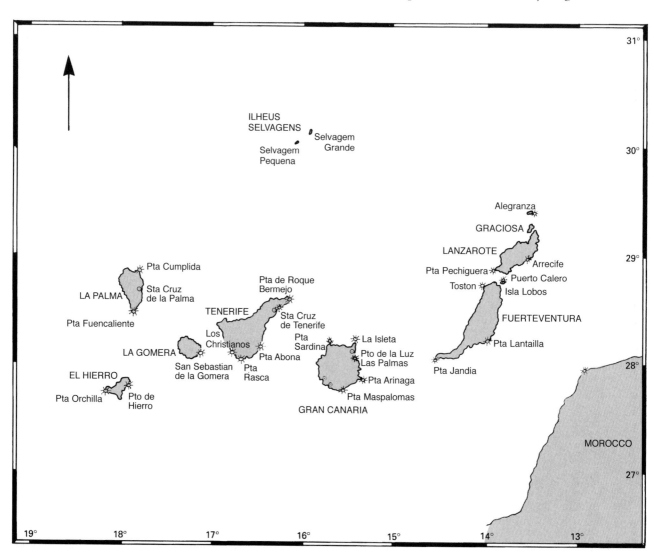

*Chart 9* The Canary Islands. Based on Admiralty Publication NP131.

relied upon. Information about changes in light characteristics can take a very long time to reach the Hydrographic Offices of other countries. Do not trust even the most recent charts to be entirely accurate.

The chief appeal of the Cape Verdes lies in the fact that they are largely undeveloped, and nearer in spirit to Africa (from which much of the population originally came) than to Portugal, the colonial power before independence in 1975. They are also desperately poor, and for this reason precautions should be taken against petty theft. Tourism is still a fairly new concept, though cruise ships call at São Vicente, and the local people are always friendly if sometimes overly curious.

Storing facilities are poor and all food except fresh fish is expensive, making it wise to do the bulk of stocking up for the transatlantic passage in Madeira or the Canaries. Good drinking water may also be hard to come by in the dry, northern islands. The southern chain is generally wetter, and both water and fresh stores may be more readily available.

Few visitors remain indifferent to the Cape Verdes. Most are fascinated; a few cannot reconcile themselves to the poverty, dirt and lack of facilities. In comparison, the Caribbean islands will seem like the centre of civilisation. Try to visit before the situation changes.

## Formalities

Customs and immigration formalities differ between the groups. The Madeiran group, being Portuguese, takes paperwork seriously and it is necessary to clear in and out of each island – sometimes each anchorage. In theory, the advent of the European Union should mean fewer formalities for yachts entering Madeira from EU countries, but the theory may not always match the practice. The Canaries are not part of the EU, but usually the relaxed Spanish attitude is taken and formalities are at a minimum. It is wise to obtain some sort of documentary evidence of leaving to present to the customs on arrival in the Lesser Antilles – a marina receipt or similar document will normally be sufficient to establish that the yacht has recently crossed from Europe. The Cape Verdean authorities also take customs (and particularly immigration) seriously, though the visa requirement for yachtsmen not staying ashore overnight is waived. For full details see Part III.

## Sailing directions and yachtsmen's guides

In addition to the official publications mentioned in Part I, one yachtsmen's guide covers the entire area while

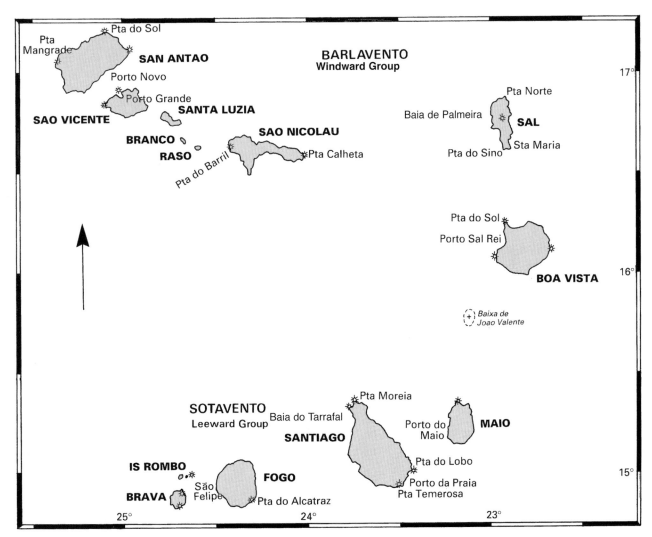

*Chart 10*  The Cape Verdean archipelago. Based on a plan in the *Atlantic Islands*.

The popular yacht anchorage at Baia do Tarrafal, Ilheu Santiago, in the Cape Verdes seen on one of the few cloudy days of the year. *Photo: Anne Hammick*

another two detail individual island groups. See Appendix B, page 217, for publishers' details.

*Atlantic Islands*, Anne Hammick
*Madeira and Porto Santo Cruising Guide*, Gwenda Cornell
*Canary Islands Cruising Guide*, Gwenda Cornell

## Relevant ports covered in Part III

# 14 THE TRADE WIND CROSSING

While for European yachts the trade wind Atlantic voyage generally receives the bulk of the anticipation and planning, it is often the most trouble-free passage of the entire circuit. This crossing has not been nicknamed the 'milk run' for nothing. There are a number of possible routes in terms of departure, arrival and distance, but all run pretty well parallel and are governed by the same prevailing conditions. For that reason they will be taken together rather than separately.

| Passage | Approx distance | |
|---|---|---|
| Madeira to Antigua | 2900 | miles |
| Canaries to Barbados | 2700 | miles |
| Cape Verdes to Barbados | 1900 | miles |

## Passage planning charts

| Latitudes | Admiralty | US |
|---|---|---|
| Southern North Atlantic | 4012 (1:10,000,000) | 120 (1:6,331,100) |

Remember that magnetic variation alters as one crosses the Atlantic, from approximately 7°30′W in Madeira and the Canaries to 13°W in the vicinity of the Cape Verdes, 18° in the middle and around 14°30′ in the Lesser Antilles. All these values are changing gradually, not necessarily at the same speed. The chart will therefore show nothing but the true compass rose, plus isogonic lines linking the places which have the same amount of variation, and details of annual change. It is worth calculating and applying these accurately, as even

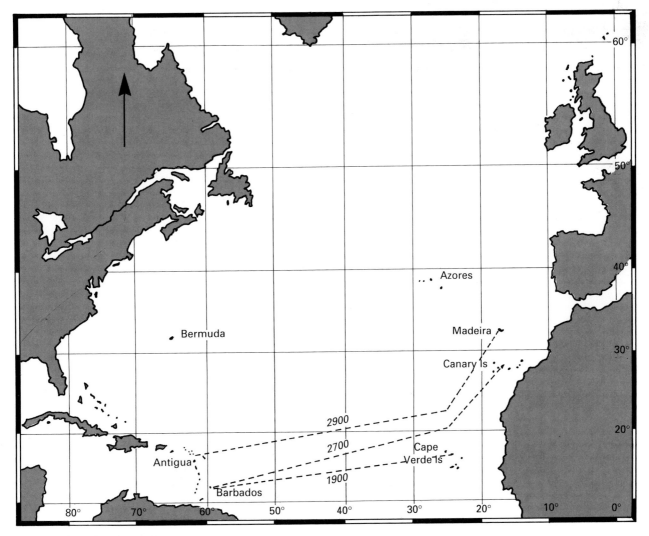

*Chart 11*   Typical trade wind routes.

a few degrees of error can produce a sizeable divergence over several days run.

## Timing

The majority of yachts make the trade wind crossing in November or December to give the maximum time in the Caribbean. Before mid-November hurricanes are possible and the winds are likely to be unreliable. However there is no good reason why this passage should not be made in January, February or even later, and some of the fastest crossing times have been recorded at this time of year. In general, the later the crossing the stronger the winds are likely to be.

## The trade wind belt

Whichever departure point is chosen, the objective is to get well into the belt of the established north-east trades as soon as possible. The northern limit of this belt varies with the seasons – from about 30°N in summer to 25°N in winter – and also from year to year. For those without large reserves of fuel it is usually a mistake to head west too soon and risk getting caught in the 'light 'n' variables' which predominate towards the centre of the Atlantic's massive high pressure system. Even when established, the trade wind, contrary to popular belief, does not always blow from the same quarter or at the same strength. Sometimes it does not blow at all, and the crew who do not experience a day or two of mid-ocean calm are very fortunate. It is, however, less fickle than winds in many other parts of the world. Its strength rarely exceeds force

6 (25 knots) and averages nearer force 4 (15 knots).

As mentioned, the northern limit of the trade wind belt varies each year. On occasions the trades become established almost as far north as the Canaries, and yachts staying near the direct route to the Caribbean make fast passages. A position of 25°N 25°W is often quoted as being the point to make for and in some years this is good advice – in other years it may be necessary to go much further south to find the trades. A good general rule is to head south-south-west on leaving the Canaries, aiming to pass some 150–200 miles north-west of the Cape Verde Islands, only turning west when the trades have definitely been encountered and the yacht is at least 200 miles south of their northern limit. Once certain that one is well within the trade wind belt, course can be shaped for the chosen landfall.

When the trade is fully established the sky is usually speckled with small clouds, like puffs of steam from an old-fashioned railway engine. Any large mass of cloud, lower and darker than the rest and coming up astern, is likely to denote a squall. At best, this may give the ship a welcome burst of speed; at worst, you might need to shorten sail. Sometimes these squalls bring a sharp downpour of rain, occasionally with thunder and lightning, though the worst of these thunderstorms seem to take place north of the trade wind route and one is often a spectator at an impressive but reassuringly distant display.

## Ocean currents and swell

The Canary Current, as it approaches the Cape Verde Islands, changes its course and changes its name. It turns

Bound for the Caribbean, *Wrestler* runs fast under double headsail rig in the north-east trades. *Photo: Anne Hammick*

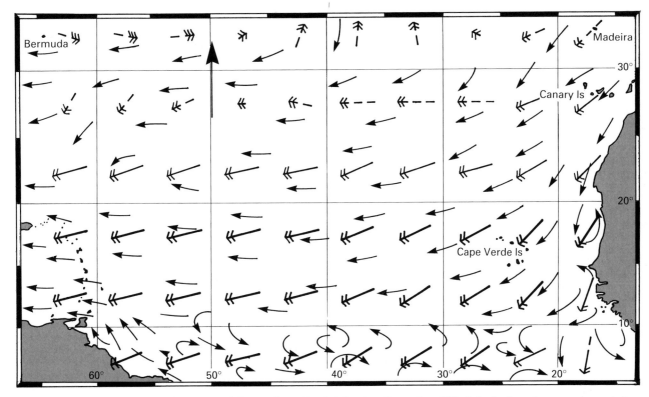

*Chart 12*   Prevailing winds and currents of the southern North Atlantic – December. (Winds in feathered arrows, currents in solid arrows.) Based on information from the *Atlantic Pilot Atlas*.

increasingly westward and becomes known as the North Equatorial Current. Both movement and reliability tend to increase throughout the winter season, though speed at any given point cannot be predicted.

Even an apparently calm ocean is seldom totally without swell, which may suddenly increase for no apparent reason. Usually it arises from a storm many thousands of miles away and is in itself harmless, though if running down from the North Atlantic, as commonly happens, may catch a yacht under running sails on the beam, causing her to roll horrendously. When sizeable swells and locally created seas oppose each other troublesome crests will be created, some of which may come aboard.

If skirting the windward side of an island at the end of a transatlantic passage, making generous allowance for current and leeway takes on particular importance. More than one yacht has driven ashore because forces which had contributed to forward progress during the downwind passage, and therefore went largely unnoticed, were ignored on altering course on to the wind.

## Caribbean approach and landfall

The traditional island on which to make landfall after a trade wind crossing is Barbados, not least because it lies more than 80 miles to windward of the rest of the archipelago and to call later would involve a long and tedious beat into the trade wind. The island is well worth a visit, with good shopping and other facilities. Details of the capital, Bridgetown, will be found in Part III. Other popular islands on which to make landfall are Antigua, Martinique, St Lucia and Grenada. Boats coming from the South Atlantic usually opt for Grenada or Trinidad. Suitable ports of entry are included in Part III.

Although few Caribbean islands are well lit in terms of navigational aids, considerable ambient light is produced by airports, hotels, domestic and street lighting. This is particularly true of Barbados, Martinique and Antigua, though all three are fringed by windward reefs, which could prove hazardous in poor visibility. Usually the weather is clear and heavy rain, which is the only thing likely to cut down visibility, will normally be in the form of short-lived squalls, which soon move away.

Many people, years after returning from a one-year Atlantic circuit, remember the trade wind crossing as the high point of the entire cruise. For most, it will be the longest ocean passage they ever make. It is as well that it is also usually one of the most enjoyable.

It is beyond the scope of this book to cover the South Atlantic in detail, not least because of the relatively small numbers of yachts which cross it each year. Other than those beginning their cruise in South Africa itself, the majority will be circumnavigators making the long haul up from Cape Town to the Caribbean, or occasionally from the Cape to Europe – the latter not technically an Atlantic crossing but nevertheless one of the longest Atlantic passages around.

This chapter therefore contains only a broad outline of South Atlantic weather and currents outside those areas most frequently traversed by yachts, plus brief details of the commonly used 'feeder' routes into the North Atlantic and the islands at which these passages may be broken.

## Winds and weather

The South Atlantic, like its northern counterpart, is dominated by a central area of high pressure and the wind and current systems that circulate around it. These run anticlockwise, and are constrained by both the land masses of the African and South American continents and the prevailing westerlies – the 'Roaring Forties' – which circle the globe south of latitude 40°S. The south-east trades form a belt between the Equator and about 20°S, swinging more easterly as they progress westwards, to become northeasterly off the coast of South America. There is less annual movement of this belt than is the case in the North Atlantic, and the south-east trades are also considered

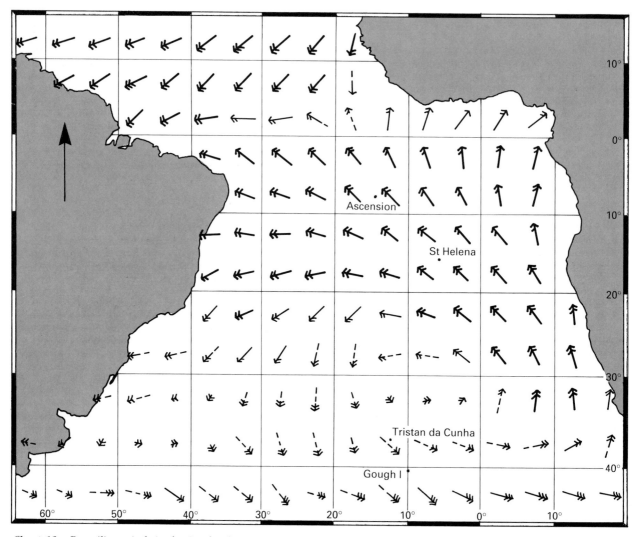

*Chart 13*    Prevailing winds in the South Atlantic – January. Based on information from the *Atlantic Pilot Atlas.*

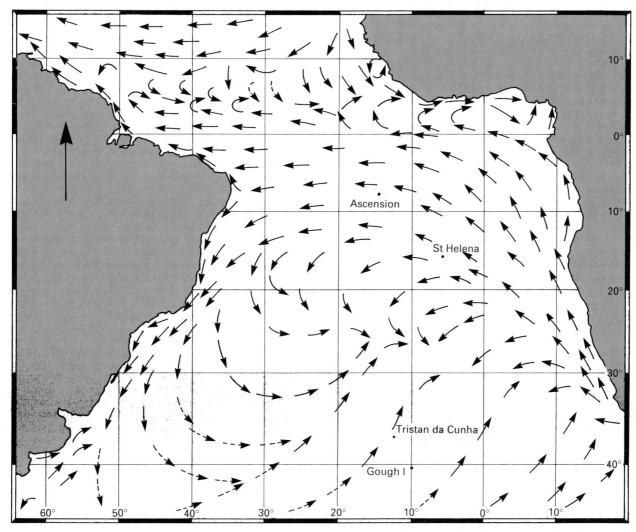

*Chart 14* General direction of current flow in the South Atlantic. Based on information from the *Atlantic Pilot Atlas*.

more dependable than their northern counterpart.

Between the two circulating systems of the North and South Atlantic lie the Doldrums, an area of light easterly winds where calms punctuated by occasional squalls are common. The band is considerably wider in the eastern part of the Atlantic, where it may stretch from the Equator to around 10°N, but narrows off further west. Occasionally it may disappear completely near the coast of Brazil allowing yachts to pass directly from the south-east into the north-east trades. Although technically lying in the North Atlantic, the Doldrums are included here as being more relevant to trans-equatorial routes.

One significant difference between the two oceans from the yachtsman's point of view is that hurricanes do not occur in the South Atlantic.

## Ocean currents

Current flow in the South Atlantic is affected by the two dominant wind systems – the high pressure circulation outlined above and the strong westerlies further south. Thus while a west-going current is generally to be found north of about 20°S, the east or north-easterly set which sweeps around Cape Horn may sometimes extend beyond 15°N, particularly in the centre of the ocean. Nearer the

African coast the west-going Agulhas Current is constricted as it passes around the Cape of Good Hope and, becoming known as the Benguela Current, runs north-westwards up the coast to join the water circulation set up by the south-east trades. As this cold water from the southern latitudes moves northwards it may give rise to fog, though visibility over the rest of the South Atlantic Ocean is generally good.

Sandwiched between the two west-going Equatorial Current systems is the Equatorial Counter Current, a relatively narrow band of east-going water centred around 6°N. It flows most strongly in the eastern Atlantic, fading out westwards where the two more powerful systems combine as they approach the South American continent.

## Routes, seasons and timing

The unsettled and often stormy weather to be found around the Cape of Good Hope abates slightly during the southern summer. Thus the majority of yachts arriving in Cape Town do so between December and February. Those heading for the Caribbean usually depart again within a few weeks, but if sailing direct to Europe it may be better to leave slightly later, in order to avoid reaching the Azores before early summer.

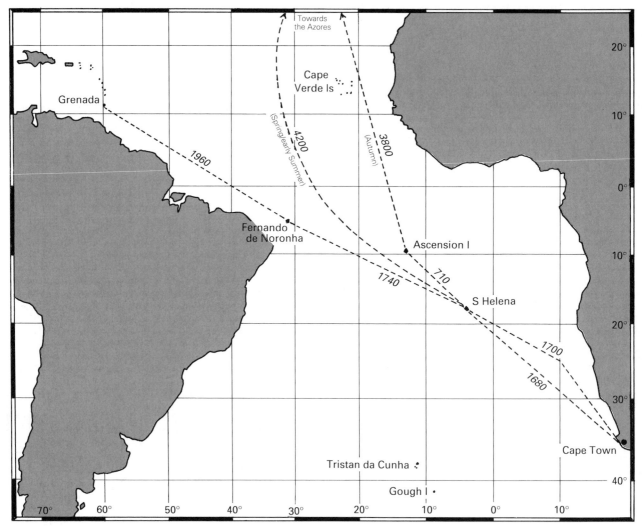

*Chart 15*  Most commonly used routes in the South Atlantic.

Once again only the most popular passages and land-falls are covered, leaving the skipper to interpolate as necessary.

| Passage | Approx distance | |
|---|---|---|
| Cape Town to St Helena | 1680 | miles |
| St Helena to Ascension Island | 710 | miles |
| St Helena to Fernando de Noroñha Island, Brazil | 1740 | miles |
| Fernando de Noroñha to the Lesser Antilles | 1960 | miles |
| St Helena to the Azores | 4000 | miles |

## Passage planning charts

| Coverage | Admiralty | US |
|---|---|---|
| Northern section | 4012 (1:10,000,000) | 120 (1:6,331,100) |
| Central section | 4022 (1:10,000,000) | 22 (1:10,000,000) |
| Eastern section | 4021 (1:10,000,000) | 21 (1:10,000,000) |
| Western section | 4020 (1:10,000,000) | 20 (1:10,000,000) |
| Gnomonic (great circle) | 5096 (1:13,500,000) | 24 (Variable scale) |

## Cape Town to St Helena

After leaving Cape Town on a favourable forecast the best bet is generally to keep slightly east of the rhumb line at first, to make the most of both wind and current. From a position around 25°S 10°E a direct course can be shaped for St Helena. However as already mentioned, visibility near the coast may be poor, and if south-westerly gales threaten it will obviously be necessary to work offshore in order to maintain searoom. For this reason many yachts simply take the rhumb line, gaining in distance saved what they may lose in speed.

St Helena may often be seen from 50 miles or more, appearing very square and solid rather than formed of individual peaks. Approach round the north coast is generally advised, due to Speery Ledge which lies about 1.5 miles off the southern tip of the island with less than 3 m (10 ft) of water. Due to its position squarely in the path of the south-east trade winds, the only feasible anchorages are on the north-west coast. The chief of these is James Bay – see page 159 in Part III for further details.

## St Helena to Ascension Island

This passage should be a straightforward continuation of

the north-westerly route from Cape Town via St Helena with both wind and current favourable, and there is no reason to sail any course other than the rhumb line.

Ascension Island can generally be seen from a good distance, but is bypassed by most yachts largely because its function as a military base and communications centre inevitably means that they are not particularly welcome. The anchorage at Clarence Bay on the north-west coast is particularly rolly, sometimes catching a swell running down from the North Atlantic, and landing dryshod at the Pierhead steps notoriously difficult. Best anchorage is to be found north-east of the pier in about 11 m (36 ft), and on no account should yachts anchor south of the two spar buoys which mark a shoal patch, or anywhere that might obstruct shipping movements.

All formalities are carried out by the Administrator at the Police Office in Georgetown, which gives on to Clarence Bay. Only a brief stop of 48 hours is normally permitted, though this may be extended if necessary repairs must be completed. There are few attractions ashore – no bars or cafés, no readily available transport, and a requirement that crews be back aboard by 1900 hours each evening. Both water and fresh stores are likely to be limited, and may be unavailable to yachts even if on sale to islanders. Diesel can normally be obtained through the wharfmaster. There is no civilian airport.

## St Helena to Fernando de Noroñha Island, Brazil

Fernando de Noroñha lies some 200 miles off the northeast coast of Brazil, at approximately 3°50′S 32°20′W, and conveniently breaks the long passage for yachts heading towards the Caribbean. Both wind and current on this

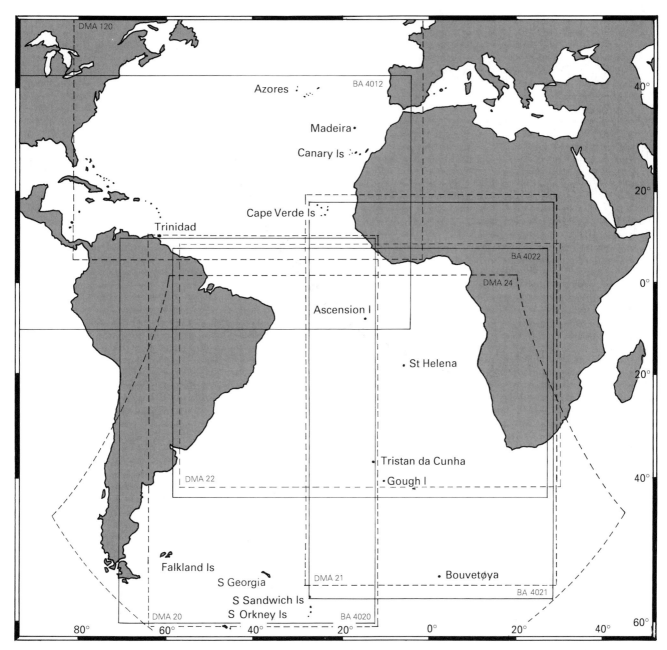

*Chart 16* Passage planning charts for the South Atlantic. (Admiralty in continuous lines, US DMA in broken lines.)

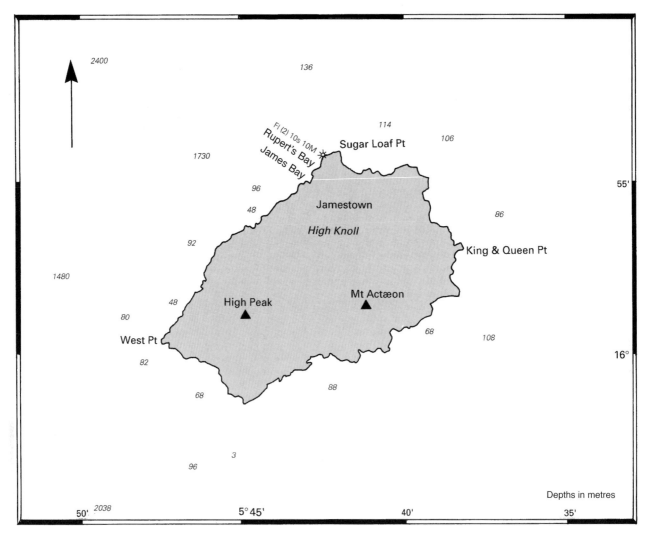

2400

136

Fl (2) 10s 10M ☀
Rupert's Bay
James Bay

Sugar Loaf Pt

114

106

1730

96

48

Jamestown

High Knoll

86

92

King & Queen Pt

1480

48

High Peak ▲

Mt Actæon ▲

80

West Pt

68

108

82

68

88

3

96

2038

Depths in metres

55'

16°

50'     5°45'     40'     35'

*Chart 17*   St Helena. Based on Admiralty Chart No 1771.

route are generally favourable, though winds are on average lighter than is the case further east. The current sets almost due west, and may on occasion be found to have some south in it.

Fernando de Noroñha is not an official port of entry although customs and immigration officials are stationed there. In the past yachts were permitted to visit the island before clearing into mainland Brazil, but this is no longer the case and those attempting to do so may be turned away. The anchorage at São Antônio Bay is rolly though reasonably sheltered, and construction of a small breakwater for local craft has greatly eased the problem of landing by dinghy in the surf. The western half of the island is a nature reserve fringed by an underwater park, with restricted access. Both water and fuel are available by can, but fresh stores are very limited.

## Fernando de Noroñha to the Lesser Antilles

The last leg of the Cape Town to Caribbean route crosses the Equator and, to the extent that they exist so far west, the Doldrums. Winds can be expected to back from southeast on departure through east into the north-east, making this a generally fast passage except in years when the Dol-

drums are unusually extensive. Currents are also favourable. On approaching the angular 'corner' of the South American land mass the west-going South Equatorial Current splits, one branch running north-west up the coast towards the Caribbean at speeds of up to two knots while the other follows the land south-west, eventually to rejoin the major circulatory system. The current can be a major factor, giving a free ride of as much as 400 miles over the entire passage. It appears to be strongest around the 200 metre line.

## St Helena to the Azores

Although not strictly a transatlantic passage, a number of yachts make the long haul from the Cape to northern Europe each year. Almost all break the voyage at St Helena and again in the Azores, and the first and third legs of this passage are thus covered elsewhere.

The main question must be at what longitude to cross the Equator. Further west there is a better chance of avoiding or at least minimising the Doldrums, extra easting on the other hand will be invaluable once into the north-east trades. In general the best point appears to be between 25°W and 30°W in spring and early summer, further east as the summer progresses, until by the autumn it may even

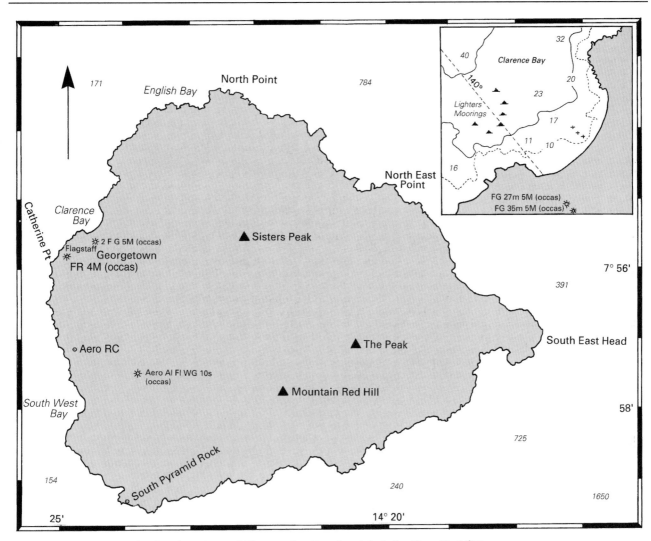

The following labels appear on the chart:

- North Point
- English Bay
- 171
- 784
- Clarence Bay (inset)
- 40
- 32
- 140°
- Lighters Moorings
- 20
- 23
- 17
- 11
- 10
- 16
- FG 27m 5M (occas)
- FG 35m 5M (occas)
- North East Point
- Catherine Pt
- Clarence Bay
- ▲ Sisters Peak
- ☀ 2 F G 5M (occas)
- Flagstaff
- ☀ Georgetown
- FR 4M (occas)
- 7° 56'
- 391
- ○ Aero RC
- ▲ The Peak
- South East Head
- ☀ Aero Al Fl WG 10s (occas)
- ▲ Mountain Red Hill
- 58'
- South West Bay
- 725
- 154
- South Pyramid Rock
- 240
- 1650
- 25'
- 14° 20'

*Chart 18*  Ascension Island with an inset of Clarence Bay. Based on Admiralty Chart No 1691.

The yacht anchorage and dinghy landing at São Antônio Bay, Fernando de Noroñha Island, Brazil.

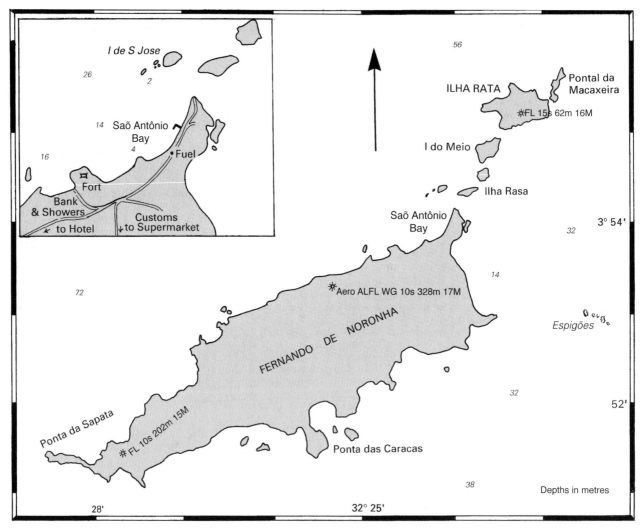

Chart 19   Fernando de Noroñha with an inset of Saõ Antônio Bay. Based on Admiralty Chart No 388.

be worth sailing between the Cape Verde Islands and the African mainland. Whatever course is shaped it is inevitable that much of the later part of this passage will be hard on the wind – a wind which may lighten or die entirely both in the Doldrums and further north on approaching the Azores. Currents will also be largely unfavourable. This is the only Atlantic passage likely to take more than a month, and the fifty days taken by a 35 ft ketch in 1990 is not untypical.

## Formalities

The above routes cover departure or arrival in the waters of at least six different countries. Formalities vary accordingly, and are covered in the port information in Part III. Where this is not the case – ie Ascension Island and Fernando de Noroñha – very brief details have been included with the passage notes.

## Sailing directions and yachtsmen's guides

Compared to its northern counterpart, there is little published material available for the South Atlantic. Official publications covering the area are mentioned in Part I, and *British Admiralty Routeing Charts* are the most comprehensive source of climatic information. There is no yachtsmen's guide to the area, but both the *South African Nautical Almanac* compiled by Tom Morgan and *South Atlantic South America* by Pete and Annie Hill (which includes Fernando de Noroñha) may prove useful in their respective areas. See Appendix B, page 217, for publishers' details.

## Relevant ports covered in Part III

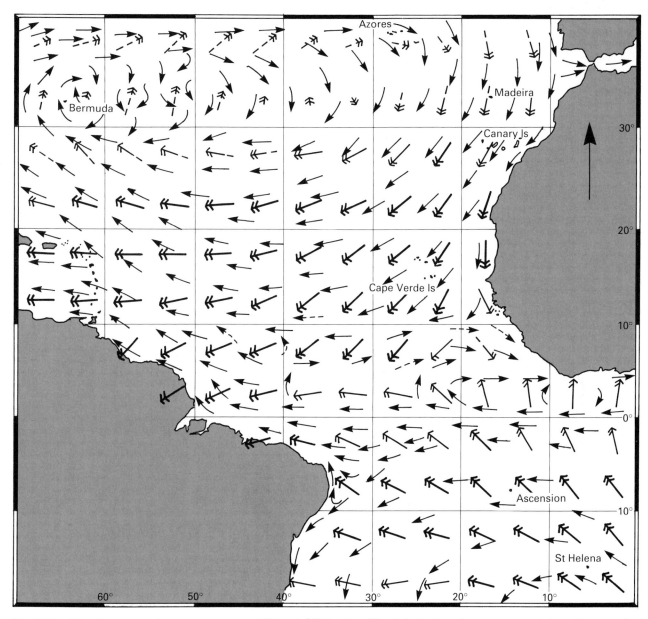

*Chart 20* Atlantic winds and currents between 20°S and 40°N – May. (Winds in feathered arrows, currents in solid arrows.) Based on information from the *Atlantic Pilot Atlas*.

For many Europeans, the chance to spend time cruising the Caribbean islands provides the main incentive for an Atlantic crossing. Situated as they are in the trade wind zone and within the tropics, their waters afford some of the world's best sailing conditions.

## History

Although the (misnamed) West Indies are often thought of as having been discovered by Columbus, recent archaeological research has proved the existence of much earlier human occupation. The Caribs, who were in possession of much of the Caribbean before the Europeans took over, represented the second or third wave of Indian emigration from South America. In most of the islands they were wiped out within a few hundred years, but some still live in a reserved territory on the windward side of Dominica. The vast majority of the local people today are descended from the slaves who were brought over from Africa in the seventeenth and eighteenth centuries to work in the sugar plantations.

Nearly all the islands have small museums, but that in St John's, Antigua, is particularly notable for its comprehensive collection of pre-Columbian artefacts.

## The trade wind

Although the trade wind dominates Caribbean weather, there are subtle but important variations throughout the cruising season. From December until early April the winds are remarkably constant in both strength and direction, averaging about 15–20 knots out of the east or north-east. However force may increase dramatically in sudden squalls (usually, though not invariably, signalled by an advancing line of purple-grey clouds), or where the trade wind funnels down valleys or around the ends of islands. From time to time, the entire Caribbean experiences a winter with lighter winds than normal. There is a local tradition that winds become stronger in late December and early January, the so called 'Christmas winds'. It may be necessary to adapt the itinerary to suit the prevailing conditions.

From mid-April to the beginning of the hurricane season in June or July (see Chapter 10) the winds become

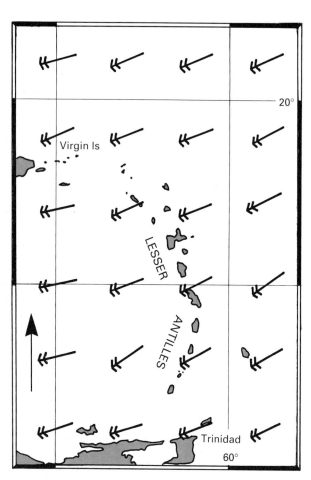

*Chart 21*  Prevailing winds in the Lesser Antilles – January. Based on information from the *Atlantic Pilot Atlas*.

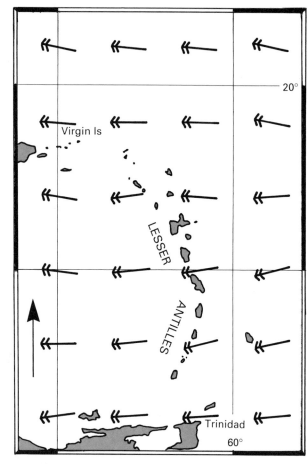

*Chart 22*  Prevailing winds in the Lesser Antilles – May. Based on information from the *Atlantic Pilot Atlas*.

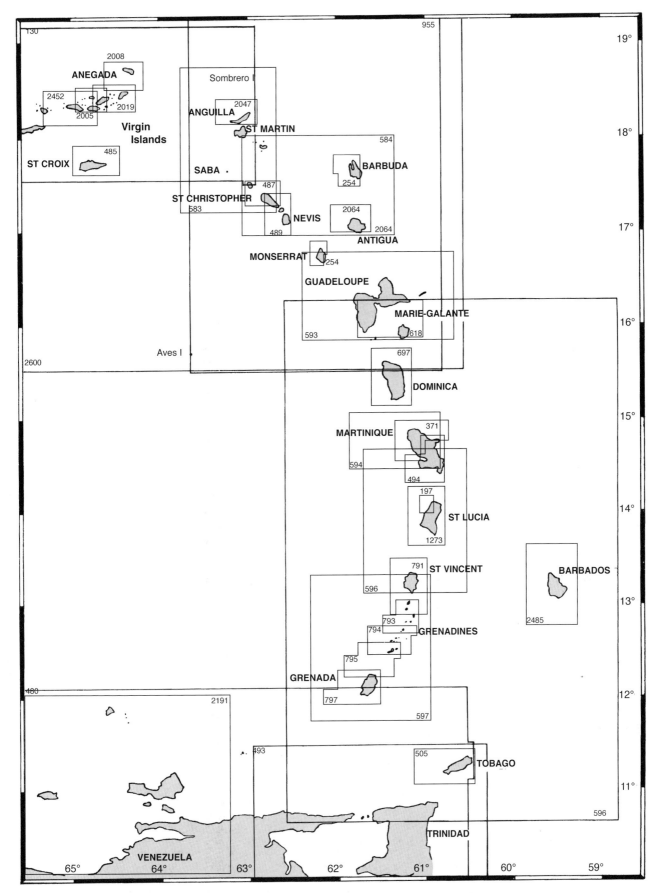

*Chart 23* British Admiralty Charts for the Eastern Caribbean. Based on Admiralty Publication NP 131.

## Current and swell

The North Equatorial Current sets westward between the islands, often attaining a knot or more. Though tidal streams may increase or decrease the rate of flow they are seldom strong enough to overcome it completely. It is easy to overlook this and find that one has been set a long way to leeward when sailing between the islands.

## Navigation and pilotage

Except for Barbados, which lies to the east of the main archipelago, each island is within sight of its immediate neighbours and navigation can be mostly by eye if so minded. Navigation aids are few, their maintenance is often poor and they cannot be relied upon. What buoyage there is throughout the islands follows the IALA B system (red right returning). There are some cardinal marks.

Night sailing is often hazardous due to the number of fish-pot floats to be found even well offshore, and often clustered particularly thickly in the approaches to many anchorages. These floats may be of fibreglass or plastic, white or coloured, or simply be stoppered bottles or chunks of expanded polystyrene. Others may be the old traditional bamboo floats, six or eight feet long, and sometimes waterlogged and floating a few inches below the surface. All are a hazard when one is moving under power. Under sail they are less of a menace, but can still wrap themselves around an exposed rudder or free-wheeling propeller. At night small fishing boats seldom show navigation lights and may be completely unlit. Any lights that are displayed are unlikely to be in accordance with International Regulations!

## Anchorages

To those used to ever-changing winds and strong reversing tidal streams, it may go against the grain to anchor in a position protected through only half the compass or less. However due to the constancy of the trade winds the islands afford a reliable lee on their western coasts and many of the traditional anchorages are quite open in this direction. The best afford both shelter from the wind and swell, but this is not always the case and quite often a certain amount of rolling may have to be endured. This is particularly true of those anchorages chosen more because of shoreside convenience than actual shelter, such as Carlisle Bay, Barbados, and the anchorages off St Pierre, Martinique and Roseau, Dominica – all worth visiting for different reasons.

## Formalities

On approaching land, allow time to brush up your knowledge of the entry procedure for the particular island to which you are going. All are different. Except for the French, Dutch and American islands, most have been granted their independence and nearly every island that was formerly a British possession is now a country in its own right, with its own national colours. For the visiting yacht this means a lot of different courtesy flags as well as a lot of formalities.

Nearly all the islands take entry and clearance procedures seriously. The authorities will wish to see clearance

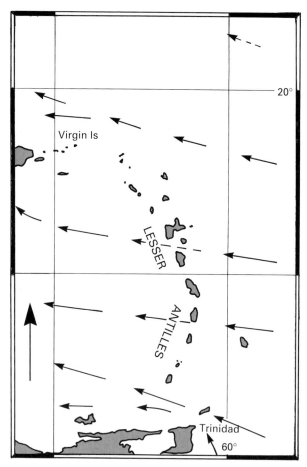

*Chart 24*  Currents in the Lesser Antilles – March. Based on information from the *Atlantic Pilot Atlas*.

less consistent. Antigua Race Week, held at the end of April, is renowned for producing everything from flat calms to gusts resulting in knock-downs, quite often on consecutive days. By May the winds will be definitely lighter, particularly in the northern part of the area. As they moderate they also veer slightly, swinging from north-east through east to slightly south of east, a definite boon for yachts leaving the islands for the United States or Bermuda.

Even when the open water trades are blowing strongly, calms often lurk in the lee of the higher islands – effectively all those of any size between Grenada and Guadeloupe. To make progress under sail one must either keep as close inshore as is safe – ideally within a few tens of yards of the land – or else pass at least five miles offshore. Neither of these methods is guaranteed to find the wind and sometimes the route to windward of an island is the only way to achieve reasonable progress under sail.

Conversely, it is easy to ghost or motor towards the end of an island forgetting that once out of the lee, the flat water and gentle breeze may suddenly be replaced by very boisterous conditions with gusty winds and an ocean swell. This change can occur within a few boat lengths. During the day, the deteriorating conditions can usually be seen ahead, but at night they can be a hazard and it may be wise to reduce sail in anticipation whilst conditions are light.

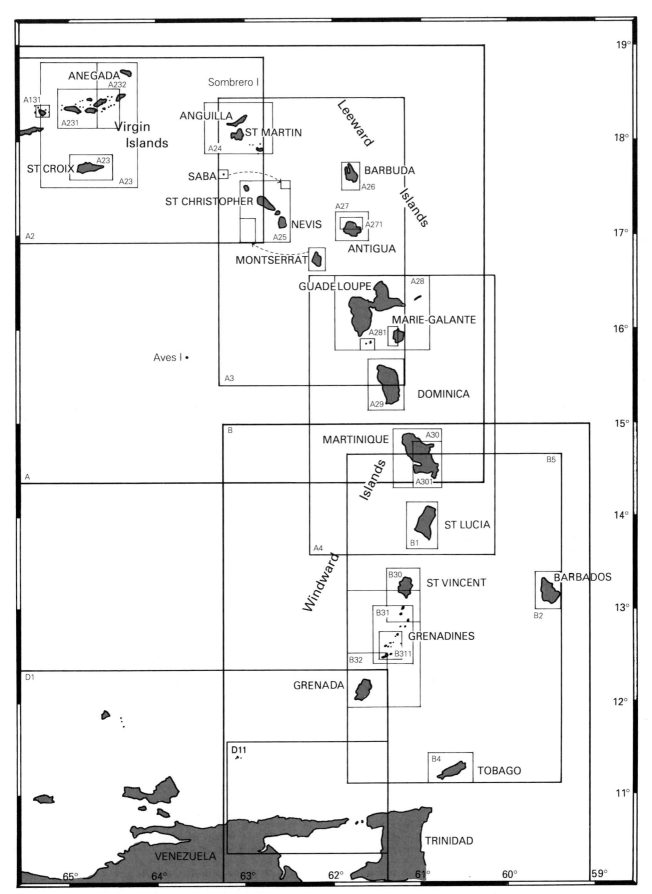

*Chart 25*    Imray–Iolaire charts for the Eastern Caribbean. Based on information from Imray Laurie Norie & Wilson.

Sun, sand and crystal clear water. Visions of such perfect Caribbean anchorages may be the first steps in the plans for an Atlantic crossing. *Photo:Anne Hammick*

papers from the last port of call and failure to produce these may result in being turned away until they are produced, and will probably lead to a fine as well. In some islands there is only one port of entry, in others there are several. All the ports listed in Part III are official entry ports.

Procedures vary from island to island and sometimes from year to year. Local pilot books give specific details, but in general the following principles should be adhered to. Ensure that the correct courtesy ensign and the Q flag are being flown before arrival, together with the yacht's ensign. After anchoring or berthing, the skipper alone should go ashore and complete the formalities. If arriving at night it may be possible to delay this until the following day, but in most islands it is preferable to arrive and depart during office hours. Arriving at other times may incur 'overtime' charges even though the actual formalities are completed during office hours.

The skipper should take with him the clearance papers from the last port, the ship's papers and the passports of all on board, together with any necessary visas. There may be several authorities to visit (customs, immigration and perhaps the harbour authority) and numerous forms to complete, usually in duplicate or triplicate; taking a few sheets of carbon paper can speed the process. There will probably be some charges to pay, both on entering and clearing, so some cash in the appropriate currency should be carried, though US dollars are normally accepted. Fees are usually modest and it is unreasonable to expect officials in a small office to be able to deal with large-

denomination banknotes. Firearms and ammunition must be declared and on most islands will be impounded; they will have to be collected on departure from the port of entry, which is not always convenient. If any crew members are leaving the yacht during the visit, this should be stated on entry. There will almost certainly be some formalities to be completed before the authorities will accept that they have left, or will leave, the country legitimately and are not attempting to become unauthorised immigrants. Often valid airline tickets must be produced, and passports endorsed. Failure to comply with these regulations will cause considerable problems when the yacht comes to clear out.

Generally speaking, the authorities on the islands are fair and tolerant in their treatment of yachts. However the officials, quite reasonably, expect to be taken seriously. It will be considered discourteous if the visitor presents himself at customs wearing clothing more appropriate for the beach than a government office and officers may decline to deal with him. Rudeness and incivility will lengthen the procedures, and impatience will certainly be counterproductive. Deliberate deceit or attempted bribery is likely to lead to arrest.

The yachtsman who deals with the officials in the islands in the same honest and fair manner that he would adopt towards the same officials in his own country is likely to encounter few problems. It is worth remembering that one is a visitor, whom no country is obliged to admit. Officials have considerable powers to make life difficult for yachtsmen and it is foolish to antagonise them.

### Formalities in the US Islands

Foreign yachts must clear into and out of the US Virgin Islands and Puerto Rico as they would in any other country. Views vary between officials as to whether it is necessary to complete formalities if travelling directly between them and it is sensible to enquire before departure. In theory, once cleared into Puerto Rico (but not the USVI) one may sail directly to mainland USA without clearing, but it would be sensible to clear out of Puerto Rico in case an unscheduled stop needs to be made en route. The USVI are considered a single group, and clearance is not necessary when travelling between islands.

Although access to the USA by airline is relatively formality free, all foreign visitors (except Canadians) arriving in the country *by yacht must be in possession of a valid visa. This also applies to Puerto Rico and the USVI.* Visas should be obtained from the US embassy in one's own country, as in the Caribbean they can only be issued in Trinidad, Barbados and Nassau. It should be noted that even indefinite visas now expire after ten years and must then be renewed. Arriving without a visa will lead to a fine.

Regulations for US flagged yachts and nationals entering and leaving Puerto Rico and the USVI are currently under review. Enquiries should be made before leaving mainland USA, or on arrival.

## Currency

In most of the islands from Grenada to Antigua the Eastern Caribbean dollar (EC) is used, currently pegged to the US dollar at a rate of EC$2.40 to US$1. The only ex-British island to have its own currency is Barbados, with a dollar roughly equal in value to the EC dollar but not acceptable outside Barbados. All the French islands use the French franc, in Dutch St Maarten either Dutch guilders or US dollars are accepted with equal alacrity, while in both the US and British Virgin Islands the US dollar is the official currency.

In point of fact the US dollar is acceptable throughout all the English-speaking islands, and if a price seems particularly reasonable check that you have not been quoted in US dollars. Most confusion is sheer misunderstanding on both sides, but occasionally the less scrupulous may ask for payment in US dollars and then attempt to give change, dollar for dollar, in EC.

All but the smallest islands have banks, usually the national bank of that particular country and often a branch of a major international chain as well. Cash can normally be obtained using either Visa or MasterCard. The acceptance of these cards as payment for services is growing fast and it is as well to carry both. Passports are likely to be required to cash traveller's cheques or to obtain cash with a card, but the use of automated cash withdrawal machines is on the increase.

## Facilities

Services and facilities for yachtsmen throughout the eastern Caribbean are excellent, largely due to the ever-growing charter boat and tourist industries.

All islands other than the very smallest now have

Nelson's Dockyard in English Harbour, Antigua, seen here during the festivities of Sailing Week, is one of the Caribbean's most famous cruising crossroads. *Photo: Anne Hammick*

reasonable food shops, many have large supermarkets, and most sport bustling local produce markets which not only offer variety and good value but are great fun to visit. Hotels, restaurants and cafés of all persuasions and prices have mushroomed, though many of the best are among the old-established.

Boatyard facilities have also improved drastically, and throughout the region yards capable of hauling and carrying out repairs abound. Most will be busy during the cruising season and in particular it may be necessary to make an advance booking for a haulout in St Lucia around the end of the ARC and in Antigua before or during (and after!) race week. It is possible that a European yacht on a one-year circuit of the North Atlantic might get away without hauling out for antifouling, but the ban on TBT paints has made this unlikely. Even with frequent swimming to scrub, fouling on the homeward passages would probably be severe.

The best facilities for major repairs or maintenance are in St Maarten, Antigua and St Lucia. Of these, St Maarten has the advantage of minimum customs formalities for the importation of spare parts, a process which at present is tedious and expensive on the other two islands.

## Medium and large scale charts

The Lesser Antilles are particularly well covered by medium and large scale charts with, in addition to those published by the British Admiralty (Chart 23, page 87) and US Defense Mapping Agency, the Imray-Iolaire series of yachtsmen's charts (Chart 25, page 89) and French publications covering Martinique, Guadeloupe, St Barts and St Martin.

## Sailing directions and yachtsmen's guides

In addition to the official publications mentioned in Part I, there are numerous yachtsmen's guides to the Lesser Antilles, listed here by area. Very few cover the entire Lesser Antilles, and as each approaches its locality in a different fashion there is much to be said for carrying several. See Appendix B, page 217, for publishers' details.

*Reed's Nautical Almanac: Caribbean Edition*

*A Cruising Guide to the Caribbean*, William T Stone & Anne M Hays
*Cruising Guide to Trinidad and Tobago*, Chris Doyle
*The Cruiser's Guide to Trinidad and Tobago*, Norma C Hoover & George B Gliksman
*Venezuela*, Donald M Street Jr
*Cruising Guide to Venezuela and Bonaire*, Chris Doyle
*Martinique to Trinidad*, Donald M Street Jr
*The Lesser Antilles*, RCC Pilotage Foundation
*A Cruising Guide to the Leeward Islands*, Chris Doyle
*A Sailor's Guide to the Windward Islands*, Chris Doyle
*Yachtsman's Guide to the Windward Islands*, Julius M Wilensky
*Anguilla to Dominica*, Donald M Street Jr
*VIP Cruising Guide – St Maarten to Antigua*, William J Eiman
*Puerto Rico, the Passage Islands, the US and British Virgin Islands*, Donald M Street Jr
*Virgin Anchorages*, Nancy & Simon Scott
*Cruising Guide to the Virgin Islands*, Nancy & Simon Scott
*Yachtsman's Guide to the Virgin Islands*, Meredith Fields

## Chart packs

*BBA chart kit*: No 10, The Virgin Islands

*CGP Caribbean charts*:
    No 1, The Virgin Islands (St Thomas to Sombrero)
    No 2, The Northern Leewards (Anguilla to Antigua)
    No 3, The Southern Leewards (Guadeloupe to Martinique)
    No 4, The Windwards (St Lucia to Grenada)

## Relevant ports covered in Part III

| | | |
|---|---|---|
| **16** | Chaguaramas Bay, Trinidad | page 161 |
| **17** | Prickly Bay, Grenada | page 164 |
| **18** | Bridgetown, Barbados | page 166 |
| **19** | Rodney Bay, St Lucia | page 169 |
| **20** | Fort de France, Martinique | page 171 |
| **21** | English Harbour/Falmouth Bay, Antigua | page 174 |
| **22** | Road Harbour, Tortola/Virgin Gorda Yacht Harbour, British Virgin Islands | page 178 |

The Bahamas, together with the adjoining Turks and Caicos Islands, form an extensive chain of rocky islands surrounded by coral reefs and sandbanks. They extend from about 21°N to 27°30′N and from 71°W to 79°W, covering an area of more than 5000 square miles, much of it with depths of less than 1.8 m (6 ft). Columbus made his first landing in the New World at San Salvador in 1492. The archipelago is best cruised from east to west. Both prevailing winds and currents set this way, and for much of the day the sun will be aft, enabling water colours indicating shoals and coral heads to be most easily read.

## Caution

Although in the past the Bahamas have had an unenviable reputation for violent crime the situation has improved markedly over recent years and in this respect the area is probably now no more hazardous to yachts than any other. Much of the problem in the past was concerned with drug smuggling; it has been chiefly through surveillance by the US government agencies that this has been controlled. The US Coast Guard continues its surveillance and officers frequently board and search private yachts in the course of their work. This is a routine matter that should be accepted as such, and is almost invariably carried out politely and professionally. The Coast Guard has authority from the Bahamian government to search all vessels within their waters, regardless of nationality.

## Weather and currents

Prevailing winds are easterly, with a northerly component from October to January or February and an increasingly southerly trend from June until September. May is the transition month when cold fronts from North America cease and frontal waves from the tropical Atlantic begin. These may cause local but intense weather systems between the Virgin Islands and the Bahamas, and the Bahamas themselves often experience at least one severe storm during May. Several different weather forecast transmissions cover the area and these should be listened to with care. The Bahamas lie squarely in the hurricane belt and it would therefore be very wise to plan to be out of the area by early June.

A north-west going current averaging about 0.5 knots follows the trend of the Bahamas until it merges with the

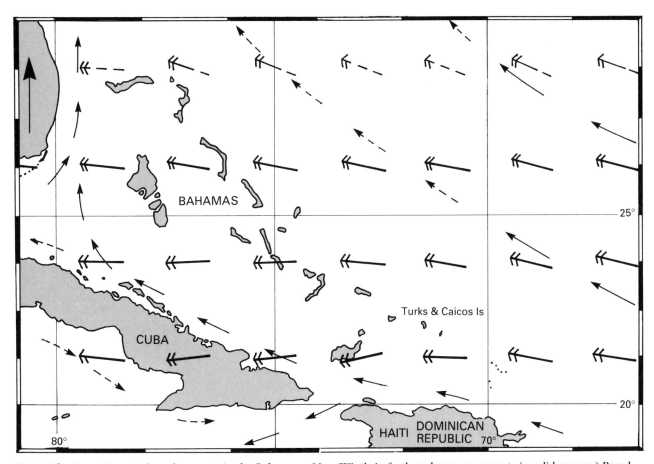

*Chart 26* Prevailing winds and currents in the Bahamas – May. (Winds in feathered arrows, currents in solid arrows.) Based on information from the *Atlantic Pilot Atlas.*

**The Bahamas   93**

Gulf Stream north of the islands. In places it may run with considerably greater speed, setting on to and across shoals and reefs, and is a good reason for avoiding passagemaking after dark. In the NW Providence Channel currents are unpredictable and much influenced by wind. In the Florida Strait the Gulf Stream runs at 3.5 to 4 knots in mid stream, rather less at the edges, and if heading for Miami or Fort Lauderdale, allowance must be made for it.

## Navigation and pilotage

The shallow waters dotted with coral heads and sand banks, combined with unpredictable currents and tidal streams, all call for what is known locally as 'eyeball navigation'. It cannot be emphasised too strongly that errors in these waters may be dangerous and that the greatest care must be exercised. Yachts drawing more than 1.5 m (5 ft) will be constrained in the areas they can visit.

Charts are frequently out-of-date or inaccurate and markers and beacons few and far between. Those with most experience advise as follows:

1 Avoid night passages if possible, but if you find yourself at sea at nightfall heave-to in open water to await daylight.
2 Navigating from east to west, try to make passages across shoal waters before noon, with the sun at your back so that you can see the submerged coral heads.
3 Avoid inter-island passages from west to east, to windward with the sun in your eyes. If forced to go in this direction it may well be better to make an ocean passage.
4 Remember that tides and currents may not only be stronger than indicated but may set in the opposite direction to that which is forecast. Consult local opinion whenever possible, especially among the skippers of fishing and inter-island trading craft.

## Formalities

Clearance must be obtained at an official entry port - prior to that a yacht may sail through the islands but cannot anchor overnight. The Q flag should be hoisted 3 miles off and, in theory, everyone is expected to stay aboard until officials come out to grant clearance. In practice it will be necessary to go ashore and complete formalities. A Cruising Permit will be issued, which remains valid for up to six months. There are severe penalties for not observing clearance formalities.

Firearms must be declared and kept locked away until departure. Animals will need valid rabies inoculation certificates.

## Facilities

The Bahamas has its own currency, the Bahamas dollar (B$). This is at par with the US dollar, which is also widely accepted.

Facilities depend almost entirely on where you are. At Nassau on New Providence Island they are excellent, with several marinas and chandleries catering for the yacht owner plus several large supermarkets. The same is true of Freeport on Grand Bahama Island and also in the Abaco group. However some of the outer islands are fairly basic, down to those which are no more than a sand bar supporting a few palm trees. Consult one of the cruising guides.

## Sailing directions and yachtsmen's guides

In addition to the official publications mentioned in Part I, the following yachtsmen's guides and chart books, listed by area, are available. See Appendix B, page 217, for recommendations and publishers' details.

*Reed's Nautical Almanac: Caribbean Edition*
*The Exuma Guide*, Stephen Pavlidis
*Exumas: Explorer Charts*, Monty Lewis
*The Bahamas Cruising Guide*, Mathew Wilson
*Yachtsman's Guide to the Bahamas*, Meredith Fields
*The Central and Southern Bahamas Guide*, Stephen Pavlidis
*The Cruising Guide to Abaco, Bahamas*, Steve Dodge

## Chart packs

*BBA chart kit*: No 9, The Bahamas

Most cruising yachts leave the Lesser Antilles in April or May, in order to be well north before the start of the hurricane season in June. The incidence of hurricanes in that month is in fact very low (see Chapter 10), but departure in good time enables yachts to reach their next cruising ground on the North American coast, or make the transatlantic passage back towards Europe, at the best time of year.

Yachts heading for America may follow the Bahamas to Florida, sail direct to some point further north, or make the passage via Bermuda. A few of those returning to Europe will sail directly to the Azores, but most will also call at Bermuda, and then visit the Azores before making their final landfall in the British Islands or mainland Europe. These latter passages are dealt with in Chapter 22. Wherever yachts are headed, nearly all will be aiming for higher latitudes in which summer cruising can be undertaken and tropical storms avoided.

| Passage | Approx distance | |
| --- | --- | --- |
| Virgin Islands to Florida via the Bahamas | 1000 | miles |
| Virgin Islands to Beaufort, North Carolina | 1200 | miles |
| Virgin Islands to Bermuda | 850 | miles |
| Antigua to Bermuda | 940 | miles |
| Bermuda to Newport, Rhode Island | 650 | miles |
| Virgin Islands to the Azores (recommended route) | 2500 | miles |

## Passage planning charts

| Coverage | Admiralty | US |
| --- | --- | --- |
| BA to 42°N | 4012 (1:10,000,000) | |
| US to 45°N | | 120 (1:6,331,100) |
| To 45°N and 60°W | 4403 (1:3,500,000) | 108 (1:3,500,000) |

## Virgin Islands to Florida via the Bahamas

This route cuts ocean passagemaking to a minimum, linking as it does with the Intracoastal Waterway running parallel to the Eastern Seaboard of the United States. However with depths throughout much of the Bahamas no more than 1.8 m (6 ft) it calls for meticulous navigation, and both charts and cruising guides will need to be studied with care. See Chapter 17 for further details of the Bahamas.

If time is limited or draught prevents passage through the Bahamas themselves, a second possibility is to sail up the Atlantic side of the chain until Eleuthera is abeam, then pass through the NE and NW Providence Channels and across the Strait of Florida to Miami or Fort Lauderdale.

Both these passages should enjoy favourable winds and currents, though the latter are unpredictable and have caused the loss of more than one yacht. Winds between April and June are predominantly easterly at 10–15 knots, becoming south-east as the season progresses. Unsettled weather is most likely to be encountered during May.

The US Coast Guard monitors all vessels entering US waters and it is possible that a yacht will be boarded at sea and searched.

## Virgin Islands to Beaufort, North Carolina

This should be another largely downwind passage, with south-easterly winds veering into the south and a 2.5 knot current following the trend of the coast. If sailing the rhumb line course in May or June there is an outside chance of encountering a hard blow, but a greater percentage likelihood of calms particularly during the mid portion of the passage. Plenty of fuel should be carried. The alternative is to sail a dog-leg, shaping a course to a point near 28°N 37°W before swinging northwards, in order to avoid the edge of the central Atlantic high pressure system with its associated light winds and calms.

If taking the direct route towards Beaufort, North Carolina, care should be taken to allow for the effects of the Gulf Stream. If set too far to the north it will be hard work indeed to return against both wind and current.

## Virgin Islands to Bermuda

Bermuda lies almost due north from the Virgin Islands at just short of 65°W, and is well within the possible path of early season hurricanes. Therefore this is another passage which should be completed before mid-June.

Departing from the Virgin Islands in May or June, south-easterly trade winds should aid the initial stages of the passage. However as progress is made northwards winds are likely to become less reliable, with a high probability of light variables or calms later in the passage. Occasionally a late-season *norther* may come through, but this is unusual after mid-April. Winds associated with cold fronts generally blow up sharply from the north-west, veering through north, east and south to finally blow themselves out in the south-west.

A north-west going current of about 0.5 knots can be expected until within 100 miles of Bermuda, after which it will vary in both speed and direction. Plenty of fuel should be carried, some of which should be earmarked for the final approach. Although Bermuda has a bad name as a landfall because of the extensive coral reefs which surround it, yachts coming from the south have the least difficult approach (see Chapter 20).

The passage between the Virgin Islands and Bermuda traverses the western edge of the Sargasso Sea - technically not a sea at all, but the static area around which the vast North Atlantic current systems sweep. Large carpets of brown Sargasso seaweed will be encountered and

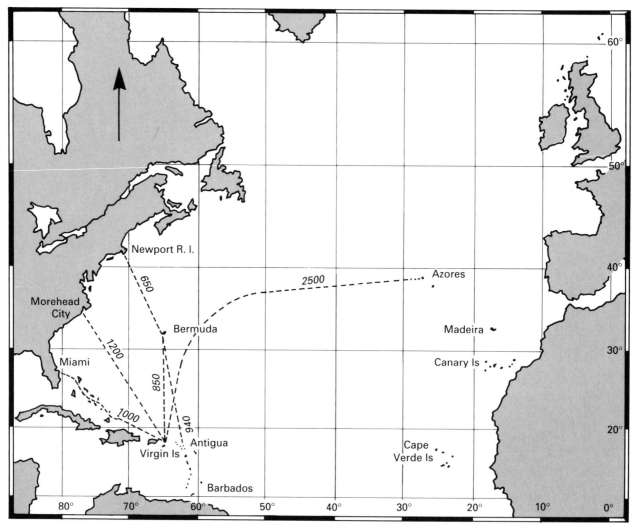

*Chart 27* Typical routes north from the Lesser Antilles.

towed and impeller logs are likely to be frequently fouled.

## Antigua to Bermuda

Very similar to the above, but typically sailed slightly earlier in the season by yachts departing at the beginning of May after Antigua Week. Winds are likely to be easterly or even north of east on departure, to some extent offsetting the advantage of leaving from a point further to windward. They are likely to veer south of east as progress is made northwards, becoming light and variable. The skipper with a schedule to maintain should carry plenty of fuel.

## Bermuda to Newport, Rhode Island

Although Newport has been chosen, as it is a frequent destination, remarks for this passage apply equally if bound for any destination north of New York. The route lies within the hurricane belt, making a landfall by the end of June highly desirable. Winds in that month are likely to be south or south-westerly for much of the passage, though should a cold front move eastward off the American continent strong west or north-west winds, often accompanied by driving rain, can be expected.

Particularly unpleasant seas will be produced where the wind runs against the Gulf Stream. They may become dangerous.

Currents are likely to be variable until around 35° N where the full force of the Gulf Stream will be met. Between Bermuda and Newport this sets east or north-east at up to 1.5 knots. The width of the main stream varies from a mere 20 or 30 miles to 300 or more. The advent of oceanographic satellites means that its position can be determined with considerable accuracy, and as changes from day to day tend to be small, it is worth studying the latest Gulf Stream chart before leaving Bermuda. Those with weatherfax receivers can obtain updates en route.

The last 100 miles or so of the passage will be affected by the cold Labrador Current, which flows past Newfoundland and Nova Scotia, and continues south-west along the coast before petering out around the latitude of the Chesapeake. The northern edge of the Gulf Stream, where it meets the cold Labrador Current flowing south-west, is typically marked by a wall of fog. In June and July visibility of less than two miles can be expected for more than 20 per cent of the time in the later stages of the passage. If heading north of Cape Cod fog is almost certain to be encountered.

## Virgin Islands to the Azores

The direct distance from the Virgin Islands to the Azores is about 2200 miles, whereas the recommended route adds some 300 to 400 miles. This is because the great circle course passes through the large area of high pressure which dominates the central Atlantic and where light and variable winds are almost guaranteed. It should only be attempted by yachts able to make good progress in very light winds. Even those whose sailing performance is sparkling in these conditions – a small minority of ocean cruisers – should carry fuel for at least 1000 miles as areas of absolute calm may extend for several hundred miles.

The more usual procedure is to shape a course to pass within 200 to 300 miles of Bermuda before swinging north-eastwards. Exactly how far to continue before heading east is open to argument, and will depend both on the conditions for the year and the preferences of those aboard – sail the rhumb line after reaching 35°N and run the risk of prolonged calms, or keep going to 38°N or 40°N in search of stronger winds and a faster passage? See Chapter 22 for more details on the later part of this route.

Even those taking this more traditional route are likely to encounter some calms and plenty of fuel should be carried. In some years, this passage may take a yacht with limited range under power as much as 35 days. When it is calm it is likely to be extremely hot. Water consumption will be noticeably greater than on previous passages and this should be allowed for.

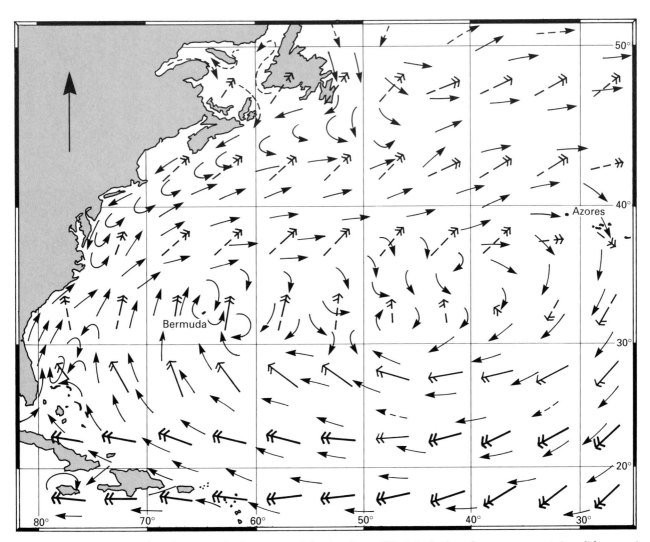

*Chart 28*   Prevailing winds and currents in the western Atlantic – June. (Winds in feathered arrows, currents in solid arrows.) Based on information from the *Atlantic Pilot Atlas*.

# 19 THE NORTH AMERICAN COASTLINE

## Weather and currents

The continent of North America has a coastline stretching from the Tropic of Cancer to the Arctic Circle, though few yachts venture beyond 60°N. Regional weather patterns and particularly temperature vary accordingly.

One of the few generalisations that can be made is that, during the summer cruising season, winds generally blow either offshore or parallel to the coast. Thus strong on-shore gales, familiar to the European yachtsman, are seldom a problem. A more frequent hazard north of about 40°N is poor visibility, caused by the cold Labrador Current bringing arctic water south in a narrow stream almost to the latitude of Cape Hatteras. As the cold water encounters the warm air, it literally steams, giving rise to the notorious fogs of the Newfoundland Banks, Nova Scotia and Cape Cod. Unlike poor visibility around British or European coasts, which is often associated with high pressure and therefore light winds or calms, thick fog allied with winds of 20–30 knots is not unusual off the American and Canadian coasts.

Visibility is at its worst in summer, with a 20 per cent likelihood of less than two miles in all areas north of Block Island, with a 40 per cent likelihood off Nova Scotia and Newfoundland. Yachts without radar are at a disadvantage in these waters, and those planning to cruise the area will save themselves anxious hours by fitting a set.

Further south, the warm Gulf Stream parallels the coast, running at up to four knots in the Florida Strait but slowing as it fans out into the Atlantic. When strong northerly winds oppose the north-east-going current particularly vicious seas can form, which have been responsible for the loss of more than one yacht. Satellite surveillance now enables the position of the stream and its associated eddies to be known with accuracy. Details are broadcast by fax and voice.

## Ice

The Labrador Current is also responsible for carrying icebergs south past Newfoundland, but only very occasion-

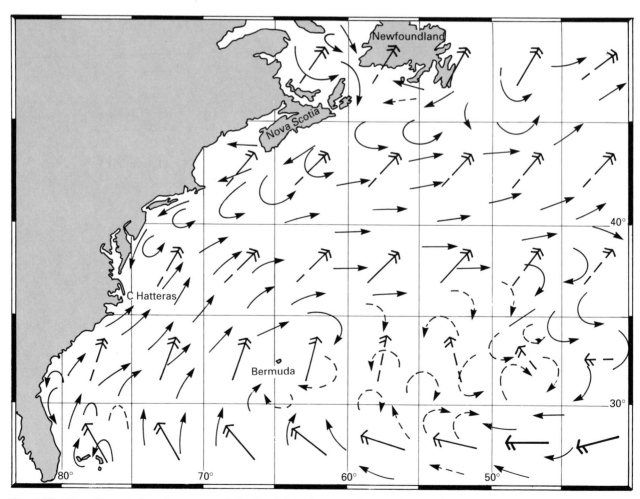

*Chart 29* Prevailing winds and currents off the North American coastline – July. (Winds in feathered arrows, currents in solid arrows.) Based on information from the *Atlantic Pilot Atlas*.

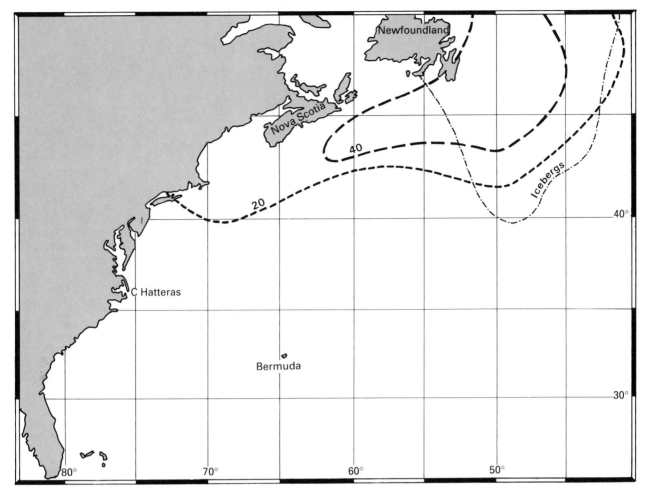

*Chart 30*　Iceberg limits and percentage likelihood of less than two mile visibility off the North American coastline – July. Based on information from the *Atlantic Pilot Atlas*.

ally do bergs reach as far south as 40°N before melting. They are seldom encountered east of 40°W or west of 60°W, their range being most widespread in April and May and shrinking throughout the summer. The occasional rogue berg or growler which comes further south is usually well tracked and its position broadcast to shipping.

There can be a concentration of bergs east of Cape Race, where the big ones go aground on the Grand Banks. As the season progresses and the icebergs begin to melt, they float off and move further south, finally reaching the northern edge of the Gulf Stream where they disperse and melt completely. Ice is therefore most prevalent in the northern and eastern parts of the Grand Banks early in the year and on their southern side later on. The International Ice Patrol co-ordinated by the US and Canadian Coast Guard services broadcasts daily reports of the location and drift of bergs. A report can be obtained before sailing by telephoning (902) 426 5665.

## Tides and tidal streams

Tidal influence varies enormously along the North American coastline, from a bare 1.3 m (4 ft) in Florida to the massive 15 m (50 ft) tides of the Bay of Fundy. The appropriate tide and tidal current tables should be consulted.

## Approach and landfall

Conditions on approaching the coast will be dictated to a great extent by the specific latitude and area chosen. It would plainly be impossible to detail all feasible landfalls, so only those associated with the passages outlined in Chapters 18, 22 and 23 will be covered. A suitable pilot book should be consulted for more detailed information.

Much of the US eastern seaboard is fringed by a wide and relatively shallow continental shelf, with depths of 36 m (120 ft) or less being found 50 miles offshore in many areas. Depths then drop off very suddenly to 3000 m (10,000 ft) or more, and in bad weather very confused seas can result. It is important not to get caught in this area by the onset of heavy weather on approaching the coast, and equally important to make offing as rapidly as possible on departure in order to get into deep water before there is any chance of meeting heavy weather.

The main problem on approaching the Canadian and northern US coasts is the high incidence of fog, and the fact that it can be prolonged. It therefore may not be practicable to stand off and wait for conditions to improve; one must be prepared to continue and enter port in bad visibility.

Cape Race and the east coast of Newfoundland are within the iceberg zone in the early part of the season. This, combined with fog, will call for great caution when approaching this coast. The coasts of Nova Scotia and the United States can generally be regarded as being to the west of the iceberg zone.

The Grand Banks and the waters off Nova Scotia are popular fishing grounds for fleets of trawlers and coastal fishing boats. A sharp lookout should be maintained for them, and also for both nets and lines of pots marked by floats, which may be found well offshore. The gear itself will be submerged, and thus the buoy the only danger. The increasing reliance on radar by shipping means that merchant vessels seldom reduce speed much in poor visibility, even though small craft may not be spotted on the screen. The main concentrations of shipping may be expected off Cape Race, the approaches to Halifax, the Nantucket Light Vessel, and to the north of Cape Cod where the routes to Boston and the Cape Cod Canal will be crossed.

### Newfoundland

St John's is the nearest port to Europe and full details of approach and entry are given in Part III. Cape Race (46°39'N 53°04'W) may be used as a landfall by those on the northern or great circle routes. Virgin Rocks and the nearby Eastern Shoals, lying 100 miles east of Cape Race, are a potential hazard on the approach.

Offshore the current sets southerly at about one knot, but runs westerly around Cape Race. There can be a strong northerly eddy off the south coast of Newfoundland. If close inshore beware of the tides and the possibility of being swept into the bays along the southern coast. Many wrecks have occurred in fog on the south-eastern and southern coasts of Newfoundland, owing to the indraught or to the current setting north-eastward.

### Nova Scotia

Sable Island (43°55'N 59°50'W) lies just under 100 miles off the coast of Nova Scotia and must be given a wide berth – it is a graveyard for ships, with strong and unpredictable currents and shoal water. In the southern part of Nova Scotia a strong indraught has been reported in the vicinity of Cape Sable. Oil rigs may be encountered in the area. Halifax is the recommended port for entering Nova Scotia and full details will be found in Part III.

### Nantucket Shoals

Many yachts on passage from Europe or coming up from Bermuda make landfall at the Nantucket Shoals Lanby (40°30'N 69°26'W), 50 miles south-east of Nantucket Island with its offlying shoals. Probably the majority continue to Newport, Rhode Island, for which harbour and final approach details will be found in Part III. Nantucket Shoals Lanby carries a 13-mile range light standing 13 m (43 ft) above sea level, and is also equipped with a horn. Care must be taken in the vicinity of the Lanby as it also marks the separation zone for the shipping lanes in and out of New York (see Chapter 10).

The Nantucket Shoals, which stretch more than 30 miles south-east of Nantucket Island, have a least depth of 1.25 m (4 ft) and frequently break in bad weather. Strong tidal streams set over the Shoals, and though they can be crossed in calm weather via the marked channels this is not advised. In any case, only a slight deflection to the west of the rhumb line will be needed if heading for

Newport, and none at all for Block Island or further west. If heading northwards the choice is between closing the coast at Buzzards Bay and traversing the Cape Cod Canal, or heading north-east from the Lanby to shape a course between Nantucket Shoal and Georges Bank, where oil rigs may be encountered.

### Cape Hatteras

While Cape Hatteras (35°15'N 75°31'W) may be broadly defined as a target area for yachts coming west from Bermuda or north from the Lesser Antilles or Bahamas, its coastline is highly dangerous with many offlying banks and strong and unpredictable currents. Cape Hatteras itself deserves to be given a wide berth.

A popular route for northbound yachts is to join the Intracoastal Waterway at Beaufort, North Carolina, passing through the Sounds inside Cape Hatteras en route to the Chesapeake Bay. The principal requirement when making the approach is to avoid the Lookout Shoals.

Southbound yachts should either stand well offshore around Cape Hatteras, or enter the Chesapeake and thence the Intracoastal Waterway at Norfolk, Virginia.

## Formalities: Canada

Arrival should be made at an official port of entry, and if possible notified by VHF. Otherwise the skipper should go ashore alone to contact customs and immigration. The usual paperwork and details are required, together with (for a foreign yacht) an intended itinerary and approximate departure date. In the case of many nationalities, including British, a cruising permit can then be issued, removing the need to clear again at subsequent ports. Firearms must be declared on arrival, but most single-shot weapons are permitted. Animals must have valid rabies vaccination certificates, but even so are not allowed ashore and will have to remain on board.

## Formalities: the United States

Yachts entering the United States should be aware that US customs agents handle both yachts and large ships. There is no simplified procedure specifically for yachts.

It is necessary to clear in at a designated port of entry. Normally, clearance is carried out at any public access berth (such as a municipal pier or marina dock), or at a yacht club jetty. If in doubt, the local Coast Guard will advise on procedure. Yachts are expected to seek clearance immediately upon arrival, and most foreign yachts are then boarded for inspection. While US customs agents have been known to board yachts at sea, this is very rare. A Coast Guard boarding at sea has nothing to do with inward customs clearance, which must still be completed after arrival.

Unless the entire crew are US citizens, an immigration officer will normally accompany a customs officer to the arrival inspection. Ship's papers, clearance from the previous port and a crew list will be required. The USA is one of the few major countries for which nearly all nationalities (including all Europeans) must have a visa. While fresh perishable foods (especially fruits and vegetables) may not be imported, it is rare for agriculture inspectors to visit yachts unless animals are aboard.

Firearms must be registered upon arrival, and only

One of the many lifting bridges along the US intracoastal waterway. The fixed bridges have a clearance of at least 65 ft.
*Photo: Gavin McLaren*

hunting and sporting firearms may be brought in without restriction. Individual state firearms' laws also apply, and these may be more restrictive. Animals do not need rabies certificates if arriving from rabies-free countries, but will otherwise require them, and rabies does exist in some islands of the Lesser Antilles. Pet birds will be put into quarantine. There are also restrictions on various animal products from declared endangered species – few yachts are likely to have furs aboard, but many people may have bought souvenirs of tortoise or turtle shell jewellery, scrimshaw on whalebone or ivory, or simply have picked up some coral.

Yachts of most nationalities, including those from Britain and northern Europe, may apply for a 'cruising permit'. This remains valid for up to a year, and exempts the yacht from further clearance whilst in US waters. A condition of the cruising permit is that yachts notify US customs when they move from one customs port sector to another. While penalties for failure to do so are very rare, notification is simple and may be made by calling the tollfree phone number 1-800-973-2867.

American-registered yachts returning home must also report arrival to customs, but are less likely to be boarded for inspection, unless the yacht has a foreign crew. There is no specific requirement for US vessels to clear outwards, though it may be wise to do so since the authorities of most other countries will wish to see evidence regarding date and port of departure.

## The US Coast Guard

Confusion can sometimes arise over the role and responsibilities of the US Coast Guard, which have a much wider brief than the British service of the same name.

Whereas the British Coastguard are largely land-based the US Coast Guard are very active afloat. Their responsibilities include policing their own and nearby international waters for drug smugglers (in the course of which private yachts are frequently boarded and searched), the maintenance of navigational aids, and generally ensuring that all vessels proceed in an orderly manner. Unlike Britain, where lifeboats are the responsibility of the Royal National Lifeboat Institution, in the USA the Coast Guard also run their own search and rescue vessels and aircraft. They will respond if a vessel is in immediate danger, but where there is no risk to life or craft the Coast Guard will usually turn the job over to a private contractor for assistance – which is likely to be expensive.

The US Coast Guard monitor VHF channels 16 and 22 A, the latter being their working channel. Except in an emergency initial contact should be made on 22 A. European yachts should note that it is illegal to call the Coast Guard (or anyone else) on channel 16 solely for a radio check.

The Coast Guard are also responsible for small craft safety, and if one is boarded by them they are likely to inspect the safety equipment carried. The list of requirements includes several items not normally found aboard

European yachts. In theory, foreign yachts are governed by exactly the same regulations as US registered ones; in practice a reasonable approach is usually taken and, provided the authorities are not antagonised, a well equipped ocean cruiser should have few problems.

## Sewage disposal

The Federal Government has charged the US Coast Guard with the inspection of sewage disposal arrangements on yachts. The rules in US waters are an amalgam of Federal, State and local regulations. Many yacht harbours have been designated 'No Discharge Areas' where disposal of even treated sewage is strictly prohibited. Local harbourmasters or State marine police are usually responsible for enforcing the regulations. The usual recourse for visiting yachts is to fit a valve at the heads, in order that sewage can be pumped directly overboard when offshore and into a holding tank in harbour. Holding tanks can be emptied via a deck fitting at pumpout stations at many marinas and yacht clubs, or the tank may be discharged overboard when the yacht is well clear of the harbour. Heads without holding tanks must show evidence of being secured from use whilst in harbour – it has been suggested that a cable tie securing the discharge seacock in the shut position would suffice.

## Facilities

Facilities in America equal the best to be found in the world. The larger yachting centres of Canada are not far behind. Equally, both countries still offer cruising grounds with dozens of miles between loaves of bread.

All those harbours detailed in Part III have good facilities for yachts, though many of the best-known yachting centres are outside the scope of this book. Local cruising guides should be consulted.

## Sailing directions and yachtsmen's guides

In addition to the official publications mentioned in Part I, the following almanacs, yachtsmen's guides and chart books, listed by area, are relevant to the North American coastline. See Appendix B, page 217, for publishers' details.

*Reed's Nautical Almanac: North American East Coast*
*Eldridge Tide and Pilot Book*, Marion Jewett White
*Atlantic Coast*, Embassy Marine
*Light List & Waypoint Guide: Maine to Texas*, J & L Kettlewell
*Cruising Guide to the Florida Keys*, Frank Papy
*Waterway Guide, Southern Edition*
*Intracoastal Waterway, Facilities Guide*, R D Smith
*The Intracoastal Waterway Chartbook*, J & L Kettlewell
*The Intracoastal Waterway, Norfolk to Miami*, Jan & Bill Moeller
*Florida's East Coast*, Embassy Marine
*Cruising Guide to Eastern Florida*, Claiborne S Young
*Cruising Guide to Coastal South Carolina and Georgia*, Claiborne S Young

*Cruising Guide to Coastal North Carolina*, Claiborne S Young
*Waterway Guide, Mid-Atlantic Edition*
*Guide to Cruising the Chesapeake Bay*, Chesapeake Bay Magazine
*Cruising the Chesapeake: A Gunkholer's Guide*, W Shellenberger
*Chesapeake Bay Cruising Guide: Vol 1, Upper Bay*, Tom Neale
*A Cruising Guide to New Jersey Waters*, Donald M Launer
*Waterway Guide, Northern Edition*
*Long Island Sound*, Embassy Marine
*Cruising Guide to Narragansett Bay & the South Coast of Massachusetts*, Linda & Patrick Childress & Tink Martin
*Rhode Island, Maine and New Hampshire*, Embassy Marine
*Cruising Guide to Maine, Vol 1: Kittery to Rockland*, Don Johnson
*Cruising Guide to Maine, Vol 2: Rockport to Eastport*, Don Johnson
*Cruising Guide to the Maine Coast*, Hank & Jan Taft & Curtis Rindlaub
*Cruising Guide to the New England Coast*, Roger F Duncan, John P Ware & Wallace Fenn
*The Coast of New England*, Stan Patey
*Cruising Guide to the Bay of Fundy and the St John River*, Nicholas Tracy
*Yachting Guide to the South Shore of Nova Scotia*, Arthur M Dechman
*Cruising Guide to the Nova Scotia Coast*, John McKelvy
*A Cruising Guide to Nova Scotia*, Peter Loveridge
*The Cruising Guide to Newfoundland*, Sandy Weld
*Cruising Guide to the Labrador*, Sandy Weld

## Chart packs

*BBA chart kits*: No 2, Canada to Block Island
No 3, New York to Nantucket
No 4, Chesapeake & Delaware
No 6, Norfolk to Jacksonville
No 7, Florida East Coast

*BBA Compact chart kits*: Cape Sable to Clearwater
Cape Cod Canal to Cape Elizabeth
Narragansett to Nantucket
Long Island Sound
Upper Chesapeake Bay
Jacksonville to Miami

## Relevant ports covered in Part III

Bermuda is Britain's oldest colony and is self-governing. It has its own currency, the Bermuda dollar, which is at par with the US dollar. Its economy is closely linked to the American tourist trade, and the two currencies are interchangeable. The islands consist of a low-lying group of small coral islets, many of which are joined by causeways, surrounded by extensive reefs.

## Weather and currents

Weather in Bermuda is influenced by the position of the Azores high, the Gulf Stream, and the weather systems on the eastern seaboard of the United States. Winds typically box the compass during the year, being generally westerly from December through until April, backing into the south around May, and gradually swinging through south-west, west and north from September onwards. In June and July, when the majority of yachts pass through, an average of 15–20 knots may be expected though a sudden increase to 30–40 knots may accompany the passage of a frontal wave moving from the American coast. The islands lie well within the hurricane belt (see Chapter 10) and passagemaking yachts should endeavour to be out of the area by the end of June. Temperatures vary from around 17°C (62°F) in February to 28°C (82°F) in August.

Currents in the vicinity are unpredictable, though a northerly set is the most common. The islands lie within a few hundred miles of the eastern wall of the Gulf Stream, which frequently sets up large eddies, and though currents seldom exceed 0.5 knots they may reverse direction within a matter of days.

## Approach and landfall

Due to the reefs which extend up to ten miles off the north-east, north and west coasts of Bermuda, the only

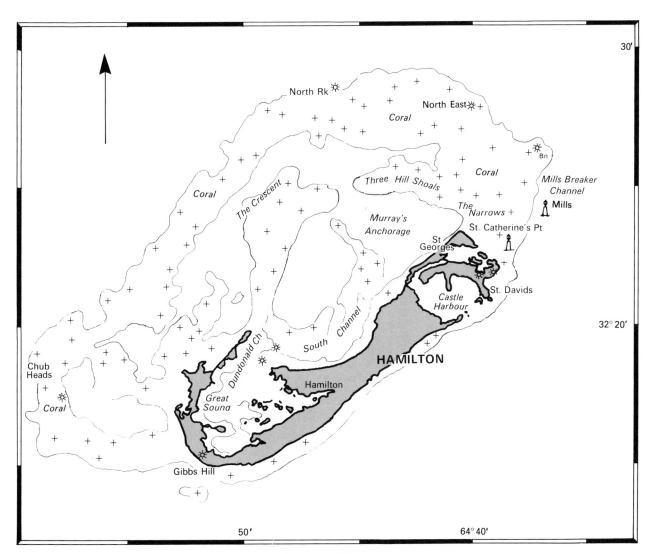

*Chart 31*   The Bermuda islands. Based on Admiralty Chart No 1073.

safe approach is from a position south or south-east of the group. Here the coast is very steep-to, with the 200 m (650 ft) sounding lying within a mile of the coastline in places. There is also a local magnetic anomaly, which may give a possible error of up to 6°.

Yachts will be called by Bermuda Harbour Radio on VHF channel 16 as they approach the islands. This station can often be received as far as 50 miles south of Bermuda. Details of various equipment carried must be given, including the serial numbers of EPIRBs on board, so it is as well to have these details to hand. Channel 16 should be monitored throughout the approach to St George's as the harbour will be closed during the movement of large cruise liners through the narrow cut at its entrance.

Details of the approach and entry to St George's Harbour will be found in Part III.

## Formalities

Although reduced in recent years, clearance charges at Bermuda are higher than those of most other countries around the Atlantic. Entry must be made at St George's – full details will be found in Part III. The Q flag should be flown when entering and until pratique has been granted, after which boats may proceed to Hamilton or elsewhere. St George's must again be visited for clearance out prior to departure.

Visitors are normally allowed to remain for an initial period of three weeks, but if a longer stay is desired application must be made to the Department of Immigration. If any crew members are leaving or joining in Bermuda then the Immigration authorities should be contacted well in advance, preferably several months. Various forms must be completed, and without them it is unlikely that a single airline ticket to the island can be obtained.

Firearms, including flare pistols and spear guns, must be declared and may be impounded until departure or placed under seal aboard. Medically prescribed drugs must also be declared. There are severe penalties for the possession of illegal drugs.

## Facilities

Bermuda is a sophisticated island with all manner of shopping facilities for both the tourist and the yacht owner. All slipping and repair services are available, and bonded stores may be obtained prior to departure. However, almost everything must be imported, making food and other stores extremely expensive. Services are priced to match. Canned foods are available, but variety may be limited as locally great reliance is placed on chilled and frozen foods. For the yacht without refrigeration this creates a problem, since chilling fruit or vegetables badly impairs their keeping properties. It may be possible by asking around to find a source of locally laid eggs which have been neither washed nor chilled, and some locally grown vegetables.

Cruising yachts and ocean liners share the harbour at St George's, Bermuda. *Photo: Georgie McLaren*

Yachts share St George's Harbour, Bermuda with the rotting hulls of old iron sailing ships, but all obstructions are very well charted. *Photo: Anne Hammick*

## Sailing directions and yachtsmen's guides

In addition to the official publications mentioned in Part I, and a section in *Reed's Nautical Almanac: Caribbean Edition*, a 20 page information sheet is published bi-annually by the Bermuda Department of Tourism (PO Box HM 465, Hamilton HM BX, Bermuda). This gives detailed information on buoyage and navigation, clearance, facilities, etc, and will be sent free on request. If intending to cruise Bermuda and its surrounding reefs a copy of Edward Harris's *Yachting Guide to Bermuda* will be invaluable. See Appendix B, page 217, for publishers' details.

## Relevant port covered in Part III

The Azores form an autonomous region of Portugal (and are thus within the EU), where Portuguese is spoken with an accent which varies from island to island. Currency is the Portuguese escudo.

Compared with other island groups in the Atlantic the Azores are thinly spread. The nine islands lie in three distinct groups stretching over more than 300 miles of ocean, and show surprising diversity in terms of both landscape and populace. All are of volcanic origin, and ancient *caldeira* craters are a feature of nearly every island. Only Pico retains its original cone, the dramatic 2351 m (7713 ft) summit being visible at 50 or 60 miles in clear weather.

Several new harbour developments are taking shape throughout the islands, and though naturally intended primarily for the use of local people, visiting yachtsmen will also benefit. Until recently only Horta on Faial and Ponta Delgada on São Miguel could be regarded as safe under nearly all conditions, but the completion of an extensive

double breakwater at Praia da Vitoria on Terceira has added a third harbour to the list. A yacht marina is under construction in the northern part of the bay and already offers some facilities. There are also many less well protected bays and harbours where a yacht can lie at anchor in settled conditions.

The Azores have long been regarded by most yachtsmen simply as a convenient place to break the Atlantic passage, and their merits as a cruising ground largely overlooked. If at all possible, at least two or three weeks should be spent in the islands, not all of them in Horta.

## Weather and currents

During the sailing season, effectively from June until mid September, the climate is dominated by the Azores High. In most years this becomes strongly established, resulting in prolonged periods of light winds or calms, but sometimes the High remains weak so that windier, more

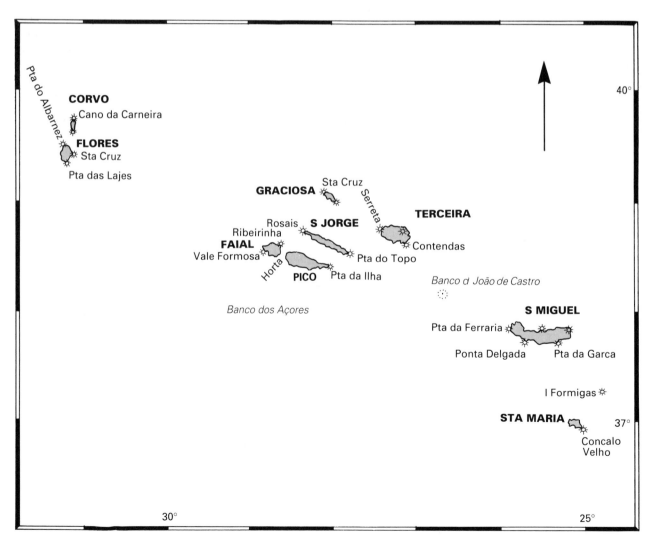

*Chart 32*   The Azores archipelago. Based on Admiralty Chart No 1950.

changeable weather predominates as it does at other seasons. Winds between south-west and north are the most common throughout the year, but almost every other direction is likely to be experienced at some time. As in Atlantic Europe, south-easterly winds usually foretell an approaching front. There is a six per cent likelihood of calms between June and August, decreasing to four per cent in September.

Summer temperatures typically rise to around 23°C (74°F), though heatwaves can occasionally produce a sizzling 30°C (86°F) for days at a time. However nights can feel chilly, particularly to those who have spent the previous months in the tropics.

Visibility is generally good, though southerly winds may produce hazy conditions which limit the field of view to five miles or so while still apparently giving a sharp horizon. This is particularly common around the western islands of Flores and Corvo. Like the *harmattan* in the Cape Verdes, it can be most misleading.

The Azores are affected by that branch of the North Atlantic Current setting south-east towards the Iberian coast which later becomes the Canary Current. Flow in open waters seldom exceeds half a knot, but this may double around the ends of the larger islands, and when ocean and tidal currents combine, races may form. Ocean swell can be a factor when picking an anchorage, as it frequently runs in from the west even when winds are light. For this reason, the majority of Azorean harbours are on south or east-facing coasts.

## Tides and tidal streams

Tidal range is relatively small throughout the Azores and nowhere exceeds 1.8 m (6 ft). However streams can run with surprising speed and may reach two knots in the

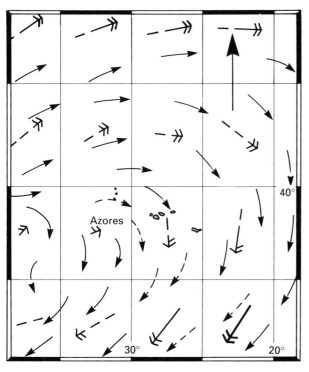

*Chart 33* Prevailing winds and currents around the Azores – July. (Winds in feathered arrows, currents in solid arrows.) Based on information from the *Atlantic Pilot Atlas*.

Canal do Faial between Faial and Pico. Tides set north or north-east on the flood, south or south-west on the ebb.

## Approach and landfall

Approach to the Azores is straightforward and neither Flores nor Faial, the two most popular landfall islands for transatlantic yachts, have any serious outliers. The usual course is to skirt their southern coasts, and if approaching Faial in darkness it should be noted that the Vale Formoso lighthouse at its western end is widely regarded as being considerably less powerful than stated, with a range of nearer 5 miles than the claimed 13 miles. Yachts approaching from Europe often make landfall on São Miguel which again is steep-to.

Buoyage (such as it is) follows the European IALA A system, in contrast to that found in North America and the Caribbean.

## Formalities

The Portuguese seem to like their paperwork, and entry can be a long drawn-out affair. Furthermore, it is necessary to clear in and out of each island individually, though the Q flag need only be flown on first arriving from abroad.

In theory, the advent of the EU should mean fewer formalities for EU owned and registered yachts arriving from mainland Europe, but in practice this represents such a small percentage of total arrivals that it is likely all yachts will be expected to follow the same clearance procedures for some time to come.

On arrival the skipper should take passports and ship's papers to the *Capitania do Porto* (Port Captain), proceeding to the *Guarda Fiscal* (immigration) office, the *Policia Maritima* and in some cases the *Alfandega* (customs). A *Livrete de Transito* (transit log) may be issued, in which all further movements of the yacht will be recorded until she leaves the islands. It is generally necessary to visit the *Capitania*, *Policia Maritima* and possibly the *Guarda Fiscal* again before leaving.

Clearance is much less effort in Horta and São Miguel than elsewhere, as all the necessary offices are in the marinas (see pages 211 and 214) whereas in other harbours it may entail a longish walk. In addition, several of the officials speak excellent English. However even when the language barrier presents almost insurmountable difficulties the officials are invariably courteous, and there is no doubt at all that a smile will speed things along much more effectively than any show of impatience.

A Portuguese courtesy flag should be flown, and many visiting yachtsmen like to hoist the blue, white and gold Azorean flag beneath it.

## Facilities

Although repair and other facilities for yachts have improved considerably over recent years, the islands remain relatively unsophisticated in this respect. Almost any work needed on a yacht *can* be done, but it may be a time consuming and expensive process. By far the best facilities are at Horta and at Ponta Delgada, both of which have small but well run marinas with helpful, English-speaking staff who would almost certainly assist with recommendations and/or translation as necessary. Further

The construction of a breakwater at Lajes on Flores encourages east-bound yachts to visit this beautiful island before continuing to Horta. *Photo: Ann Bradshaw-Smith*

details of both these harbours will be found in Part III. Mid Atlantic Yacht Services, although located in Horta, can deal with problems in all the islands and may prove the best initial contact if in difficulties or needing repairs.

Food shopping has improved considerably over the past decade, though many of the smaller towns still offer little more than the basics. It would be fair to say that while all normal day-to-day needs are likely to be met, it would be unwise to expect to do any major stocking up in the Azores. Nearly all the islands have markets and the fresh produce is excellent – both temperate and tropical fruit and vegetables thrive, and seasonal gluts of plums and figs may test the toughest digestion. Particularly good cheese is also produced, notably on Pico and São Jorge.

## Sailing directions and yachtsmen's guides

In addition to the official publications mentioned in Part I, there are two yachtsmen's guides to the archipelago. See Appendix B, page 216, for publishers' details.

*Atlantic Islands*, Anne Hammick
*Azores Cruising Guide*, Gwenda Cornell

## Relevant ports covered in Part III

There is a wide variety of possible routes if sailing from the USA or Canada to the UK and Europe, some of which break the voyage at one or more of the mid-Atlantic island groups. Probably the majority of cruising yachts elect to take the voyage in stages. Others make the passage direct, usually keeping further north. It is broadly true to say that eastward routes tend to keep further south so as to make maximum use of the North Atlantic Current. It is certainly more pleasant to cross the northern Atlantic from west to east than vice versa, with a good chance of favourable winds for most of the passage. Yachts heading westwards must either stay well north and face the likelihood of severe weather, or remain further south in the hope of lighter weather but at the expense of mileage lost to the current.

Inevitably, many of the following remarks that refer to one passage will also apply to others with a similar departure point or landfall. It is therefore suggested that readers should study all those passages taking a similar or parallel course, in addition to the one they actually intend to sail.

| Passages eastwards | Approx distance | |
| --- | --- | --- |
| USA to Bermuda | 650 to 700 miles | |
| Bermuda to Horta, Azores | 1820 | miles |
| Newport, Rhode Island to Horta, Azores | 1980 | miles |
| Halifax, Nova Scotia to Horta, Azores | 1635 | miles |
| St John's, Newfoundland to Horta, Azores | 1240 | miles |
| Horta, Azores to Falmouth, UK | 1250 | miles |
| Ponta Delgada, Azores to Spain or Portugal | 750 to 820 miles | |
| Ponta Delgada, Azores to Gibraltar | 960 | miles |
| Newport, Rhode Island to Falmouth via the mid latitudes | 2940 | miles |
| Halifax, Nova Scotia to Falmouth via the mid latitudes | 2600 | miles |
| Newport, Rhode Island to Falmouth via the great circle | 2850 | miles |
| Halifax, Nova Scotia to Falmouth via the great circle | 2390 | miles |
| St John's, Newfoundland to Falmouth via the great circle | 1900 | miles |

| Passages westwards | Approx distance | |
| --- | --- | --- |
| Falmouth, UK to the Azores – see Chapter 12 | 1200 | miles |
| Horta, Azores to Bermuda | 1820 | miles |
| Bermuda to Newport, Rhode Island – see Chapter 18 | 650 | miles |
| Falmouth to Newport, Rhode Island via the mid latitudes | 2940 | miles |
| Falmouth to Halifax, Nova Scotia via the mid latitudes | 2600 | miles |
| Falmouth to Newport, Rhode Island via the great circle | 2850 | miles |
| Falmouth to Halifax, Nova Scotia via the great circle | 2390 | miles |
| Falmouth to St John's, Newfoundland via the great circle | 1900 | miles |
| Falmouth to Newport, Rhode Island via the Northern Route | 2870 | miles |
| Falmouth to Halifax, Nova Scotia via the Northern Route | 2230 | miles |
| Falmouth to St John's, Newfoundland via the Northern Route | 2050 | miles |

NB: many of the above distances are approximations, due to the wide variety of possible routes.

## Passage planning charts

| Coverage | Admiralty | US |
| --- | --- | --- |
| Northern North Atlantic | 4011 (1:10,000,000) | 121 (1:5,870,000) |
| Southern North Atlantic | 4012 (1:10,000,000) | 120 (1:6,331,100) |

It is important to note that magnetic variation differs as one crosses the Atlantic, reaching more than 20° of westerly variation near 50°W. The amount of variation fluctuates slowly, rates varying from place to place. Ocean passage charts show isogonic lines, linking those places with equal variation, and also give details of annual changes.

## Weather patterns

Except in the immediate vicinity of Bermuda, the passages discussed in this chapter lie between 35°N and 55°N or 60°N. Those routes in higher latitudes, perhaps visiting Greenland or Iceland en route to Norway, are the preserve of the experienced yachtsman and should be carefully researched using the relevant *Sailing Directions* and Admiralty *Routeing Charts* or US *Pilot Charts*.

The latitudes in which crossings are most often made are dominated by the prevailing westerly and south-westerly winds, created by low pressure to the north and the mid Atlantic High Pressure system to the south. This typically stretches from Bermuda to the Azores throughout the summer, but in some years may remain further south than usual, allowing the passage of depressions also to veer unusually far south. Less frequently, associated cells of high pressure not only form but persist further north, giving light winds and calms over large areas for weeks at a time. Thus while some features – such as fog – tend to be true of a particular area or latitude at all times, others may shift their area of influence from one year to the next. Whereas the movements of the trade wind belt can be predicted with a fair degree of accuracy, weather affecting

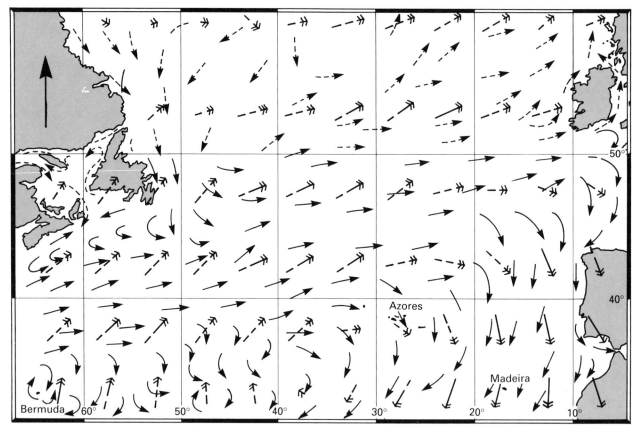

*Chart 34* Prevailing winds and currents between 30° and 58°N – June. (Winds in feathered arrows, currents in solid arrows.) Based on information from the *Atlantic Pilot Atlas*.

all crossings in the middle and northern latitudes is less predictable.

Short term weather over the entire area is dominated by the west to east passage of Atlantic depressions, as they move from North America towards Europe. These give rise to those rapidly changing conditions familiar to European yachtsmen; south-east winds veering into the south-west together with a falling barometer as the depression approaches, a period of south-westerlies and heavy rain as the warm front passes, followed by a sudden shift into the north-west as the cold front comes through, often accompanied by sharp, squally showers but soon clearing to give blue skies and clear visibility.

Not only do Atlantic depressions generally move more slowly in summer than in winter, but almost without exception they are much less intense and generate correspondingly less powerful winds. Thus by far the best season for all crossings north of the Atlantic high pressure system is between mid-May and mid-August. Unfortunately visibility off the coasts of Canada and the northern USA is at its worst in the summer, and the iceberg limit is also at its greatest extent (see Chapter 19). However these drawbacks are far outweighed by the almost certain promise of lighter winds – from a ten per cent plus chance of winds over 35 knots on any one day between October and April, down to an average of only one per cent in July. Naturally, the chance of encountering a gale is always greater in northern latitudes than further south. Although it is rare for a hurricane to track beyond 40°N 60°W, the possibility should be borne in mind and careful attention paid to weather forecasts.

## Ocean currents

The northern North Atlantic is dominated by the vast clockwise circulation described in Chapter 10. The Gulf Stream sets north-east in a clearly defined band off the North American continent, continuing to flow east or slightly north of east at around half a knot over much of the ocean between 35° and 55°N, by which time it is known simply as the North Atlantic Current. On reaching about 20°W this current splits, one arm continuing past Scotland towards Norway and the other setting south-east and then south off the coasts of Spain and Portugal. Minor branches flow into the English Channel and Bay of Biscay.

The only major exception to the generally east-going circulation is the Labrador Current, which sets south or south-west down the coasts of Canada and the northern United States (see Chapter 19). From 50°W westwards the interface between the Gulf Stream and the Labrador Current is known as the Cold Wall and is normally very noticeable because of the change both in water temperature and in colour – the cold Labrador Current is light green whereas the warm Gulf Stream is a deep blue. However, there will not be a sharp and unbroken dividing line at all times – rather, bulges and eddies where the warm and cold waters mix.

## USA to Bermuda

Departure can be made from whichever US port is most convenient and a direct course normally sailed. In order to clear the Bermuda area before the onset of the hurricane

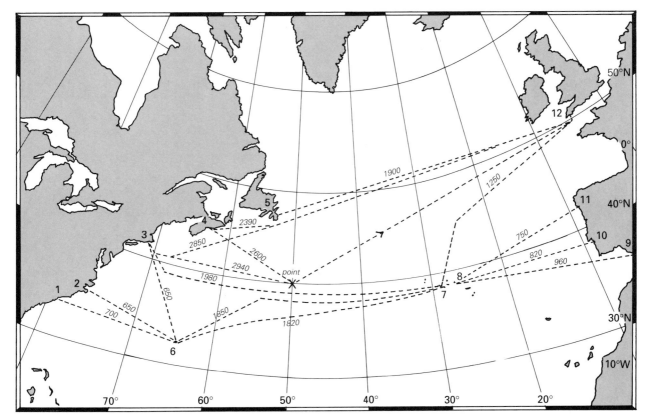

*Chart 35* Typical routes eastwards in the middle and northern latitudes. Projection based on Admiralty Chart No 5095. Key to numbered departure/arrival ports: (1) Charleston, S Carolina; (2) Norfolk, Virginia; (3) Newport, Rhode Island; (4) Halifax, Nova Scotia; (5) St John's, Newfoundland; (6) St George's, Bermuda; (7) Horta, Azores; (8) Ponta Delgada, Azores; (9) Gibraltar; (10) Lisbon, Portugal; (11) Bayona, Spain; (12) Falmouth, UK.

season many yachts make the passage in May, when south-westerly winds of 15 to 25 knots alternate with stronger winds from the north or north-east. When these oppose the Gulf Stream dangerous seas can be created. By June, the incidence of northerlies is less, but the chance of an early season hurricane must be considered.

The further north the departure point the more wind-ward work is likely to be called for, and it may be worth diverging from the rhumb line course in order to cross the Gulf Stream as quickly as possible, having made additional westing while still in the Labrador Current. Although the *Routeing* and *Pilot Charts* show the Gulf Stream in this area as running at an innocuous 1–1½ knots, many observers have experienced much higher rates, together with eddies and offshoots totally uncharted and inexplicable. For comfort – and also for safety – avoid crossing the Stream in a strong northerly wind.

The corridor between Bermuda and the US coast is a favourite hurricane track, those later in the season tending to run further inshore than early season hurricanes, which (though far less likely to start with) have a statistically greater chance of approaching Bermuda itself. Hurricane forecasting has become a fine art, and if you leave the US coast with a favourable forecast, although there is no guarantee of reaching Bermuda unscathed, neither is there any reason to be caught unawares. Both speed and track become more predictable than is the case earlier in the hurricane's existence and the meteorologists should give enough warning for evasive action to be taken. Although a hurricane can occur any time between June and Novem-ber, the worst period is from July to September. For that reason departure eastward from Bermuda should be made by mid-June.

Details of approach and landfall on Bermuda will be found in Chapter 20. St George's harbour is covered in Part III.

## Bermuda to the Azores

There are two choices regarding this passage. The first is to head north-east after departure until 38°N or 40°N is reached, before turning due east for the Azores. Unless a major cell of high pressure has formed much further north than is usually the case this should put one firmly into the belt of the Westerlies. There is also a good chance of a favourable current. The disadvantages are an increased distance to sail, and the fact that gales are common in these latitudes, particularly in May and June.

The alternative is to sail a course much nearer to the great circle, though it would still be wise to make some northing early on. On this route the likelihood of calms is considerably greater, but the chance of gales corres-pondingly less. The current will also be much less predictable, particularly in the earlier stages of the pas-sage. Although the general trend of the North Atlantic Current in this area is between east and south, giant eddies may form, setting at up to half a knot in almost any direction and frequently altering from day to day. Plenty of fuel may be needed if the passage is not to be a slow one. Choice of route will obviously depend on the size of

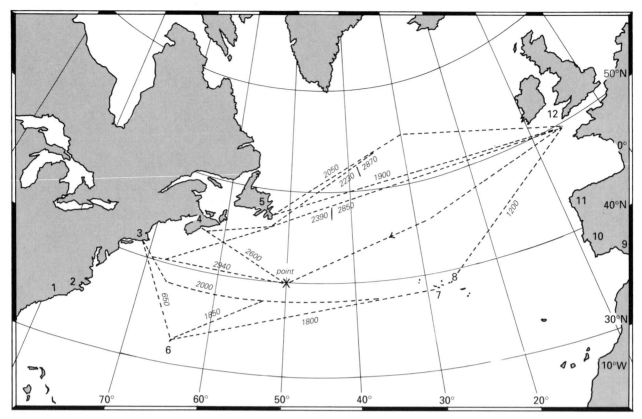

*Chart 36* Typical routes westwards in the middle and northern latitudes. Projection based on Admiralty Chart No 5095. Key to numbered departure/arrival ports: (1) Charleston, S Carolina; (2) Norfolk, Virginia; (3) Newport, Rhode Island; (4) Halifax, Nova Scotia; (5) St John's, Newfoundland; (6) St George's, Bermuda; (7) Horta, Azores; (8) Ponta Delgada, Azores; (9) Gibraltar; (10) Lisbon, Portugal; (11) Bayona, Spain; (12) Falmouth, UK.

yacht and the strength and priorities of her crew.

The Azores are well known for the extensive calm which often surrounds them and if possible enough fuel should be kept in reserve to motor the last 100 or so miles. Details of the approaches to the islands are given in Chapter 21, and entry details for the harbours of Horta and Ponta Delgada in Part III.

## USA or Canada to the Azores

This is most likely to be the choice of yachts leaving from the Chesapeake Bay or further north, and much of what has been said under the previous two headings will apply equally to the direct route.

From south of New York it should be possible to sail a great circle course, and enjoy favourable winds and currents most of the way. From further north the standard procedure is to head south-east to make a good offing and get well clear of the Labrador Current with its attendant fogs. Once around 40°N a direct course can be shaped for the Azores, though some skippers may prefer to continue a little further south. The first part of the passage will be within the hurricane zone, and it would be wise to be east of 55°W before mid-June.

## Azores to northern Europe

It is often necessary to leave the Azores under engine, and if fuel is limited the wind is most likely to be found first by motoring due north. Even if leaving with a good wind every opportunity should be taken to make northing until at least 45°N, aiming to cross it near 20°W. A direct course from this position should make the most of the east-going current (and avoid the south-east set towards Iberia) and there is a reasonable chance of favourable winds. In some years it may be necessary to work even further north before reaching the westerlies – it is worth listening to the BBC shipping forecasts even before the area covered is reached as the Atlantic synopsis may be useful.

If at all possible, landfall should be made before the end of August. The south-western approaches to the English Channel – and the rest of northern Europe for that matter – are notorious for the severe gales which often come through early in September. If entering the English Channel in such a gale, which is almost certain to come up from the south-west and later veer into the north-west, by far the best harbour to make for will be Falmouth, tucked behind the shelter of the Lizard peninsula. Details of both Falmouth and Plymouth will be found in Part III.

## Azores to Iberia or Gibraltar

There are two likely reasons for heading east from the Azores. Crews from northern Europe who are in no particular hurry may choose to break the passage homewards on the coast of north-west Spain, waiting there for a good forecast before crossing the Bay of Biscay. Others may be planning to cruise the west coast of Iberia before heading east to Gibraltar and thence into the Mediterranean. A few may cruise as far as Vilamoura or even Gibraltar before departing south-west for Madeira, the Canaries and the trade wind crossing.

Whatever the reason, there is a good chance of this being a pleasant passage, with northerly winds and a south-going current, both of which are apt to be quite strong. As the chance of north-easterlies increases on closing the coast, it would be wise to keep well to windward of the intended destination, to avoid a last minute slog against both wind and current. If continuing direct to Gibraltar, after rounding Cape St Vincent the current will tend towards the Straits as there is a permanent flow into the Mediterranean caused by the high rate of evaporation in that warm area. Winds may be variable.

There is certain to be considerable shipping off the coasts of Spain and Portugal, where poor visibility may also be encountered – see Chapter 11. There is also heavy traffic through the Straits of Gibraltar, where a Traffic Separation Scheme is in force.

## USA or Canada to Europe via the mid latitudes

The mid latitudes, so far as this passage is concerned, may be defined as a track passing south of Sable Island and the Newfoundland Grand Banks but well north of the Azores high pressure system. If the yacht is lying west of Cape Cod, the choice is either to sail south of the Nantucket Shoals or transit the Cape Cod Canal and leave from further north.

In either case, to reduce the time spent in fog and avoid possible icebergs, make for the vicinity of 40°N 50°W – point X on Chart 35. Up-to-date weather and ice reports may make it possible to shift this point further north and reduce the distance to be sailed, but the track may then coincide with the main shipping routes which it is preferable to avoid. If ice has moved particularly far south, it may be necessary to continue south of point X.

From point X, a great circle course can be sailed for most European destinations. Winds will be predominantly westerly, but may veer right around the compass as depressions pass through. West of 30°W up to a knot of north-easterly current may be experienced, but both the strength and northerly component diminish further east.

Those remarks regarding landfall made in the section entitled *Azores to northern Europe* apply equally to this passage, and to the following one.

## USA or Canada to Europe via the great circle

From anywhere in the north-eastern United States the great circle route to northern Europe runs close past the coast of Nova Scotia (well inside Sable Island) and thence to Cape Race on the south-east tip of Newfoundland. The winds are likely to be fair, but there can be a high incidence of fog and there will also be the weak adverse Labrador Current on this part of the route. St John's Harbour, 60 miles north of Cape Race, makes a good final port for provisions and stores. An up-to-date ice report should also be obtained.

From Cape Race or St John's, a great circle course can be shaped. Icebergs and/or fog may have to be contended with until around 40°W (crossed on this route at about 49°N), but east of 40°W normal North Atlantic conditions can be expected with a predominance of fair winds and current. Unfortunately, the Atlantic depressions spawned off Nova Scotia also favour the great circle route on their way to north-west Europe, and there is a good chance of at least one severe gale if crossing this far north. Larger seas may also be expected for much of the passage than if crossing further south.

## Passages westward

Any passage westward in the higher latitudes involves a lot of windward sailing and adverse currents with, in the latter stages, the chance of meeting ice and the certainty of fog on and to the west of the Grand Banks. For this reason few cruising yachtsmen opt to sail directly from northern Europe to Canada or the United States, more often going via the Azores and possibly Bermuda. The direct routes are largely the preserve of entrants in the single and two-handed races run biennially from Plymouth, UK to Newport, Rhode Island, who are in the main experienced yachtsmen well able to decide their own routes and prepared to take their chances with the weather. Whatever route is chosen, gale-force headwinds may be met repeatedly as depressions track past and at least some progress will be lost to the current.

A potential problem further south is the outside chance of encountering a hurricane – see *USA to Bermuda*

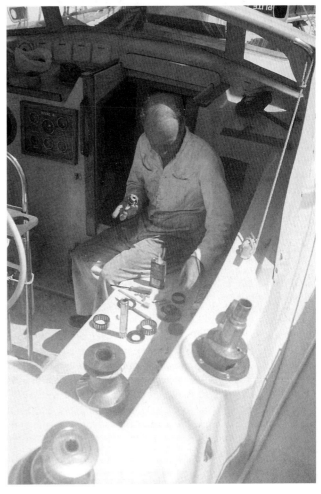

Routine maintenance is an ongoing activity and time must be allowed for it before and after the ocean crossing.
*Photo: Georgie McLaren*

above. Weather forecasts should be monitored carefully, particularly later in the season, and the yacht should be readied to take evasive action if necessary. Ideally, landfalls on the American coast south of 40°N should be made before the end of June.

## Azores to Bermuda

The route from Europe to the Azores (see Chapter 12), and thence either to Bermuda or direct to the United States, is the summer choice of most cruising yachtsmen. Though headwinds and an adverse current are inevitable for much of the passage it will at least be warm, and yachts with a good range under power may consider taking the rhumb line or great circle course along the ridge of high pressure which normally lies between Bermuda and the Azores. Extensive calms and flat to glassy seas can be expected on this route, and it will be very hot.

Yachts with less range under power would be wise to head due west, at least until beyond 50°W, only ducking further south if the forecast indicates that reliable winds are likely to be found – certainly both timing and route planning for this passage are easier than they used to be due to better weather forecasting. If departing from Horta, a long-term forecast can usually be obtained from the marina office.

It must be remembered that Bermuda lies well into the hurricane belt, as does the area between Bermuda and the North American mainland. The passage should be timed accordingly.

Details of the approaches to Bermuda will be found in Chapter 20, with St George's harbour covered in Part III. Onward routes are considered in Chapter 18.

## Azores to USA or Canada

Unless the destination is very far north, the first part of this route will be much the same as if heading for Bermuda. The best plan is to remain at around 38°N until south or south-east of one's landfall in order to minimise time spent in fog. A high proportion of headwinds and adverse current can be expected and plenty of fuel, stores and water should be carried. Details of approach and landfall are given in Chapter 19, but the remaining sections of this chapter are also relevant.

## Europe to USA or Canada via the mid latitudes

This passage follows much the same route as its reciprocal from west to east. Its objectives are also largely the same – to keep well north of the Azores high pressure system, but south of the Grand Banks and Sable Island. If the destination is west of Cape Cod the Nantucket Shoals should either be left well to starboard or landfall made north of the Cape and the passage continued close down the coast and through the Cape Cod Canal.

Exactly what route is taken in order to reach 40°N

50°W – point X on Chart 36 – will depend on individual choice. The shortest will obviously be the great circle, but many cruising yachtsmen will opt to keep further south in the hope of avoiding some of the strong headwinds likely to be found near 50°N. However heading too far south early on risks the boat becoming caught in the calms which so often surround the Azores – it would be wiser to keep at least 300 miles north of the islands. Whatever latitude is chosen, this passage will be largely to windward with an opposing current.

While point X is quoted as a suitable point from which an onward course can be shaped to the final destination, this could be altered in the light of up-to-date ice reports. While the temptation will always be to get out of the opposing Gulf Stream and into the favourable Labrador Current as soon as the ice situation permits, this also means heading into the worst of the fog.

## Europe to USA or Canada via the great circle

To sail the great circle from one's departure port to Cape Race at the south-western extremity of Newfoundland will be the shortest route in terms of distance, but not necessarily the fastest option and certainly not the most pleasant. Winds will be mainly from between north-west and south-west, and there is a high probability of heavy weather as Atlantic depressions track towards Europe. Landfall is likely to be made in poor visibility (Cape Race has a 40 per cent incidence of visibility of under two miles in July) and from 40°W onwards ice may be encountered.

## Europe to USA or Canada via the northern route

This cold, windy route is largely the preserve of entrants in various transatlantic races – and most cruising people would probably consider them welcome to it. The object is to go north of the succession of lows, which track across the Atlantic from west to east, in the hope of picking up easterly winds on their northern perimeters. A typical point to head for is 55°N 30°W, after which a great circle can be shaped to Cape Race, Newfoundland and beyond, giving Sable Island a wide berth. It is likely to be cold and the weather heavier than on the more southerly routes, but offers the potential of a fast passage. This is not guaranteed however, as if the lows pass unusually far north, bitter headwinds will be encountered.

The latter part of the voyage goes straight through the centre of the fog and iceberg zones, and many competitors in the transatlantic races have spoken of sudden and unnerving sightings. There is also a considerable amount of traffic, both merchant ships and fishing vessels making radar extremely useful. Jock McLeod, an intrepid singlehander with many ocean races to his credit, has this to say about the northerly route: 'It could be described as a long thrash to windward with a permanently foul tide, and should not be undertaken lightly'.

# PART III - PORT INFORMATION

## Selection

The following ports have been selected primarily as being suitable for landfall or departure, and most also have reasonable facilities for yachts. No attempt has been made to cover all viable harbours, for which local cruising guides should be consulted. Where possible ports have been chosen which, with due caution, may be approached and entered even in bad conditions.

## Coordinates

The coordinates given for each port, rounded to the nearest half minute, correspond with the lines of latitude and longitude shown on the appropriate port plan. However, users of GPS and other electronic position fixing systems should be aware that there may occasionally be a considerable discrepancy between the charted position of a feature and that given by their instrument. This is particularly true in the Cape Verde Islands and parts of the Caribbean.

Bearings, where given, are in true from seaward.

## Local time

Local time, in relation to Greenwich Mean Time, is quoted for each port. In many places, including Great Britain, clocks are advanced during the summer months. The dates when this operates are decided by the government of each country and may vary from year to year. The times quoted are therefore subject to the appropriate adjustment for local 'summer' time if applicable.

## Tides

Tidal heights quoted are Mean Level above Datum, as listed in the *British Admiralty Tide Tables* NP 202. All heights are given in metres.

## Charts

For most ports only British Admiralty and US Defense Mapping Agency charts are listed, together with the Imray-Iolaire Caribbean series where applicable and Canadian charts for Nova Scotia and Newfoundland. Others, sometimes on a larger scale, may be produced by the hydrographic office of the country concerned but are often difficult to obtain. Chart numbers change from time to time with the publication of new editions and an up-to-date Catalogue of Charts should be consulted before placing an order.

Where a chart is listed twice with different scales this indicates a relevant larger scale insert on a chart of an overall smaller scale.

## Buoyage

The IALA A system (red to port, green to starboard, plus cardinals) is standard in European waters, including the Azores, Madeira and the Canaries. The IALA B system (green to port, red to starboard, plus cardinals) is used throughout American waters, as well as Bermuda and the Caribbean, though few cardinal buoys will be found.

## Chartlets and harbour plans

The chartlets and harbour plans in this book should not be used for navigation: they are intended only to illustrate the text. In many areas developments are taking place which could render information out of date at any time. Current charts, pilot books and yachtsmen's guides should be consulted before attempting to enter any harbour for the first time.

## Caution

Ocean cruising yachtsmen should be aware that maintenance of navigation aids is poor in some areas, and even major lights may sometimes be out of service for long periods. Where a change is notified, it may also take several months for it to appear in *Notices to Mariners* and therefore on newly bought charts. If approaching in darkness and in any doubt at all about entry it is always prudent to stand off until daylight.

## Mailing addresses

It is always wise to arrange mailing addresses in advance, though in most cases mail will be held for all yachts. *Poste restante* is used in Europe, General Delivery in American-influenced areas, and the words 'Please hold for arrival' can do no harm. Wording should be kept clear and simple, without titles or honorifics, and the sender's address always given on the envelope (though by no means all uncollected letters will be returned).

## Duty free imports

Many countries allow yacht equipment or spares for a visiting foreign yacht to be imported duty free. It is always wise to enquire about current regulations concerning paperwork, labelling and notification before despatch, and any such parcel should be clearly labelled 'STORES FOR VESSEL IN TRANSIT' (unless other wording is specified locally). Personal imports are nearly always subject to duty.

# Ports

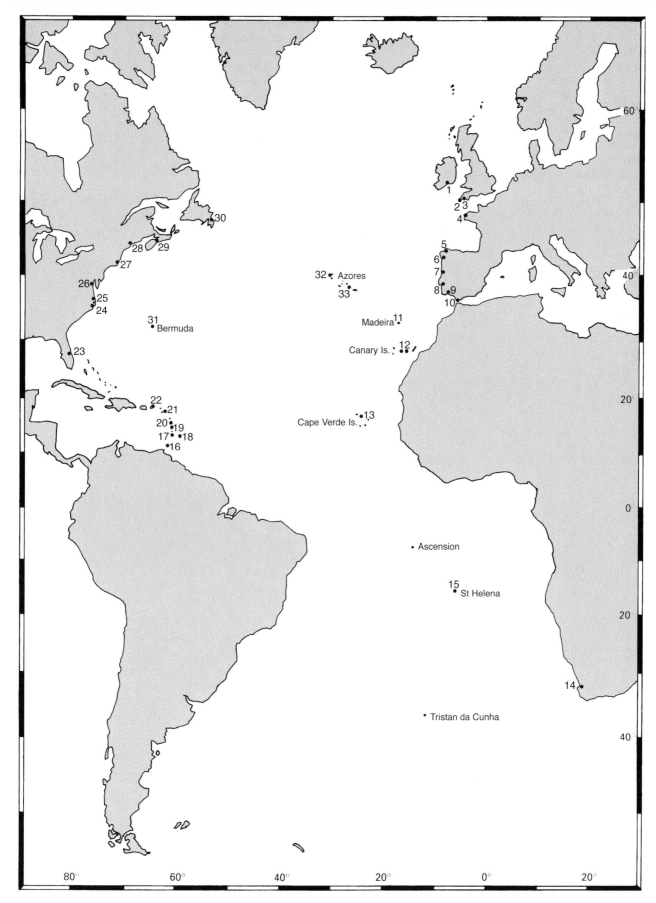

*Chart 37*   The North Atlantic showing ports covered in Part III.

| | | |
|---|---|---|
| *Springs*: 4.2 m/13 ft 10 in | *Flag*: Republic of Ireland | |
| *Neaps*: 3.3 m/10 ft 10 in | *Currency*: Punt (Irish pound) | |

*Tel/fax – Country code*: 353, *Area code*: (0) 21

| Charts | Admiralty | US |
|---|---|---|
| General | 2424 (1:150,000) | 35400 (1:150,000) |
| Approach | 1765 (1:50,000) | 35424 (1:50,000) |
| Harbour | 1777 (1:12,500) | 35421 (1:12,500) |

## General

On the south coast of Ireland and 60 miles east of Fastnet Rock, Cork Harbour is one of the world's finest natural harbours and a busy commercial port. Crosshaven on the Owenboy River is on the west side within the entrance. It is the home of the Royal Cork Yacht Club, and offers good shelter in all weathers. It is said that Sir Francis Drake once evaded the Spanish fleet by taking his ships up the Owenboy River to Drake's Pool.

Buoyage follows the European IALA A system.

## Approach

The distinctive promontory known as the Old Head of Kinsale [Fl(2) 10s 72m 25M] lies some 15 miles south-west of Cork entrance and is easily identified if closing the coast from the south or south-west. On approaching Cork

Harbour itself, landfall marks are a 24 m (79 ft) high hammer-headed water tower about 1.5 miles east of Roche's Point, and a high chimney with red and white horizontal bands and vertical red lights north-east of Corkbeg which shows clearly east of Roche's Point. A pillar buoy marking safe water is situated some five miles south of the entrance.

## Dangers

Pollack Rock with a least depth of 7.6 m (25 ft) lies 1.25 miles east-south-east of Power Head, itself 3.25 miles east of the entrance to Cork Harbour. The rock is buoyed and covered by a red sector of Roche's Point light. Daunt Rock with a least depth of 3.5 m (11 ft) lies nearly five miles south-south-west of Roche's Point. It too is buoyed and covered by a red sector of Roche's Point light.

## Radio

Cork Harbour Radio monitors VHF channel 16, working channels 12 and 14. The Royal Cork Yacht Club and Crosshaven Boatyard both monitor channels 16 and M.

## Entrance

Entry is between Weavers Point and Roche's Point, on a heading slightly west of north. At this point the entrance is about 0.8 miles wide, narrowing to 0.5 miles between Fort Meagher and Fort Davis. There are two well buoyed channels divided by Harbour Rock, but as this has a least

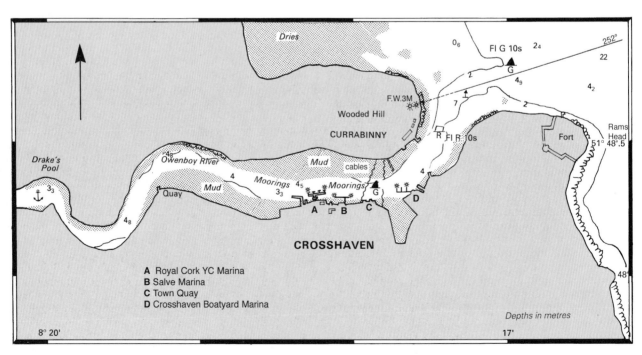

A  Royal Cork YC Marina
B  Salve Marina
C  Town Quay
D  Crosshaven Boatyard Marina

*Chart 38*   Crosshaven, Ireland. Based on Admiralty Chart No 1777.

ABOVE The west to east crossing by any of the northern routes can produce strong winds and fast sailing. *Photo: Jill Vasey*

LEFT Calm weather in mid-ocean, between Bermuda and the Azores. *Photo: Georgie McLaren*

BELOW A typical scene on Scotland's west coast: the most magnificent cruising ground in Europe. *Photo: Gavin McLaren*

Voyaging people rally round to help each other out. Here several yachts are assisting in clearing a badly fouled anchor. *Photo: Georgie McLaren*

LEFT Evening at Cape Clear on Ireland's magical south-west coast. This pretty harbour is typical of the many small, friendly ports in the area. *Photo: Georgie McLaren*

Fishing boats at Puerto del Son in the Ria de Muros fly regional and national flags in honour of a local festival. *Photo: Anne Hammick*

A stop amongst the skyscrapers of downtown Baltimore offers an interesting interlude during the passage up the American East Coast. *Photo: Liz Hammick*

LEFT The fall is the best time to cruise in the Chesapeake. Countless anchorages can be found where the yacht will be surrounded by magnificent colours. *Photo: Gavin McLaren*

BELOW The US Intracoastal Waterway provides an interesting, sheltered and convenient route between the Chesapeake and Florida. *Photo: Georgie McLaren*

With Grenada on the skyline, courtesy and quarantine flags are hoisted at the end of a passage up from the South Atlantic. *Photo: Mark Scott*

RIGHT Blue skies, sunshine and steady winds make Caribbean sailing a delight. *Photo: Michael Beaumont*

BELOW Anchored between islands in the Grenadines, the crew come ashore to enjoy the perfect beach. *Photo: Anne Hammick*

The marina at Horta in the Azores is a major cruising crossroads for the transatlantic yachtsman. *Photo: Georgie McLaren*

LEFT Maine, the finest summer cruising ground on the US East Coast. *Photo: Georgie McLaren*

The unmistakable skyline of New York is especially memorable when seen from the deck of one's own yacht. *Photo: Georgie McLaren*

With superb snorkelling and a breezy but sheltered anchorage, the Tobago Cays are amongst the most popular stops in the Grenadines. *Photo: Margaret Honey*

Approaching English harbour, Antigua, with the distinctive 'Pillars of Hercules' on the starboard bow. The entrance is almost invisible until well inshore, one of the reasons it found such favour with the British navy. *Photo: Anne Hammick*

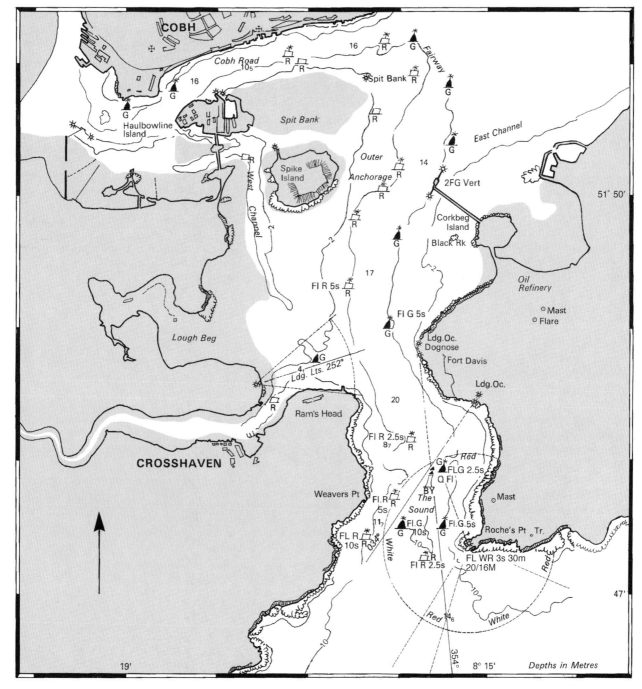

*Chart 39* Cork Harbour, Ireland. Based on Admiralty Chart No 1777.

depth of 5.2 m (17 ft) both buoyed channels and leading lights (two sets) can normally be ignored by yachts. Rock ledges extend up to 180 m (600 ft) offshore on either side. Two rocks, the Cow which always shows and the Calf which dries 1.3 m (4 ft), extend 180 m (600 ft) south of Roche's Point.

Tidal streams can run strongly in the entrance, reaching two knots at springs, though the strength of the ebb can be somewhat lessened by keeping to the west side of the channel.

On reaching Fort Meagher, allow at least 180 m (600 ft) clearance around Ram's Head before altering course westwards for the Owenboy River, passing close to the green cone buoy which marks the east end of the spit dividing the west channel from the Crosshaven channel. The latter is narrow, and no liberties should be taken with the buoyage or unlit perches. If approaching at night and unfamiliar with the area it would be wise to anchor and await daylight.

## Anchorage and moorings

There is no good anchorage in the lower river, which is crowded and has cables and numerous old chains fouling the bottom, but a mooring may be available through the Royal Cork Yacht Club or Salve Marina Ltd. Drakes Pool, 1.5 miles up the river, offers secure anchorage in delightful surroundings but has no facilities.

## Berthing and marinas

There are three marinas, run (progressing upstream) by the Crosshaven Boatyard (tel: 831161, fax: 831603) with about 100 berths, Salve Marina (tel: 831145, fax: 831747) with about 50 berths, and the largest, at the Royal Cork Yacht Club (tel: 831023, fax: 831485), with about 300 berths. All are on the south side of the river with depths of 2.0 m (6 ft) or more (Salve Marina can offer up to 4.5 m (15 ft), and usually have berths available for visitors.

## Formalities

Entry requirements may be waived in the case of an EU registered yacht arriving direct from another EU country (including the Azores), but if in any doubt it would be wise to check procedure with customs. In the case of a non-EU registered vessel, or if arriving from a non-EU country or with non-EU nationals aboard, hoist the Q flag on closing the land. Customs and immigration may be contacted through any of the marina offices or through the police station situated across the road from the Royal Cork Yacht Club.

## Facilities

*Boatyard* The Crosshaven Boatyard has a 40 ton travel lift, covered and open boat storage areas, and can handle most repairs and maintenance including rigging. Salve Marina call in a mobile crane if required
*Engineers* Salve Marina and Crosshaven Boatyard
*Sailmaker* UK McWilliams Sailmaker (tel: 831505, fax: 831700) just outside Crosshaven are the only sailmakers/repairers in the area and will collect and deliver
*Chandlery* At Crosshaven Boatyard and several in Cork

*Yacht club* The Royal Cork Yacht Club is the oldest in existence, having been founded in 1720. It has a fine clubhouse overlooking the river and an established reputation for hospitality to visiting yachtsmen
*Diesel* At all three marinas
*Water* At all three marinas and the town quay
*Electricity* At all three marinas
*Bottled gas* At Power's shop in Crosshaven
*Showers* At all three marinas
*Laundry/launderette* In Crosshaven
*Banks* One in Crosshaven (no credit card facilities) and many in Cork
*General shopping* Limited in Crosshaven, but excellent in Cork some 12 miles away
*Provisioning* Two stores in Crosshaven, more on the road to Cork and in the city itself
*Restaurants/hotels* Several locally, and a wide choice in Cork and the surrounding countryside
*Medical services* Hospitals in Cork

## Communications

*Mailing address* C/o any of the marinas (name + Crosshaven, Co Cork, Republic of Ireland) by prior arrangement
*Post Office* In Crosshaven
*Telephones* At the yacht club and elsewhere
*Bus/rail services* Buses to Cork, linking with the rail network
*Ferry services* Car ferry to Swansea in South Wales and to Roscoff in Brittany
*Taxis/car hire* Can be arranged by telephone
*Air services* Cork airport with flights to the UK and the Continent about ten miles distant. Train from Cork to Limerick for Shannon airport and transatlantic flights

| Charts | Admiralty | US |
|--------|-----------|-----|
| General | 2665 (1:150,000) | 36140 (1:200,000) |
| Approach | 154 (1:35,000) | 36181 (1:75,000) |
| | | 37041 (1:35,000) |
| Harbour | 32 (1:12,500) | 37042 (1:12,500) |

*Springs*: 5.3 m/17 ft 4 in     *Flag*: British (Red Ensign)
*Neaps*: 4.2 m/13 ft 9 in      *Currency*: £ sterling

*Tel/fax – Country code*: 44, *Area code*: (0) 1326

## General

Falmouth is the most westerly of the larger English Channel ports and is convenient for departure and landfall for passages south and west. It is one of the finest natural harbours in Europe, with much sheltered deep water and several inlets and creeks. There are sometimes shipping movements (tug assisted) entering and leaving the harbour and dock area, and also some commercial fishing. The entrance is well marked and safe under all conditions.

## Approach

After passing the Lizard [Fl 3s 70m 25M] the only danger is the group of rocks known as the Manacles, clearly marked on the chart and with an East Cardinal buoy to seaward. An easterly wind combined with a flood tide can produce a race between Black Head and the Manacles on the direct course to Falmouth. In these conditions, after rounding the Lizard, head towards the Lowland Buoy in about 50°N 5°W and thence east of the race towards Falmouth. Lobster pot marker buoys may be encountered anywhere in the area, either singly or in attached strings, and may be found well offshore. They are often poorly marked and constitute a hazard to a yacht under power, particularly at night.

## Radio

Falmouth Harbour Radio monitors VHF channel 16, and

Falmouth harbour, looking north-west. The commercial docks are on the right, with the river (buoyed as far as Falmouth Marina) winding up towards Penryn. *Photo: Falmouth Harbour Commissioners*

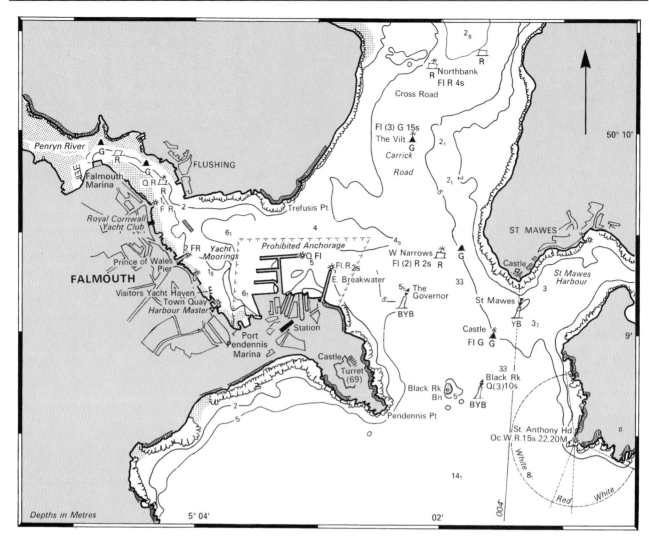

*Chart 40*  Falmouth, England. Based on Admiralty Chart No 32.

uses 11, 12 and 14 as working channels. The harbour launch *Killigrew* operates on channel 12. Both marinas monitor channels M1 and M2.

## Entrance

The entrance is passable under all conditions – even with a southerly gale and ebb tide a yacht can enter in safety if not comfort. The main channel lies between St Anthony Head and the East Cardinal buoy marking the unlit Black Rock Beacon, and should be used after dark. In daylight a yacht can safely pass either side of Black Rock with an offing of 100 m (350 ft).

There is local racing in Carrick Roads on two or three afternoons each week in summer. This is taken very seriously, particularly by the skippers of the gaff-rigged Falmouth Working Boats, and it would be most unwise to cut through the racing fleet.

## Anchorage and moorings

The main yacht anchorage is in the south-west of the harbour off the Town Quay, though anchoring too close to the docks is prohibited (see plan). Holding is generally good in firm mud, though there are a few soft patches, and protection adequate. In northerly winds more shelter may

also be found east of the moorings which run between Flushing and Trefusis Point.

The Royal Cornwall Yacht Club (tel: 312126, fax: 211614) has six visitors' moorings able to take up to 12 m (40 ft). The Harbour Commissioners (tel: 312285/314379, fax: 211352) have 18 moorings (with green pickup buoys) in the northern part of the harbour, some able to take yachts up to 24 m (80 ft). A detached island pontoon, to which yachts raft up, is normally in place from April until early October.

Land at either the Visitors' Yacht Haven or the Royal Cornwall Yacht Club.

## Berthing and marinas

There are two marinas in Falmouth in addition to the smaller Visitors' Yacht Haven run by the Harbour Commissioners. The latter is normally in place between April and October and can accommodate up to 50 boats, maximum length 12 m (40 ft). Some parts shoal to less than 1.5 m at low water springs.

Falmouth Marina (tel: 316620, fax: 313939) with about 330 berths is situated about 0.7 miles up the Penryn River. The approach channel carries a minimum of 2.0 m at all states of the tide, but though the river is buoyed the dredged channel at the marina is narrow and the beacons must be followed. Secure to the clearly marked reception pontoon until directed to a berth by marina staff. Falmouth Marina accepts some liveaboards and is a pleasant marina in which to winter.

Port Pendennis Marina (tel: 311113, fax: 313344), a marina village development with space for a few visiting yachts, lies in the southern part of the harbour between the docks and the town. The marina basin, containing about 60 berths, is enclosed within a single tidal barrier with access for about half the tide. An outer section is due for completion by 1998, and will offer a further 70 or so berths with some reserved for visitors.

## Formalities

Entry requirements are waived in the case of an EU registered yacht arriving direct from another EU country (including the Azores).

In the case of a non-EU registered vessel, or if arriving from a non-EU country or with non-EU nationals aboard, hoist the Q flag at sea and telephone customs on 0345 231110 immediately on arrival.

## Facilities

Falmouth has excellent facilities for yachts, and is a good place to make final preparations for an Atlantic crossing. All the following companies are in or near Falmouth itself – others exist elsewhere on the estuary:

*Boatyards/engineers* Many – Falmouth Boat Construction (tel: 374309, fax: 377679) across the water at Flushing can haul boats of up to 80 ft into a covered work area; though not a boatyard as such, Falmouth Marina (tel: 316620, fax: 313939) has a 30 ton travel lift; Port Falmouth Boatyard (tel: 313248, fax: 319395) has an 18 ton hoist and a large area of hardstanding; Challenger Marine (tel: 377222, fax: 377800) which uses a local crane service; and finally Pendennis Shipyard (tel: 211344, fax: 319253) in the docks area, which specialises in large to seriously mega-yachts
*Electronics* Sea-Com Electronics Ltd (tel: 376565, fax: 377465) in Penryn, about a mile from Falmouth Marina
*Riggers* Falmouth Boat Construction Ltd (tel: 374309, fax: 377679), plus the Boathouse chandlery (tel: 374177, fax: 318314) and Islington Ropeworks (tel/fax: 372838), both in Penryn
*Sailmakers* SKB Sails (tel: 372107, fax: 373792) and South West Sails (tel: 375291, fax: 376350) both in Penryn, and Penrose Sailmakers (tel/fax: 312705) who also specialise in traditional sails
*Chandleries* Marine Instruments (tel: 312414, fax: 211414) on the waterfront in Falmouth; The Boathouse (tel:

374177, fax: 318314) in Penryn with a branch at Falmouth Marina, and Challenger Marine on the Penryn road. Millers Maritime Bookshop (tel: 314542, fax: 318024) carries a good stock of cruising guides, etc
*Admiralty chart agent/compass adjusters* Marine Instruments
*Yacht clubs* The Royal Cornwall Yacht Club welcomes visiting yachtsmen and has a launch service, dinghy landing, showers, a bar and an excellent restaurant (tel: 311105). Closed on Monday
*Diesel* Falmouth Marina and the Visitors' Yacht Haven (summer only). The fuelling barge *Ulster Industry* is usually moored south-west of Trefusis Point
*Petrol* The Visitors' Yacht Haven, or by can from a filling station directly behind Falmouth Marina
*Water* On pontoons at both marinas and the Visitors' Yacht Haven, or by can from the Royal Cornwall Yacht Club
*Electricity* Falmouth Marina and Port Pendennis Marina
*Bottled gas* Falmouth Marina, the Visitors' Yacht Haven, Marine Instruments and elsewhere
*Showers* Falmouth Marina, Port Pendennis Marina, the Visitors' Yacht Haven and the Royal Cornwall Yacht Club
*Laundry/launderette* At both marinas and the Visitors' Yacht Haven, and in the town
*Banks* Several, with credit card facilities
*General shopping* Good, and anything lacking can generally be found in Truro about 10 miles away
*Provisioning* Several supermarkets, including a Pioneer close to Falmouth Marina and a large Asda at Penryn
*Restaurants/hotels* Dozens, at all levels
*Medical services* Falmouth Health Centre (tel: 317317) or Treliske Hospital in Truro. Many doctors, dentists and opticians

## Communications

*Mailing addresses* C/o Falmouth Marina, North Parade, Falmouth, Cornwall TR11 2TD; Port Pendennis Marina, Falmouth, Cornwall TR11 3YE; Falmouth Harbour Commissioners, 44 Arwenack Street, Falmouth, Cornwall TR11 3JQ or the Royal Cornwall Yacht Club, Greenbank, Falmouth, Cornwall TR11 2SW, all by prior agreement
*Fax service* At Falmouth Marina (tel: 313939)
*Post Offices* Several
*Telephones* Numerous, both coin and card operated
*Bus/rail services* Buses to Truro and other nearby towns. Trains to Truro for connections to London, etc
*Taxis* No problem
*Car hire* AVIS (tel: 211511) at Falmouth Marina
*Air services* Daily flights to London from Newquay airport about 30 miles away

| Springs: 5.5 m/18 ft | Flag: British (Red Ensign) |
| Neaps: 4.4 m/14 ft 5 in | Currency: £ sterling |

*Tel/fax – Country code: 44, Area code: (0) 1752*

| Charts | Admiralty | US |
| --- | --- | --- |
| General | 442 (1:150,000) | 37070 (1:200,000) |
| Approach | 1267 (1:75,000) | 37043 (1:75,000) |
| | | 37046 (1:75,000) |
| Harbour | 30 (1:12,500) | 37044 (1:12,500) |
| | | 37045 (1:5,000) |

## General

Plymouth is one of England's larger maritime cities with excellent facilities for yachtsmen and good communications. Local yards and suppliers are used to meeting the needs of long distance voyagers of all nationalities. Plymouth is a busy naval, commercial and fishing port but this does not conflict with the yachtsman's needs.

## Approach

The Eddystone Lighthouse [Fl(2) 10s 41m 20M] marks a small area of breaking rocks ten miles south-south-west of Plymouth. It is conspicuous by day or night and can be passed on either side at a distance of 500 m (0.3 miles). Rame Head and Penlee Point to the west of the entrance and the Mewstone to the east are prominent features. In clear weather, the high land of Dartmoor to the north-east and the radio masts on Staddon Heights on the eastern shore of the Sound assist identification. There is a gunnery range to the east of the entrance – call Wembury Range on VHF channel 16, transferring to channels 10 or 11, to check on firing times.

## Radio

Plymouth is under the jurisdiction of the Queen's Harbour Master – call Longroom Port Control on VHF channel 16, transferring to channels 08, 12 or 14. Devonport Naval Dockyard works on channels 13 and 73, and the ferry terminal at Millbay Docks on channels 12, 13, 14 and 16. Of the marinas, Mayflower International and Clovelly Bay both monitor channels M1 and M2, Queen Anne's Battery Marina and Sutton Harbour Marina channel M1 only. Sutton Harbour Lock monitors channel 16 and works on channel 12.

## Entrance

Plymouth Sound is nearly two miles wide at its entrance, over half of this being blocked by a detached stone breakwater. Although the breakwater is lit at both ends it would not be impossible for a stranger entering in bad conditions to spot the large fort in the middle, mistake it for one of the ends, and run up on the breakwater. The Western Channel can be used in all conditions, though gales from a southerly quarter may cause sizeable breaking seas off the breakwater end. Thence the recommended approach lies north-east across the Sound leaving Drake's Island to port. The whole area is very well buoyed.

Bridge Channel to the west of Drake's Island makes a convenient short cut if heading for the Mayflower Marina, but should not be attempted without either local knowledge or a large scale chart.

## Anchorage and moorings

There are no protected anchorages convenient to the city itself, though quiet anchorages and good shelter, depending upon wind direction, can be found in Cawsand Bay to the west of the detached breakwater, Jennycliff Bay beneath the prominent Staddon Heights radio masts and Barn Pool to the west of Drake's Island. The Tamar and Lynher Rivers afford some interesting exploring and many protected but remote anchorages. There are very few moorings available to visitors, though both the yacht clubs have a few.

## Berthing and marinas

There are four larger marinas in the Plymouth area, plus several smaller ones:

1  Longest established is the Mayflower International Marina (tel: 556633/567106, fax: 606896) which can take deep draught yachts up to 30 m (100 ft). About 30 of its 270 berths are reserved for visitors. The staff are helpful and facilities and security excellent, but without transport it is some distance from the city. Tidal streams run strongly across the approach, and in severe south-westerly gales the marina can become uncomfortable.

2  Queen Anne's Battery Marina (tel: 671142, fax: 266297) on the northern shore of the Cattewater can take yachts up to 45 m (150 ft) and 4.5 m (15 ft) draught, with 50 of its 240 berths reserved for visitors. A passenger ferry crosses to the Mayflower Steps in the historic area of the city or one can walk via the Sutton Harbour lock gate. Several major races, including those organised by the Royal Western Yacht Club of England, begin and/or end using the marina. There are clear written rules and, amongst other things, long-term living aboard is not permitted.

3  Sutton Harbour Marina (tel: 664186, fax: 223521) is entered via a 24 hour access lock (*see Radio, above*) situated north of the entrance to Queen Anne's Battery Marina. There is a floating pontoon inside the lock, which is floodlit at night. The marina is very convenient to the old city with its restaurants, shops and nightlife,

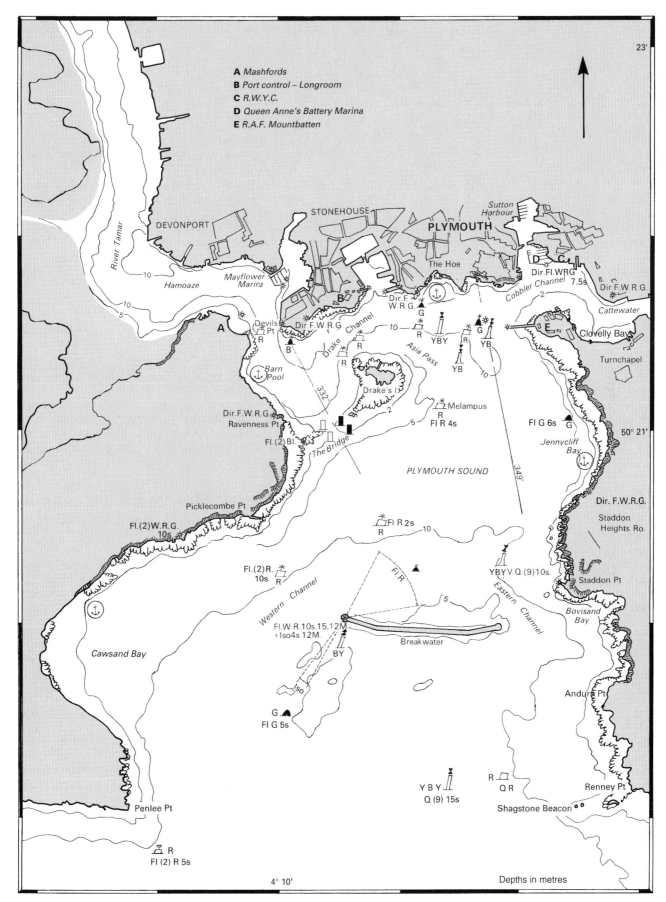

A Mashfords
B Port control – Longroom
C R.W.Y.C.
D Queen Anne's Battery Marina
E R.A.F. Mountbatten

23'

DEVONPORT

STONEHOUSE

PLYMOUTH

Sutton Harbour

River Tamar

Hamoaze

10

Mayflower Marina

The Hoe

D

C

Dir.Fl.WRG 7.5s

Dir.F.W.R.G.

Cattewater

B

Dir.F.W.R.G.

Devils Pt

R

Dir.F W.R.G.

G

10

R

YBY

R

YB

Cobbler Channel

2

E

Clovelly Bay

A

Barn Pool

Drake Channel

R

R

Asia Pass

YB

Turnchapel

332

Drake's I.

Melampus
R
Fl R 4s

10

Dir.F.W.R.G.
Ravenness Pt

2

5

Fl G 6s
G

50° 21'

Fl.(2) Bl.

The Bridge

PLYMOUTH SOUND

349

Jennycliff Bay

Picklecombe Pt

Fl.(2)W.R.G.
10s

Fl R 2s
R

10

Dir. F.W.R.G.

Staddon Heights Ro.

Fl.(2)R.
10s
R

Western Channel

Fl.R.

YBY V.Q.(9)10s.

Staddon Pt

Eastern Channel

5

Bovisand Bay

FlWR.10s.15,12M
+Iso4s.12M

BY

Breakwater

Iso

Andura Pt

Cawsand Bay

G
Fl G 5s

Penlee Pt

YBY
Q(9)15s

R
Q R

Shagstone Beacon

Renney Pt

R
Fl(2)R 5s

4° 10'

Depths in metres

*Chart 41*  Plymouth, England. Based on Admiralty Charts Nos 30 and 1267.

and as a result its two dozen or so visitors' berths are usually occupied. Sutton Harbour Marina is unsuitable for vessels of more than about 15 m (50 ft) overall.

4   Clovelly Bay Marina (tel: 404231, fax: 484177) lies opposite QAB on the south bank of the Cattewater, and is the newest of Plymouth's larger marinas. It was undergoing expansion at the end of 1997, including dredging to 2.25 m throughout and an increase in the already good facilities. There is a regular ferry service across the Cattewater to the Barbican.

Of the smaller marinas, Millbay Marina Village (tel/fax: 226785), in the eastern entrance to the old Millbay Dock opposite the Brittany Ferries terminal, is a residential development with berthing for property owners. There is limited space for visiting yachts, though berths may occasionally be available if arranged in advance.

Torpoint Yacht Harbour (tel: 813658) on the west bank of the River Tamar largely caters for annual berthholders but may sometimes have a vacant pontoon berth available. The same is true of Southdown Marina (tel/fax: 823084), also at Torpoint, which reserves five of its 50 berths for visitors.

## Formalities

Entry requirements are waived in the case of an EU registered yacht arriving direct from another EU country (including the Azores).

In the case of a non-EU registered vessel, or if arriving from a non-EU country or with non-EU nationals aboard, hoist the Q flag at sea and telephone customs on 0345 231110 immediately on arrival.

## Facilities

Many historic voyages have begun or ended in Plymouth, from the time of the Pilgrim Fathers onwards. It is hard to imagine anything a yacht might require which could not easily be found.

*Boatyards/engineers* Mashford Brothers Ltd at Cremyll (tel: 822232) is the largest yacht yard with slip facilities and capacity to service yachts up to 250 tons, 37 m (120 ft) LOA, 7.0 m (23 ft) beam and 3.5 m (12 ft) draught. There is a 25 ton travel lift plus boatyard facilities at Mayflower International Marina; 20 ton lift and facilities at Queen Anne's Battery Marina, 65 ton lift due to replace 25 ton lift at Clovelly Bay Marina, and 50 ton crane at Southdown Marina

Independent yards include A Blagdon (tel: 561830) on Richmond Walk near the Mayflower International Marina, A S Blagdon & Sons (tel: 228155) on Embankment Road, K R Skentlebury & Son (tel: 402385) at Laira Bridge Boatyard to the east of the city and the Multihull Centre (tel: 823900) at Millbrook

*Electronics* Plymouth Marina Electronics (tel: 227711) at Queen Anne's Battery; Ocean Marine International (tel: 500121) at Mayflower International, plus others

*Sailmakers* Ösen Sails (tel: 255056) will collect and deliver to all marinas, also Clements (tel: 562465) and Westaway Sails out at Ivybridge (tel: 892560)

*Chandleries* Seven or eight, including at least one at each of the larger marinas and Cloads on the Barbican (tel: 663722)

*Admiralty chart agent* The Sea Chest, Queen Anne's Battery (tel: 222012), which also has a wide selection of new and secondhand books

*Yacht clubs* Royal Western Yacht Club of England (tel: 660077) occupies upper floor rooms at Queen Anne's Battery; the Royal Plymouth Corinthian YC (tel: 664327, fax: 256140) has premises at the east end of The Hoe. Both make visitors very welcome

*Weather forecast* Posted daily at the larger marinas

*Diesel/petrol* Available at all larger marinas and Mashfords Boatyard

*Water* All marinas

*Electricity* All marinas

*Bottled gas* Mayflower International, QAB and Clovelly Bay marinas, and in the city

*Showers* All marinas

*Launderettes* Mayflower, QAB and Clovelly Bay marinas, and in Plymouth itself

*Banks* All major British banks, with credit card facilities

*General shopping* Excellent, as befits a major city

*Provisioning* Excellent

*Restaurants/hotels* Numerous at all prices, including at least one handy to each of the larger marinas

*Medical services* Freedom Fields Hospital (tel: 668080). Many doctors, dentists and opticians

## Communications

*Mailing addresses* C/o Royal Plymouth Corinthian YC, Madeira Road, Plymouth PL1 2NY; Royal Western Yacht Club of England or QAB Marina, both at Queen Anne's Battery, Plymouth PL4 0LP; Mayflower International Marina, Ocean Quay, Richmond Walk, Plymouth PL1 4LS or Clovelly Bay Marina, The Quay, Turnchapel, Plymouth PL9 9TF, all by prior arrangement

*Fax services* At Mayflower International (fax: 606896) and Clovelly Bay marinas (fax: 484177)

*Post Offices* Several

*Telephones* At all marinas and in the city

*Bus/rail services* Local bus services, coaches and mainline trains to London and elsewhere

*Ferries* Services to Brittany and northern Spain

*Taxis* Numerous private firms

*Car hire* All major agencies

*Air services* Plymouth airport, with regular services to London and the Continent

| | | | |
|---|---|---|---|
| *Springs*: 7.5 m/24 ft 7 in | | *Flag*: France | |
| *Neaps*: 5.9 m/19 ft 5 in | | *Currency*: French franc | |

*Tel/fax – Country code*: 33, *Area code*: (0) 2

| Charts | Admiralty | US |
|---|---|---|
| General | 2643 (1:200,000) | 37320 (1:150,000) |
| Approach | 798 (1:60,000) | 37328 (1:50,000) |
| | 3427 (1:30,000) | |
| Harbour | 3428 (1:15,000) | 37325 (1:15,000) |
| | | 37326 (1:7,500) |

## General

Brest has long been France's primary naval base, no doubt partly due to its protected and easily defensible position inside the relatively narrow Goulet de Brest some ten miles from the open sea. The Rade de Brest makes an interesting cruising ground, though some parts are reserved for naval use with the movement of yachts restricted and anchoring prohibited.

Brest is a large city of considerable historic interest, with excellent facilities.

## Approach

If approaching from northwards down the Chenal du Four, after rounding Pointe de St Mathieu Les Vieux Moines tower, Le Coq and Charles Martel buoys should all be left to port. The twin light towers of Le Petit Minou [Fl(2) WR 6s 32m 19/15M] should by then be visible, and be brought in transit with the grey tower of Pointe du Portzic [Oc(2) WR 12s 56m 19/15M] on 086°. Veer to starboard on approaching Le Petit Minou, but remain on the northern side of the Goulet to clear the Plateau des Fillettes shoal in mid-channel, well marked with buoys and beacons.

If entering from the south-west the Plateau des Fillettes shoal may be left to port, but good clearance must be allowed around the Pointe des Espagnols to clear La Cormorandiere wreck and white beacon.

## Radio

French coastal stations do not answer an initial call on VHF channel 16 unless it is a Mayday call. The commercial port working channel is channel 12, with channel 74 used in the military port. The Marina du Moulin Blanc may be contacted on channel 9, between 0800 and 2000 (0900–1200 and 1400–1900 on public holidays).

## Entrance

On approaching Pointe du Portzic the city, together with the large naval and commercial port complex, will be seen some two miles beyond. Yachts are unwelcome here, and should continue the further three miles to the Marina du Moulin Blanc, on the eastern edge of reclaimed land near the mouth of the Elorn River. The marina is approached via a narrow dredged channel, and the buoyage should be observed. A minimum of 2.5 m is carried even at low water springs.

## Anchorage and moorings

There are many sheltered anchorages within the Rade de Brest, but not adjacent to the port of Brest itself where anchoring is generally either forbidden, or the water too shallow.

## Berthing and marinas

The Marina du Moulin Blanc (tel: 980 22002, fax: 984 16791) is a large marina complex containing more than 1300 berths, of which one hundred are reserved for visiting yachts of up to 30 m. A central breakwater divides the marina into two parts, with reception, fuelling and visitors' pontoons on its northern side. The *Capitainerie* (harbour office) is near the root of this breakwater.

## Formalities

It is not necessary for a yacht registered in the EU to report to customs if arriving from another EU country, but failure to do so implies a formal declaration that the vessel complies with all the detailed customs and health regulations. Non-EU registered yachts, those arriving from a non EU-country or those with non-EU nationals aboard should report arrival without delay. All yachts must carry some form of registration, and it is important that this document is in date. Officials may visit yachts, sometimes boarding at sea.

## Facilities

*Boatyard* With 14 tonne travel lift and 6 tonne crane at the Marina du Moulin Blanc
*Engineers/electronics* At the marina and the Port du Commerce
*Sailmaker* At the marina and the Port du Commerce
*Chandlery* At the marina and the Port du Commerce
*Chart agent* At the Port du Commerce
*Compass adjusters* At the Port du Commerce
*Weather forecast* Posted daily at the harbour office
*Diesel/petrol* At the marina
*Water* On pontoons at the marina
*Shore power* On pontoons at the marina
*Bottled gas* At the marina, and many places in the city (Camping Gaz only available)
*Ice* At the marina
*Showers* At the marina

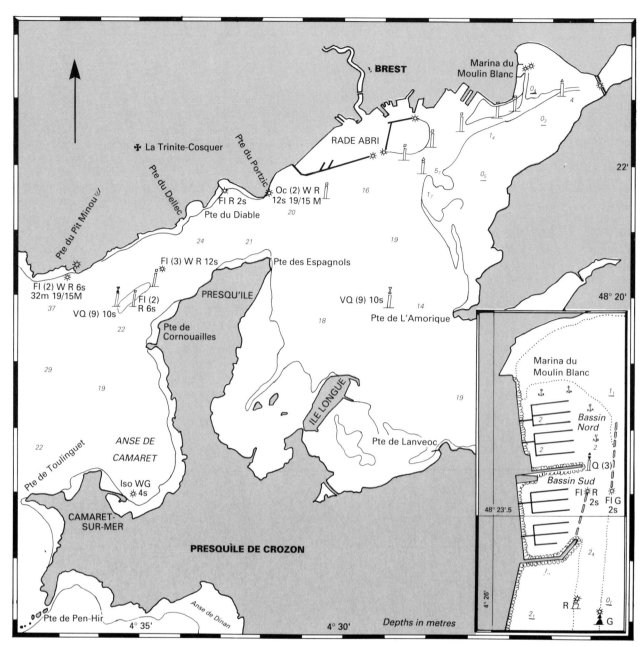

*Chart 42*  Brest, France. Based on Imray Chart No C36.

*Laundry/launderette* At the marina

*Banks* Currency exchange available at the harbour office, many banks in the city

*General shopping* Shops of all varieties in the city

*Provisioning* Grocery store in the marina, large supermarket on the road into Brest, plus many others

*Restaurants/hotels* Restaurant in the marina complex, plus many others

*Medical services* Good, as befits a large city

## Communications

*Mailing address* C/o Port de Plaisance du Moulin Blanc, 29200 Brest, France by prior arrangement

*Post Office* In the city

*Telephones* Kiosks at the marina and in the city

*Bus/rail services* Frequent buses into the city (although the marina lies three miles beyond the Port du Commerce, it is little more than a mile from the city by land). Trains from Brest to Morlaix, Rennes and beyond

*Taxis/car hire* Agency at the marina, plus bicycle hire

*Air services* Twice daily flights to Paris (not Sundays). Guipavas airport 10 km from city centre

# 5 LA CORUÑA, Spain

| | | | |
|---|---|---|---|
| *Springs*: 3.6 m/11 ft 10 in | | *Flag*: Spain | |
| *Neaps*: 2.8 m/9 ft 2 in | | *Currency*: Spanish peseta | |

*Tel/fax – Country code*: 34, *Area code*: (9) 81

| Charts | Admiralty | US |
|---|---|---|
| General | 1104 (1:1,000,000) | 37034 (1:300,000) |
| Approach | 1111 (1:200,000) | 37505 (1:156,800) |
| Harbour | 1114 (1:25,000) | 37506 (1:25,000) |

## General

La Coruña is a major city of Galicia with roots going back to Roman times, and although the newer parts of the city are largely commercial the older quarters are very picturesque and well worth exploring. La Coruña is a busy fishing and commercial port, also visited by cruise ships, and facilities are in general good.

Of the four marina pontoons the northern two are administered by the Sporting Club Casino, the southern two by the Real Club Náutico, an arrangement which can occasionally cause confusion. There has long been talk of turning the inner basin known as the Dársena de la Marina into a yacht harbour but so far it is no more than talk.

## Approach

Yachts on passage southwards across the Bay of Biscay may make landfall anywhere on the coast between Pta Estaca de Bares [Fl(2) 7.5s 99m 25M] nearly 40 miles to the north-east of La Coruña and Islas Sisargas [Fl(3) 15s 108m 23M] just over 20 miles to the west. An even better landfall would be Cabo Prior [Fl(1+2) 15s 105m 22M], about ten miles north of La Coruña entrance. The Torre de Hércules [Fl(4) 20s 104m 23M], which stands on the peninsula to the west of the harbour, was originally built by the Romans and is the world's oldest operational lighthouse. There are various banks and shoals in the approaches which, although not of depths to trouble yachts, can cause the seas to break severely in bad weather. In these conditions approach is best made from the west, on a bearing of no more than 145° on the Torre de Hércules.

Yachts anchored inside the Dique de Abrigo at La Coruña. The white port authority tower is visible from well offshore.
*Photo: John Melling*

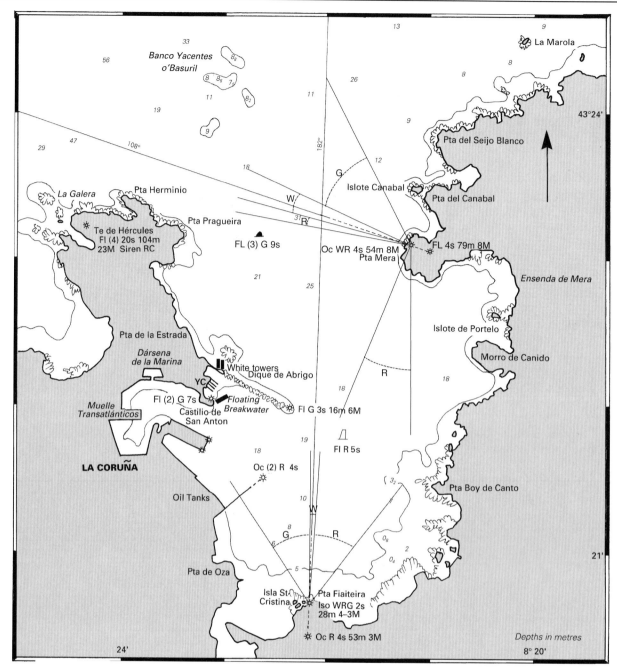

*Chart 43*    La Coruña, Spain. Based on a plan in *Atlantic Spain and Portugal*.

## Radio

Dársena Radio Torre de Hércules and La Coruña Port Control operate on VHF channels 12, 13, 14, 16 and 70. Both sections of the marina monitor channel 09.

## Entrance

The entrance is straightforward by day or night, with leading lights and marks easily seen. The Dique de Abrigo is a solid affair, visible from some distance and lit at its eastern end. The tall, white double tower near its root houses the port authorities as well as a restaurant with spectacular views. A floating breakwater some 200 m long lies off the Castillo de San Antón, running on an axis of 065°–245°. It is intended to protect the marina from wash, but is low in the water and may be difficult to see, particularly at night.

## Anchorage and moorings

There are a limited number of mooring buoys controlled by the two yacht clubs – consult the appropriate club boatman. It is also possible to anchor further out, in about 12 m over mud. However there is little shelter, holding is patchy and a tripline advisable. There appears to be no objection to landing by dinghy on the marina pontoons, whether on a mooring or anchored off.

Various other anchorages exist in the Ria de la Coruña, but none are convenient to the city.

## Berthing and marinas

As stated above, there is a relatively small marina shared between the Sporting Club Casino (tel: 209007, fax: 213953) and the Real Club Náutico (tel: 207910, fax:

203008). A few of the 250 or so berths are reserved for visitors. Parts of the marina are shallow and rocky. Berthing in both sections is either bow or stern-to with a holding off line provided.

The various basins to the west of the Castillo de San Anton, including the Dársena de la Marina, are currently used by fishing and commercial vessels. Yachts are generally not welcome, and the basins tend in any case to be unpleasantly oily and dirty.

## Formalities

In theory it is not necessary for a yacht registered in the EU to report to customs if arriving from another EU country unless there are non-EU nationals aboard, and in any case formalities in Spain have always been relaxed. However it can do no harm to check in, and non-EU registered yachts should report arrival without delay. Enquire at the yacht club as to current procedure.

## Facilities

*Boatyard* With 25 tonne travel lift at the Real Club Náutico
*Engineers/electronics* Enquire at the Real Club Náutico
*Sailmaker* Toldos Jar, at Calle Merced 40-42, a taxi-ride across the city
*Chandlery* Yacht chandlery at Regata, at Pasio Dársena, 13 Bajo; larger items from Effectos Navales Pombo on Avenida Primo de Riveira
*Yacht clubs* The Real Club Náutico (tel: 207910, fax: 203008) and Sporting Club Casino (tel: 209007, fax:

213953) both have premises by the marinas
*Diesel/petrol* In the marina
*Water* At marina berths
*Electricity* At marina berths (220 volt 50 Hz)
*Bottled gas* Camping Gaz readily available in the city. Calor Gas cylinders must be taken to a plant some miles to the south for refilling
*Showers* In both clubs
*Laundry/launderette* In the Real Club Náutico
*Banks* Many in the city, with credit card facilities
*General shopping* Excellent
*Provisioning* For a major stock-up it may be worth taking a taxi to the hypermarket outside the city. Otherwise there is good provisioning in the city, with a particularly good fruit, vegetable and fish market just a few minutes' walk from the marina
*Restaurants/hotels* Many and varied
*Medical services* Hospital outside the city

## Communications

*Mailing addresses* C/o the main post office (the *poste restante* office has a separate entrance around the back) or the Real Club Náutico by prior arrangement
*Post Office* This imposing building is on the main thoroughfare leading past the Dársena de la Marina
*Telephones* At the marina and throughout the city
*Bus/rail services* Local buses, trains to Madrid and elsewhere
*Taxis/car hire* No problem
*Air services* The airport at Santiago de Compostela about 60 km away handles many international flights

| Charts | Admiralty | US |
|---|---|---|
| General | 3633 (1:200,000) | 51100 (1:200,000) |
| Approach | 2548 (1:42,000) | |

*Springs*: 3.5 m/11 ft 6 in    *Flag*: Spain
*Neaps*: 2.7 m/8 ft 11 in    *Currency*: Spanish peseta

*Tel/fax – Country code*: 34, *Area code*: (9) 86

## General

Although the town is relatively small, Bayona is one of the most popular and useful harbours on this coast for the cruising yachtsman. The surrounding area is attractive with some pleasant walks, and the town contains many old buildings. The city of Vigo lies less than eight miles away as the crow flies (though considerably further by road), and any requirement that cannot be satisfied in Bayona can probably be met in Vigo.

Bayona was Columbus' first Iberian landfall on his return from the Caribbean in 1493 aboard the *Pinta*, after a less than warm reception in the Azores.

## Approach

Approach may either be made from the north, passing inside the Islas Cies and with Cabo de Home and Punta Robaleira [Fl(2) WR 7.5s 25m 11/9M] to port, or from the west, to the south of the Islas Cies and leaving the Islote Boerio (or Agoeiro) [Fl(2) R 8s 21m 6M] to port.

If coming from south of west Cabo Silleiro [Fl(2+1) 15s 83m 24M] may be the landfall, but it should be noted that the lighthouse is situated nearly a mile south of the headland of the same name, from which offlying rocks extend some distance northwards.

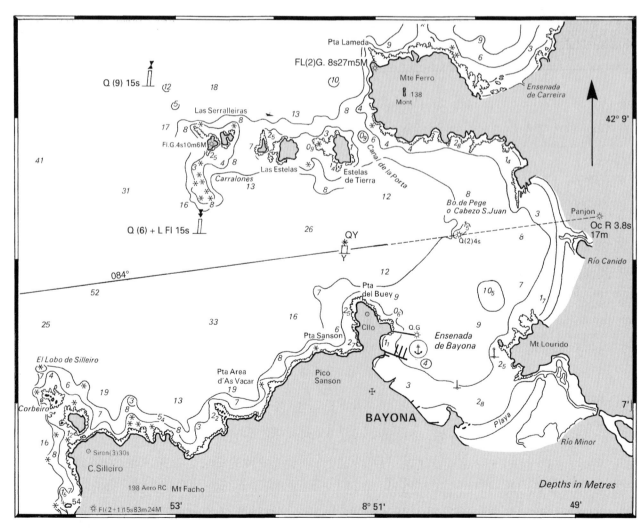

*Chart 44*  Bayona, Spain. Based on Spanish Hydrographic Office Chart No 9241.

The harbour and town of Bayona looking northwards with Monte Ferro in the background. *Photo: John Melling*

## Radio

The Monte Real Club de Yates, which runs the marina, monitors VHF channels 09 and 16.

## Entrance

If approaching from inside the Islas Cies, the intrepid may wish to try a passage, known as the Canal de la Porta, which leads between Monte Ferro and the easternmost of the three Estelas islands. However it shoals to 0.9 m so a large scale chart will be needed.

Most yachtsmen will prefer to use the main entrance, leaving Las Serralleiras [FlG 4s 9m 6M] and its attendant buoys marking the western extremity of the Ilas las Estelas well to port. The leading lights then bear 083°, the front one, Cabezo de San Juan, being on a shoal almost in the centre of the bay. In daylight both Pta del Buey and the breakwater head can be left close to starboard.

## Anchorage and moorings

The yacht anchorage, which has excellent holding, is to the south and south-west of the mole, outside the mooring buoys. The fairway leading to the fishermen's mole south of the marina should be left clear. The moorings are administered by the yacht club – consult their berthing master. The club does not like dinghies from anchored yachts being left tied to its pontoons, but there is generally space to leave a dinghy on the pontoons at the fishermen's mole.

## Berthing and marinas

The marina pontoons are administered by the Monte Real Club de Yates (tel: 355576, fax: 355061). The reception and fuelling berths are on the south side of the main jetty, and though much of the marina is occupied by local boats the berthing master is usually able to arrange a visitor's berth.

Alternatively there are two disused pontoons on the inside of the Dique de Abrigo, at one time administered by the Grupo des Puertos de Pontevedra. These are currently in a poor state of repair, with no facilities (but no charge either).

## Formalities

In theory it is not necessary for a yacht registered in the EU to report to customs if arriving from another EU country and crewed only by EU nationals, and in any case formalities in Spain have always been relaxed. However it can do no harm to check in, and non-EU registered yachts should report arrival without delay. Enquire at the yacht club as to current procedure.

## Facilities

*Boatyard* Repair facilities and a 15 tonne travel lift at the Monte Real Club de Yates. For major work, try Astilleros Lagos, Avda de Eduardo Cabello 2, 36208 Vigo (tel: 232626, fax: 291833), a family-run boatyard with a high reputation for quality where good English is spoken

*Engineers/electronics* Some facilities at the yacht club,

but for major work it may be necessary to go to Vigo

*Chandlery* In Vigo

*Yacht club* The Monte Real Club de Yates (tel: 355576, fax: 355061) occupies an imposing building overlooking the marina and bay. It has a large and comfortable bar and good restaurant

*Weather forecast* Posted daily at the yacht club

*Diesel/petrol* Fuelling berth on the south side of the marina main jetty

*Water* At marina berths

*Electricity* At marina berths (220 volt 50 Hz)

*Bottled gas* Camping Gaz available in the town. Calor Gas cylinders must be taken some distance for refilling

*Ice* At the yacht club

*Showers* In the basement of the yacht club

*Laundry/launderette* One road back from the waterfront

*Banks* Several in the town, with credit card facilities

*General shopping* Somewhat limited – Bayona is a tourist resort rather than a commercial centre or major town

*Provisioning* Several grocery stores plus a fresh produce market. Quite adequate to replenish supplies, but not equal to a major stocking-up

*Restaurants/hotels* Numerous. The Parador, a hotel converted from the Castillo de Monte Real, has attractive walks, a restaurant and a bar, all open to non-residents

*Medical services* Limited – best to go to Vigo if possible

## Communications

*Mailing address* C/o the Monte Real Club de Yates, Bayona, Galicia, Spain by prior arrangement

*Post Office* In the town

*Telephones* Booths at the yacht club and in town

*Bus/rail services* Buses to Vigo, linking with the rail network

*Taxis/car hire* Enquire at the yacht club

*Air services* National airport at Vigo, or international flights from Santiago de Compostela

| Springs: 3.5 m/11 ft 6 in | Flag: Portugal |
|---|---|
| Neaps: 2.7 m/8 ft 11 in | Currency: Portuguese escudo |

*Tel/fax – Country code*: 351, *Area code*: (0) 2

| Charts | Admiralty | US |
|---|---|---|
| General | 3634 (1:200,000) | 51100 (1:200,000) |
| | | 51120 (1:200,000) |
| Approach | 3254 (1:50,000) | 51109 (1:50,000) |
| Harbour | 3254 (1:10,000) | 51109 (1:15,000) |

## General

Leixões, with its well protected entrance, is the only real port of refuge on this stretch of the coast and can be entered in almost any weather. There is a small marina in the northern corner of what is otherwise a rather grim oil, fishing and general commercial port. Inevitably it can sometimes be rather dirty.

Leixões lies only a few miles north of the ancient city of Porto (Oporto) on the Rio Douro, the approach to which can be dangerous in onshore winds or swell.

## Approach

Compared to the coastline further north, the area around Leixões is somewhat featureless. The oil refinery 1.5 miles to the north is a good mark by day or night, with the powerful Leça light [Fl(3) 14s 57m 28M] lying between it and the town. South of Leixões the city of Oporto can be seen from well offshore.

## Radio

The Radar Station controls navigation within 18 miles of the port approaches, working on VHF channels 01, 04, 09, 10, 11, 12, 14, 16, 18, 20, 61, 63, 67, 68, 69, 71, 79, 80, 84. Port control uses channels 11, 13, 16, 19, 60, 61, 64, 74 and the pilots work on channels 14 and 16. The Marina monitors channels 16 and 62.

## Entrance

If approaching from the north, harbour regulations state that vessels must give the northern breakwater a berth of at least one mile. Not all fishing boats observe this, though there are dangers 200 m to its seaward side. During westerly gales the swell at the entrance may be heavy, but this is lost once within the breakwater. Head for the middle of the passage between the two inner moles on about 355°. At night the breakwater light may be difficult to identify against the bright shore lights, but from south of Leixões the Leça light on 350° leads through the inner moles. The marina mole has been extended and is now lit.

## Anchorage and moorings

It is possible to anchor in the angle formed by the marina's south-west wall and the main breakwater in 4.0 m or less.

## Berthing and marinas

The Marina Porto Atlântico (tel: 996 4895, fax: 996 5899) occupies the old fishing harbour in the northern corner of the main harbour. The south-east facing entrance is less than 50 m wide. All its 250 berths are normally occupied, but space will probably be found.

On arrival secure to the reception pontoon (to starboard on entry) and visit the marina office on the north mole. (Open 0900–1830 daily, or 2000 from mid-June to mid-September.) Berthing is either bow or stern-to with a holding off line provided.

## Formalities

The advent of the EU should in theory mean fewer formalities for EU registered yachts arriving from another EU country, but as of 1997 Portugal still required all foreign yachts to report their arrival, and their movements once within the country, to the relevant authorities. In this instance visit the marina office, taking passports, ship's papers and insurance documents. The Administração do Portos do Douro e Leixões occupies the upper floor. It may also be necessary to visit the administration office sited in the fort about 200 m from the marina on the main road.

## Facilities

*Boatyard/engineers/electronics* Practically any repair can be made at the larger yards, though geared more to fishing vessels than yachts. There is a 6.5 tonne travel hoist at the marina itself
*Sailmaker* In Oporto
*Yacht clubs* The Clube Vela Atlântico (tel: 995 2725) and Clube Nautico de Leça (tel: 995 1700) overlook the marina
*Diesel* On the south-west wall of the marina
*Petrol* By can from filling stations
*Water* On the marina pontoons
*Electricity* On the marina pontoons (220 volt 50 Hz)
*Bottled gas* Camping Gas available in the town
*Showers* Unisex showers in the marina building, otherwise at the Clube Vela Atlântico
*Banks* In the town, most with credit card facilities
*General shopping* Reasonable, but better in Oporto
*Provisioning* As above. There is a market at Matosinhos, best reached by taxi
*Restaurants/hotels* The Clube Vela Atlântico serves meals, but much more choice in Oporto
*Medical services* Best to go to Oporto if possible

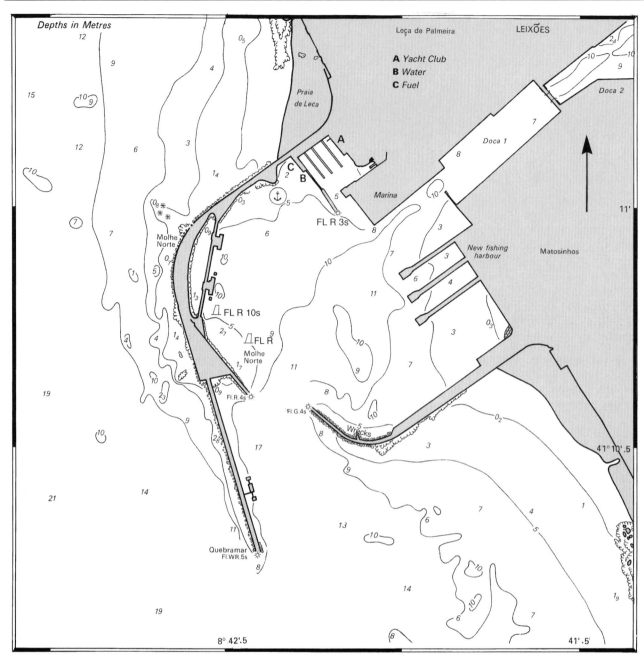

*Chart 45*   Leixões, Portugal. Based on Portuguese Hydrographic Office Chart No 58.

## Communications

*Mailing address* C/o the Marina Porto Atlântico, Molhe Norte, Leça de Palmeira, 4450 Matosinhos, Portugal, by prior arrangement, or the main post office

*Post Office/telephones* In Leixões

*Bus/rail services* The 44 bus runs from near the marina gate into Oporto, and links with the rail network

*Taxis* Readily available

*Car hire* In Oporto, or can be arranged through the marina office

*Air services* International airport at Oporto

| Charts | Admiralty | US |
|--------|-----------|-----|
| General | 3635 (1:200,000) | 51150 (1:300,000) |
| Approach | 3263 (1:25,000) | 51142 (1:75,000) |
| Harbour | 3264 (1:25,000) | 51143 (1:15,000) |

*Springs*: 3.8 m/12 ft 6 in      *Flag*: Portugal
*Neaps*: 3.0 m/9 ft 10 in      *Currency*: Portuguese escudo

*Tel/fax – Country code*: 351,  *Area code*: (0) 1

## General

Lisbon has been the capital of Portugal for more than 700 years. It occupies a splendid site on the north bank of the Rio Tejo (River Tagus) which allows sizeable ships to berth in front of one of the main squares, and is an intriguing city with Arabic undertones and a history of seafaring and exploration. The maritime museum (just inland from the Torre de Belém) is fascinating and not to be missed.

Provision for yachts visiting Lisbon is improving rapidly, and any remaining shortcomings are more than compensated for by the sheer interest of berthing in the heart of one of Europe's more handsome capital cities.

## Approach

If making landfall from north or west, the high cliffs of Cabo de Roca [Fl(4) 18s 164m 26M] are likely to be the first indication that the latitude of Lisbon has nearly been reached. Some five miles further south the lower headland of Cabo Raso [Fl(3) 15s 22m 20M] is rounded to port, the town of Cascais soon becoming visible.

In settled conditions there is a pleasant anchorage off Cascais, but it is exposed to wind or swell from south or west and is frequently rolly. A large marina is currently under construction close east of Santa Marta light, which it is hoped will be operational for the summer of 1999.

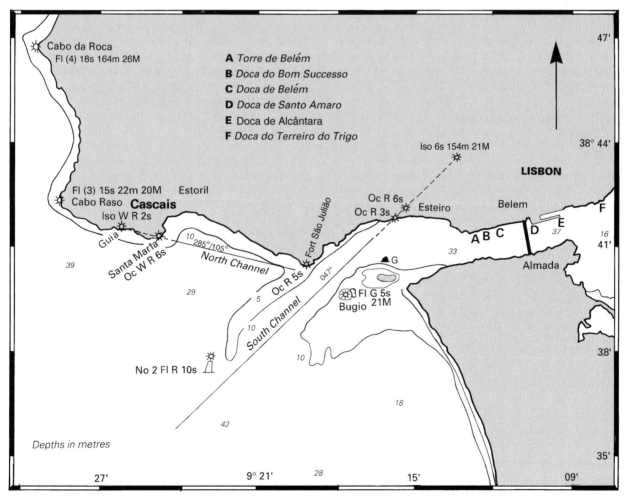

*Chart 46*  Lisbon, Portugal. Based on Admiralty Chart No 3263.

## Radio

Lisbon Port Control operates on VHF channels 01, 04, 09, 10, 11, 12, 13, 16, 20, 63, 67 and 69, with the harbour police on channel 11 and pilots on channels 14 and 16. The Doca de Alcãntara lock and swing bridge (NOT the marina) operate on channels 05 and 12.

## Entrance

The Rio Tejo is entered between Fort São Julião on the north bank and Fort Bugio to the south-east. The main channel lies on a bearing of about 050° from No 2 buoy, or follow the leading lights of Gibalta and Esteiro up 047°. Do not be tempted to cut Fort Bugio too close or turn too soon – best water is found near the northern bank. Tidal streams run at three knots at springs (more on the ebb after heavy rain) and in strong south-westerly winds there may be rollers on the bar.

There is a second channel close under Fort São Julião much used by fishing boats and other small vessels, particularly in thick weather or if stemming an ebb tide. However, the sandbanks of the bar may shift from time to time, and in addition to current large scale charts one eye should be kept on the depth sounder. Once inside the mouth, the Rio Tejo is deep with no unmarked hazards. The Ponte de 25 Abril suspension bridge has a clearance of 70 m (220 ft) – unlikely to worry any yacht!

## Anchorage and moorings

There is no yacht anchorage convenient to Lisbon itself, though there are a number of possible areas further upriver where it widens into the Mar de Palha (literally 'Sea of Straw', or reeds).

## Berthing and marinas

There are currently five marinas in Lisbon, not all of which accept visitors, with a sixth under construction further east. As the situation regarding visiting yachts appears to change relatively frequently, brief details of all are given below.

All the yacht harbours are built inside old commercial docks – be prepared for the tidal set across their often narrow entrances. Not only will it set the yacht sideways, but may also tend to slew her round during those seconds when the bow is in the calm water of the entrance and the stern still in the moving river.

Taken from west to east, those docks used by yachts comprise:

1 The Doca do Bom Successo (tel: 301 3227), just upstream of the ornate (and largely original) Torre de Belém which is floodlit at night. Once the preferred berth for foreign yachts it is now full of local boats. Depths are claimed as 3.0 m, and fuel is available.
2 The Doca de Belém (tel: 363 1246), just beyond the striking monument to Prince Henry the Navigator, which is also floodlit. Again, chock-a-block with local yachts. Fuel is available, but depths shoal to 1.5 m at low water.
3 The Doca de Santo Amaro (tel: 392 2011/2, fax: 392 2038), just east of the suspension bridge (which can

make it noisy). There is a reception pontoon opposite the (narrow) entrance, and a few of the 300 or so berths are normally reserved for visitors. Depths shoal from 4.0 m at the entrance to 0.5 m at the back.
4 The Doca de Alcântara (tel: 392 2011, fax: 392 2038), which contains some 200 berths, many of them reserved for visitors, and is currently the first place to try. The dock itself is more than 0.5 miles long and it seems likely that further pontoons may be added in the future. It is entered about a mile upstream of the suspension bridge via an entry channel crossed by a swing bridge. Until recently it was a purely commercial dock and is still used by ships of considerable size – for this reason it can sometimes be oily. The marina is at the far (western) end of the basin. The pontoons are equipped with fingers and have water and electricity but fuel is not available. Security is good via a gated fence.

The swing bridge (NOT the marina) operates on channels 05 and 12. Opening times appear to change every year, but are normally once every hour during the morning and about every two hours in the afternoon, slightly less frequently at weekends. There is a waiting pontoon in the entrance close east of the bridge.
5 The Doca do Terreiro do Trigo, which is also known as the Marina Aporvela (tel: 887 6854, fax: 887 3885), and is considerably further upstream near the old part of the city, just beyond the Doca de Marinha which is reserved for naval use. It is run by the Portuguese Sail Training Organisation, and although normally occupied by their vessels may occasionally have space for a few visiting yachts. Depths are less than 2.0 m at low water springs, though the bottom is such soft mud that it hardly matters.
6 A new 500 berth marina is under construction in the Doca dos Olivais, further up the estuary. It is hoped that its opening will coincide with Expo 98.

## Formalities

The advent of the EU should in theory mean fewer formalities for EU registered yachts arriving from another EU country, but as of 1997 Portugal still required all foreign yachts to report their arrival, and their movements once within the country, to the relevant authorities. The skipper should initially report to the marina office with ship's papers and all crew's passports, and may then have to visit both *Guarda Fiscal* (immigration) and *Alfandega* (customs).

A Port Control launch may intercept the yacht while entering Lisbon and officials come aboard. It would be as well to have all necessary paperwork to hand. This does not exempt the skipper from formal clearance once berthed.

## Facilities

*Boatyards/engineers/electronics* Good facilities are available in Lisbon, though two of the yards, Estaleiro Venancio at Amora and Estaleiro Jose Gouveia at Porto Brandao, are on the south bank of the Tejo. There are many others – ask marina staff or enquire at the Associação Naval de Lisboa at the Doca de Belém, where there is a boatyard with travel lift and also a scrubbing grid

*Sailmaker* Velamar in Rua do Giestal, or enquire at the marina office

*Chandlery* J Garraio, Avenida 24 Julho 2 (tel: 347 3081), and Gordhino, both in the Cais Sodré area near the Estoril train terminal

*Charts* The Instituto Hidrografico (tel: 395 5119/5124, fax: 396 0515), Rua das Trinas 49 (the shop door is on the side of the building, on Rua Garoa de Orta), publishes Portuguese charts and pilots. Also Godhino and Garraio (see above), or G Vieria, Travessa do Carvalho 15-1, 1200 for US DMA charts

*Yacht club* The Associação Naval de Lisboa has premises overlooking the Doca de Belém. Aporvela have their headquarters at the Doca do Terreiro do Trigo

*Weather forecast* A five-day forecast is available, in English, from the Lisbon meteorological office on tel: 848 3961. A small charge is made

*Diesel* Not available at either the Doca de Alcântara or Doca de Santo Amaro. The Shell wharf on the south bank about a mile below the suspension bridge will serve yachts

*Water* In all the marinas

*Electricity* In all the marinas (220 volt 50 Hz)

*Bottled gas* Camping Gaz readily available in Lisbon. Calor Gas bottles must be taken to the filling plant outside the city

*Showers* At the Doca de Belém and Doca do Terreiro do Trigo, plus a shower block between the Doca de Santo Amaro and Doca de Alcântara shared by both marinas

*Laundry/launderette* Several in the city

*Banks* Many, with credit card facilities. Banking hours 0830–1200 and 1345–1430

*General shopping* Excellent

*Provisioning* Very good – there are several large supermarkets in the city, one within five minutes' walk of the Doca de Alcântara, and a hypermarket on the road to Cascais

*Restaurants/hotels* Many and varied. Some bars and restaurants feature live *fado* singing

*Medical services* The British Hospital, Rua Saraiva de Carvalho 49 (tel: 363 161)

## Communications

*Mailing address* Probably best c/o the Doca de Alcântara, 1300 Alcântara, Lisbon, Portugal by prior arrangement, though there is an entire building adjacent to the main post office given over to nothing but *poste restante*

*Post Office/telephones* Many. Stamps can be bought at any shop displaying the green *correio* sign

*Bus/tram/rail services* Frequent buses and trams between the Belém area and central Lisbon. Trains to Cascais every 30 minutes via Belém and Estoril

*Taxis/car hire* No problem

*Air services* Lisbon has an international airport

Yachts berthed in the Doca de Alcântara, within walking distance of Lisbon city centre. Several ships can be seen in the commercial part of the vast 900 m long basin. *Photo: Anne Hammick*

| Charts | Admiralty | US |
|---|---|---|
| General | 89 (1:175,000) | 51160 (1:300,000) |
| | – | 51155 (1:150,000) |

*Springs*: 3.6 m/11 ft 10 in     *Flag*: Portugal
*Neaps*: 2.8 m/9 ft 2 in     *Currency*: Portuguese escudo

*Tel/fax – Country code*: 351, *Area code*: (0) 89

## General

Begun in 1971, Vilamoura Marina is one of Portugal's old-est purpose-built yacht harbours, dredged in a lagoon just inside the coastline and fringed by a large development of villas, hotels, a casino and a golf course. There is a good beach within a short dinghy ride, or within walking dis-tance if berthed on the west side of the basin.

Vilamoura is a popular and relatively safe place to leave a yacht – possibly between a summer passage southwards and the late autumn passage to Madeira, the Canaries and beyond – in which case its proximity to Faro airport is likely to be a significant advantage.

## Approach

The Algarve coast is low and relatively featureless, but the white Hotel Dom Pedro building just to the east of the entrance may be visible from some distance. Further east are the tower blocks of Quarteira and Faro airport. Vilamoura has its own powerful light [Fl 10s 17m 19M], and is bracketed by Ponta de Alfanzina [Fl(2) 15s 61m 29M] some 17 miles to the west and Cabo de Santa Maria [Fl(4) 17s 49m 25M] about 12 miles to the south-east.

## Radio

Harbour control operates on VHF channels 20 and 62 from 0900–2100 except Sundays. Hours are slightly shorter out of season. English is spoken.

## Entrance

Two 500 m moles converge to form an entrance 100 m wide and facing south-east, which can become dangerous in strong southerlies. Although the moles are lit, the many moored fishing boats and empty moorings in the outer harbour are not. The entrance to the inner harbour is about 60 m wide, with a long reception pontoon on its western side in front of the marina office and control tower (from which Vilamoura light operates).

In 1998 it was reported that depths at datum in the entrance were no more than 1.6 m. Although plans for dredging were in hand, no date had yet been set.

## Anchorage and moorings

All berths are alongside.

## Berthing and marinas

As elsewhere it is worth contacting Vilamoura Marina (tel: 302923/7, though it is unlikely that there will not be a berth available. Secure to the reception pontoon and call at the marina office which overlooks it to complete for-malities and be assigned a berth. Depths vary from 3.3 m to 2.0 m, with 4.0 m in the entry basin. The helpful staff speak English, German and other languages.

## Formalities

All formalities are handled at the marina office, which lies just behind the reception pontoon on the west side of the

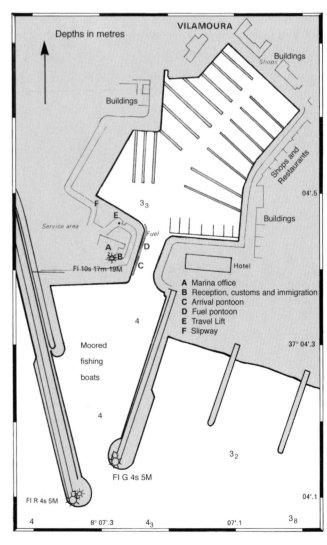

*Chart 47*   Vilamoura, Portugal. Based on a plan by the Marina de Vilamoura.

entrance. In the past Vilamoura had a reputation for particularly bureaucratic customs and immigration officials, but thankfully this is no longer the case. Even so, a careful if discreet watch is kept on the movement of all yachts on the Algarve coast due to the activities of drug smugglers from North Africa.

## Facilities

*Boatyard* Near the marina office, with 60 tonne travel lift and 6 tonne mobile crane. Yachts can be laid up ashore but there are no undercover facilities

*Ramp/drying grid* Tidal grid for boats drawing less than 2 m/6 ft 6 in, or dry out on the beach in the south-west corner of the marina. Check at low water first

*Engineers/electronics/sailmaker* In the boatyard area. Most major diesel engine manufacturers have agents in Faro or Portimão

*Chandlery* Overlooking the boatyard area

*Yacht club* There is a Club Náutico (tel: 302536), with bar and restaurant, next to the marina office. Crews of visiting yachts have free membership

*Diesel* Fuel pumps at the north end of the reception pontoon

*Water* At all berths and the fuel pontoon

*Electricity* At all berths and the fuel pontoon (220 volt 50 Hz)

*Bottled gas* At the chandlery. Camping Gaz exchanges and Calor Gas cylinders refilled

*Ice* At the supermarkets and the chandlery

*Showers* Behind the marina office, and on the east side of the marina basin. Access by card only

*Launderettes* In the shower blocks and in the commercial area north-west of the marina

*Banks* Several around the marina, with credit card facilities

*General shopping* Tourist and general shops surround the marina basin

*Provisioning* Several small supermarkets near the marina, plus a large market in Quarteira

*Restaurants/hotels* Overlooking the marina, and in Quarteira

*Medical services* English-speaking doctor(s) in Faro. Consult the marina office

## Communications

*Mailing address* C/o Marina Vilamoura, 8125 Quarteira, Algarve, Portugal, by prior arrangement

*Fax service* At the marina office (fax: 302928)

*Post Office* In Quarteira, though stamps can be bought at any shop displaying the green *correio* sign

*Telephones* Several booths around the marina basin, accepting either money or cards. Mobile phones can be rented from the marina office

*Bus/rail services* Bus services to Faro (40 minutes) and Lisbon (4 1/2 hours)

*Taxis/car hire* In the commercial area or through the marina office

*Air services* Faro international airport is 20 minutes by taxi, 40 minutes by bus. There is also a small airport at Vilamoura itself

*Springs*: 1.0 m/3 ft 3 in    *Flag*: British (Red Ensign)
*Neaps*: 0.7 m/2 ft 3 in    *Currency*: Gibraltar £ and £ sterling

*Tel/fax – Country code*: 350, *Area code*: none

| Charts | Admiralty | US |
|--------|-----------|-----|
| General | 92 (1:400,000) | 52040 (1:300,000) |
| | 773 (1:300,000) | |
| Approach | 142 (1:100,000) | 52039 (1:100,000) |
| Harbour | 1448 (1:25,000) | 52043 (1:15,000) |
| | 144 (1:10,000) | |

## General

Gibraltar is a British colony, self-governing through an elected House of Assembly. It has withstood a number of Spanish sieges, but since 1985 the border with Spain has been open on both sides. Tourism is the major industry, though its importance in banking and as a tax haven is growing. The population is an ethnic mixture of all the Mediterranean races as well as British, and while English is the official language much Spanish is also spoken.

Though somewhat off the beaten track so far as the average Atlantic cruise is concerned, Gibraltar is a good place for major repairs or to lay up, particularly for those with a limited command of foreign languages. It is also considerably quicker and easier to get imported items through customs in Gibraltar than in many other places – yacht equipment sent from abroad addressed to the yacht and marked 'Ship's Stores In Transit' will normally be admitted duty free, though personal imports are usually subject to duty. It may actually be cheaper to have equipment flown in than to buy locally.

## Approach

The Rock of Gibraltar is totally unmistakable from both west and east. After dark the Aeromarine light flashes the letters GB in Morse from high on the rock itself [R 10s 405m 30M], with the sectored Europa Point light [Iso W 10s 49m 21M, Oc R 10s 17m and FR 44m 17M] near its southern tip. The airport, just to the north of the customs berth and two of the three marinas, is also well lit.

Gibraltar Bay has deep water everywhere except for the offshore reefs on its western side, from Pta Carnero to just south of Algeciras. Depths in the area north of the airstrip (where a new, Spanish-owned marina has recently been completed) also shelve gradually.

## Radio

Port Control operates on VHF channels 06, 12, 13, 14 and 16, and the pilots on channels 14 and 16. Marina Bay and Queensway Quay Marina operate daily on channel 73,

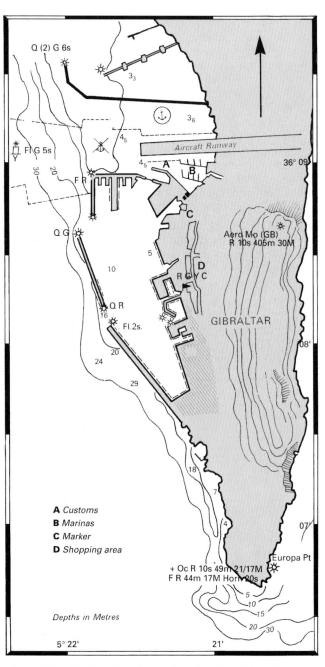

*Chart 48*    Gibraltar. Based on Admiralty Chart No 144.

0830–2230 and 0830–2145 respectively with slightly shorter hours in winter. Sheppard's Marina operates on channel 71, weekdays only, 0900–1255 and 1430–1800.

## Entrance

If making for one of the two northern marinas, head north-east into Gibraltar Bay past the long breakwaters of the naval and commercial port. The airport runway will be seen ahead – both Marina Bay and Sheppard's Marina lie in the angle formed between the North Mole and the run-

Marina Bay, Gibraltar, with Sheppard's Marina behind. *Photo: Anne Hammick*

way. Note that before securing at either marina yachts must first call at the reporting station opposite – *see Formalities, below*.

If heading for Queensway Quay Marina, pass between the south mole and the detached mole (both lit), from which the marina entrance (also lit) will be seen about 650 m ahead. This entrance can be confusing if approached for the first time after dark, as two long floating pontoons produce a very distinct 'S' bend (an attempt to keep swell out). If berthing at Queensway Quay Marina the requirement to first visit the reporting station is waived – *see Formalities, below*.

## Anchorage and moorings

It is possible to anchor north of the runway, though this is not encouraged. Holding is good in 4–5 m over sand. As the border runs close north of the runway most of this anchorage is actually in Spain.

## Berthing and marinas

Three marinas serve Gibraltar, the northern two being old-established while Queensway Quay is relatively new. All tend to be full and it is wise to telephone in advance. Otherwise contact via VHF on approach.

*Marina Bay* (tel: 73300, fax: 42656) is the largest of the three with about 200 berths. The reception berth is alongside the office towards the outer end of the main pier – office hours are 0800–2000 daily. Proof of insurance will be required.

*Sheppard's Marina* (tel: 75148/77183, fax: 42535) was established in 1961 and is very much a working boatyard with comprehensive repair and maintenance facilities. Arrivals berth alongside the pontoon extending south-west from the main pier. Many of its 140 berths are bow or stern-to without finger pontoons. Office hours are 0900–1255 and 1430–1800, weekdays only.

*Queensway Quay Marina* (tel: 44700, fax: 44699) opened in March 1994 as part of a rather attractive wharfside development. It has the advantage over the older marinas of greater distance from the dust and noise of the airport, and being a bare five minute walk from the town centre. The staff are noted for being particularly helpful and friendly. Problems with swell entering the marina in westerly gales have led to the dog-leg entrance described above and the re-siting of the main pontoons from a north/south axis to an east/west axis, which appear to have done the trick. Office hours are 0830–2145 in winter and 0830–2015 in summer.

## Formalities

Gibraltar is not a part of the EU and all yachts must observe the formalities. If making for Marina Bay or Sheppard's Marina yachts must first call at the reporting station (WATERPORT) on the north mole opposite the western end of the airport runway. The station flies the 'Q' flag by day and has an illuminated sign at night. Visitors to Queensway Quay Marina may complete customs formalities by fax from the marina office. In both cases normal particulars of vessel and crew will be required. Any crew member leaving the yacht, whether to move ashore, to another vessel or to leave by air, must be reported by the skipper to the police and the crew list amended accordingly. The same applies to new arrivals. Yacht departures are notified to the marina office, which informs the relevant authorities. Quarantine restrictions no longer apply to animals aboard yachts, though they should be declared on arrival.

## Facilities

*Boatyards* Gun Wharf Ltd (further south inside the main commercial harbour) can handle vessels up to 200 tonnes. It has an excellent reputation but is not cheap. Sheppard's Marina has a 40 tonne travel hoist and a 10 tonne crane, and permits DIY work

*Engineers/electronics* At Sheppard's Marina and elsewhere

*Sailmakers* At Gun Wharf and elsewhere

*Chandleries* At all three marinas, a branch of Pumpkin Marine & Leisure at 15 Watergardens (tel: 71177, fax: 42610), and others

*Chart agent* Gibraltar Chart Agency Ltd, 4 Bayside Road, Gibraltar (tel/fax: 76293)

*Yacht club* The old-established Royal Gibraltar Yacht Club (tel: 78897) welcomes visiting yachtsmen as honorary members while in port

*Weather forecast* Posted at the marinas, and broadcast on the English-language radio stations

*Diesel* At the Shell jetty near the customs office

*Water* At the Shell jetty and at marina berths

*Bottled gas* Camping Gaz exchanges in town. Calor Gas cylinders (butane) can be refilled at four hours' notice at the Shell jetty. Tanks over five years old require a test certificate

*Ice* At the marinas

*Showers* At the marinas

*Laundry/launderette* At Marina Bay and Queensway Quay, and in the town

*Banks* At Marina Bay and in the town, with credit card facilities

*General shopping* A wide range of shops, many shutting between 1300 and 1500

*Provisioning* Several supermarkets, including a vast Safeway on the Varyl Begg Estate opposite Sheppard's Marina. Also shops specialising in Spanish and Mediterranean foods

*Restaurants/hotels* Wide choice at all prices

*Medical services* St Bernards Hospital (casualty, tel: 73941). Health Clinic, Casement Square (tel: 78337/ 77603)

## Communications

*Mailing addresses* C/o the Post Office; Marina Bay Complex Ltd, PO Box 80, Gibraltar; H Sheppard & Co Ltd, Waterport, Gibraltar or Queensway Quay Marina, PO Box 19, Gibraltar, by prior arrangement

*Post Office* On Main Street

*Telephones* At the marinas and in town. Some marina berths have telephone points

*Bus/rail services* Buses to La Linea, connecting with Spanish bus and railway services

*Ferry service* Regular ferries to Tangier

*Taxis* Plentiful

*Car hire* Several agencies. Hire cars can be taken across the border into Spain

*Air services* Gibraltar Airport has several flights daily to the UK, and hourly flights to Tangier in summer. There are still no flights to Spain

| | | | |
|---|---|---|---|
| *Springs*: 2.4 m/7 ft 11 in | | *Flag*: Portugal | |
| *Neaps*: 1.9 m/6 ft 3 in | | *Currency*: Portuguese escudo | |

*Tel/fax – Country code*: 351, *Area code*: (0) 91

| Charts | Admiralty | US |
|---|---|---|
| General | 1831 (1:150,000) | 51261 (1:150,000) |
| Approach | 1689 (1:15,000) | 51263 (1:10,000) |
| Harbour | 1689 (1:7,500) | 51263 (1:5,000) |

## General

Funchal is a favourite harbour with many ocean cruising yachtsmen, and as a result is very crowded during the migrant season. The city of Funchal is somewhat touristy, but the island itself quite beautiful and worth exploring.

There has long been talk of building a second yacht marina, most probably at Machico in the eastern part of the island though possibly at an unspecified location west of Funchal.

## Approach

Most yachts will approach from the east around Pta de Garajau, topped by a huge statue of Christ which is flood-lit at night. The city and harbour are unmistakable by day or night, and Funchal Bay has deep water everywhere.

## Radio

The port authority operates on VHF channels 11, 12, 13 and 16, with tugs using channels 09, 10 and 69 and pilots working on channels 14 and 16. The marina monitors channel 62.

## Entrance

Very straightforward, though it would be unwise to cut the end of the main breakwater too close. If entering at night there are a great many shore lights which could cause confusion, but on the other hand the ambient light will be helpful in spotting unlit mooring buoys or anchored yachts.

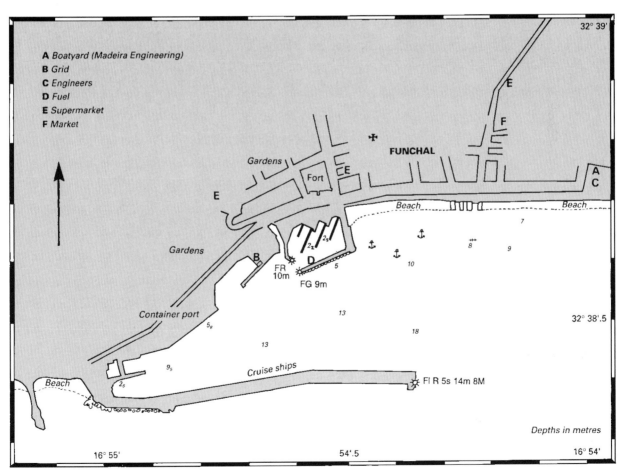

A Boatyard (Madeira Engineering)
B Grid
C Engineers
D Fuel
E Supermarket
F Market

*Chart 49*   Funchal, Madeira. Based on a plan in the *Atlantic Islands*.

Funchal marina from the public gardens to the west. Several cranes are at work in the foreground, almost masking the marina entrance on the right of the photograph. *Photo:Anne Hammick*

## Anchorage and moorings

Yachts may anchor to the east of the *Cais* in a somewhat exposed position, untenable in strong onshore winds when the only adequate shelter would be inside the marina. Depths of 10 m or more are found close inshore and the holding is poor in places. A First World War wreck lies directly off the easternmost of the two small river mouths some 400 m east of the *Cais* and the area should be avoided.

*Caution*: Particular care must be taken if anchoring, as the prevailing north-easterly wind eddies around the mountains and frequently blows parallel to the south coast, generally from the west but occasionally from the east. If combined with an onshore sea breeze during the afternoon this will take on a southerly component, which will not only swing yachts through 360° each day but may set them ashore should they drag.

## Berthing and marinas

The construction of a marina (tel: 225281/225188, fax: 225524) in the mid 1980s was much welcomed by visiting yachtsmen, but since then the administration has not always been of the best. Four jetties with finger pontoons provide berths for around 160 local craft, but visiting yachts lie alongside the southern wall, frequently eight or ten abreast. Depending on wind direction, the marina can collect floating debris and warps may become oily.

In November 1997 about half the length of the southern wall was taken up by local yachts moored bows-to. Most of these were at least 11 m (36 ft) overall, and reflect the increasing prosperity of many islanders.

## Formalities

Madeira is part of Portugal and therefore of the EU. In theory this should mean fewer formalities for EU registered yachts arriving from another EU country, but as of 1997 all foreign yachts were still required to report their arrival to the relevant authorities, all of which have offices in the marina. Start at the marina office and work through the *Capitania do Porto* (port captain), the *Guarda Fiscal* and the *Alfandega* (customs). Crew arrivals and/or departures while the yacht is in Madeira must be documented through the *Policia Maritima*. All three offices must be visited again before departure.

## Facilities

*Boatyard/engineers/electronics* Madeira Engineering Lda, at the eastern end of Avenida do Mar, has a good reputation and some employees speak English. It would be wise to get a firm quotation in advance. There are several outboard engine workshops – enquire at the marina office

*Ramp/drying grid* Inside the mole to the west of the marina, capable of handling yachts up to about 11 m/36 ft and draught 2.0 m

*Sailmaker* Enquire at the marina office

*Chandlery* Mare at 26 Rue Fontes for fittings and equipment, or Brendle on Rue das Pretas for tools and hardware

*Compass adjustment* To check the yacht's compass:

   1  The eastern end of the breakwater and the eastern end of the harbour office are in line on a bearing of true north

   2  From a position east of the breakwater, the lamp standards are in line on a bearing of true west

*Yacht club* The Clube Naval do Funchal (CNF) has its clubhouse two miles west of Funchal at Quinta Calaca

*Weather forecast* Posted daily in the window of the *Capitania do Porto* office and at around noon in the marina office

*Diesel* At the western end of the marina wall, 1630–1800 Monday to Friday only

*Petrol* From a pump in the marina

*Water* At the marina wall. Madeiran water is exceptionally pure and sweet

*Shore power* A few power points on the marina wall (220 volt 50Hz)

*Bottled gas* Camping Gaz available in town. HINTON on Rua Til handles refills of Calor Gas, etc

*Ice* From the fish dock at the western end of the harbour

*Showers* In the marina complex. They are currently kept locked and access is by key

*Laundry/launderette* Several in the town

*Banks* Many, open 0830–1145 and 1300–1445 weekdays only. Most have credit card facilities and a few have automated money changing machines

*General shopping* Good and varied, though with a strong bias towards tourist items

*Provisioning* Several well-stocked and reasonably priced supermarkets. The fresh produce market in the eastern part of the town is a must – flowers, vegetables and fruit on two levels, with a busy fish market at the rear. Take your own egg boxes and plastic bags (and camera)

*Restaurants/hotels* Very wide choice at all levels

*Medical services* There is a health services information centre for visitors at 1 Rua das Pretas, plus several well-equipped hospitals

## Communications

*Mailing address* C/o the main post office or the Marina do Funchal, Funchal 9000, Madeira, Portugal

*Fax service* At the marina office (fax: 225524) and the main post office

*Post Office* on Avenida Zarco. Open 0830–2000 weekdays, 0900–1230 Saturdays. Stamps can be bought at any shop displaying the green *correio* sign

*Telephones* At the main post office, the marina office and elsewhere

*Bus service* Cheap and reliable. A timetable is available from the Tourist Office

*Taxis/car hire* Wide choice

*Ferry service* Regular ferries to Porto Santo

*Air services* Direct flights to London and Portugal. Santa Cruz Airport is 20 km from Funchal

*Springs*: 1.8 m/5 ft 11 in < 2.2 m/7 ft 3 in    *Flag*: Spain
*Neaps*: 0.7 m/2 ft 4in < 1.1 m/3 ft 7 in    *Currency*:
Spanish peseta

*Tel/fax – Country code*: 34,
*Area codes*:   (9)28 (Lanzarote, Fuerteventura, Gran Canaria)
(9)22 (Tenerife, La Gomera, La Palma, El Hierro)

| Charts | Admiralty | US |
|--------|-----------|-----|
| General | 1869 (1:300,000) | 51380 (1:263,900) |
|  | 1870 (1:300,000) | 51260 (1:300,000) |

## General

Mention has already been made in Part II of the difficulty – if not impossibility – of finding an empty berth in many Canarian marinas. This is because nearly all the private marinas were built alongside holiday complexes, and in most cases a high proportion of the berths were sold together with the properties. The vast majority of the remaining berths are let annually.

For this reason, rather than covering one or two harbours in detail it has been felt more appropriate to describe four, scattered over as many islands. As of early 1998 all anticipated having berths available for transient yachts even during the busy autumn season. However it should be stressed that this situation may change and that it is always worth telephoning ahead.

The main criteria for inclusion is that all offer secure alongside or bow/stern-to berthing, can be entered in all normal conditions and can meet at least day-to-day shopping needs. Two – Puerto de la Luz at Las Palmas de Gran Canaria and Marina Atlantico at Santa Cruz de Tenerife – are close to major cities where a yacht can readily be stored up for the Atlantic passage. Puerto Calero, Lanzarote and San Sebastian de la Gomera are smaller and more remote, but also cleaner and more peaceful. Harbours are taken on a general north-east to south-west trend since few skippers will choose to pass through the islands in any other direction.

It should not be assumed that no other harbours are worth visiting. If conditions are favourable La Sociedad (Caleta Sebo) on Isla Graciosa north of Lanzarote makes a delightful landfall, provided almost nothing is required ashore. For those who do not mind the noise and smells of a busy fishing harbour, the anchorage inside Puerto de Naos (Lanzarote) gives total protection from the elements and convenient access to the city of Arrecife. Gran Canaria has possibly the most crowded marinas of the archipelago, though either Pasito Blanco or Puerto Rico may be able to find space for a visitor and both have well run boatyards. Mogan has long been a favourite with British yachtsmen, but seldom has a berth available.

On Tenerife, the small marina at Radazul can sometimes take visitors and has good workshop facilities. Further west there are anchorages at Las Galletas and Los Cristianos, though the latter is technically closed to yachts other than those waiting for the travel lift (strictly DIY, but with the lowest prices in the Canaries). Puerto Colon no longer accepts visiting yachts, but Los Gigantes can sometimes take one or two.

On the smaller islands, Santa Cruz de la Palma offers pleasant, relaxed surroundings in which to make final preparations for the Atlantic passage, together with good shopping facilities and excellent tap water (rare in the Canaries). However, visitors, though welcome, are currently berthed alongside the main breakwater – a real problem for smaller yachts. On El Hierro, smallest and least visited of the Canaries, Puerto de la Restinga in the south offers a last stop before the Atlantic Ocean, together with some yard facilities. If planning to cruise the Canaries in any detail the purchase of a cruising guide will be more than justified.

## Shelter from stress of weather

The requirement to shelter a yacht at risk from heavy weather is generally honoured, though she may be requested to leave as soon as conditions have moderated. However there appears to be no formal definition of 'heavy weather', presumably leaving a decision to the discretion of harbour staff.

## Puerto Calero, Lanzarote
## 28°55′.1N 13°42′W

| Charts | Admiralty | US |
|--------|-----------|-----|
| Approach | 886 (1:75,000) | – |

## General

A spotlessly clean but expensive private marina, Puerto Calero is currently expanding from some 250 to 420 berths – hopefully in time for autumn 1998. The marina is surrounded by a small tourist complex including supermarket and restaurants, but it would be necessary to organise a hire car or taxi to Arrecife for serious shopping.

## Approach and entrance

Puerto Calero is situated some 9 miles west-south-west of Arrecife. The harbour opens to the west but is somewhat protected by the curve of the coast towards Punta Gorda and Punta Papagayo. It is best identified from offshore by the white upper part of the octagonal marina office near the end of the south mole.

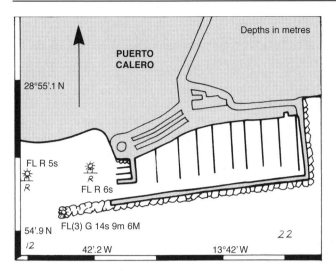

*Chart 50*   Puerto Calero. Based on a plan provided by Puerto Calero.

On closing the coast the bottom shelves suddenly and steeply, but a pair of red buoys warn against continuing too far north before the sharp starboard turn into the marina. Entrance is straightforward and visitors should secure to the reception berth beneath the office.

VHF watch is kept on channels 09 and 16 from 0800–2000 daily. (Tel: 511285, fax: 514568.)

## Facilities

*Boatyard/engineers/electronics* Small but active boatyard, with contractors available. The 75 tonne travel lift is to be replaced by an even larger machine

*Sailmaker* Drizas Velas in the marina complex, or Lanzarote Sail Repairs (tel: 592351)

*Chandlery* Jewel Marine Services next to boatyard (tel: 512468, fax: 512777) for electronics; Efectos Navales Duarte (tel: 811117, fax: 802108) at Puerto de Naos

*Fuel* At the reception berth

*Water* Throughout the marina, but unpleasant to drink

*Shore power* Throughout the marina. Both 220 and 380 volt available

*Bottled gas* From the DISA plant north of Puerto de Mármoles. Any cylinder can be filled, generally while you wait. Camping Gas exchanges may be available in the Alamar supermarket

*Showers* Well maintained and open 24 hours a day

*Launderette* At the supermarket

*Bank* In Puerto del Carmen, about 6 miles by road. Small quantities of currency can be exchanged at Alamar

*General shopping/provisioning* Small supermarket near the harbour. Otherwise in Puerto del Carmen

*Restaurant* In the octagonal grey building near the root of the north mole, and several others

*Medical services* Cruz Roja post in the marina

## Communications

*Mailing address* C/o Puerto Calero, PO Box 45, 35510, Puerto del Carmen, Lanzarote, Islas Canarias, España

*Fax service* At Alamar (fax: 514382)

*Post Office* In Puerto del Carmen (stamps at Alamar)

*Telephones* At Alamar and elsewhere

*Taxis* Available by phone. No buses

*Car hire* In Puerto del Carmen, or arrange via Alamar

*Air services* International airport west of Arrecife, some 10 miles by road

---

# Puerto de la Luz, Las Palmas de Gran Canaria 28°07′.7N 15°25′.4W

| Charts | Admiralty | US |
|---|---|---|
| Approach | 1856 (1:75,000) | 51344 (1:30,000) |
| Harbour | 1856 (1:12,500) | 51244 (1:10,000) |

## General

A large yacht marina with all the usual facilities, but sharing its approach with that of Gran Canaria's largest commercial harbour. Both marina breakwaters are to be extended in an effort to overcome the resulting problems. Puerto de la Luz is very crowded in late November before the start of the ARC rally, when non-participating yachts have to wait at anchor outside, but can normally accommodate visitors at other times. Over the next few years the marina is due to increase its 827 berths by 420 to a massive 1247, which should ease the overcrowding.

## Approach and entrance

The solid buildings of Las Palmas are unmistakable for many miles offshore. Head for a point some half mile south-west of the head of the Dique Reina Sofia (the main outer breakwater) keeping a good watch for commercial traffic, then turn north-west for the outer head of the marina breakwater. Note that changes are expected in the marina approach – see plan.

In early 1998 a short extension had been run north-east from the end of the old breakwater, and the angled floating pontoon which previously ran out from the mainland shore to terminate north-west of the breakwater head was being dismantled and its piles removed. A solid replacement was to be positioned on much the same line but jutting out further north-east than its predecessor and angled to protect the marina entrance from swell and wash. It was not known exactly when this work would be finished, but possibly by winter 1998.

Arrivals generally secure to the Texaco fuel berth on the breakwater; alternatively call on either VHF channel 16 (ready to switch to a working channel) or channel 09.

## Berthing

Currently most visitors are berthed on pontoons 9 or 10, though this may change when the extra berths are available. Large yachts are usually berthed stern-to against the outer wall just south of the fuel berth. Visitors' berths are provided with buoys and lazy lines to the pontoon, the finger pontoons in the southern part of the basin being reserved for local boats.

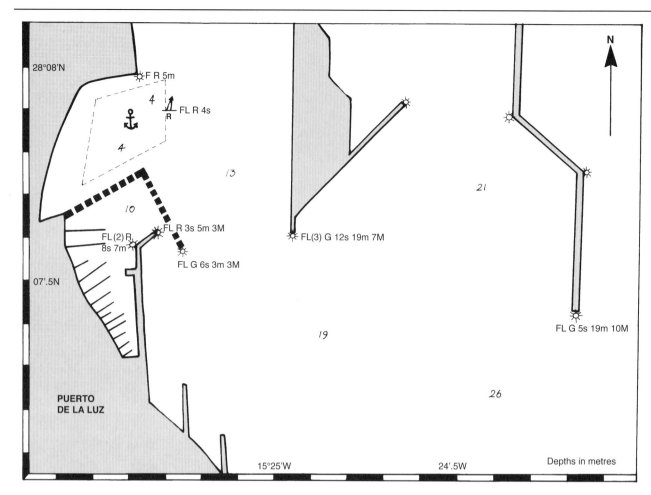

*Chart 51*   Puerto de la Luz. Based on Admiralty Chart No 1856.

## Anchorage

Anchoring (a small charge is made) is permitted north of the marina. Holding is said to be good, but a trip line might be advisable. Protection will be much improved with the completion of the new north breakwater.

## Formalities

The marina office (tel: 300464, 300480, fax: 300466), where customs and other formalities are also handled, is at the south end of the basin beside the road which leads (via a tunnel) out of the harbour. Ship's papers and crew passports are held until departure.

## Facilities

*Boatyard* Serious boatyard in the north-west part of the harbour, where major wood and grp repairs can be carried out. Equipment includes a 60 tonne travel lift

*Engineers* Ask at the marina office. There are local agents for Perkins, Volvo, Evinrude, Johnson, Mercury, Suzuki and Yamaha

*Sailmakers* Charles Linton of Velas Linton (tel/fax: 291934), Olivier Youf of O'Sails (tel/fax: 261553) and Velas Benoit Claveau (tel: 280939)

*Chandlery* Alcorde, at Calle Luis Antunex 51 (tel: 242484, fax: 249526) and others

*Liferafts* Can be serviced by Ocean Products Española (tel: 270962, 272716) on Muelle de Rivera near the root of the Dique del Léon y Castillo

*Fuel* All varieties, plus oils etc, at the Texaco fuel dock

*Water* At all berths, but unpleasant to drink

*Shore power* 220 volt at all berths, with 380 volt south of the fuel dock

*Bottled gas* Exchange or refills available via the fuel dock. The latter (refilled at the DISA plant south of Las Palmas) may take several days

*Showers* Built into the wall near the harbour office and opposite pontoon 10, with a card entry system

*Laundry* At the corner of Calle de Sagasta and Isla Hierro

*Banks* Many, with credit card facilities

*General shopping* Three large supermarkets: El Corte Ingles, Supersol and Hiperdino, plus a produce and fish market near the commercial harbour. The small store at the fuel dock stocks bread, milk, wine etc

*Restaurants, bars and hotels* A very wide choice, some handy to the marina

*Medical services* Hospital near the marina

## Communications

*Mailing address* C/o Oficina del Puerto, Muelle Deportivo, E-35004 Las Palmas de Gran Canaria, Islas Canarias, España

*Fax service* At the marina office (fax: 300466)

*Post Office* In the town

*Telephones* On the fuel dock and near the port office, as well as in town

*Bus service* To the airport etc

*Taxis/car hire* Readily available
*Ferry service* Jetfoil to Fuerteventura and Tenerife plus inter-island car ferry
*Air services* International airport 10 miles south of Las Palmas

## Marina Atlantico, Santa Cruz de Tenerife
### 28°27′.5N 16°14′.8W

| Charts | Admiralty | US |
|--------|-----------|-----|
| Approach | 1858 (1:75,000) | 51341 (1:50,000) |
| Harbour | 1857 (1:12,000) | 51341 (1:10,000) |

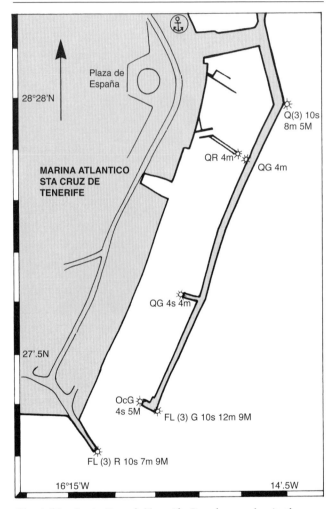

*Chart 52*   Santa Cruz de Tenerife. Based on a plan in the *Atlantic Islands*.

## General

Several years ago plans were produced for a large, full service marina in the Dársena de los Llanos, the southernmost of Santa Cruz's four commercial basins. A barrier was installed near the head of the basin – the outer part is still used by container and Ro-Ro traffic – and two pontoons installed, but since then work appears to have come to a standstill. However there is a possibility that it may be resumed in the next two or three years.

Although marina facilities are almost non-existent, Marina Atlantico is very convenient to the city and visiting yachts can generally either squeeze in on one of the pontoons or secure to the wall. The older Marina Tenerife, situated in the Dársena Pesquera to the north, seldom has space for visiting yachts.

## Approach and entrance

The Dársena de los Llanos lies at the southern end of the harbour complex, less than a mile north of the chimneys and fuelling berths of Puerto Caballo. Its entrance opens almost due south, with leading lights on 353°. The basin is used by commercial shipping and providing lights and buoys are observed should present no problems to a yacht. However it should be noted that only the eastern of the two entrances to the marina is passable – the western is narrow with what appears to be a wave baffle, presumably to limit wash from the commercial harbour.

## Formalities

The port office is north of the marina, overlooking the Dársena Sur (tel: 605472, fax: 605481). Visit with the usual ship's papers and passports.

## Facilities

*Boatyard* No yacht yards in Santa Cruz (though several shipyards). Hauling is best done at Los Cristianos, where there is a 60 tonne travel lift operated by the fishermen's cooperative (tel: 790014, 793912, fax: 751785). Engineers at Puerto Radazul about 6 miles south-west of Santa Cruz
*Sailmaker* Spinnaker (tel: 243975, fax: 293830), which also handles stainless steel rigging
*Chandlery* Good selection – Spinnaker (see above), La Marina (tel: 271246, fax: 247246), Sucesores Tomás Fernandez Blanco (tel: 275014, 275058, fax: 279769) and H Oscar Martín Fariña (tel: 281550/4, fax: 285174)
*Fuel* None at the Marina Atlantico, but available in the Dársena Pesquera from the rear of the filling station about halfway up the harbour on the inner side
*Water* On the pontoons, but unpleasant to drink
*Shore power* On the pontoons
*Bottled gas* Camping Gas exchanges at Tomás Fernandez Blanco and elsewhere. Other cylinders can be filled at DISA (tel: 224966) next to the Palacio de Ferias
*Showers* No showers at the Marina Atlantico
*Launderettes* Several in the city including Lavandería la Rosa (tel: 283382)
*Banks* Many, with credit card facilities
*General shopping/provisioning* Excellent supermarkets and other shops in Santa Cruz. Also several freezer warehouses near the Dársena Pesquera which sell a wide range of frozen fish and meat at good prices with no minimum quantity restrictions
*Restaurants/hotels* Many in the town
*Medical services* Several hospitals plus a first aid station

## Communications

*Mailing address* C/o the main post office: *Poste Restante,* Correos de Santa Cruz, Plaza de España, Santa Cruz de

Tenerife, Islas Canarias, España
*Fax service* At the port office (fax: 605481)
*Post Office* Across the road from the marina
*Telephones* At the port office and elsewhere
*Bus service* Regular bus service, including to both airports
*Taxis/car hire* Readily available
*Ferry service* Jetfoil to Gran Canaria and Fuerteventura. Car ferries to Gomera and La Palma
*Air services* International flights mainly from Reina Sophia in the south, inter-island services from Los Rodeos in the north

## San Sebastián de la Gomera
## 28°05′N 17°06′.5W

| Charts | Admiralty | US |
|--------|-----------|-----|
| Harbour | 1858 (1:10,000) | – |

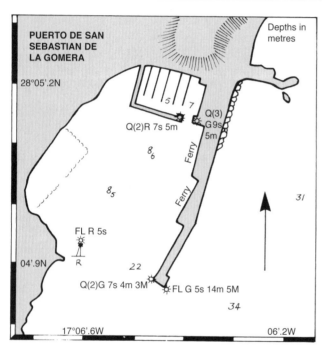

*Chart 53* San Sebastián de la Gomera. Based on Admiralty Chart No 1858.

## General

San Sebastián is a small commercial harbour with car ferries to Tenerife and El Hierro. Tucked inside is a 275 berth marina which welcomes visiting yachts. Anchoring in the harbour is no longer permitted. The marina is reported to suffer from swell in strong southerlies.

The town has strong links with Columbus, whose house is now an art gallery. The Church of Our Lady of the Assumption, where Columbus and his crew said Mass before their departure, is on the main street (though rebuilt a number of times). San Sebastián still is an excellent place from which to leave for the Atlantic crossing.

## Approach and entrance

From north-east the radio mast makes a fine landmark. The lighthouse is less conspicuous and the breakwater and town are concealed by the headland. From south or east the town on the north side of the valley can be seen and the breakwater will be raised on close approach. There are no outlying dangers and course can be set to clear the breakwater end. Keep a lookout for the hydrofoil and car ferry and keep well clear if either is entering or leaving. The marina entrance is close west of the breakwater root and well marked by day or night. There is normally someone on duty until 2100, otherwise arrivals should berth either on the head of the pontoon nearest the entrance or alongside the eastern quay.

## Formalities

The port office (tel: 870357, fax: 141310) is on the second floor of the building at the root of the main breakwater. Closed at weekends, when a smaller office is manned in the marina itself. Both monitor VHF channel 09. Visit with the usual ship's papers and passports.

## Facilities

*Boatyard/engineers* Enquire at the port office. Several small workshops, but not a place for major work. No travel lift by March 1998 though a dock was provided
*Chandlery* Nothing – best to order from Tenerife (see Marina Atlantico, above)
*Fuel* In cans from CEPSA filling station on main road
*Water* Good drinking water on the pontoons, with hoses provided
*Shore power* On the pontoons
*Bottled gas* Bottles can be refilled at a plant in the south-west part of the town. Allow plenty of time
*Showers* Good showers in the marina
*Laundry* Lavandería Hecu on Calle del Medio
*Banks* Several, with credit card facilities
*General shopping/provisioning* Two or three supermarkets plus a produce/fish market where purchases can be frozen to order
*Restaurants/hotels* All grades, including the four star Parador
*Medical services* Hospital in the town

## Communications

*Mailing address* C/o Puerto Deportivo, CP 38800/ Autoridad Porturia, San Sebastián de la Gomera, Islas Canarias, España
*Fax service* At the port office (fax: 141310)
*Post Office* Near the church
*Telephones* In the square opposite the marina, on the breakwater and elsewhere
*Bus service* Around the island. Details from the tourist office
*Taxis/car hire* In the ferry booking office on the breakwater
*Ferry service* To Tenerife and El Hierro
*Air services* The airport has still to be completed

*Springs*: 1.2 m/3 ft 11 in  *Flag*: Republic of Cape Verde
*Neaps*: 1.0 m/3 ft 3 in    *Currency*: Cape Verdean escudo

*Tel/fax - Country code*: 238, *Area code*: none

| Charts | Admiralty | US |
|--------|-----------|-----|
| General | 366 (1:500,000) | 51500 (1:250,000) |
| Approach | 367 (1:150,000) | - |
| Harbour | 367 (1:17,500) | 51500 (1:20,000) |

## General

After years of receiving a bad press - if mentioned at all -

the Cape Verde Islands are at last being recognised as an interesting port of call for Atlantic voyagers. Porto Grande (also known as Mindelo) is an excellent natural harbour and facilities for yachts are very gradually improving.

Many of the local people are desperately poor, and both theft from yachts and harassment by 'boat boys' is on the increase. Dinghies in particular are a tempting target, and padlocks should be employed on outboard and oars as well as to secure the dinghy to the yacht or landing.

## Approach

Most yachts will approach from the north through the Canal de São Vicente. The small and rocky Ilhèu do Pássaros [Fl(3) 13s 86m 14M] can be passed on either side.

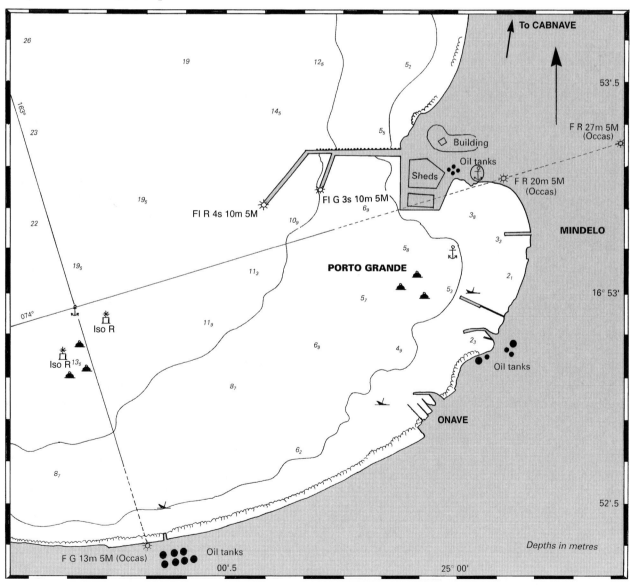

*Chart 54*  Porto Grande, São Vicente, Cape Verdes. Based on Admiralty Chart No 367.

*Caution*: Refer to the warnings in Chapters 12 and 13 regarding frequent poor visibility and the unreliability of lights and other navigational aids.

## Radio

The port authorities operate on VHF channel 13, with the pilot service using channels 13 and 16.

## Entrance

Very straightforward both by day and night, with good depths throughout the northern part of the bay. The grey stone breakwaters are deep close-to, and well lit. A new jetty, with steps and a slipway, has been built near the yacht anchorage. Various ships' mooring buoys, mostly unlit, are scattered in the southern part of the bay while a number of wrecks line the beach.

In 1998 it was reported that a new passenger terminal was under construction, to extend some 120 m southward from the south-west corner of the main quay. In addition, the inner breakwater arm was to be extended 40 m south-east and the area between the two dredged. Extra care should be taken on entry until all work is finished and charts brought up to date.

## Anchorage and moorings

The yacht anchorage is in the north-east corner of Porto Grande Bay, with good holding in sand. Depths of 5–6 m in the outer part of the anchorage shoal gradually towards the beach. There are no moorings.

## Berthing

It may be possible to lie alongside in the inner harbour, though the east side of the inner breakwater is used by ferries. No yacht lying alongside should ever be left unattended – employing a watchman does not give complete security.

## Formalities

Fly the Q flag on arrival. Officials from the Port Captain's office and immigration may board the yacht or it may be necessary to seek them out ashore – try and ascertain current procedure from earlier arrivals. If a courtesy flag is not already hoisted they will be delighted to sell you one.

Ship's papers are held ashore until departure, but a receipt will be issued on request. Passports are no longer retained and visiting yachtsmen do not require visas. There is a small departure tax.

## Facilities

*Boatyards/engineering/electronics* The CABNAVE shipyard (tel: 314122/314233/314389, fax: 312874) in the bay north of Porto Grande has good facilities including well-equipped engineering and electronics workshops, can haul anything from a yacht to a 3000 tonne ship and will carry out repairs in wood, fibreglass, steel and aluminium. It is one of the few places in the archipelago where a yacht might safely be laid up ashore. Several of the senior management speak English. ONAVE (tel: 312270, fax: 312522), about half a mile

Porto Grande harbour and the city of Mindelo. The ruinous state of many of the jetties is all too obvious. *Photo: Anne Hammick*

south of the anchorage, is a smaller concern but has diesel engineers

*Sailmaker* None as such, though a local seamstress might be able to repair lightweight sails

*Chandlery* Very limited stock at 12 Traversa da Praia

*Yacht club* The Clube Náutico occupies the low white building with two gables immediately opposite the anchorage and beach

*Diesel* Available alongside, by pre-arrangement with the Shell office, or from filling stations in the town

*Petrol* From filling stations in the town

*Water* Either by can from a tap on the new jetty beside the anchorage, or by hose, arranged via an office on the fuelling jetty. Quality is variable, and it would be wise to conserve Madeiran or Canaries water for the Atlantic crossing

*Bottled gas* Camping Gaz cylinders can be exchanged at the Shell garage, and other bottles taken to ENACOL just south of town for refilling

*Ice* From the fish-freezing plant in the dock area (icebox rather than drinks quality)

*Showers* Try one of the larger hotels

*Laundry/launderette* Launderette at 56 Avenida Unidade Africana. Laundry done by local women is not always returned either clean or dry

*Banks* Two, where foreign currency or traveller's cheques can be exchanged and cash drawn against a credit card (no machines). Identification will be required

*General shopping* Most needs can be met, but prices tend to be high

*Provisioning* Much improved since the late 1980s, but still limited compared to Madeira or the Canaries. Several small supermarkets, and a rebuilt produce market described as being 'a cross between an African market and Sainsburys'! The fish market is good, or fish may be bought directly from the boats

*Restaurants/hotels* Several, at reasonable prices

*Medical services* Hospital east of town, reported in 1996 to be more than satisfactory. Some English is spoken

## Communications

*Mailing address* C/o the main post office

*Post Office* At the south end of the Praça Amilcar Cabral. Open weekdays only, 0800–1200 and 1430–1700

*Telephones* At the post office, but open 0800–2200 weekdays, 0800–1130 and 1500–1700 Saturday, and 0800–1130 Sunday. Some card-operated phone booths

*Bus service* Services link different parts of the island, but may not return the same day

*Ferry service* The regular inter-island service employs two purpose-built vessels. There is also a daily service to Santo Antão

*Taxis/car hire* Readily available, but rates should always be negotiated in advance and include hidden extras such as tax, mileage and fuel

*Air services* Daily flights from the small airfield at San Pedro to Ilha do Sal, from which there are international services, and to other Cape Verde Islands. Credit cards cannot yet be used to pay for flights

| *Springs*: 1.8 m/5 ft 11 in | *Flag*: Republic of South Africa |
| *Neaps*: 1.3 m/4 ft 3 in | *Currency*: South African rand |

*Tel/fax – Country code*: 27, *Area code*: (0) 21

| Charts | Admiralty | US |
|--------|-----------|-----|
| General | 2082 (1:300,000) | 57480 (1:249,000) |
| Approach | 636 (1:100,000) | 57484 (1:36,000) |
| | 1920 (1:37,500) | – |
| Harbour | 1846 (1:10,000) | 57488 (1:10,000) |

## General

Cape Town is one of South Africa's oldest settlements, and vessels have been using the harbour under Table Mountain since the days of the Portuguese explorers. It is now visited by everything from yachts through supertankers to cruise liners, and has facilities to match. It is possible to get almost anything done in Cape Town.

## Approach

Cape Town will most often be approached from the south via Cape Agulhas and the Cape of Good Hope, the latter marked by Cape Point light [Fl(2+1) 30s 86m 32M]. It should be given generous clearance as shoal water extends more than two miles offshore.

Cape Town lies some 25 miles north of the Cape itself, but do not turn northwards until Slangkop Point light [Fl(4) 30s 40m 30M] can be seen, bearing 338°. The coast can then be followed at a distance of at least 0.5 miles to clear all hazards, passing Twelve Apostles and Lion's Head mountains before turning eastwards into Table Bay harbour.

Lights and buoyage follow the European IALA A system.

## Radio

On approach to the harbour yachts should contact Table Bay Port Control on VHF channel 16, to request permission to proceed to the yacht basin. They also operate on channels 09, 11, 12, 13, 14 and 29.

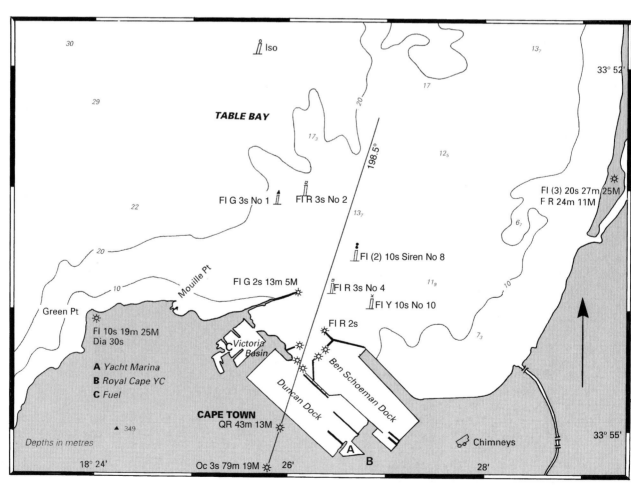

*Chart 55*    Cape Town, South Africa. Based on Admiralty Charts Nos 1920 and 1846.

The Royal Cape Yacht Club's marina is well sheltered in the south-east corner of the harbour. *Photo: Anne Hammick*

## Entrance

The harbour entrance is clear and well lit. Follow a course of about 200° through the outer harbour, turning to port once inside the inner harbour (Duncan Dock). The yacht basin is in the south-eastern corner. Upon entering the yacht basin, turn immediately to starboard and proceed along the Royal Cape Yacht Club marina to the floating fuel dock until a berth can be allocated.

## Anchorage and moorings

Anchoring is not permitted in Cape Town harbour, though in a strong south-easterly it is possible to pick up one of two moorings outside the basin and the floating anti-pollution barrier.

## Berthing and marinas

The Royal Cape Yacht Club (tel: 211354, fax: 216028), whose office is open during normal business hours, can usually arrange berthing in their marina. The first three slots inside the entrance are reserved for visitors – if these are occupied secure to the fuel dock until a berth is allocated. The marina has an overflow area in the Eliot Basin (at the south-west corner of Ben Schoeman Dock) to which visitors may be sent during busy periods, but this is some distance from the city and walking between the two after dark could be unwise.

The Royal Cape Yacht Club's custom of making no charge for the first five days' berthing is, sadly but understandably, a thing of the past. However club facilities such as showers can be used free for the first month, after which temporary membership is expected.

In 1997–8 a new marina, likely to offer berthing for visitors, was under construction in the old quarry at the Victoria and Alfred Dock, Cape Town's rejuvenated waterfront area.

There are minimal harbour dues after one month in all South African ports, unless one stays at the yacht club.

## Formalities

Whether arriving from another South African port or coming from foreign, customs and immigration should be notified. In the former case, and if staying at the Royal Cape Yacht Club, they will contact customs and immigration for you. Otherwise the officials will be found on the fifth floor of the Customs and Excise Building immediately outside Adderley Street Customs Gate.

To clear out one must obtain a clearance certificate from the Royal Cape Yacht Club and take this first to immigration (passport control) and then to the Harbour Revenue Office, both in the Customs and Excise Building. The last stop is customs, located at the Adderley Street entrance, where a port clearance will be issued. A yacht leaving at the weekend must obtain port clearance by 1200 on Friday.

## Facilities

*Boatyard* Several, with good haulage facilities
*Engineers/electronics* Enquire at the yacht club for recommendations
*Sailmakers* Both North and Doyle have lofts in Cape Town
*Chandleries* Small chandleries at the yacht club and in the Woodstock area (across the pedestrian bridge northeast of the yacht club), plus Central Boating in the city
*Yacht club* The Royal Cape Yacht Club overlooks the yacht basin in the inner harbour, and welcomes visiting yachtsmen

*Weather forecast* Displayed daily at the yacht club

*Diesel* Foreign yachts can obtain duty free fuel at nearly half price from the Joint Bunkering Services in the Victoria and Alfred Basin, across from Bertie's Landing. Open Monday to Friday 0800–1600. The ship's papers must be produced but port clearance is not required. Exact change is necessary. Fuel is also available from Enza Marine at the yacht club

*Water* On the yacht club marina pontoons

*Shore power* On the yacht club marina pontoons (220 volt 50Hz)

*Bottled gas* Enquire at the yacht club

*Showers* At the yacht club

*Laundry/launderettes* In the southern part of the city and in Woodstock. Alternatively, Action Yachting offer a full laundry service, charged by weight. Contact via the yacht club reception desk

*Banks* Many in Cape Town, with credit card facilities

*General shopping* Excellent

*Provisioning* Particularly good. Some of the larger supermarkets will give a tax refund for major purchases on production of the ship's papers. Given a day's notice the Tableview Pick-n-Pay Superstore will deliver to the yacht club, and will attempt to order any items which are not on the shelves

*Restaurants/hotels* A wide choice at all levels and prices, including a good restaurant at the Royal Cape Yacht Club itself

*Medical services* Excellent. The District Surgeon on Plein Street can organise yellow fever immunisation, necessary if planning to visit Brazil

## Communications

*Mailing address* C/o the Royal Cape Yacht Club, PO Box 772, Cape Town 8000, Republic of South Africa. They will hold or forward on request

*Post Office* In the city

*Telephones* At the yacht club and in the city

*Rail service* Connections throughout South Africa

*Taxis/car hire* Widely available

*Air services* Direct flights to Europe from Cape Town (D F Malan) international airport. Air services to the USA via Miami

*Springs*: 1.6 m/5 ft 3 in    *Flag*: British (Red Ensign)
*Neaps*: 1.1 m/3 ft 7 in    *Currency*: St Helenian £ and £ sterling

*Tel/fax – Country code*: 290, *Area code*: none

| Charts | Admiralty | US |
|---|---|---|
| General | 1771 (1:125,000) | 57485 (1:200,000) |
| Approach | – | 57485 (1:26,530) |
| Harbour | 1771 (1:15,000) | – |

## General

St Helena is a favourite staging post for yachts crossing the South Atlantic from Cape Town to Brazil or the Lesser Antilles. It has been variously described as 'fascinating', 'unusual' and 'friendly'. One couple remarked that 'visiting by yacht in 1997, after an interval of six years, we noticed a significant and encouraging increase in motivation and enterprise on St Helena, combined with the same friendly welcome as previously'.

St Helena has long been a British colony, and to many people it will always remain famous primarily as the island to which Napoleon was exiled after defeat at Waterloo. There is only one settlement of any size, at Jamestown on the north-west coast. Two useful guides to the island are available from the information office situated above the museum on Main Street.

## Approach

Details of the approach to St Helena, together with a plan of the island, will be found in Chapter 15 under the heading *Cape Town to St Helena*. It is not well lit, the only powerful lighthouse being at Buttermilk Point [Fl(2) 10s 37m 10M] just west of Sugar Loaf Point, the island's most northerly promontory.

## Radio

Radio St Helena monitors VHF channel 16 between 0800–2000, 1900 on Sundays.

## Entrance

After rounding Buttermilk Point, first Rupert's Bay and then James Bay will be sighted. Both are open anchorages but the buildings of Jamestown make the latter unmistakable. The leading lights for James Bay bear 171°, but it can safely be entered on any course between west and north. The 1910 wreck of the steamship *Pamanui* lies in the centre of the bay, her sternpost still breaking the surface, and there is at least one other wreck plus a number of unlit ships' mooring buoys.

## Anchorage and moorings

The yacht anchorage is in the eastern corner of the bay. There are also some large steel drum moorings available which require a stern anchor to be set. Even so, one generally lies beam on to the swell and some rolling is inevitable. This can be minimised by tucking as close in to the beach as prudence and the moored fishing boats allow.

The dinghy landing is often subject to surge, but the new landing steps completed in 1996 make getting ashore dry much less of a challenge than previously. Tenders must be hauled out, making an inflatable the best bet. There is also a small ferry which operates 24 hours a day, primarily for the fishermen.

## Formalities

Fly the Q flag on arrival. Ship's papers, passports and previous port clearance papers should be taken to the

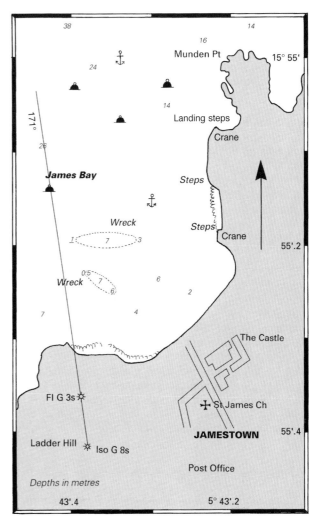

*Chart 56*   James Bay, St Helena. Based on Admiralty Chart No 1771.

James Bay, St Helena, seen from the anchorage. The new landing steps can just be seen beyond the yacht's bow.
*Photo: Liz Hammick*

harbourmaster (the pale blue building on the wharf) and customs and immigration (at the police station in the main square). In 1997 clearance fees were £16 for the vessel and £10 per person. Passports may be held at the police station until departure, and firearms, spear guns and scuba gear will be impounded against departure. Animals are not allowed ashore under any circumstances.

## Facilities

*Boatyard* None as such, but in an extreme emergency the harbour crane can lift up to 30 tons

*Engineers/electronics* Try the workshop which maintains the local boats

*Sailmaker* None, but local dressmakers are willing to machine light sails

*Diesel* Small quantities available by container from the filling station in the town, larger quantities – 200 litres (44 gallons) or more – from the fuel barge

*Water* By container from a tap on the quay

*Bottled gas* Cylinders can be refilled at the Shell station

*Showers* Near the landing steps

*Laundry/launderette* DIY facilities on the quay, or by machine at Anne's Place, through the public gardens

*Banks* No banks but a government-run cash desk at the castle. Neither credit cards nor personal cheques are accepted, but traveller's cheques can be cashed or major currencies (including the SA rand) exchanged

*General shopping* Much improved, with prices similar to the UK

*Provisioning* Several small supermarkets and grocery stores. A wide variety of tins, packets, dry staples, bread and eggs are always to be found. Fresh fruit and vegetables from the market open from 0900 weekdays. Occasional problems with the regular steamship service from South Africa may affect the availability of food, to which (quite reasonably) local people get first access

*Restaurants/hotels* Anne's Place is highly recommended for quality and value (book in advance). The Consulate Hotel Bar serves snacks and has a full restaurant

*Medical services* Small general hospital in Jamestown and also a dental surgery

## Communications

*Mailing address* Of limited use as a mailing address as there is no airmail service

*Fax service* At Cable & Wireless (fax: 2206) on the main street

*Post Office* On the main street

*Telephones* At the post office. There is direct dialling to most countries

*Bus service* No buses, but lifts are freely offered

*Taxis* Island tours can be arranged at very modest cost

*Car hire* Easily arranged and good value

*Ferry service* The Royal Mail ship MV *St Helena*, which also carries over a hundred passengers, calls every six weeks or so

*Air services* None

| | | |
|---|---|---|
| *Springs*: 0.8 m/2 ft 7 in | *Flag*: Trinidad | |
| *Neaps*: 0.5 m/1 ft 8 in | *Currency*: Trinidad & Tobago dollar | |

*Tel/fax - Country code*: 1–868, *Area code*: none

| Charts | Admiralty | US | Imray/Iolaire |
|---|---|---|---|
| General | 493 (1:300,000) | 25400 (1:250,000) | B (1:745,000) |
| | | 24404 (1:175,000) | |
| Approach | 484 (1:50,000) | 24405 (1:75,000) | D11 (1:240,700) |
| Harbour | 479 (1:25,000) | 24406 (1:17,500) | – |

## General

Over the past five years Trinidad has developed into one of the south-east Caribbean's leading yachting centres. Its position south of the normal hurricane belt increases its appeal as a safe venue to leave a boat during the summer – and makes it acceptable to most insurers. Yachting services are largely concentrated in the north-west of the island, many of them in the Chaguaramas Bay area where marinas and boatyards offer extensive facilities for haulout, lay-up and servicing. Foreign yachts are frequently stored ashore while their owners return home on one of the regular flights to the UK, USA and Canada.

Carnival – in theory held over the three days preceding Lent but with a build-up starting around New Year – is also a major attraction. Described with only slight exaggeration as 'the greatest show on earth', many local people spend the entire year planning costumes. Equally, visiting yachtsmen are more than welcome to take part and costumes can often be hired.

## Approach and entrance

Chacachacare Light [Fl 10s 26M] on the island of that name is the principal navigation light for the approach to Trinidad. From the north the light should be kept well to starboard until close to land to counter west-flowing currents.

Yachts approaching from the north usually pass through the Boca de Monos, the most easterly of the three *bocas* (literally 'mouths'). Le Chapeau rock [Fl(3) 10s] lies on the starboard hand in the entrance, after which a course of 170° clears Têteron Rock [Fl G 4s 7m 4M] at the southern end of the *boca*. There is good water between the islands of Caspar Grande and Gasparillo, leading directly into Chaguaramas Bay.

Yachts arriving from Venezuela generally enter the Gulf of Paria via either the Boca de Navios, east of Chacachacare Island, or south of Chacachacare Island and its two companions. Again there are no particular hazards.

## Radio

North Port Radio and Chaguaramas Bay customs both monitor VHF channel 16. Of the commercial concerns, CrewsInn Marina and Boatyard uses channel 77, Power Boats channel 72 and Peake Yacht Services channel 69. The smaller yards share channel 68 with both clubs as well as businesses ranging from chandleries to taxis.

## Anchorage and moorings

There is a designated yacht anchorage in the eastern part of Chaguaramas Bay marked by large white buoys, and a hefty fine will be imposed for ignoring them. Holding is patchy in sand and mud and a chain scope of at least 5:1 is advised locally.

The Trinidad & Tobago Yachting Association (tel: 634 4210, 4519, fax: 634 4376) on Carenage Bay to the east of Point Gourde has 16 visitors' moorings – another possibility is to anchor off the Trinidad Yacht Club (tel: 633 7420, fax: 633 6388) further east on Cumana Bay.

## Berthing and marinas

At least seven companies of varying size offer berthing on the shores of Chaguaramas Bay. Taken anti-clockwise these include:

1 CrewsInn Marina and Boatyard (tel: 634 4384/5, fax: 634 4542), the biggest and newest concern in the area which caters purely for visiting yachts. The marina has 60 berths capable of taking vessels up to 40 m (130 ft).
2 Tropical Marine (tel: 634 4502, fax: 634 4453), Tardieu Marine (tel: 634 4534) and Calypso Marine Services (tel: 634 4551), all relatively small boatyards each with some berthing available. They share the eastern corner of the bay, the latter two in a narrow and well-sheltered creek.
3 Humming Bird Marine (tel/fax: 634 4046), sometimes referred to as Stella Maris, also situated in the corner creek and owned by Harold La Borde, well-known in Caribbean sailing circles for having circumnavigated twice during the last 25 years, both times in home-built yachts. Humming Bird Marine has recently expanded and now provides 17 stern-to berths on its new jetty as well as nine or ten slots alongside.
4 The much larger Power Boat Mutual Facilities (tel: 634 4303, fax: 634 4327), generally known as simply 'Power Boats', immediately west of the creek with 20 stern-to berths for yachts up to 21 m (70 ft).
5 Peake Yacht Services (tel: 634 4405, 4420, 4423, 4427, fax: 634 4387), further west again, offering 16 stern-to berths for yachts up to 30 m (100 ft).

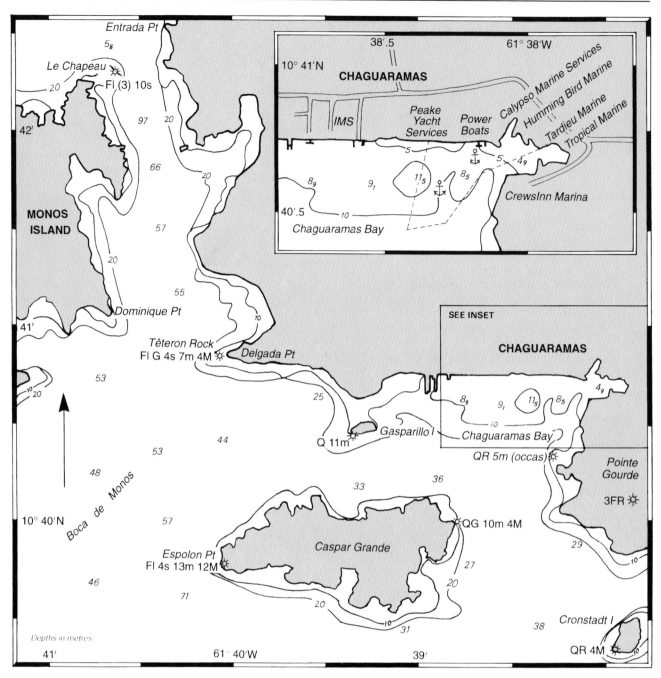

*Chart 57*  Chaguaramas Bay, Trinidad. Based on Admiralty Chart No 479.

In addition the Trinidad Yacht Club (tel: 633 7420, fax: 633 6388), situated four miles to the east on Cumana Bay, reserve 40 of their 80 berths for visiting yachts up to 17 m (55 ft).

## Formalities

Entry formalities are completed at Chaguaramas customs and immigration office in the CrewsInn Marina complex, where there is a dedicated customs jetty which arriving yachts must use. The office is manned around the clock and the entire crew is expected to present themselves without delay. However, sizeable overtime fees are charged for arrival outside normal office hours (0800–1200 and 1300–1600, weekdays only), apparently also levied for *entering territorial waters 12 miles off-*

*shore* outside these hours. More modest dues are payable for each 30-day period spent in the country. The officials are friendly and efficient, but in peak periods the offices can be under-staffed.

## Facilities

Although based at Power Boats, the Yacht Service Association of Trinidad and Tobago (tel/fax: 634 4938) represents most yacht-related businesses in the country. They can recommend who to go to for what (if not covered below), as well as supplying current haulage and lay-up charges, etc to those considering sailing to Trinidad for this purpose.

*Boatyards* CrewsInn Marina and Boatyard (tel: 634

4384/5, boatyard fax: 634 4828) has a 200 ton travel lift plus a 60 ton crane with 43 m (140 ft) boom, backed by comprehensive yard facilities and a large lay-up area, some of it under cover. All work is done by boatyard staff and DIY work is not normally permitted.

Power Boats (tel: 634 4303, fax: 634 4327) has a 50 ton lift and dry storage space for 160 boats. Other than actual hauling, work is normally subcontracted out to carefully vetted specialists, some of them based in the yard. Semi-skilled labour is available and DIY work permitted. Peake Yacht Services (tel: 634 4427/3, fax: 634 4387) use a 150 ton lift. They can take around 300 yachts ashore and also have large covered workshops. Again DIY work is permitted. Industrial Marine Services (IMS) (tel: 634 4328, fax: 634 4437) have a 70 ton lift and room for some 130 boats ashore. Most work is carried out by Atlantic Yacht Services (tel: 634 4337, fax: 634 4437), which is based in the yard.

Finally, all the smaller yards previously listed under *Berthing and marinas* offer space for maintenance ashore, generally with a DIY option

*Engineers/electronics* Bowen Marine at the CrewsInn Marina Boatyard, plus several engineering concerns on and around the Power Boats site and at Peake Yacht Services

*Sailmaker* Ocean Sails International (tel/fax: 634 4560) at IMS can make or repair sails of all sizes. Also Barrow Sail Loft (tel/fax: 634 4137) at Power Boats, and Soca Sails (tel: 634 4384, ext 117) at the CrewsInn Boatyard. Rigging services are available at Ocean Sails, Peake Yacht Services and CrewsInn Boatyard

*Chandlery* Very good stocks at Peake Yacht Services Chandlery, at Budget Marine (tel/fax: 8634 4382) in the Formula III Building on Western Main Road, and at the Boat Shop II (tel: 634 2628, tel/fax: 634 4148) at Power Boats. All are willing to order items not in stock

*Yacht clubs* The Trinidad & Tobago Yachting Association (tel: 634 4210, 4519, fax: 634 4376) and the Trinidad Yacht Club (tel: 633 7420, fax: 633 6388) are both situated east of Point Gourde, facing on Carenage Bay and Cumana Bay respectively. Both make bona fide visiting yachtsmen very welcome

*Diesel* Fuel jetties at Power Boats and the CrewsInn Marina, Peake Yacht Services is supplied by a fuel truck

*Water* At all marinas, boatyards and clubs

*Electricity* At all marinas, boatyards and clubs. Normally 110 volt, though 220 volt is sometimes available

*Bottled gas* Propane is readily available, but pure butane is not obtainable – a propane/butane mix is normally used to fill yachtsmen's cylinders

*Ice* Plentiful everywhere

*Showers* At all marinas, boatyards and clubs

*Launderettes* At Power Boats, Peake Yacht Services and IMS. Also Chin's Laundry and Dry Cleaning (tel: 622 3733), which offers free pick-up and delivery

*Banks* At Peake Yacht Services and CrewsInn Marina, with credit card facilities, plus many elsewhere

*General shopping* Excellent, with several American-style shopping malls in and around Port of Spain

*Provisioning* Grocery stores at or near Peake Yacht Services, Power Boats and CrewsInn Marina (which also has a range of other shops). An even better choice further afield, with a wide range of domestic and imported produce available

*Restaurants/hotels* Something for every pocket, including a café, and/or restaurant at each of the larger marinas and boatyards. Peake Marine Services and CrewsInn boast hotels, with rental apartments at Power Boats

*Medical services* Several hospitals and medical centres in and around Port of Spain

## Communications

*Mailing addresses* C/o CrewsInn Marina and Boatyard, PO Bag 518, Carenage; Power Boat Mutual Facilities, PO Box 3163, Carenage; Peake Yacht Services, PO Box 3168, Carenage; the Trinidad & Tobago Yachting Association, PO Box 3140, Carenage; or the Trinidad Yacht Club, Bayshore, and others (in all cases followed by 'Trinidad, West Indies') by prior arrangement

*Fax services* At Power Boats (fax: 634 4327), Peake Yacht Services (fax: 634 4387), CrewsInn Marina and Boatyard (marina fax: 634 4542, boatyard fax: 634 4828), Humming Bird Marine (tel/fax: 634 4046), both the yacht clubs and elsewhere

*Post Office* On Carenage Bay east of Point Gourde. Power Boats sells stamps and will take visitors' mail to the post office

*Telephones* Card operated telephones at all marinas, boatyards and clubs, where cards are also on sale

*Bus service* Local people favour 'maxi-taxis' – minibuses which operate much as regular buses would elsewhere. They normally stop only at marked bus stops, and must be waved down. Like private taxis they have 'H' number plates – confirm that you are boarding the type you intend

*Taxis* Readily available, but private taxis are much more expensive than the shared variety

*Car hire* Mark's Rentals (tel: 632 8984) at Power Boats and Convenient Rental (tel/fax: 634 4017) at Peake Yacht Services (where bicycles can also be hired). Driving is on the left

*Air services* The island is served by regular flights to USA, Canada and London, as well as to other Caribbean countries

| | | | |
|---|---|---|---|
| *Springs*: 0.7 m/2 ft 3 in | | *Flag*: Grenada | |
| *Neaps*: 0.6 m/2 ft | | *Currency*: EC dollar | |

*Tel/fax – Country code*: 1-473, *Area code*: none

| **Charts** | **Admiralty** | **US** | **Imray/Iolaire** |
|---|---|---|---|
| General | 597 (1:175,000) | 25400 (1:250,000) | B5 (1:510,700) |
| Approach | 797 (1:60,000) | 25481 (1:60,000) | B3 (1:162,000) |
| | | | B32 (1:86,000) |
| Harbour | 797 (1:25,000) | – | B32 (Inset) |

## General

Prickly Bay, also known as L'anse aux Epines, is one of the few recommended harbours which does not have a town, or at least a village, nearby. However, it is only a short bus or taxi ride from the capital, St George's, and until facilities improve in that harbour Prickly Bay offers a far preferable port of call for yachts. It is particularly attractive even by the high standards of the Caribbean, and is an official port of entry.

## Approach

The majority of yachts approach from the north, down the western (lee) side of Grenada. If a course is shaped directly for Point Salines at the western extremity of the island all outliers will be cleared, but if coming from the direction of St George's, Long Point Shoal to the north-west of Long Point (itself at the western end of the spectacular Grande Anse beach) carries less than one metre. The old, striped lighthouse at Point Salines fell victim to the airport development and the replacement [Q(9) 15s 7M] is a poor substitute. After rounding Point Salines, Prickly Point to the east of Prickly Bay should be seen about 2.5 miles distant, extending further south than the intermediate headlands. Glover Island can be left on either side.

If approaching from eastwards, or from the south, the chief hazard is The Porpoises, a group of breaking rocks about 0.7 miles south of Prickly Point. They are unmarked and unlit, and have claimed more than one yacht. In fact lights along this entire coast are poor, and if approaching in darkness there is much to be said for taking the traditional line and heaving-to until daylight, but beware of being set past the island by the strong current.

## Radio

Spice Island Marine Services monitors VHF channels 16 and 68.

## Entrance

There are reefs close to both sides of the entrance, but these generally present no problem. More dangerous is the isolated coral patch in the centre of the bay, west of Spice Island Marine Services, which is *sometimes* marked by an inconspicuous buoy. The water in Prickly Bay, though clean, is often cloudy, and if in doubt keep well east, towards the Spice Island Marine pontoon. There is a second shoal close inshore on the eastern part of the bay just north of the boatyard.

## Anchorage and moorings

Most yachts anchor either in the north-east corner of the bay or off Spice Island Marine, the best place for landing by dinghy. Otherwise choose almost any part of the bay in 10 m or so over mud and sand, though anchoring within 100 m (300 ft) of the beach at the Calabash Hotel at the head of the bay is forbidden. Some swell may find its way in from the south, but Prickly Bay is often both flat and breezy – the best possible Caribbean combination. As with all Caribbean anchorages, keep a careful watch for swimmers if going ashore by outboard-powered dinghy.

## Berthing and marinas

Spice Island Marine offers stern-to berthing for two dozen or so yachts, as well as providing dinghy dockage and other services to those anchored off. It must be one of very few top Caribbean destinations to have remained operational but unspoilt by the yachting explosion of the last two decades, and with its lawns, flowers and trees, long may it remain so.

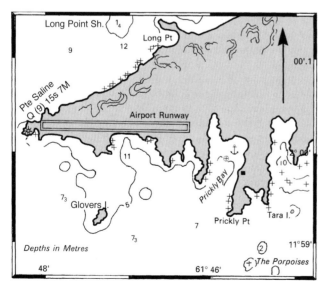

*Chart 58*   The south-west coast of Grenada. Based on Admiralty Chart No 797.

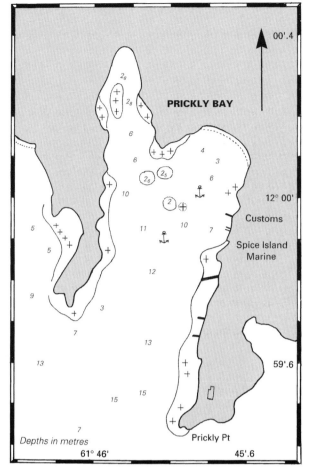

*Chart 59* Prickly Bay, Grenada. Based on a plan in the *Lesser Antilles*.

## Formalities

Customs and immigration inhabit the upper floor of the building just to the north of the disused slipway. All the usual documents are required, but the attitude is pleasant and relaxed. Office hours are 0800–1145 and 1300–1545 weekdays only, and as overtime fees are likely to be accompanied by separate taxi fares for several officials, the charge can mount dramatically.

## Facilities

*Boatyards* Spice Island Marine Services (tel: 444 4257/4342, fax: 444 2816) has a 35 ton travel lift and allows DIY work

*Engineers/electronics* At Spice Island Marine, or McIntyre Bros (tel: 440 3944, fax: 444 2899) on the road to the airport

*Sailmaker* Michael at Spice Island Marine. Jeff Fisher (tel/fax: 440 2556) is agent for Neil Pryde sails of Hong Kong, which claims six week delivery. Also Johnny Sails & Canvas (tel: 444 1108/9619, fax: 444 1108) on the St George's road, which also deals with rigging etc

*Chandlery* Well stocked chandlery at Spice Island Marine

*Yacht club* The Grenada Yacht Club (tel: 440 3050, fax: 440 4128) has long been one of the best reasons for taking a yacht to St George's. Their new, full-service, 30 berth dock facility was opened in September 1997, while their premises overlooking the Carenage and Lagoon are famed as a venue from which to see the 'green flash'

*Diesel* On the pontoon at Spice Island Marine

*Water* On the pontoon at Spice Island Marine, plus taps elsewhere in the boatyard. Grenada has some of the sweetest water in the Lesser Antilles

*Electricity* Available (220 volt 50Hz) if berthed stern-to

*Bottled gas* Propane refills available at Spice Island Marine or at Huggins on the Carenage in St George's

*Ice* At Spice Island Marine

*Showers* At Spice Island Marine. A small charge is made if not berthed in the marina

*Laundry/launderette* At Spice Island Marine

*Banks* Several in St George's, with credit card facilities

*General shopping* Not too much locally, but a good range in St George's

*Provisioning* Essentials mini-market at Spice Island Marine, with a wider choice at several supermarkets on the road into St George's. Local ladies sometimes bring baskets of fresh produce out to the boatyard, but nothing rivals the excellent and colourful market in the centre of St George's – go early, and take a camera and several bags

*Restaurants* Pleasant bar/restaurant at Spice Island Marine (with really good local steel band on Friday nights). Just down the road are the long-established Red Crab Restaurant (tel: 444 4424), the Choo Light (tel: 444 2196) which also does take-aways, and the Bolero (tel: 444 1250). In town the Nutmeg, overlooking the Carenage, deserves a visit – try their calaloo soup and rotis

*Hotels* Many at all levels, including several overlooking Prickly Bay

*Medical services* Hospital outside St George's

## Communications

*Mailing addresses* C/o General Delivery at the main post office, or c/o Spice Island Marine Services, Prickly Bay, L'Anse aux Epines, St George's, Grenada, West Indies

*Fax service* At Spice Island Marine Services' office (fax: 444 2816)

*Post Office* On the waterfront in St George's

*Telephones* At Spice Island Marine and elsewhere

*Bus service* Irregular buses from the boatyard, or walk up the road to the T junction for more frequent services

*Taxis* Plenty, both cars and mini-buses. Many of the drivers are delighted to double as tour guides

*Car hire* McIntyre Brothers (tel: 440 3944) and others. Driving is on the left

*Air services* The airport at Point Salines has direct flights to the UK, USA and Canada as well as inter-island services

*Springs*: 0.8 m/2 ft 7 in          *Flag*: Barbados
*Neaps*: 0.7 m/2 ft 3 in          *Currency*: Barbados dollar

*Tel/fax – Country code*: 1–246, *Area code*: none

| Charts | Admiralty | US | Imray/Iolaire |
|---|---|---|---|
| General | 956 (1:644,000) | – | B5 (1:510,700) |
| Approach | 2485 (1:100,000) | 25485 (1:100,000) | B2 (1:56,900) |
| Harbour | 502 (1:12,500) | 25485 (1:25,000) | B2 (Inset) |
| | | 25487 (1:10,000) | |

## General

Barbados was once a popular island for an Atlantic landfall – it is reasonably well lit, offers some of the best general shopping of any ex-British island in the West Indies and has direct flights to Britain, the USA and Canada among other countries. However clearance procedures are more complicated and time consuming than in most other islands, and Carlisle Bay, the usual yacht anchorage, can be unpleasantly rolly. There is no marina, though one has been under discussion for many years.

The fact remains that, with Barbados lying nearly 100 miles to the east of the main chain of islands, if it is to be visited at all it is logical to do so first, though boats do occasionally beat out from Martinique or St Lucia. And of course a call at Barbados cuts at least a day off the Atlantic passage.

## Approach

Barbados differs from most West Indian islands in that it is low lying with only one high point, Mount Misery, at 329 m (1069 ft). Bridgetown lies near the south-west tip of Barbados and is most often approached around the south of the island, though there is no reason why it should not be approached from either end. Along parts of the south-east coast depths shoal rapidly, from 100 m or more to breaking reef in considerably less than 0.5 miles, and if approaching after dark it is unwise to close the windward coast. Even using GPS, a good half mile should be allowed outside charted dangers to allow for possible datum errors. The airport is well lit, as is South Point [Fl(3) 30s 44m 17M], and once these have been identified the course should be altered to remain south of the latter by at least a mile, an offing maintained until off Bridgetown.

A large bank known as The Shallows, with a least depth of 60 m (200 ft), lies about four miles south-east of South Point. This area can be very rough when a westerly swell meets an east-going current and should be avoided.

## Radio

Barbados Radio monitors VHF channel 16 and uses channel 12 as its working channel.

## Entrance

On arrival yachts must go straight to the Deepwater Harbour to clear. The most convenient berth is in the far south-eastern corner, opposite the customs and immigration office, but there is frequently a swell and the quayside is rough, so large fenders will be needed. See *Formalities*, below.

## Anchorage and moorings

After clearance has been granted most yachts return to anchor in Carlisle Bay, in good holding with 10 m or less over sand. Although in some ways a classic Caribbean anchorage, with clear blue water backed by a long sandy beach, Carlisle Bay frequently suffers from swell, causing monohulls to roll and making landing by dinghy a distinctly wet affair. If surf is breaking on the beach it may be best to take the dinghy into the Careenage. Otherwise,

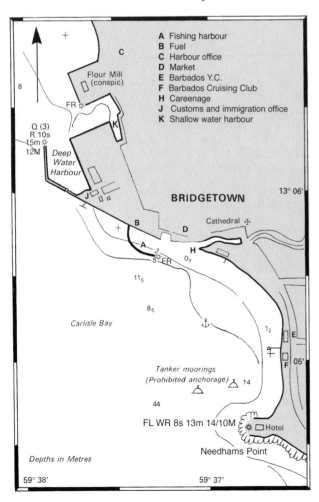

A  Fishing harbour
B  Fuel
C  Harbour office
D  Market
E  Barbados Y.C.
F  Barbados Cruising Club
H  Careenage
J  Customs and immigration office
K  Shallow water harbour

Flour Mill (conspic)

Deep Water Harbour

BRIDGETOWN

13° 06'

Cathedral

Carlisle Bay

Tanker moorings (Prohibited anchorage)

FL WR 8s 13m 14/10M

Hotel

Needhams Point

Depths in Metres

59° 38'          59° 37'

*Chart 60*   Bridgetown, Barbados. Based on Admiralty Chart No 502.

The anchorage at Carlisle Bay, Barbados. *Photo: John Melling*

until you've got the measure of it, avoid carrying cameras (except the waterproof kind) or other valuables, and transport money, shoes etc in sealed polythene bags.

## Berthing and marinas

Yachts are sometimes allowed to lie in the Shallow Water Harbour to the north of the town but it is dusty, inconvenient, and usually reserved for local use. Another possibility is to berth in the Careenage, for which permission will be needed from the Barbados Port Authority (tel: 436 6883), though the frequent surge will put severe strain on warps and fenders. However most crews will want to celebrate their arrival in the Caribbean by swimming from the boat, impossible in either of the above.

## Formalities

Fly the Q flag on approaching Barbados. As already mentioned, yachts must go into the Deep Water Harbour to clear customs and immigration. Call Bridgetown Harbour Signal Station on VHF channel 12 for clearance to enter the harbour or, if out of hours, to anchor in the Quarantine holding area south of the Careenage Molehead.

Customs and immigration are housed in a large building just to the south of the Deep Water Harbour and function from 0600 to 2200 seven days a week. The usual papers, including outward clearance from the previous port, will be required and a charge of around US $25 made, covering boat and crew. Anchorage and light dues are also payable.

It is normally necessary to return to the Deep Water Harbour *with the yacht* to obtain outward clearance, which remains valid for 24 hours. However it seems this rule may sometimes be relaxed and outward clearance granted to skippers who have walked over from Carlisle Bay – check the current position when clearing in. Once cleared from the Deep Water Harbour the yacht must leave directly to sea towards her next port of call and cannot return to the anchorage.

## Coastal cruising

Customs clearance is required to cruise northwards along the coast and dues may also be payable. If intending to do this check the procedure either on arrival or through the Coast Guard on VHF channel 16.

## Facilities

*Boatyard* The Boatyard (previously Knowles Marine) on Carlisle Bay provides excellent service though it does not have haulage facilities which are only available in the main harbour

*Engineers/Electronics* Enquire at The Boatyard

*Sailmaker* Doyle Sailmakers Caribbean (tel: 423 4600, fax: 423 4499) at 6 Crossroads, St Philip are a major sailmaker, exporting throughout the Caribbean and worldwide

*Chandlery* Two in Bridgetown

*Yacht club* Both the Barbados Yacht Club (tel: 427 1125) and the Barbados Cruising Club (tel: 426 4434) have premises facing the southern part of Carlisle Bay. Both are friendly and helpful towards visiting yachtsmen

*Diesel* In the Shallow Water Harbour or the Fishing Harbour (preferably go in the morning when the fishing boats are out)

*Petrol* From the service station near The Boatyard

*Water* In the Careenage, the Deep Water Harbour (whilst clearing in) or the Fishing Harbour (where water is free if also taking on diesel). Unless large quantities are required it may be easier to carry it by can from The Boatyard

*Bottled gas* The Boatyard, or the Texaco tank farm north of Deep Water Harbour. Propane and butane are both available

*Ice* The Boatyard and most filling stations

*Showers* The Boatyard

*Laundry/launderette* The Boatyard

*Banks* Several, with credit card facilities. Both Barbados and US dollars are used, but the former are not accepted elsewhere in the Caribbean so change any remaining for US dollars before departure

*General shopping* Relatively good, though inevitably slanted towards the thousands of cruise ship and hotel tourists

*Provisioning* Several large supermarkets, mostly stocking American brands, plus good produce and fish markets

*Restaurants/hotels* A vast choice. The bar/restaurant at The Boatyard is a favourite evening venue with cruisers, and there are dozens more in Bridgetown

*Medical services* A small private hospital, The Diagnostic Clinic, is situated within walking distance of the Barbados Yacht Club. There is a large modern hospital just outside Bridgetown

## Communications

*Mailing addresses* C/o General Delivery at the main post office (identification will be required on collection), either of the yacht clubs, or The Boatyard, Bay Street, Bridgetown, Barbados, all by prior arrangement

*Post Office* A large building with General Delivery occupying its own floor

*Telephones* At The Boatyard, the post office and elsewhere

*Bus service* Buses all over the island – a cheap, fun, way to travel

*Taxis* Plentiful until a cruise ship arrives, when they vanish

*Car hire* Several agencies. Driving is on the left

*Air services* International air services to Europe and the Americas, and local air services to Eastern Caribbean islands. Grantley Adams airport is 20.8 km from Bridgetown

*Springs*: 0.6 m/2 ft

*Neaps*: 0.5 m/1 ft 8 in

*Flag*: St Lucia

*Currency*: EC dollar

*Tel/fax – Country code*: 1–758, *Area code*: none

| Charts | Admiralty | US | Imray/Iolaire |
|--------|-----------|-----|---------------|
| General | 596 (1:175,000) | – | B5 (1:510,700) |
| Approach | 1273 (1:60,000) | 25521 (1:75,000) | B1 (1:72,000) |
| Harbour | 197 (1:25,000) | – | B1 (Inset) |
|  | 197 (1:5,000) |  |  |

## General

Rodney Bay Marina, St Lucia, inside the lagoon at Rodney Bay (also known as Gros Islet Bay), has become a popular Atlantic landfall over the last few years. Certainly the range of on-the-spot facilities is the widest in the southern Antilles, and several large charter fleets are based here. It is currently the arrival port for the annual ARC (Atlantic Rally for Cruisers).

The lagoon's most obvious disadvantages are in being some way from Castries – though this is partly offset by excellent shopping etc nearby – and even further from the international airport. The protection offered by the narrow entrance also means that the water inside is

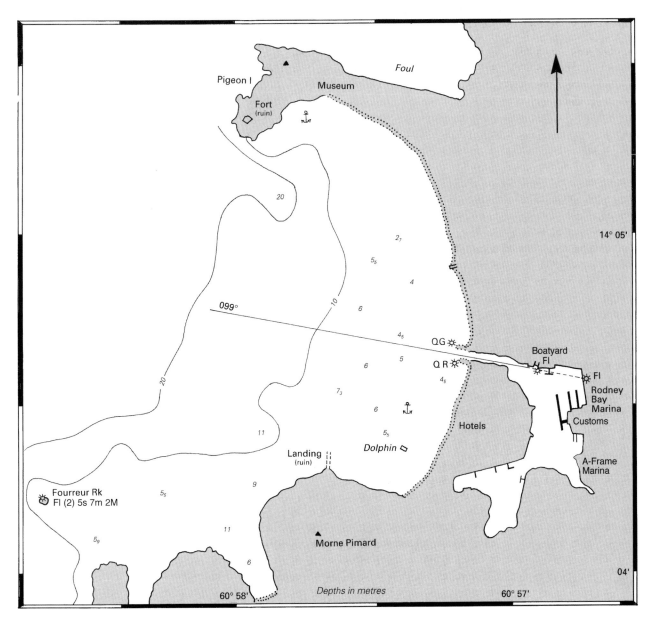

*Chart 61*    Rodney Bay, St Lucia. Based on a plan in the *Lesser Antilles*.

stagnant and unsuitable for swimming, though admittedly it is only a short walk or dinghy ride to the beach. It all comes down to priorities.

## Approach

Rodney Bay lies within a couple of miles of the northern end of St Lucia, one of the more mountainous of the Lesser Antilles. Although Pointe du Cap at the extreme north of the island has no outlying hazards, neither is it lit, and the light at Cape Marquis [Fl(2) 20s 60m] three miles further south on the windward coast is of unspecified range.

Having rounded Pointe du Cap, Pigeon Island will be seen rising to over 100 m (356 ft) at the end of a low artificial causeway. Beyond is Rodney Bay, where fish traps with their associated floats and lines can be a hazard.

## Radio

Rodney Bay Marina operates on VHF channel 16 with Rodney Bay Marina Boatyard on channel 68. The A-Frame Marina uses channels 16 and 17. As is usual in the Caribbean, a number of other concerns ranging from charter companies to restaurants monitor VHF, generally channel 16.

## Entrance

The entrance to the lagoon lies near the middle of the bay, between Gros Islet village to the north and Reduit Beach to the south. It is not hard to identify by daylight and is lit at night, but the channel is narrow and if approaching after dark the first time visitor might do better to anchor outside and enter in daylight. There is 2.5 m (8 ft) or more in the entrance channel and in much of the lagoon itself.

## Anchorage and moorings

It is possible to anchor to the south of the marina in the main lagoon in 2.5–3 m, or in the slightly shallower inner lagoon to the south-west. Both offer reasonable holding in mud and a guaranteed escape from rolling, but can be buggy if the wind is down. The alternative is to return to the outer bay after completing formalities and anchor either off Reduit Beach or to the south-east of Pigeon Island, but both may be subject to swell.

## Berthing and marinas

If intending to berth at Rodney Bay Marina (tel: 452 0324, fax: 452 8363/0185) it is best to telephone or call up on VHF channel 16 before arrival to be allocated a berth, as there is no reception pontoon. Failing this, secure in any space available until a berth can be arranged. Security is good.

The smaller A-Frame Marina (tel: 452 8725) is situated to the south of the larger marina, with most of its 20 berths stern-to.

## Formalities

Rodney Bay is one of four ports of entry in St Lucia. There is a clearance berth opposite the customs and immigration office, but only if planning to anchor off is it necessary to secure here first. If staying in the marina the skipper can take the usual papers and go on foot. Office hours are 0800–1800, but overtime is charged after 1600.

## Facilities

*Boatyard/engineers/electronics* Rodney Bay Marina Boatyard (tel: 452 8215, fax: 452 9725) has the best boatyard facilities in the southern Antilles, including a 50 ton travel lift and large lay-up area. DIY, or hire local labour. Also Rodney Bay Ship Services (tel: 452 9973, fax: 452 9974) at the A-Frame Marina

*Electronics* Cay Electronics (tel: 452 9922, fax: 452 8524) has branches throughout the islands

*Sailmaker* At Sunsail charters (tel: 452 8848/8648, fax: 452 0839), who will also deal with rigging problems

*Chandlery* Rodney Bay Marine Hardware (tel: 452 9973, fax: 452 9974) has extensive stocks, as have Sunsail charters

*Diesel* On the fuel dock to the north of the marina (available duty free following outward clearance)

*Water* On pontoon berths and at the fuel dock, also at the A-Frame Marina

*Electricity* On pontoon berths (220 volt 50Hz)

*Bottled gas* At Sunsail charters (most types of propane cylinder)

*Ice* Block ice from Sunsail, cube ice from stores and the mini-market

*Showers* In the marina complex and at the A-Frame Marina

*Laundry/launderette* In the marina complex

*Banks* In the marina complex, with credit card facilities

*General shopping* Plenty of tourist shops, boutiques etc locally, but for wider variety go to Castries

*Provisioning* Several supermarkets and bakeries etc in the marina complex and a large shopping centre and more supermarkets on the Castries road, but for the best fresh produce visit the market in Castries

*Restaurants* Dozens within walking or dinghy distance

*Hotels* Many, scattered throughout the island

*Medical services* Various clinics, plus a hospital south of Castries

## Communications

*Mailing address* C/o Rodney Bay Marina, PO Box 1538, Castries, St Lucia, West Indies

*Fax service* At the marina office (fax: 452 8363)

*Post Office* In Castries

*Telephones* In the marina complex and elsewhere

*Bus service* Buses to Castries

*Taxis/car hire* In the marina complex. Driving is on the left

*Air services* Inter-island flights from Tapion airport at Vigie Cove near Castries, but long-haul carriers use Hewannora airport, adjacent to Vieux Fort at the south end of the island

*Springs*: 0.8 m/2 ft 7 in     *Flag*: France
*Neaps*: 0.6 m/2 ft             *Currency*: French franc

*Tel/fax – Country code*: 596, *Area code*: none

| Charts | Admiralty | US | Imray/Iolaire |
|--------|-----------|-----|---------------|
| General | 594 (1:175,000) | – | A4 (1:388,000) |
|         | 596 (1:175,000) |   |                |
| Approach | 371 (1:79,700) | 25524 (1:75,000) | A30 (1:92,000) |
| Harbour | 494 (1:12,000) | 25527 (1:15,000) | A30 (Inset) |

## General

Fort de France is one of the very few cities in the Lesser Antilles which truly merits the title in terms of both size and atmosphere. It became the capital of Martinique in 1902 following the eruption of Mt Pelée and destruction of the previous capital, St Pierre, and has more than made up for lost time. Facilities are generally excellent, and not surprisingly landfalls in Martinique, and to a lesser extent Guadeloupe, are very popular among French-speaking yachtsmen.

All the French islands of the Lesser Antilles are technically part of France and receive large subsidies from their parent country, some of which appear to go into the comprehensive and generally well maintained system of buoys and lights. Much of the infrastructure comes from France, along with the legal and education systems plus, somehow, that indefinable chic in dress and bearing which so many French West Indian ladies share with their Parisienne counterparts. Not for nothing did Napoleon's Empress Josephine come from Martinique.

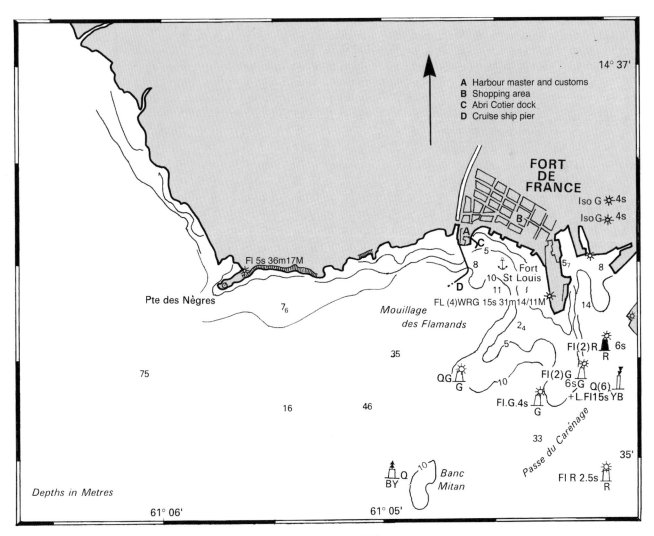

*Chart 62*     Fort de France, Martinique. Based on Admiralty Chart No 494.

The waterfront and anchorage at Fort de France, with the cathedral spire neatly framed by the raked masts of a schooner.
*Photo: Anne Hammick*

## Approach

Martinique is one of the more mountainous islands of the Lesser Antilles, and Fort de France lies on the northern shores of a large bay somewhat south of its centre. If making landfall there after a transatlantic passage it therefore makes sense to approach around the southern end of the island, if only to avoid the long and often windless stretch from Pte du Macouba in the extreme north. Reefs and offlying islets fringe much of the windward coast, which should be given a wide berth.

If approaching around the south, Ilet Cabrits [FlR 5s 43m 16M] can be cleared at a mile or so and Rocher du Diamant (Diamond Rock) at the same distance. This will avoid the 4.0 m (13 ft) Banc du Diamant shoal where the seas can be rough. The south-west coast has no outlying hazards.

## Radio

Fort de France Radio monitors VHF channel 16 and uses channels 12 and 13 as its working channels.

## Entrance

The entrance to the Baie de Fort de France is more than three miles wide, between Pointe des Nègres [Fl 5s 36m 17M] in the north and Ilet a Ramiers (unlit) in the south. An unlit red buoy, Banc du Gros Ilet, lies almost in the centre of the mouth to mark shoals carrying a least depth of 3.5 m (11 ft). Other buoys, mostly lit, mark other shoals to the east of the main yacht anchorage.

## Anchorage and moorings

The most popular yacht anchorage is in the Mouillage des Flamands, to the west of Fort Saint Louis and directly off the city and public gardens. However with the two ferry piers to the east, and the new but seldom-used cruise ship pier to the west, space is tight. Some moorings have also been laid in the area, contributing to the chronic overcrowding. It may be possible for a smaller yacht to find space close inshore, but crews of larger yachts (or those needing scope for a nylon anchor rode) may be faced with a long dinghy ride. Dinghies can be left free of charge at the floating pontoon near the Abri Cotier dock. Holding is reasonably good in mud.

Winds from south of east make the Mouillage des Flamands uncomfortable, and an alternative is to cross to Anse Mitan, sheltered by Pte du Bout on the southern shore, from which a regular ferry service runs to Fort de France.

## Berthing and marinas

It may be possible to lie stern-to at the Abri Cotier dock, but this is usually fully occupied by charter boats.

## Formalities

The customs and immigration office is situated near the new cruise ship pier. Office hours are 0700–1100 and 1430–1700 daily.

## Facilities

*Boatyards* The Ship Shop at Quai Ouest (tel: 737399, fax: 701302) has a 30 tonne travel lift, Polymar (tel: 706288, fax: 601097), next to the Ship Shop slipway, specialises in GRP yachts, and Chalmessin Enterprises (tel: 600375/600379, fax: 634967) specialises in metalwork

*Engineers* Madia Boat (tel: 631061, fax: 634870), Multicap Caraibes (tel: 714181, fax: 714183) Martinique Diesel (tel: 511613/513433) and several others

*Electronics* Carib Electronic Engineering (tel: 600700, fax: 636014) for electronics, and Cadet Petit (tel: 637918) for electrical work

*Sailmaker* R Helenon (tel: 602205, fax: 631763) who has premises overlooking the Riviere Madame, and North Sails Martinique (tel: 680334, fax: 685069)

*Chandlery* The Ship Shop (tel: 714340, fax: 701302) is one of the best chandleries in the Lesser Antilles, plus Sea Services (tel/fax: 702669) who also have a rigging workshop, Multicap Caraibes and several others. Used bargains at Puces Nautique (tel: 605848, fax: 637331)

*Yacht club* The Yacht Club de la Martinique is situated in the military and commercial port on the eastern side of the Fort St Louis peninsula. It has its own small marina, but vacant berths are extremely rare

*Diesel/petrol* Currently no fuel available alongside in Fort de France. Try Ponton du Bakoua (tel: 660545, fax: 660950) in Anse Mitan

*Water* At the Abri Cotier dock

*Bottled gas* Camping Gaz exchanges readily available. Calor Gas and other non-standard bottles can be filled at Antilles Gas (tel: 503330) in the industrial area

*Ice* At the Abri Cotier dock or Glaciers Modernes

*Showers* At the Abri Cotier dock and at the yacht club

*Laundry/launderette* In the city

*Banks* Many, with credit card facilities

*General shopping* Excellent – the place to treat yourself

*Provisioning* Up to the best French standards, with cheese and paté abounding, and a good place to stock up on wine. Several of the larger supermarkets will deliver to the Abri Cotier dock. Don't miss the large covered produce market, and the fish market on the banks of the Riviere Madame to the west of the city

*Restaurants* Many and excellent, at all prices

*Hotels* At all levels

*Medical services* Large modern hospital outside the city

## Communications

*Mailing addresses* C/o Ship Shop, Baie des Tourelles, 97200 Fort de France, Martinique, French West Indies or c/o *Poste restante* at the main post office

*Post Office* On the main road opposite the attractive Place de la Savanne public gardens

*Telephones* Many around the city, using cards bought in post offices

*Bus service* Minibuses run all over the island from the square next to the customs office

*Ferry service* Regular ferries to Anse Mitan

*Taxis* From the same square as the minibuses. Communal taxis are the norm, and very economical – you specify where you want to go, but the driver can then pick up more passengers en route. Sole use taxis are expensive

*Car hire* Several agencies. Driving is on the right

*Air services* International airport to the east of the Baie de Fort de France with flights to the USA, Canada and Europe

| | | |
|---|---|---|
| *Springs*: 0.6 m/2 ft | *Flag*: Antigua | |
| *Neaps*: 0.4 m/1 ft 4 in | *Currency*: EC dollar | |

*Tel/fax – Country code*: 1–268, *Area code*: none

| Charts | Admiralty | US | Imray/Iolaire |
|---|---|---|---|
| General | 584 (1:175,000) | 25550 (1:250,000) | A3 (1:394,000) |
| Approach | 2064 (1:50,000) | 25570 (1:75,000) | A27 (1:57,600) |
| Harbour | 2064 (1:20,000) | – | A27 (Inset) |

## General

English Harbour, Antigua, features high on the 'must visit' list for most British and American cruising yachtsmen. Semi-derelict until the 1950s, Nelson's Dockyard and its surrounds are now one of the busiest yachting centres in the Lesser Antilles, particularly during Antigua Race Week at the end of April. Probably less than a quarter of the yachts present actually race but there is plenty going on ashore and, if you don't mind crowds, it provides a fun contrast to the 'deserted beaches' aspect of the Caribbean. (If you can't stand crowds and adore deserted beaches, clear in at Antigua and then sail on to Barbuda, its smaller and much less developed sister island to the north.)

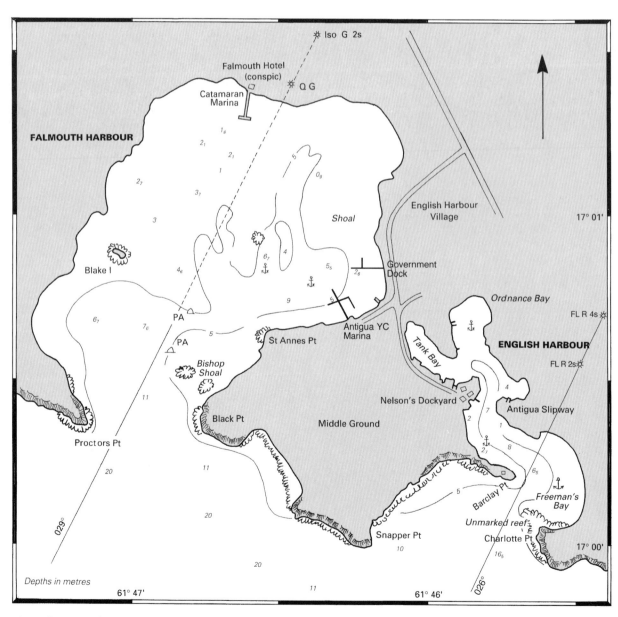

*Chart 63*   English Harbour/Falmouth Bay, Antigua. Based on a plan in the *Lesser Antilles*.

The classic shot of English Harbour, taken from Shirley Heights. Falmouth Bay can be seen in the background.
*Photo: Anne Hammick*

English Harbour is never deserted. Until a decade or so ago most visiting yachts used the same small protected anchorage favoured by the eighteenth-century British fleet, but since then ever-increasing numbers have turned to the adjoining Falmouth Bay, preferring the open, breezy anchorage of Falmouth to its more enclosed neighbour.

Almost all the development fringing both harbours is yacht or tourist related, and with nearly all requirements met locally it would be possible, though a pity, to spend several weeks in Antigua without ever visiting the capital, St John's, or venturing more than a mile from one's boat.

## Approach

At one time Antigua had a poor reputation as an Atlantic landfall, not least because its vicious windward reefs are unmarked by lights of any kind. While this is still true, the bright lights of V C Bird International Airport in the north of the island now effectively announce Antigua's presence from afar. They appear to burn all night, and should be quite sufficient to prevent the unwary from running up on the island unawares. If Antigua is sighted at dusk consideration should be given to reducing speed or even heaving-to for the night, but this might be said of many Caribbean landfalls.

The entrances to English Harbour and Falmouth Bay lie almost in the centre of the south coast, somewhat easier to identify when approaching from eastwards than from the south. Coming in from the east in daylight the bluff promontory of Cape Shirley [Fl(4) 20s 150m 20M] is

unmistakable, though the light atop may be unreliable. This headland is the place to close the coast, and a mile or so onwards the entrances first to English Harbour and then to Falmouth Bay will open up.

From the south the approach is straightforward although the entrances are not always easy to pinpoint. Inland there are rolling hills, but the lower, slightly darker patch in front is Middle Ground, which separates the two entrances. On closer approach the sandstone cliffs of Cape Shirley and Shirley Heights will be seen to terminate at their western end (Charlotte Point) in some unusual vertical columns, aptly named The Pillars of Hercules. If coming in from the south be careful not to get set too far to the west – Middle and Cade Reefs lurk off the south-west tip of Antigua and have claimed several yachts.

## Radio

English Harbour Radio, operated by Nicholson's Yacht Charters, normally operates on VHF channel 68, moving to a working channel once contact is established. Channels 06, 12, 14 and 16 are also used.

## Entrance

*English Harbour:* to the north-west the low crenellations of Barclay Point are unmistakable from nearby, while to the south-east Charlotte Point is marked by the equally distinctive Pillars of Hercules. A reef extends north-west from Charlotte Point directly towards Barclay Point, and best depths will be found by keeping between half and three quarters of the way across the gap – ie nearer to Barclay Point.

The old leading marks on 055° fell victim to a hurricane a few years ago, and have been replaced by a pair of orange boards positioned further to the north which transit on approximately 026°. Their lights should not be relied upon, and first time entry after dark is best avoided.

*Falmouth Bay*: although much larger, wide stretches of Falmouth Bay are shallow and there are several isolated coral patches. Bishop Shoal extends nearly 0.5 miles offshore on the starboard hand soon after entering and often breaks, the central shoal (supposedly buoyed) does not. Again there are leading lights, and again they do not always work so avoid entering the bay in darkness.

## Anchorage and moorings

*English Harbour*: pick any spot that offers swinging room and does not impede the channel to Antigua Slipway and Nelson's Dockyard. Some prefer the breeze and cleaner water of Freeman's Bay, some the greater convenience of being nearer the Dockyard, perhaps in Ordnance Bay on its northern side. Dinghies can be landed on the beach in Freeman's Bay or at the purpose-built dinghy landing by the boundary wall of the old Dockyard.

*Falmouth Bay*: again a case of finding a convenient spot, though the majority of yachts favour the south-east corner of the bay near the Antigua Yacht Club Marina. Dinghies can be left at the pontoon near the customs building.

## Berthing and marinas

*English Harbour*: a limited number of yachts can berth stern-to at Nelson's Dockyard (tel: 463 1053/1379/1380), but space is not always available. Call up on VHF channel 68 before arrival. The Dockyard is administered by the National Parks Authority, PO Box 1283, English Harbour. A few yachts may also be able to lie alongside at Antigua Slipway (tel: 463 1056, fax: 460 1156) on the eastern shore but this is usually reserved for boats undergoing work.

*Falmouth Bay*: the long-established Antigua Yacht Club has branched out into the marina business (tel: 460 1544, fax: 460 1444) with a pontoon to which about thirty yachts (some of them mega-yachts) can moor stern-to. The Catamaran Club (tel: 460 1503/1505, fax: 460 1506) runs a marina in the northern part of the bay, but it is usually full and is at a distance from many of the shoreside facilities.

## Formalities

After entering with the Q flag hoisted the skipper should go ashore with ship's papers, passports and previous port clearance to the combined customs and immigration office at the eastern end of the balconied Officers' Quarters building in Nelson's Dockyard. Hours are 0800–1630 daily, with dues payable for anchoring and for a cruising permit (whether or not you plan to cruise the island). Before departure a receipt must be obtained from the Harbour Office before outward clearance will be granted.

## Facilities

*Boatyards* Antigua Slipway can haul yachts up to 125 tons and has a travel hoist for the rest of us. They do not normally allow DIY work. Crabbs Marina (tel: 463 2113, fax: 463 3750) at Parham Harbour on the north coast have a 50-ton travel lift and do allow DIY work

*Engineers* Antigua Slipway; Pumps & Power (tel: 460 1242) at the head of Falmouth Bay; Seagull Services (tel: 460 3050, fax: 460 1767) at Falmouth Harbour, who also handle rigging; Marine Power Services (tel: 460 1850, fax: 460 3602) at Falmouth Harbour and Caribbean International Yacht Services (tel: 462 9525, fax: 462 9526) on the road between the Dockyard and Falmouth Harbour

*Electrical/electronics* The Signal Locker (tel: 460 1528, fax: 460 1148), which has an excellent reputation and is the local agent for a wide variety of British and US manufacturers, and Dockyard Electrics (tel: 460 1133) are both at English Harbour. Marionics (tel: 460 1780, fax: 460 1135) operate from the Catamaran Club Marina

*Sailmaker* Antigua Sails (tel: 460 1527, fax: 460 1526) near the head of Tank Bay, or A & F Sails (tel: 460 1522, fax: 460 1152) in Nelson's Dockyard

*Chandlery* Good stock upstairs at Antigua Slipway, also The Chandlery (tel: 460 1225, fax: 460 1226) at Falmouth (near Pumps & Power) and at Crabbs Marina

*Chart agent* The Map Shop (tel: 460 3993, fax: 460 3995) on St Mary's Street in St John's stocks BA, US DMA and Imray-Iolaire charts plus local cruising guides. The chandlery at Antigua Slipway also holds Imray-Iolaire charts

*Yacht club* Antigua Yacht Club on Falmouth Bay organises evening racing throughout the winter season, and has a relaxed bar and good restaurant

*Weather forecast* Broadcast by English Harbour Radio on VHF channel 06 at 0900 local time following an announcement on channel 68

*Diesel/petrol* Antigua Slipway, Antigua Yacht Club Marina and at the Catamaran Club Marina

*Water* At all the above, plus hoses to yachts lying stern-to in the Dockyard

*Electricity* Stern-to in Nelson's Dockyard, and at Antigua Slipway, Antigua Yacht Club Marina and the Catamaran Club Marina

*Bottled gas* Hinckley Yacht Services (ex-Antigua Yacht Services, tel: 460 2711, fax: 460 3740) or Pumps & Power – propane only, and allow several days

*Ice* Antigua Slipway, Antigua Yacht Club Marina and the Catamaran Club Marina

*Showers* At the marinas and in Nelson's Dockyard, where a charge of US $2 is currently made

*Laundry/launderette* Sam & Dave Laundry (tel: 460 1266) at Falmouth, plus several local ladies who can be found in the Dockyard

*Banks* Two in the Dockyard area and others in St John's, with credit card facilities

*General shopping* Mostly tourist shops locally, but a wider selection in St John's

*Provisioning* Malone's store opposite the head of Tank Bay, which is owned by Seventh Day Adventists (closed Saturday, open Sunday). Also a mini-market at Antigua Yacht Club Marina. Several larger supermarkets in St John's, plus a fresh produce market opposite the bus terminal

*Restaurants* Spoilt for choice. The Admiral's Inn (tel: 460 1027/1153, fax: 460 1534) has the atmosphere, The Lookout on Shirley Heights (tel: 460 1785) the view, but neither are cheap. Many, many others at all levels

*Hotels* At least three overlooking English Harbour with many more throughout the rest of the island. Antigua's economy depends heavily on tourism

*Medical services* Doctors and dentists in St John's, plus a modern hospital outside the town

## Communications

*Mailing addresses* C/o Nicholson's Yacht Charters, English Harbour Post Office, English Harbour, Antigua, West Indies; Caribbean International Yacht Services, Stanley's Tavern, English Harbour, Antigua, West Indies; Hinckley Yacht Services, PO Box 2242, St John's, Antigua, West Indies (although located at English Harbour) or Antigua Yacht Club Marina, Falmouth Harbour, Antigua, West Indies, all by prior arrangement

*Post Office* In the building just outside the Dockyard gates and in St John's

*Fax services* At Hinckley Yacht Services (fax: 460 3740) and Caribbean International Yacht Services (fax: 462 9526)

*Telephones* Outside the Dockyard gates, at the marinas and elsewhere

*Bus service* Minibuses to St John's from the car park outside the Dockyard gates

*Taxis* Plentiful but not cheap

*Car hire* Several agencies nearby. Driving is on the left

*Air services* Direct flights from E C Bird International Airport to the UK, USA, Canada etc

*Springs*: 0.6 m/2 ft
*Neaps*: 0.4 m/1 ft 4 in

*Flag*: British Virgin Islands
*Currency*: US dollar

*Tel/fax – Country code*: 1–284, *Area code*: none

| Charts | Admiralty | US | Imray/Iolaire |
|---|---|---|---|
| General | 130 (1:282,000) | 25600 (1:250,000) | A2 (1:416,000) |
| Approach | 2019 (1:35,000) | 25609 (1:80,000) | A231 (1:88,300) |
| | 2005 (1:35,000) | 25611 (1:30,000) | A232 (1:87,550) |
| Harbour | 2020 (1:15,000) | 25611 (1:15,000) | A231 (Insets) |

## General

Unlike anchorages such as English Harbour, Fort de France, etc, where many cruising yachtsmen stay for several weeks, once cleared into the British Virgin Islands few yachts will stay in one harbour long – the whole appeal is to explore by water.

Road Town is the capital of the British Virgin Islands and a centre for bareboat charters, and has all facilities necessary to prepare for departure northwards. However some skippers prefer to clear in and out at one of the other ports in the area, only visiting Road Town for essential shopping.

## Approach

If coming from eastwards – ie St Martin or Anguilla – aim to arrive at dawn and enter through Round Rock Passage, between Ginger Island [Fl 5s 152m 14M] and the jumbled rocks known as Fallen Jerusalem off the south end of Virgin Gorda (unlit). Then either head north for Virgin Gorda Yacht Harbour or continue down the Sir Francis Drake Channel towards Road Town, about half way along the south coast of Tortola.

Landfall from northwards – ie Bermuda or the USA – is more of a problem because of the dangers posed by the low-lying island of Anegada. Approach from the northwest and be certain to arrive in daylight. If coming from this direction it may be convenient to clear into the BVI at Great Harbour on Jost Van Dyke.

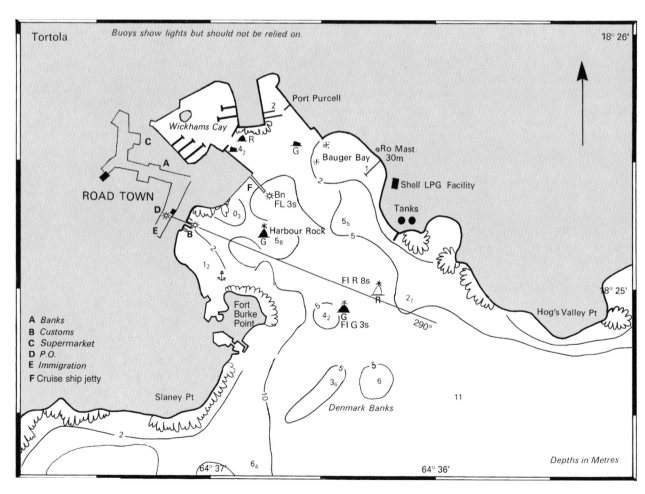

*Chart 64* Road Town, Tortola. Based on Admiralty Chart No 2020.

## Radio

Tortola Radio monitors VHF channel 16 and uses channel 27 as its working channel. The pilots operate on channels 14 and 16. Village Cay Marina and Virgin Gorda YH work on channel 16, which is also monitored by the Moorings/Mariners Inn though channel 12 is normally used in preference.

## Entrance

*Road Town*: Road Bay is unmistakable, with many buildings and a large fuel depot near its head. Although various shoal patches dot the entrance all carry at least 2.5 m (8 ft) so can be ignored by the majority of yachts. However avoid approaching Fort Burk Point too closely, and beware of Harbour Spit which runs south-east towards the middle of the harbour, supposedly marked by a lit buoy. If continuing into Wickhams Cay at the north end of the bay, having left the cruise ship dock to port keep carefully to the channel – it is narrow with a distinct dog-leg, but well buoyed. (But see *Formalities*, below.)

*Virgin Gorda Yacht Harbour*: The marina lies north of the famous Baths on the west coast of the island. The channel is buoyed, with a sharp turn first to the south and then eastwards into the marina proper.

## Anchorage and moorings

*Road Town*: Yachts anchor along the western shores of the outer harbour, with dinghy landing at the ferry pier in the north-west corner. More protected but often buggy is Wickhams Cay – anchor in the northern part being careful not to impede access to the several marinas. A notice

forbidding yachts to anchor may be visible, but no one seems to take much notice.

*Virgin Gorda Yacht Harbour*: St Thomas Bay, in 6.0 m (20 ft) or more over sand, provides pleasant temporary anchorage while clearing in etc. For both safety and comfort keep well north of the approach to the ferry pier.

## Berthing and marinas

*Road Town*: Either Village Cay Marina (tel: 494 2771, fax: 494 2773) on the west side of Wickhams Cay or The Moorings/Mariners Inn (tel: 494 2331, fax: 494 3776) to the east may have a berth available – check before arrival. Their reception pontoons are clearly marked.

*Virgin Gorda Yacht Harbour*: (tel: 495 5500, fax: 495 5706) can berth just over 100 yachts. The reception pontoon is nearly opposite the entrance and again well marked. There is little room to manoeuvre once inside, so if short on crew go in with lines and fenders ready (port side to).

## Formalities

Fly the Q flag on arrival. If wishing to clear in at Road Town it is, in theory, still necessary to anchor off the customs dock while the skipper alone goes ashore to clear, taking all the usual papers plus clearance from the last port of call. In practice it may be permissible to go on foot from a marina berth – check the current situation with the marina by radio before berthing. In Road Town the offices are at the head of the ferry and customs pier, in Virgin Gorda YH in the main administration block, and hours are 0830–1530. Outward clearance is valid for 24 hours, but if you admit that you intend to depart outside working hours you may well be charged overtime!

American citizens should note that a valid passport is now required to enter the British Virgin Islands. A birth certificate plus photographic identification is no longer sufficient.

## Facilities

*Boatyards/engineers/electronics* Both Tortola Yacht Services (tel: 494 2124, fax: 474 4707) close east of the Moorings, and Virgin Gorda YH Boatyard (tel: 495 5318, fax: 495 5685) have 70-ton travel lifts with full boatyard facilities on site

*Engineers* Parts & Power (tel: 494 2830, fax: 494 6972) at Tortola Yacht Services

*Sailmaker* Doyle Sailmakers Caribbean (tel: 494 2569, fax: 494 2034), who have a branch near the Moorings, and Tortola Yacht Services. Both in Road Town

*Chandlery* At all three of the marinas listed, and at Tortola Yacht Services

*Diesel* At all the marinas

*Water* At all the marinas. Water is scarce in the BVI and a charge will be made

*Electricity* At all the marinas

*Bottled gas* Enquire at the marina office or at Tortola Yacht Services

*Ice* At all the marinas and at many shops and filling stations

*Showers* At all the marinas. It may be possible for crews from yachts anchored off to use marina showers by arrangement, but expect to pay

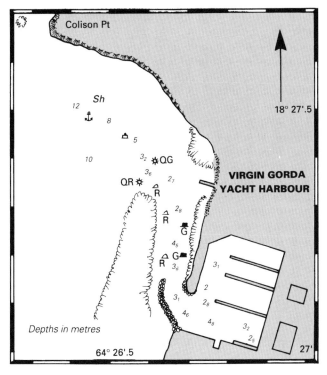

*Chart 65*   Virgin Gorda Yacht Harbour, Virgin Gorda. Based on a plan in the *Lesser Antilles*.

*Laundry/launderette* At Village Cay Marina and Virgin Gorda YH, and in Road Town

*Banks* In Road Town and at Virgin Gorda YH, with credit card facilities

*General shopping* Reasonable shopping in Road Town, though with a strong tourist slant

*Provisioning* Several large supermarkets in Road Town. Everything in Virgin Gorda must be brought over on the ferry, so although the store in the marina complex is well stocked prices are high

*Restaurants* Dozens, both tourist and local

*Hotels* Everything from small guest houses to five-star developments, including one in the Village Cay Marina complex

*Medical services* Doctors on Tortola and Virgin Gorda, hospital outside Road Town

## Communications

*Mailing addresses* C/o Road Town Post Office (not recommended); Village Cay Marina, Wickhams Cay I, Road Town, Tortola, BVI; Virgin Gorda Yacht Harbour, Spanish Town, Virgin Gorda, BVI; or Tortola Yacht Services, PO Box 74, Tortola, BVI, all by prior arrangement

*Post Offices* Near the customs building in Road Town; south of the marina at Virgin Gorda

*Telephones* At post offices, marinas and elsewhere

*Bus service* Buses to Beef Island airport and other destinations

*Taxis/car hire* No problem. Driving is on the left

*Ferry service* Frequent ferries between Road Town and Virgin Gorda

*Air services* Beef Island airport, Tortola (about ten miles from Road Town) has links with other Caribbean islands including Antigua and Puerto Rico, but no long-haul flights. There is a convenient anchorage in nearby Trellis Bay. Virgin Gorda has a small airstrip, but having seen it most yachtsmen would probably rather go by water

| Springs: 0.8 m/2 ft 7 in | Flag: USA |
|---|---|
| Neaps: 0.7 m/2 ft 3 in | Currency: US dollar |

*Tel/fax – Country code*: 1, *Area code*: (1) 954

| Charts | Admiralty | US |
|---|---|---|
| General | 2866 (1:500,000) | 11460 (1:466,940) |
| Approach | – | 11466 (1:80,000) |
| Harbour | 3684 (1:20,000) | 11470 (1:10,000) |

## General

Most yachts approaching Fort Lauderdale – or more correctly Port Everglades – will be doing so to enter the Intracoastal Waterway, which runs northwards for more than 1000 miles to Norfolk, Virginia. There is considerable commercial activity in the port, and priority must always be given to ships when entering or leaving. Fort Lauderdale's 'Miracle Mile' may hold a greater concentration of sizeable yachts than anywhere else in the United States (or the world).

## Approach

The east coast of Florida shelves gently with no offlying hazards in the Fort Lauderdale area. However nearly all the shoreline is built up, and it may be difficult to pinpoint the narrow entrance to Port Everglades from offshore, particularly in daylight. At night Port Everglades light [Fl 5s 106m 17M] on a building just north of the entrance should help with identification, allied to fixed and flashing red lights on chimneys about a mile further south.

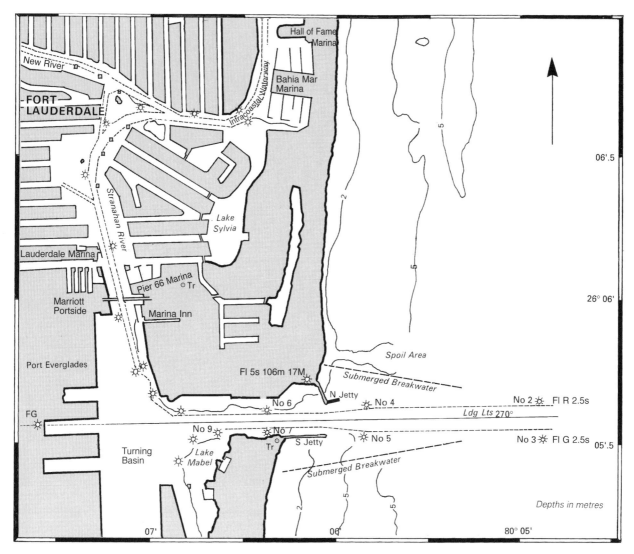

*Chart 66*  Fort Lauderdale, Florida. Based on US Chart No 11470.

## Radio

The harbourmaster monitors VHF channel 16 and operates on channels 12 and 13. The pilots use channels 12, 13, 14, 16, 18 A, 19 A and 77, and tugs work on channels 13, 14, 16, 18A and 77. The Coast Guard monitors channel 16.

All the marinas for which details are given below monitor channel 16, but working channels differ. Pier Sixty-Six, Marriott Portside and Lauderdale Marina use channel 68, Marina Inn uses channel 11, and Bahia Mar, Hall of Fame Marina and the Birch-Las Olas Docks use channel 09.

## Entrance

The red and white outer fairway buoy, marked 'PE' [Fl Mo (A)], lies about 1.5 miles due east of the harbour entrance. The first pair of channel markers – '2' to starboard and '3' to port – will be found about a mile offshore and from then on the channel, known as Outer Bar Cut, is clearly marked. Submerged breakwaters run from each side of the entrance out towards these buoys, and any yacht tempted to take a short cut must use large scale charts. Green leading lights on 270° mark the centre of the fairway.

The entrance to Port Everglades is relatively narrow, and protected by the North and South Jetties. Inside is the large Turning Basin with wharves on the western side. The marked channel turns sharply northwards, hugging the eastern shore and passing under the 17th Street Causeway Bridge to join the Stranahan River. (The bridge has an air height of only 7.6 m (25 ft), but opens on demand – if it has been closed for at least 15 minutes.) About 0.5 miles further on this converges with the New River and the Intracoastal Waterway. Currents can run strongly in this section, reaching three knots beneath the bridge.

## Anchorage and moorings

The city authorities provide a very limited number of moorings (many of them permanently occupied) in the bight opposite the municipal marina at Birch-Las Olas Docks, just south of the Las Olas Blvd Bridge. (Call the dockmaster on channel 09.) It is also possible to anchor here, though stays are limited to a few nights. Holding is good but passing traffic may make for a bumpy night. Dinghies can be left at the marina.

## Berthing and marinas

There are approaching twenty marinas in and around Fort Lauderdale. Pier Sixty-Six (tel: 728 3570, fax: 728 3588) and Marina Inn (tel: 525 3484) are situated on the east side immediately north of the bridge which marks the end of the Turning Basin, with Marriott Portside (tel: 527 6781), Everglades Marina (tel: 763 3030) and Lauderdale Marina (tel: 523 8507, fax: 524 5225) nearly opposite. Bahia Mar Yachting Center (tel: 764 2233, fax: 627 6356), Hall of Fame Marina (tel: 764 3975, fax: 779 3658) and the Birch-Las Olas Docks municipal marina (tel: 761 5423) lie a mile or two further up the Intracoastal Waterway.

Bahia Mar has, at 200, the greatest number of visitors' berths though Pier Sixty-Six, the Birch-Las Olas Docks and Marriott Portside keep 60, 38 and 33 transient berths free respectively. There are many marinas with visitors' berths

further north and south, and on the New River which branches westwards about a mile north of the entrance.

## Formalities

Fly the Q flag from offshore if arriving from abroad. The skipper only should go ashore on berthing and telephone 1 800 973 2867 (tollfree). This national centre will supply the number for the local customs office, which can (and should) be called at any time of the day or night, though normal office hours are 0800–1700. (The marina may know the number or even have a direct line.) If requested, customs will notify the immigration services.

The yacht will then be visited, by launch if necessary. There is no charge for clearance within office hours but a Cruising License, currently costing $25 and valid for one year, will be issued to a foreign yacht at the first port of call. Ship's papers, passports (with visas) and previous port clearance will be required – see Chapter 19.

## Facilities

Fort Lauderdale possesses hundreds of marine-related businesses, those listed below are merely an indication of what is available.

*Boatyards* It is necessary to go beyond the city centre for specialist services, though Everglades Marina has a 30 ton travel lift and some repair facilities

*Engineers* RPM Diesel Engine Co (tel: 587 1620) and others

*Electronics* At Everglades Marina, or Ward's Marine Electric Inc (tel: 523 2815) for electrical repairs

*Chandlery* Boat/US (tel: 523 7993) on W Broward Blvd, West Marine (tel: 527 5540) on S Federal Highway and at Pier Sixty-Six and Lauderdale Marinas. Sailorman (tel: 522 6716) on E State Road also carries used equipment

*Chart agent* Bluewater Books & Charts (tel: 763 6533) on 17th Street

*Diesel* Pier Sixty-Six, Lauderdale Marina and Bahia Mar

*Water* At all the marinas

*Electricity* At all the marinas, with both 110 volt and 220 volt generally available

*Bottled gas* Lauderdale Marina and in the city

*Showers* At all the marinas

*Holding tank pumpout* Lauderdale Marina, Hall of Fame

*Laundry/launderette* Pier Sixty-Six, Marina Inn, Marriott Portside, Bahia Mar and Hall of Fame

*Banks* Many, with credit card facilities

*General shopping* Good, nearly all needs can be met

*Provisioning* Supermarkets and shopping malls abound

*Restaurants/hotels* Hundreds, at all levels

*Medical services* Several large hospitals in the area, including Broward General Medical Center (tel: 355 4400), plus the usual doctors and dentists

## Communications

*Mailing addresses* C/o the marinas by arrangement

*Fax service* Most of the marinas provide a fax service

*Post Office* In the city

*Telephones* At the marinas and elsewhere

*Taxis/car hire* No shortage

*Air services* Fort Lauderdale International airport a few miles away, or Miami for most European flights

| | | | |
|---|---|---|---|
| *Springs*: 0.9 m/2 ft 11 in | | *Flag*: USA | |
| *Neaps*: 0.8 m/2 ft 7 in | | *Currency*: US dollar | |

*Tel/fax – Country code*: 1, *Area code*: (1) 919

| *Charts* | *Admiralty* | *US* |
|---|---|---|
| General | 2864 (1:500,000) | 11520 (1:432,720) |
| Approach | 3686 (1:100,000) | 11543 (1:80,000) |
| Harbour | 3686 (1:15,000) | 11547 (1:12,500) |

## General

Beaufort and its twin town of Morehead City to the west are popular both as stops on the Intracoastal Waterway and as an entry point for yachts heading north and wishing to avoid Cape Hatteras. They are often referred to as the US gateway to the Caribbean, as for many yachts it is a four day sail to the Bahamas, five to Bermuda and between seven and ten days direct to the Virgin Islands.

The North Carolina Maritime Museum (tel: 728 7317) on Front Street, Beaufort is particularly helpful towards visiting yachtsmen.

## Approach

For details of Cape Hatteras some 70 miles to the north-east, see Chapter 19. The later approaches to Beaufort Inlet receive good protection from Cape Lookout, just under ten miles to the south-east, though the vicinity of the Cape and its offlying shoals is dangerous and should be given wide clearance. It should further be noted that the powerful light [Fl 15s 48m 25M] is displayed from a tower about 1.5 miles north of the point itself, though the outlying shoals are well buoyed.

The coast to the west of Beaufort Inlet runs on an almost east/west axis, with good water within 0.5 miles or less of the shore.

## Radio

Pilots and port operations monitor VHF channel 16 and work on channels 10, 13, 14, 16, 81 and 83. The Coast Guard monitors channel 16 and operates on channel 22 A. All the marinas plus Bock Marine monitor channel 16 during daylight hours, and Town Creek Marina also monitors channel 08.

Beaufort Waterfront showing Taylor Creek yacht anchorage. *Photo: Tom Doe*

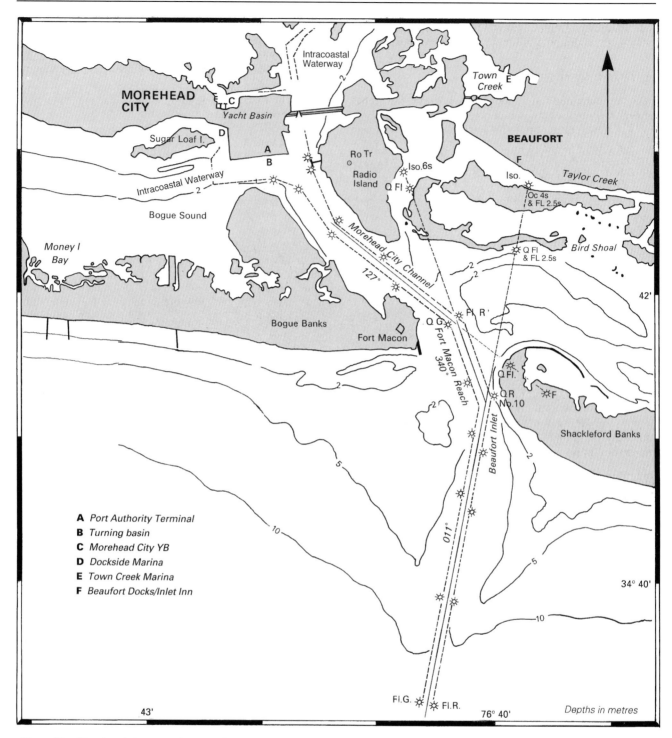

Money I
Bay

Bogue Sound

Bogue Banks

MOREHEAD
CITY

Sugar Loaf I.

Yacht Basin

Intracoastal
Waterway

Intracoastal Waterway

Ro Tr
Radio
Island

Q Fl

Town
Creek

BEAUFORT

Iso.6s

Iso.

Oc 4s
& FL 2.5s

Taylor Creek

Bird Shoal

Q Fl
& FL 2.5s

Morehead City Channel

127°

Fort Macon

G
Fort Macon
Reach
340°

Fl R

Q Fl.

Q R
No.10

F

Shackleford Banks

Beaufort Inlet

011°

Fl.G.          Fl.R.

A   Port Authority Terminal
B   Turning basin
C   Morehead City YB
D   Dockside Marina
E   Town Creek Marina
F   Beaufort Docks/Inlet Inn

42'

34° 40'

43'

76° 40'

Depths in metres

*Chart 67*   Morehead City/Beaufort, North Carolina. Based on Admiralty Chart No 3686.

## Entrance

The long, buoyed Beaufort Inlet Channel is one of the safest on the coast and begins/ends at the red and white BM seabuoy [Fl Mo (A)] almost seven miles offshore. It is entered on a bearing of 011° with leading lights at night. Once close off Shackleford Point this bearing is abandoned for one on 340°, which leads up Fort Macon Reach and into the well buoyed Morehead City Channel. Fort Macon, on the port hand when entering, is unlit.

If making for Beaufort, once in the Morehead City Channel look for red pillar buoy R 2 [Fl R 2.5s] and the nearby marker G 1 [Fl G 4s 4.5m 4M], after which the channel is buoyed on the starboard hand.

Tidal streams in the Beaufort Inlet Channel may run at 2–3 knots and an opposing wind will cause steep seas. In the vicinity of the Port Authority Terminal the stream can reach more than four knots at springs.

## Anchorage and moorings

The two best anchorages are on the south side of Taylor Creek, in a marked area opposite the Beaufort Docks, or in Town Creek to the north of Beaufort. The latter anchorage is quieter, and still convenient for the town. A spot must be chosen clear of the main channel and a Bahamian moor is essential in the strong streams. There is a public dinghy dock opposite the post office on Front Street, Beaufort.

## Berthing and marinas

There are many marinas in the area, but those with most visitors' berths are the Dockside Marina (tel/fax: 247 4890) and Morehead City Yacht Basin (tel: 726 6862, fax: 726 1939), both just west of the Port Authority Terminal in Morehead City, and Town Creek Marina (tel: 728 6111, fax: 728 4053), Inlet Inn (tel: 728 3600, fax: 728 5833) and Beaufort Docks (tel: 728 2503), which caters for visiting yachts only, on the Beaufort side.

Morehead City Yacht Basin is approached via a bascule bridge which carries the railway and is normally open unless a train is due, and a fixed bridge with 20 m (65 ft) air height. Inlet Inn is reached via a bascule road bridge which opens on the hour and at 20 minute intervals.

## Formalities

Fly the Q flag from offshore if arriving from abroad. The skipper only should go ashore immediately after berthing and telephone 1 800 973 2867 (tollfree). This national centre will supply the number for the local customs office, which can (and should) be called at any time of the day or night, though normal office hours are 0800-1700. (Alternatively, the marina may know the number or even have a direct line.) If requested, customs will notify the immigration services.

The yacht will then be visited, by launch if necessary. There is no charge for clearance within office hours but a Cruising License, currently costing $25 and valid for one year, will be issued to a foreign yacht at the first port of call. Ship's papers, passports (with visas as appropriate) and previous port clearance will be required – see Chapter 19.

## Facilities

*Boatyards* Bock Marine (tel: 728 6855) at Beaufort has a 60 ton travel lift and allows DIY work. The yard specialises in steel and aluminium boatbuilding. There is a 50 ton travel lift with full service boatyard at Town Creek Marina and a wide range of repair facilities are also available at Beaufort Docks

*Engineers* At Beaufort Docks and Town Creek Marina

*Electronics* West Marine in Morehead City and at Town Creek Marina

*Sail repairs* At Beaufort Docks

*Chandlery* Beaufort Marine Discount on Front Street and in Morehead City

*Charts* The NC Maritime Museum or Scuttlebutt, both on Front Street, Beaufort

*Weather forecast* Rolling forecast with hurricane information on VHF weather channel WX 2

*Diesel* At Beaufort Docks and Town Creek Marina

*Water* At all the marinas

*Electricity* At all the marinas; 110 volt and 220 volt available at Beaufort Docks

*Bottled gas* Propane at Dean's Gas

*Showers* At all the marinas

*Holding tank pumpout* At Beaufort Docks and elsewhere

*Laundry/launderette* On Front Street and Town Creek Marina in Beaufort, and at Dockside Marina in Morehead City

*Banks* Several, with credit card facilities

*General shopping* Somewhat limited in Beaufort, good in Morehead City

*Provisioning* No problem in Morehead City, and several grocery stores in Beaufort. On production of a driving licence the Maritime Museum will lend a car for two hours to visit the excellent shopping mall just out of town on Route 70. Several of the marinas offer a similar service

*Restaurants* A wide selection

*Medical services* Hospital in Morehead City; doctors and dentists in both Morehead City and Beaufort

## Communications

*Mailing addresses* C/o The North Carolina Maritime Museum, Front Street, Beaufort, NC 28516 or General Delivery, Main Post Office, Front Street. Otherwise c/o Town Creek Marina, 232 West Beaufort Street, Beaufort, NC 28516; Beaufort Docks, 500 Front Street, Beaufort, NC 28516 or Dockside Marina, PO Box 3398, 301 Arendell Street, Morehead City, NC 28557 by prior arrangement

*Fax service* At Town Creek Marina (fax: 728 4053)

*Post Office* On Front Street in Beaufort and in Morehead City

*Telephones* At the marinas and elsewhere

*Taxis/car hire* No problem

*Air services* National airport at New Bern, 40 miles away

*Springs*: 0.8 m/2 ft 7 in  *Flag*: USA
*Neaps*: 0.7 m/2 ft 3 in  *Currency*: US dollar

*Tel/fax – Country code*: 1,  *Area code*: (1) 757

| Charts | Admiralty | US |
|--------|-----------|-----|
| General | – | 12280 (1:200,000) |
| Approach | 2919 (1:80,000) | 12221 (1:80,000) |
| | | 12222 (1:40,000) |
| Harbour | 2813 (1:20,000) | 12245 (1:20,000) |
| | 2814 (1:20,000) | 12253 (1:20,000) |

## General

Norfolk lies at the mouth of the Elizabeth River and marks the emergence of the Intracoastal Waterway into the Chesapeake Bay, and most yachts passing through Norfolk will be either joining or leaving the Waterway. The seaward approach is via Hampton Roads – the lower stretches of the James River – where a bridge-tunnel combination links Norfolk with Hampton and Newport News on the northern shore. Hampton Roads is a busy area for both naval and commercial shipping, and the Norfolk Naval Base the largest in the world (tours of the base are run daily in summer). Although yachtsmen generally refer to the area as Norfolk, several of the marinas listed below are actually in Portsmouth, on the west bank of the Elizabeth River.

## Approach

Norfolk may be approached from further north up the Bay, or from the Atlantic via the Chesapeake Bay Channel between Cape Charles [Fl 5s 55m 24M] on the northern shore and Cape Henry [Mo(U) WR 20s 50m 17/15M] to the south. Six miles to the west of Cape Henry lies the Chesapeake Bay Bridge Tunnel Complex, with the well buoyed Thimble Shoal Channel leading through it just over three miles from the southern shore. Strong currents can run in the area, sometimes exceeding three knots, and particular care must be taken near the bridge. The Thimble Shoal Channel extends a further six miles west-north-west towards Old Point Comfort [LFl(2) W/R 12s 16m 16/14M] and the northern end of the bridge-tunnel combination linking Norfolk and Hampton. Fort Wool [Fl 4s 8s 8M] marks the southern side of the navigable area.

## Radio

Both Coast Guard and harbourmaster monitor VHF channel 16. The Chesapeake Bay pilots use channels 6, 11, 13, 14, 16 and 74. All the marinas listen on channel 16, with the Waterside Marina (and the Ocean Marine water taxi) also using channel 68.

## Entrance

A direct course can be shaped from the tunnel area past the narrow but well marked channel for Willoughby Bay and thence south-west down Entrance Reach towards

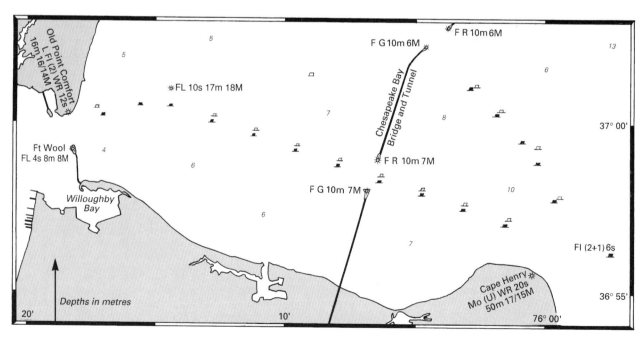

*Chart 68*  The approaches to Norfolk, Virginia. Based on Admiralty Chart No 2919.

Passing downtown Norfolk, with the grey-roofed Waterside Festival Marketplace and the Waterside Marina.
*Photo: Gavin McLaren*

Sewells Point. Norfolk Harbor Reach then leads south past the Naval Base into the Elizabeth River. The wide mouthed Lafayette River flows in from the east, before the channel narrows into the Southern Branch and the Waterway proper. The entire area is extremely well buoyed.

## Anchorage and moorings

There are several possible anchorages convenient to Norfolk and Portsmouth. The northernmost – and deepest – is on the west side of the channel opposite Lamberts Point in about 8.0 m (26 ft), with others just south of Lamberts Point and south of Hospital Point on Town Point Reach in 4.0 m (13 ft) or so. The latter offers convenient dinghy access to both Norfolk and Portsmouth city centres. Dinghies can be left at the Waterside Marina for a nominal charge, and a dinghy dock is also being installed at the Nauticus centre just north of Waterside Marina. The Ocean Marina water taxi covers the inner harbour from 0700 daily.

## Berthing and marinas

There are numerous marinas around Norfolk and Portsmouth, with more at Little Creek some seven miles further east towards the Chesapeake Bay Bridge.

Willoughby Harbor Marina (tel: 583 4150, fax: 583 1846) is located on the north side of Willoughby Bay about four miles from Norfolk city centre, near the southern end of the Hampton Roads Bridge/Tunnel. It is some distance out of town but there are good facilities locally and a courtesy car may be available. A current of up to two knots can flow in the marina basin. Much closer to the city centre on the Norfolk shore is the Waterside Marina (tel: 625 2000, fax: 623 8477), an all transient facility with fifty berths and able to take mega-yachts up to 120 m (400 ft).

On the Portsmouth side are the H&H Marina (tel: 484 6148), Scott's Creek Marina (tel: 399 2628), which has 135 berths for yachts up to 20 m (65 ft), and Tidewater Yacht Agency (tel: 393 2525, fax: 393 7845). Of these, Tidewater Yacht Agency is the largest with 325 berths for vessels up to 30 m (100 ft), a hundred of them reserved for visiting yachts, and is situated right opposite Waterside Marina and the Norfolk city centre.

## Formalities

Fly the Q flag from offshore if arriving from abroad. The skipper only should go ashore immediately after berthing and telephone 1 800 973 2867 (tollfree). This national centre will supply the number for the local customs office, which can (and should) be called at any time of the day or night, though normal office hours are 0800–1700. (Alternatively, the marina may know the number or even have a direct line.) If requested, customs will notify the immigration services.

The yacht will then be visited, by launch if necessary. There is no charge for clearance within office hours but a Cruising License, currently costing $25 and valid for one year, will be issued to a foreign yacht at the first port of call. Ship's papers, passports (with visas as appropriate) and previous port clearance will be required – see Chapter 19.

## Facilities

*Boatyards* Ocean Marine (tel: 391 3000, fax: 399 3088) at Tidewater Yacht Agency has a 60 ton travel lift and 25 m (80 ft) enclosed wet slip, and can handle all normal work. There is also a boatyard next to Willoughby Harbor Marina

*Engineers* At Ocean Marine plus a mobile mechanical

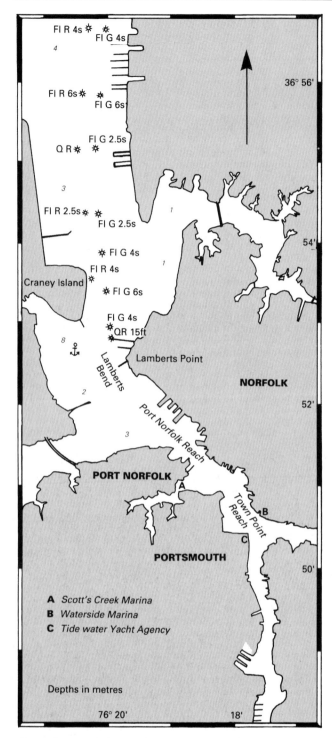

service at Waterside Marina

*Electronics* Ocean Marine

*Chandlery* West Marine (E&B Marine), a short bus ride from Waterside Marina, and at most of the marinas

*Diesel* At all the marinas

*Water* At all the marinas

*Electricity* At all the marinas, with both 110 volt and 220 volt generally available

*Showers* At all the marinas

*Holding tank pumpout* At Willoughby Harbor Marina, Waterside Marina, Scott's Creek Marina and Tidewater Yacht Agency

*Laundry/launderette* At Willoughby Harbor Marina, Waterside Marina, Scott's Creek Marina, Tidewater Yacht Agency and in the city

*Banks* Many, with credit card facilities

*General shopping* Good on both sides of the river

*Provisioning* All requirements can be met. Gene Walters' Marketplace store will collect customers from Waterside Marina

*Restaurants/hotels* A choice in both Norfolk and Portsmouth

*Medical services* Several hospitals and the usual doctors and dentists

## Communications

*Mailing addresses* C/o General Delivery, US Post Office/Customs House Station, Norfolk, VA 23514 (mark 'Hold for Arrival'), or c/o one of the marinas by prior agreement: Willoughby Harbor Marina, 1525 Bayville Street, Norfolk, VA 23503; Waterside Marina, 333 Waterside Drive, Norfolk, VA 23510–3202; H&H Marina, 3515 Shipwright Street, Portsmouth, VA; Scotts Creek Marina, 6 Harper Avenue, Portsmouth, VA 23707 or Tidewater Yacht Agency, 10 Crawford Parkway, Portsmouth, VA 23704–2606

*Fax service* At Willoughby Harbor Marina (fax: 583 1846), Waterside Marina (fax: 623 8477) and Tidewater Yacht Agency (fax: 393 7845)

*Post Offices* On both sides of the Elizabeth River

*Telephones* At the marinas and elsewhere

*Bus service* Local and airport buses

*Taxis/car hire* Readily available

*Ferry service* Two ferries link Portsmouth and Norfolk from 0700 daily

*Air services* Norfolk International airport is a few minutes away

*Chart 69* Norfolk Harbour and the Elizabeth River, Virginia. Based on Admiralty Chart No 2814.

| | | |
|---|---|---|
| *Springs*: 0.2 m/8 in | | *Flag*: USA |
| *Neaps*: 0.2 m/8 in | | *Currency*: US dollar |

*Tel/fax – Country code*: 1, *Area code*: (1) 410

| Charts | Admiralty | US |
|---|---|---|
| General | – | 12280 (1:200,000) |
| Approach | 2921 (1:80,000) | 12270 (1:40,000) |
| | | 12282 (1:25,000) |
| Harbour | – | 12283 (1:10,000) |

## General

Annapolis, Maryland, briefly the capital of the United States and the state capital since 1695, is located on the western shore of the Chesapeake Bay some 140 miles north of Newport News, Virginia. It is the yachting and sailing centre for the middle Chesapeake Bay and offers all maritime services for sail, power and commercial vessels. Within the city limits are eleven marinas, which between them provide facilities ranging from transient only to full service and do-it-yourself, and three main creeks which offer good anchorage for transient vessels. From south to north these are Back Creek, Spa Creek, and Weems Creek. College Creek, although within the city limits, is unsuitable as an anchorage. Access to all three is straightforward, and Back Creek and Spa Creek provide access to all the city's marinas.

Annapolis is also the venue of the United States Sailboat Show and the United States Powerboat Show, which run consecutively for two weeks during October. The city enjoys a thriving tourist business, with many of the homes of the early settlers restored and open for viewing.

*Caution*
There is little tidal range even at springs, and heights are affected by wind as much as by lunar forces – a strong north-westerly breeze will reduce the water level in the Bay by as much as 1.0 m.

Yachts, many of them based in Annapolis, crowd the Chesapeake Bay and Severn River. Spa Creek, with the finger-shaped City Dock, appears on the right of the photo with Back Creek beyond. *Photo: David Wallace*

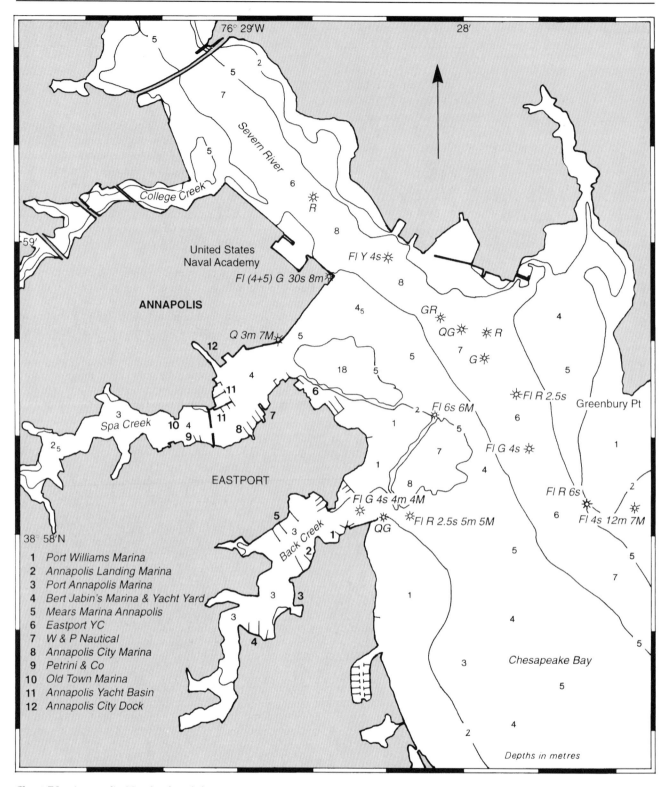

*Chart 70* Annapolis, Maryland, and the Severn River. Based on US Chart No 12283.

## Approach and entrance

Annapolis lies on the south-west shore of the Severn River about 0.7 miles from its mouth. Approach is simple from both north and south with good depths available. From the north, set a course of 212° from the centre span of the Bay Bridge to No 2 buoy [Fl R 2.5s]. Keep a careful watch for crab pots which are prolific on the westerly side of the

route. From the south, steer a course to leave marker No 1 AH [Fl G 4s 4.5m 4M] close to port. From either of the above marks head north-west towards marker No 4 [Fl R 6s] and then follow the well buoyed channel.

In July 1997 the Coast Guard renumbered and replaced several of the channel markers in the area – ensure that the large scale chart in use is dated 6 September 1997 or later.

## Radio

The harbourmaster monitors VHF channels 16 and 09 and uses others, principally channel 17, for communication. The marinas generally use one or more of channels 09, 16 and 72. The water taxi which serves Back Creek and Spa Creek monitors channel 68.

## Anchorage and moorings

Anchorage may be found in Back Creek, Weems Creek and the upper reaches of Spa Creek. Holding is generally good.

To enter Back Creek, which has a minimum depth at the entrance of 3.0 m (10 ft), turn west at marker No 4 towards No 2 E [Fl G 2.5s 4.5m 5M] and follow the channel markers into the creek. Special attention should be paid at marker No 3, which designates the end of a submerged jetty running out from the shore to the south-west. As well as providing anchoring space for transient vessels, Back Creek is home to several large marinas.

For Spa Creek, continue in the main channel to buoy No 9 [Q G] before turning west into the creek using the spire on St Mary's Church as a range marker. Good anchorage can be had in 3.5–4.5 m (12–15 ft) near its mouth, and there is ample room further upstream beyond the bascule bridge in 3.5 m (12 ft) or less.

The harbour authorities maintain 59 moorings in the creek, 40 downstream of the bridge, for yachts of no more than 13 m (43 ft) or so, and 19 beyond it in St Mary's Cove, this time limited to 10.7 m (35 ft) overall. The city moorings are white with a blue stripe and a number, and are allocated on a 'first come, first served' basis. The harbourmaster patrols the moorings during daylight hours. Dinghies can be left at the north-west end of the City Dock inlet (labelled 'Market Slip' on DMA chart 12283) for which no charge is made.

Weems Creek, the most northerly of the three, lies between the two highway bridges crossing the Severn River. Vertical clearance is 22.8 m (75 ft) at the south-east bridge and 24.3 m (80 ft) at the north-west one. The creek entrance is indicated by a red and green marker labelled 'WC'. A bascule bridge crosses Weems Creek about 0.5 miles from its mouth, severely limiting navigation, but depths of around 4.5 m (15 ft) will be carried to the bridge. It is a quiet anchorage with very limited access to the shore, though it is possible to land at a street end on the south-eastern shore, from which it is a one mile walk to a small shopping centre.

## Berthing and marinas

As already mentioned, there are eleven marinas in Annapolis. All provide the usual services and some have boatyards on site.

Clockwise around Back Creek are: Port Williams Marina (tel: 268 4197); Annapolis Landing Marina (tel: 263 0090, fax: 626 1851); Port Annapolis Marina (tel: 268 7907/269 1900, fax: 269 5856); Bert Jabin's Marina & Yacht Yard (tel: 268 9667, fax: 280 3163) and Mears Marina Annapolis (tel: 268 8282, fax: 268 7161).

Clockwise around Spa Creek are: W & P Nautical (tel: 268 7700); Annapolis City Marina (tel: 268 0660, fax: 974 9345); Petrini & Co (tel: 263 4278, fax: 263 4917); Old

Town Marina (formerly Arnold C Gay Yacht Yard) (tel: 263 9277, fax: 268 7758); Annapolis Yacht Basin (tel: 263 3544, fax: 269 1319) and the Annapolis City Dock (tel: 263 7973). This latter, which has eighteen berths in 2.5–3 m (8–10 ft) depths, is run by the harbour authorities and caters for transient yachts only.

## Formalities

Unlike all the other harbours detailed in this section, Annapolis is NOT an official port of entry. Visiting yachtsmen should clear customs and complete appropriate formalities in Baltimore, Newport News, Norfolk or elsewhere.

## Facilities

The harbourmaster (tel: 263 7973), who has his office close east of the City Dock, welcomes visiting yachts enthusiastically and will assist in any way he can. The Tourist and Visitors' Information Booth in the same building is open from 1 April to 1 November and will provide all tourist information during normal business hours.

The Port Book, which is produced annually and covers Annapolis and the Eastern Shore of Maryland, lists marine, tourist and travel services, bridge opening times, etc. It is available free of charge from the harbourmaster's office.

*Boatyards/engineers* Bert Jabin's Yacht Yard, Port Annapolis Marina, and Annapolis Yacht Yard all have travel lifts, while Mears Marina has a 50 ton crane. All have facilities for DIY or yard work

*Electronics* Bay Country Electronics (tel: 263 3000) at the City Dock and Electronic Marine (tel: 268 8108, fax: 268 8111) on 4th Street

*Sailmakers* Several international companies including Banks (tel: 266 3666), Hood (tel: 268 4663) and North (tel: 269 5662) have sail lofts within the city limits. See the Port Book

*Chandlery* Fawcett's Boat Supplies (tel: 267 8681, fax: 268 7547) and Viking Boat Supplies (tel: 268 8000, fax: 268 1532) both near the City Dock. West Marine (tel: 268 0129, fax: 431 5100) and Boat/US (tel: 573 5744) on the outskirts of the city, and others

*Chart agent* Good selection at Fawcett's Boat Supplies

*Yacht clubs* Annapolis is the home of the Annapolis Yacht Club (tel: 263 9279), the Eastport Yacht Club (tel: 267 8986) and the United States Naval Academy Sailing Squadron (tel: 293 5603)

*Weather forecast* Try the local service (tel: 301 936 1212) or the NOAA recording (tel: 859 5380)

*Diesel* At Annapolis City Marina, Annapolis Landing Marina, Annapolis Yacht Basin and the City Dock

*Water* At all marinas and the City Dock

*Electricity* At all marinas and the City Dock

*Bottled gas* Propane is available at most hardware stores, True Value, and some garages. For refills try Rental Works (tel: 268 7173) at 1919 Lincoln Drive

*Showers* At all marinas and the City Dock (the latter free if berthed in the Dock, otherwise a small charge)

*Holding tank pumpout* At most of the marinas. In addition the pumpout boat, provided by the city authorities, can be called on VHF channel 09

*Laundry/launderette* At most marinas, plus several readily available to the Spa Creek and Back Creek anchorages. The Avenue Laundromat on Maryland Avenue is within walking distance of the City Dock

*Banks* Many in the city, all with credit card facilities

*General shopping* On the Eastport peninsula between Back Creek and Spa Creek, and in the downtown area adjacent to the City Dock

*Provisioning* Two large supermarkets, within a mile of Back Creek and Weems Creek respectively. No large store handy to Spa Creek, but public transport available to the above

*Restaurants* To suit all tastes and pockets. Crab and other seafood dishes are specialities. In the downtown area excellent Japanese, Italian and French cuisine is available

*Hotels* Several

*Medical services* The hospital at Anne Arundel Medical Center in downtown Annapolis is about five minutes from Spa Creek

## Communications

*Mailing addresses* C/o The Harbormaster's Office, 1 Dock Street Annapolis, MD 21401, or General Delivery, Annapolis Post Office, Annapolis, MD 21401. In both cases mail should be marked 'Hold for Arrival'. Alternatively c/o the destination marina by prior agreement

*Fax services* Annapolis Post Box (fax: 268 6245), Eastport Copy Inc (fax: 269 6399) and Minute Man Press (fax: 263 3442) and several of the marinas

*Post Office* On Chesapeake Avenue

*Telephones* At the marinas, the City Dock and in the town

*Bus service* Local bus service plus longer distance routes

*Taxis/car hire* Not a problem

*Water taxi* The Jiffy Water Taxi (tel: 263 0033) operates from the City Dock and serves Spa Creek, Back Creek and the Severn River. It listens on channel 68

*Air services* Baltimore-Washington International airport, which provides national and international services, is about 45 minutes away and can be reached by shuttle service or public transport

*Springs*: 1.2 m/3 ft 11 in      *Flag*: USA
*Neaps*: 0.9 m/2 ft 11 in      *Currency*: US dollar

*Tel/fax – Country code*: 1, *Area code*: (1) 401

| Charts | Admiralty | US |
|--------|-----------|-----|
| General | 2492 (1:677,000) | 12300 (1:400,000) |
| Approach | 2890 (1:100,000) | 13218 (1:80,000) |
| | | 13221 (1:40,000) |
| Harbour | 2730 (1:20,000) | 13223 (1:20,000) |

## General

Newport, Rhode Island, lies to the east of the main entrance channel to Narragansett Bay. It has long been an important yachting centre and for many years was the venue for the America's Cup races. It is also the destination of the singlehanded transatlantic race run from Plymouth, England, every four years and a favourite landfall for yachts heading north from Bermuda. Newport is an official port of entry and, together with the other harbours on Narragansett Bay, offers excellent facilities of all kinds.

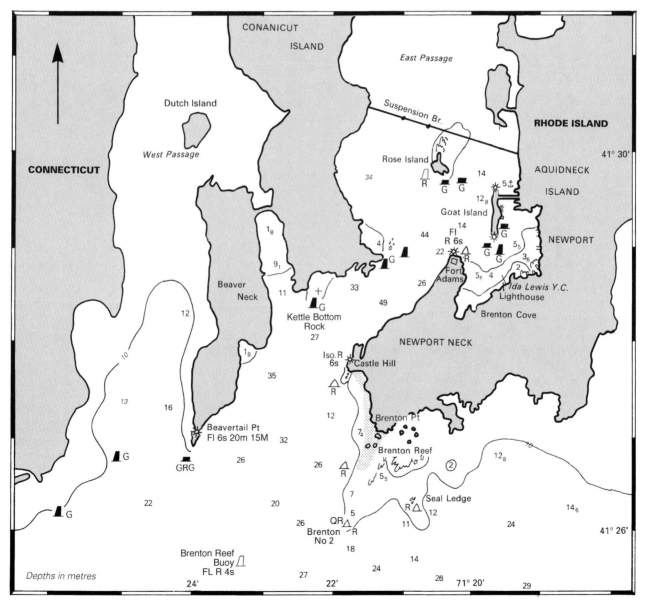

*Chart 71*    Newport, Rhode Island. Based on Admiralty Chart No 2890.

# Approach

The coast between Cape Cod and Newport is low lying, with shoal water and low islands to the south of Cape Cod. The area is very prone to fog and it can be difficult to identify the coast. If coming from the south-east or south it is advisable to make first landfall at Nantucket Shoals Lanby (see Chapter 19), thus keeping well south of the shoals themselves and ensuring an exact position from which to close the land. If approaching from the north-east most yachts will use the Cape Cod Canal, which leads into a dredged channel at the north-east end of Buzzard's Bay. A middle route, through Nantucket Sound and Vineyard Sound, is possible but not recommended.

Heavy concentrations of shipping are likely to be encountered on the approach to Newport – fishing vessels around the various banks, and commercial traffic en route to New York, Narragansett Bay and Boston.

The entrance to Narragansett Bay is well bracketed by lights, including Buzzards Bay light [Fl 2.5s 19m 17M] sixteen miles to the east, Point Judith light [Oc(3) 15s 20m 16M] six miles to the south-west and Block Island SE light [Fl G 5s 80m 20M] eighteen miles south-south-west. All have foghorns.

If approaching from the east, head for the red and white Narragansett Bay entrance buoy [F & Fl 4s] until a bearing on Beavertail Point [Fl 6s 20m 15M] on the west side of the entrance clears Brenton Reef whistle buoy [Fl R 4s] to starboard. This will take one well clear of Brenton Reef and the many fish nets in the area. In poor visibility home in on Beavertail Point until abeam of the entrance buoy. If approaching from south or south-west, head directly for the entrance buoy.

# Radio

Castle Hill Coast Guard station maintains a 24 hour watch on VHF channel 16, but can also be called direct on channel 71. The harbourmaster monitors channel 16 but communicates on channel 14. The marinas use channel 09 and/or 78, with Oldport Marine's launch listening on channel 68.

# Entrance

The outer entrance lies between Beavertail Point to the west and Brenton Point to the east. From Narragansett Bay entrance buoy steer 026° to give Castle Hill [Iso R 6s 12m 12M] good clearance to starboard. Although the rock cliff is very bold it is essential to leave Butterball Rock bell buoy, which marks a barely awash shoal south-west of Castle Hill, to starboard. A buoyed channel then leads between Fort Adams and Goat Island into Newport Harbor.

# Anchorage and moorings

Both yacht anchorages designated on BA 2730 (in Brenton Cove at the south-western corner of the harbour and between Goat Island and the town waterfront further north) are now occupied by moorings. Most yachts now anchor either just north of the Ida Lewis Yacht Club or north of the causeway to Goat Island. If using the former beware the cable area – call the harbourmaster for advice.

The harbourmaster maintains twenty moorings available on a first come, first served basis, but there is seldom one free. Others are controlled by Oldport Marine Services (tel: 847 9109 or VHF channel 09). (They also run an excellent launch service between 0800 and midnight which will pick up and deposit anywhere in the harbour for a modest fee – call up on channel 68.) Otherwise try Long Wharf Marina (tel: 849 2210 or channel 68) or Island Marine Services (tel: 8498 9648 or channel 09). Alternatively the Ida Lewis Yacht Club (tel: 849 5655 or channel 78 A) may have a visitors' mooring available. Dinghies can be left at the Municipal Dock or the Ann Street Pier.

# Berthing and marinas

There are many marinas in the Newport area. One of the largest is at Goat Island (tel: 849 5655, fax: 848 7144), situated about half way along that island's eastern shore. It is some way from the town, but a water shuttle runs twice each hour.

Perhaps more convenient for the visiting yachtsman are the Newport Yachting Center (tel: 846 1600, fax: 847 9262) and Oldport Marine Services (tel: 847 9109), both on the eastern side of the harbour and convenient for the town, or Bannister's Wharf (tel: 846 4500) or Bowen's Wharf (tel: 849 2243) which are smaller and lie just north of the other two. Further north again are Newport Harbor Marina (tel: 847 9000), which reserves sixty berths for transients, and Long Wharf Marina (tel: 849 2210). The Newport Yacht Club (tel: 846 9410) at the head of the harbour may also have berths available.

Further south will be found Christie's Restaurant & Marina (tel: 848 7950), Newport Marina (tel: 849 2293) and the new West Wind Marina (tel: 849 4300).

# Formalities

Fly the Q flag from offshore if arriving from abroad. The skipper only should go ashore immediately after berthing and telephone 1 800 973 2867 (tollfree). This national centre will supply the number for the local customs office, which can (and should) be called at any time of the day or night, though normal office hours are 0800–1700. (Alternatively, the marina may know the number or even have a direct line.) If requested, customs will notify the immigration services.

The yacht will then be visited, by launch if necessary. There is no charge for clearance within office hours but a Cruising License, currently costing $25 and valid for one year, will be issued to a foreign yacht at the first port of call. Ship's papers, passports (with visas as appropriate) and previous port clearance will be required – see Chapter 19.

# Facilities

The harbourmaster (tel: 848 6492) will assist with information and advice. The Visitors' Information Centre at 23 America's Cup Avenue is worth a visit.

*Boatyards/engineers/electronics* The American Shipyard Corporation (tel: 846 6000), Island Marine Services (tel: 848 9648), Oldport Marine Services (tel: 847 9109) and

Brewer Street Boatworks (tel: 847 0321) located at the Newport Yachting Center. Only the first has a marine railway. Diesel engineers are available at Goat Island Marina.

Little Harbor Marine (tel: 683 7100) (a Ted Hood company), about six miles up the Bay, has a major concentration of marine industries including electronics, sailmakers, sparmakers, etc

*Sailmakers* Several in the town – contact through one of the concerns listed above

*Chandlery* JT's (tel: 846 7256) at 364 Thames Street has a good range, plus many others

*Chart agent* The Armchair Sailor Bookstore (tel: 847 4252, fax: 847 1219) has comprehensive stocks and extremely helpful staff

*Yacht club* The Ida Lewis Yacht Club (tel: 846 1969), host to many America's Cup races, has premises on the southern shores of the harbour, while the Newport Yacht Club (tel: 846 9410) is at its head. Both welcome visiting yachtsmen

*Diesel* At Goat Island Marina, Bannister's Wharf and Newport Yachting Center

*Water* At all the marinas

*Electricity* Alongside at all the marinas. 110 volt and/or 220 volt may be available

*Bottled gas* Island Marine Services (tel: 848 9648). Propane only is available

*Showers* At all the marinas

*Holding tank pumpout* At the larger marinas and the Ida Lewis Yacht Club

*Laundry/launderette* At the larger marinas and Island Yacht Services

*Banks* Many in the town, with credit card facilities

*General shopping* Good, if slightly tourist orientated

*Provisioning* Several large supermarkets and many delicatessens etc

*Restaurants/hotels* Wide choice at all levels

*Medical services* Newport Hospital (tel: 846 6400) and many doctors and dentists

## Communications

*Mailing address* C/o General Delivery at the main post office or any of the marinas by prior arrangement

*Post Office* In the town

*Telephones* At the marinas and elsewhere

*Bus/rail service* Buses to Providence, Rhode Island, with rail connections to Boston, New York, etc

*Taxis/car hire* No problem

*Air services* From Providence to international destinations

| Springs: 3.4 m/11 ft 1 in | Flag: USA |
| Neaps: 2.4 m/7 ft 11 in | Currency: US dollar |

Tel/fax – Country code: 1, Area code: (1) 207

| Charts | Admiralty | US |
| --- | --- | --- |
| General | 2492 (1:677,000) | 13260 (1:378,838) |
| Approach | – | 13302 (1:80,000) |
| | | 13305 (1:40,000) |
| Harbour | – | 13307 (1:20,000) |

## General

Rockland is a large harbour which has traditionally concerned itself with fishing and commercial activities. However these have declined sharply over the past five years and considerable efforts are now being made to attract yachts. There are several marinas and boatyards and all facilities are available.

Though perhaps not an obvious choice for an Atlantic landfall, Rockland would be an excellent departure point if leaving for the eastward Atlantic passage by one of the northern routes.

## Approach

Rockland lies on the western shore of Penobscot Bay, about 150 miles from the Cape Cod Canal and about 160 miles west-north-west of Cape Sable at the south-west tip of Nova Scotia.

If approaching from southward, landfall is probably best made at Monhegan Island [Fl 15s 54m 20M]. From south-east, Matinicus Rock with its powerful light [Fl 10s 27m 20M] should be easy to identify, whilst from the east Mount Desert Rock [Fl 15s 23m 18M] is the most likely landfall. Penobscot Bay is well buoyed and lit, but vast numbers of lobster pots laid within the 50 m line make a night approach hazardous even with the aid of radar.

## Radio

The harbourmaster monitors VHF channel 09 and works on channel 11. Tugs monitor VHF channels 10, 13 and 16. Both the Coast Guard and Hurricane Island Outward Bound School (which also maintains a SAR capability) monitor channel 16.

Of the marinas, Journey's End uses channels 09, 18 and 68, Rockland Landings and Knight Marine Service work on channels 09 and 16, and Rockland Public Landing uses channel 09 only.

## Entrance

The entrance lies between the breakwater (lit) and an

unlit green can buoy 0.5 miles to the south. The buoy marks Spears Rock (1.5 m), and Lowell Ledge (drying) further inshore. Within the harbour buoyed channels indicate the deepest water but, armed with the large scale chart, yachts of normal draught can take their own route.

## Anchorage and moorings

Free anchorage may be found anywhere within the harbour. Shelter from the prevailing winds is good, and in the occasional easterly blow protection can be found behind the breakwater.

The harbourmaster maintains moorings east of the public landing – those reserved for visitors have a white buoy with blue stripe and red number, the pick-up marked with a white flag. Both Samoset Resort Inn (tel: 594 2511) and the Hurricane Island Outward Bound School (tel: 594 5548) occasionally have moorings vacant, and several of the boatyards and marinas may also have moorings available.

## Berthing and marinas

Journey's End Marina (tel: 594 4444, fax: 594 0407), situated astride the root of the granite Coast Guard Pier, has excellent facilities and is able to accommodate larger yachts – over 15 m (50 ft) – in their 'schooner berths'. Rockland Landings Marina (tel: 596 6573) close south of the Coast Guard Pier, Knight Marine Service (tel: 594

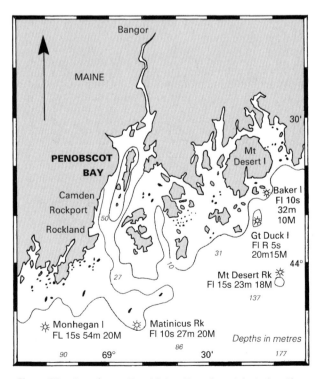

Chart 72   Penobscot Bay, Maine. Based on Admiralty Chart No 2670.

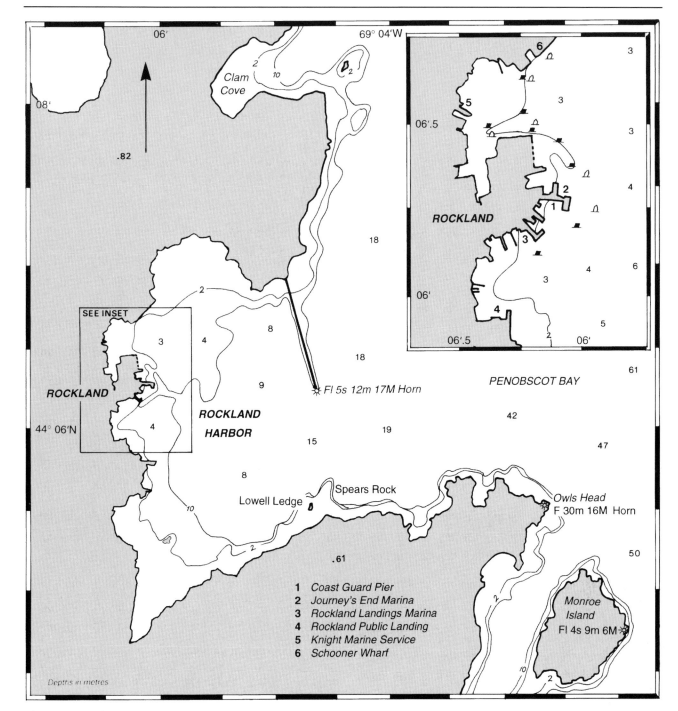

*Chart 73*   Rockland, Maine. Based on US Chart No 13307.

4068) in the cove north of the Coast Guard Pier, and Rockland Harbor Boatyard (tel: 594 4337) all have the usual marina facilities including visitors' berths. Rockland Public Landing, administered by the harbourmaster (tel: 594 0312), has some pontoon berths for visitors with water and electricity available.

From 1998 a few berths for smaller vessels may be available off the Black Pearl Restaurant close north of the public landing, and there is also a project to build a marina at Schooner Wharf, north of the Coast Guard Pier, though work had not started by December 1997.

## Formalities

Fly the Q flag from offshore if arriving from abroad. The skipper only should go ashore immediately after berthing and telephone 1 800 973 2867 (tollfree). This national centre will supply the number for the local customs office, which can (and should) be called at any time of the day or night, though normal office hours are 0800-1700. (Alternatively, the marina may know the number or even have a direct line.) If requested, customs will notify the immigration services.

The yacht will then be visited, by launch if necessary. There is no charge for clearance within office hours but a Cruising License, currently costing $25 and valid for one year, will be issued to a foreign yacht at the first port of call. Ship's papers, passports (with visas as appropriate) and previous port clearance will be required – see Chapter 19.

## Facilities

The harbourmaster (tel: 594 0312) has an office in the Chamber of Commerce building near the public landing. He and his staff welcome visiting yachts and will assist in any way they can. The Chamber of Commerce (tel: 596 0376, fax: 596 6549) provides general tourist information.

*Boatyards* Journey's End Marina (tel: 594 4444, fax: 594 0407) has a 50 ton travel lift and 750 and 1200 ton marine railways, and can carry out all repairs. Knight Marine Service (tel: 594 4068) has 35 and 20 ton travel lifts, backed by full boatyard facilities handling wood, steel and GRP. Rockland Harbor Boatyard (tel: 594 4337) has a 30 ton haulout trailer – it is the home of International Classic Yachts and specialises in wooden boat repairs. Rockland Marine (tel: 594 7860) is a shipyard dealing with large yachts and small commercial vessels (mostly steel) and major engineering work. North End Shipyard (tel: 594 8007) has a 150 ton railway and carries out wooden boat repairs

*Engineering* All boatyards plus Shaw's Yacht Service (tel: 594 5035) which has a mobile workshop. Rockland Harbor Marine (tel: 596 0706) at Journey's End Marina handles outboards

*Electronics* Omni Electronics, Lew Grant (tel: 594 7073) at Journey's End Marina and others

*Sail repairs* Haarstick-Pope Sailmakers (tel: 596 7293) on Tilson Avenue and E S Bohndell & Co (tel: 236 3549) in nearby Rockport also provide rigging services, as do Shaw's Yacht Service (tel: 594 5035). Gemini Canvas and Sails (tel: 596 7705) at Journey's End Marina specialises in canvas and upholstery

*Chandlery* Rockland Boat (tel: 594 8181) holds a mixture of fishing boat and yacht chandlery and will order items not in stock. Also good chandleries at Journey's End Marina and Knight Marine Service

*Chart agent* The Better Boating Association (tel: 617 982 4060) on Commerce Road is an agent for US DMA charts. Stocks are also held at Rockland Boat and Huston Tuttle Bookshop in Main Street

*Yacht club* The Rockland Yacht Club has, as yet, no premises or facilities

*Diesel* Journey's End Marina (north section), Rockland Landings Marina and Knight Marine Service

*Water* All marinas and the public landing

*Electricity* All marinas and the public landing

*Bottled gas* Propane refills at local garages

*Showers* All marinas and the harbour office building (for the public landing)

*Holding tank pumpout* At Journey's End Marina, Rockland Landings Marina and the public landing

*Laundry/launderette* At the harbour authority building, plus several in town

*Banks* Several, with credit card facilities

*General shopping* Usual town shops

*Provisioning* Medium-sized supermarket in town. Several larger supermarkets about 1.5 miles north on the main road

*Restaurants/hotels* To suit all tastes and pockets. Lobster

Rockland Harbor looking slightly south of west. Journey's End Marina and the grey stone Coast Guard Pier can be seen behind the breakwater

and seafood are specialities

*Medical services* The Penobscot Bay Medical Center (tel: 596 8000) in nearby Rockport

## Communications

*Mailing addresses* C/o The Harbourmaster's Office, PO Box 546, Rockland, ME 04841, or General Delivery, Rockland Post Office, ME 04841, in both cases marked 'Hold for Arrival'. Alternatively c/o Journey's End Marina, 120 Tillson Avenue, Rockland, ME 04841 by prior arrangement

*Fax service* The Chamber of Commerce (fax: 596 6549) will hold faxes provided they are clearly marked 'For visiting yacht (NAME)'

*Post Office* Off Main Street

*Telephones* At the marinas, the public landing and in the town

*Bus service* In summer a 'dollar' bus runs a shuttle service around the town and to the supermarkets - *see Provisioning, above*

*Taxis/car hire* Readily available

*Air services* Knox County airport at nearby Owl's Head has connecting flights to Boston. Bangor Intercontinental airport is 54 miles away (about 1.5 hours)

| | | | |
|---|---|---|---|
| *Springs*: 1.8 m/5 ft 11 in | | *Flag*: Canada | |
| *Neaps*: 1.5 m/4 ft 11 in | | *Currency*: Canadian dollar | |

*Tel/fax – Country code*: 1, *Area code*: 902

| Charts | Admiralty | US | Canadian |
|---|---|---|---|
| General | 1651 (1:725,000) | 14005 (1:300,000) | 4012 (1:300,000) |
| | | 14014 (1:350,000) | 4013 (1:350,000) |
| Approach | 729 (1:256,000) | 14083 (1:145,000) | 4320 (1:145,000) |
| | 2027 (1:40,000) | 14087 (1:38,866) | 4237 (1:40,000) |
| Harbour | 2028 (1:10,000) | 14091 (1:10,000) | 4203 (1:10,000) |
| | 2029 (1:10,000) | 14089 (1:10,000) | 4202 (1:10,000) |

## General

Halifax is the capital of the Canadian province of Nova Scotia. It is a large commercial port and a naval base, and an official port of entry. Yachting activity is largely centred in the North West Arm, a long narrow bay branching off just inside the main entrance before the city and waterfront is reached, and in Bedford Basin north of the city.

## Approach

The coastline of Nova Scotia is somewhat rugged and hilly with many inlets, and off-lying rocks and small islands extend up to five miles from the coast in places. It is well buoyed, but subject to fog during summer months, particularly with onshore winds. In clear weather the land will be visible well before any dangers are approached, but in poor visibility it is essential to exercise great caution when closing the coast.

If approaching from west of 63°30'W care must be taken when off Pennant Point and Sambro Island. This is an area of shoal water and isolated rocks, many of which dry or are awash, and in bad weather the sea breaks fiercely. Although it is well buoyed these may be missed in thick weather.

The final approach to Halifax is made between Chebucto Head on the western side, a 30 m (100 ft) headland of whitish granite with a light [Fl 20s 49m 14M] shown from a white tower close to the north, and Devils Island [Fl 10s 16m 13M] off Hartlen Point to the north-east. Between them lie Portuguese Shoal and Rock Head Shoal, both of which are buoyed. There are numerous other buoys and leading lights in the final approach.

## Radio

'Halifax Traffic' operates a Vessel Traffic Management System for all vessels over 20 m (65 ft) and will advise smaller craft on the proximity of shipping. It monitors VHF channel 16 and works on channels 12 and 14 (channel 14 for traffic to seaward of Chebucto Head, channel 12 in the harbour itself). The harbourmaster uses channel 65 A, with the Royal Nova Scotia Yacht Squadron on channel 68. The Canadian Coast Guard monitors channel 16, and works on 26 and 27. In addition, a continuous weather forecast is broadcast on channel 21 B.

## Entrance

Halifax is entered between Sandwich Point and McNab's Island. Shipping generally uses one or other of the tracks indicated on the plan, and as there is good water outside the channel yachts may do better to keep further west. The only possible hazard is a 2.0 m patch about 0.5 miles south-east of Sandwich Point.

The entire area is well buoyed, and if entering at night the leading lights at George's Island and Dartmouth will be useful (but keep a careful watch for shipping).

## Anchorage and moorings

All three of the yacht club marinas listed below may also have moorings available.

If entering the North West Arm there are many yacht moorings, and care must be taken at night or in thick weather. Anchorage is prohibited inside a 'no wake corridor' which runs the entire length of the inlet occupying approximately its centre third – speed must also be decreased if applicable. The clubhouse of the Royal Nova Scotia Yacht Squadron (tel: 477 5653, fax: 477 6298) lies on the south-west side, about 0.5 miles up the North West Arm, with moorings off it. Visitors can anchor off, or may go alongside the floating pontoons or the 50 m (160 ft) wharf if space permits. The Armdale Yacht Club (tel: 477 4617) is situated on Melville Island near the head of the North West Arm, with moorings off it and pontoon berths and jetties round the island's shore. Beware a rocky shoal patch 60 m (200 ft) off the western end of Melville Island.

Anchoring is not permitted in the main harbour between McNab's Island and the bridge.

## Berthing and marinas

The Canadian Forces Sailing Association (tel: 427 0550 for the military base general switchboard) has berths behind the north end of McNab's Island. They offer all usual marina facilities other than fuel.

There are two yacht club marinas in Bedford Basin north of the city – at the Dartmouth Yacht Club (tel: 468 6050) on the east side of the Basin about 1.5 miles past the Narrows, and the Bedford Basin Yacht Club (tel: 835 3729) at the head of the Basin about three miles past the Narrows. Both have all the usual marina facilities, though fuel is available only at the former.

The Dartmouth Yacht Club is close to the largest industrial park in Atlantic Canada, where a wide selection of services and equipment useful to visiting yachts is available.

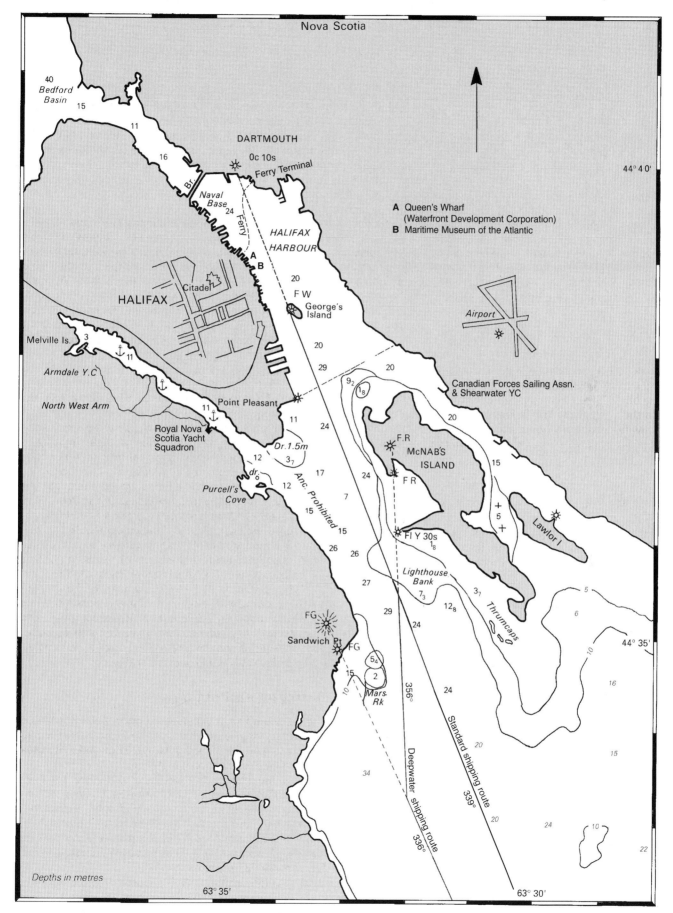

*Chart 74* Halifax, Nova Scotia. Based on Admiralty Chart No 2029.

There are two possibilities in the city itself. The Maritime Museum of the Atlantic (tel: 424 7490, fax: 424 0612) offers free berthing for up to three days (longer if there's no competition for space), on a pontoon just south of SMCS *Sackville* and CSS *Arcadia*. However there are no facilities other than water, and visiting yachts inevitably become a part of the tourist attraction. There can also be a problem with wash from passing vessels. About 200 m (660 ft) further north is the Queen's Wharf, owned and operated by the Waterfront Development Corporation (tel: 422 6591, fax: 422 7582). This is more suited to larger yachts and shore power is available, but again wash can be a problem.

Yachts can also tie up at the Dartmouth Ferry terminal on the east side of the harbour, but beware a shoal area alongside the wharf about half way along.

## Formalities

Fly the Q flag from offshore if arriving from abroad. On arrival the skipper should go ashore alone to call Canadian Customs Control on 1 888 226 7277 (tollfree) with all yacht and personal details to hand – registration number, last port, names and dates of birth of all crew, etc. This number is in operation 24 hours a day. They will want to know the yacht's exact location and will then issue a Report Number. Finally they will alert local customs who will visit the yacht to stamp the passports of non-US or Canadian nationals, for which a fee ($25 in 1997) will be charged if outside normal working hours. Note that all weapons and firearms must be declared and that there is a total ban on retaining hand guns on board.

## Facilities

*Boatyards/engineers* The Royal Nova Scotia Yacht Squadron has a 5 ton crane, and like the Armdale Yacht Club has limited facilities for slipping and repair work. All the clubs will advise visitors about alternative yards if they cannot offer the necessary service

*Electronics* Cross Marine Electronics (tel: 468 3993) in the Burnside Industrial Park at Dartmouth

*Chandlery* The Binnacle Yachting Equipment and Accessories (tel: 423 6464, fax: 479 1518) on Purcell's Cove Road, plus others in the city

*Chart agents* The Binnacle, Gabriel Aero-Marine Instruments (tel: 425 5030) and Cross Marine Electronics stock US and Canadian charts

*Yacht clubs* All five yachts clubs mentioned above have

good facilities and welcome visiting yachtsmen

*Weather forecast* Contact the Port Meteorological Office (tel: 426 6703, fax: 426 9158) whose publication *Using the Marine Forecast* includes a map of forecast areas. *See also Radio, above*

*Diesel* Available at the Royal Nova Scotia Yacht Squadron, the Armdale Yacht Club and the Dartmouth Yacht Club

*Water* Available at all five yacht clubs and the Maritime Museum

*Electricity* At the marinas and the Queen's Wharf

*Bottled gas* Propane refills are normally available – enquire at one of the yacht clubs

*Showers* At any of the yacht clubs at the discretion of the staff

*Laundry/launderette* At the Royal Nova Scotia Yacht Squadron, near the head of the North West Arm and in the city

*Banks* Several in the city, with credit card facilities

*General shopping* All one would expect in a large, modern city

*Provisioning* Supermarkets in the city and in the suburbs near the head of the North West Arm

*Restaurants* Many, including those at the yacht clubs

*Hotels* A wide choice

*Medical services* Hospitals in the city

## Communications

*Mailing addresses* C/o The Royal Nova Scotia Yacht Squadron, 376 Purcell's Cove Road, Halifax, Nova Scotia B3P 1C7, Canada; the Armdale Yacht Club, PO Box 40, Armdale, Halifax, Nova Scotia B3L 4J7, Canada; The Maritime Museum of the Atlantic, 1675 Lower Water Street, Halifax, Nova Scotia B3J 1S3, Canada; The Waterfront Development Corporation, 1751 Lower Water Street, Halifax, Nova Scotia B3J 1S5, Canada; or one of the other yacht clubs. All by prior arrangement

*Post Office* In the city, plus a sub-post office in the suburbs near the head of the North West Arm

*Telephones* At the yacht clubs and elsewhere

*Bus service* A local bus route serves the area, including the North West Arm

*Rail service* Halifax is served by the Canadian National Railway system. The main station is near the southern end of the docks

*Taxis/car hire* Plentiful

*Air services* The airport is some 25 miles north of the city and offers flights to destinations within Canada, the USA and Europe

*Springs*: 1.3 m/4 ft 3 in      *Flag*: Canada
*Neaps*: 0.9 m/2 ft 11 in     *Currency*: Canadian dollar

*Tel/fax – Country code*: 1, *Area code*: 709

| Charts | Admiralty | US | Canadian |
|---|---|---|---|
| General | 232A (1:565,700) | 14360 (1:284,330) | 4017 (1:350,000) |
| Approach | 298 (1:60,000) | 14373 (1:75,106) | 4846 (1:60,000) |
| | | 14364 (1:37,506) | |
| Harbour | 298 (1:5,000) | 14365 (1:3,609) | 4846 (1:5,000) |

## General

St John's is the capital and principal port of Newfoundland, situated on the Atlantic coast of the Avalon Peninsula near the south-east corner of the island. The harbour is landlocked and well sheltered, but is purely commercial with no real provision for yachts. Its principal importance to the transatlantic sailor is in being the nearest port to Europe. It is an official port of entry.

## Approach

The approaches to Newfoundland lie in one of the foggiest areas in the world. However it is often clear within a few miles of the shore even when there is thick fog further out. Icebergs carried south by the Labrador current

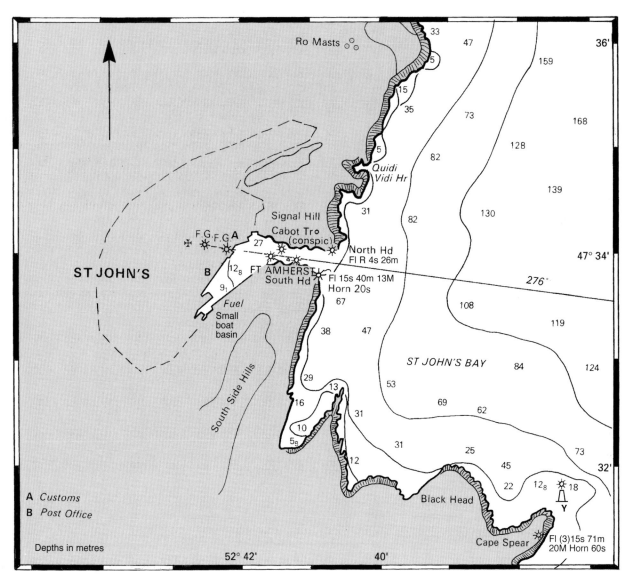

*Chart 75*   St John's, Newfoundland. Based on Admiralty Chart No 298.

may pose a further hazard (see Chapters 10 and 19).

The coastline is generally very steep, rising directly to 60 m (200 ft) in many places, with a somewhat barren appearance and few signs of habitation. Hills of 150 m to 250 m (500 ft to 800 ft) lie close inland and identification of the exact landfall can be difficult. The bluff coastline can also result in squally winds or wind shadows when close inshore. The shore is generally steep-to and clear of underwater rocks, and in thick weather can be approached using the depth sounder. The 40 m (130 ft) line lies between 0.2 and 0.5 miles offshore.

Sugarloaf Head three miles north of St John's is conspicuous – 168 m (550 ft) high with a sheer cliff face. It appears wedge-shaped when seen from north of north-east, but as a truncated cone from east-north-east round to the south-east. Cape Spear, 3.5 miles south-east of St John's, is a promontory some 80 m (262 ft) high, projecting north-eastward from the coast. A light is shown [Fl(3) 15s 71m 20M] from a 10.7 m (35 ft) white tower, with an old light structure about 200 m (660 ft) to the south-west.

## Radio

St John's Radio broadcasts weather forecasts and ice reports as well as providing radio communications, and monitors VHF channel 16. A Vessel Traffic Management System is administered from Signal Hill and may be contacted on VHF channel 11 or 14 as 'St John's Traffic'. The Canadian Coast Guard monitors VHF channels 16 and 26. In addition, a continuous weather forecast is broadcast on channel 21 B.

## Entrance

St John's harbour is entered between North and South Head. Though not easily identified from a distance, it becomes clearer as the land is closed. North Head is a steep headland of 72 m (235 ft) rising to 150 m (500 ft) immediately to its north-west as Signal Hill, topped by the conspicuous Cabot Tower. A light [Fl R 4s 26m] is shown from a mast at the entrance. South Head is marked by Fort Amherst Light [Fl 15s 40m 13M], on a square white tower. There is also a fog horn. The final approach is straightforward, with no offlying dangers other than Vestal Rock with a depth of 3.7 m (12 ft) some 65 m (213 ft) south-east of the headland.

In thick weather care must be taken not to mistake the entrance to Quidi Vidi harbour a mile further north for that of St John's. Quidi Vidi has no lighthouses or fog signals.

Enter between the two headlands on a course of 276°. There are daymarks and leading lights [F G 29m & F G 59m] on this bearing, but they are difficult to identify. The twin towers of the Roman Catholic Cathedral break the skyline on the outskirts of the city – the rear light (itself mounted on a church tower) is just to the north of these towers and almost level with their bases. If the leading line cannot be identified continue on 276° until through the narrows, observing the buoys which mark shoals in the western part of the channel. Once inside, the harbour opens up to the south-west.

## Anchorage and moorings

The harbour is busy and anchoring is only allowed under the direction of the harbourmaster. There is good holding in mud.

## Berthing and marinas

Yachts berth in the south-west corner of the harbour, where there is a small boat basin used by tourist boats. The authorities are extremely pollution conscious and the entire harbour is now very clean.

## Formalities

Fly the Q flag from offshore if arriving from abroad. On arrival the skipper should go ashore alone to call Canadian Customs Control on 1 888 226 7277 (tollfree) with all yacht and personal details to hand – registration number, last port, names and dates of birth of all crew, etc. This number is in operation 24 hours a day. They will want to know the yacht's exact location and will then issue a Report Number. Finally they will alert local customs who will visit the yacht to stamp the passports of non-US or Canadian nationals, for which a fee ($25 in 1997) will be charged if outside normal working hours. Note that all weapons and firearms must be declared and that there is a total ban on retaining hand guns on board.

## Facilities

*Boatyards* There are no yacht yards at St John's, though Down East Boat Works (tel: 576 6672) handles general boat maintenance and Dawson Newman (tel: 782 3964) repairs in GRP. The Royal Newfoundland Yacht Club has a 50 ton travel lift in Conception Bay, some 40 miles by sea from St John's

*Engineers* Machine shops at D F Barnes (tel: 579 5041), right opposite the yacht berths, and East Coast Marine (tel: 722 8600). Engine repairs by Detroit Diesel-Allison (tel: 579 7341) for Volvo and Perkins and Liftow (tel: 754 3010) for Volvo and Yanmar. Fuel systems by Diesel Injection Sales (tel: 726 6774)

*Electrical* Terra Nova Marine (tel: 747 1565)

*Electronics* Canadian Marconi (tel: 726 2422) for Raytheon and Atlantic Electronics (tel: 368 8853) for Furuno

*Sail repairs* United Sail Works (tel: 754 2131) and Creative Canvas (tel: 747 1988). IMP (tel: 722 4221) handle rigging and rope work

*Chandlery* IMP, Coastal Outdoors (tel: 747 0159) and Mercer's Marine (tel: 466 7430)

*Chart agent* Campell's Ship Supplies (tel: 726 6932)

*Yacht club* The Royal Newfoundland Yacht Club (tel: 834 5151), which welcomes visiting yachtsmen, is based at Long Pond on the western shores of the Avalon Peninsula

*Weather forecast* Contact the Port Meteorological Office (tel: 772 4798, fax: 772 2593) whose publication *Using the Marine Forecast* includes a map of forecast areas. *See also Radio, above*

*Diesel* Contact Irving Fuel (tel: 758 3000) who are willing to deliver small quantities

*Water* Water outlets in the area used by yachts. Hoses need a threaded connector

*Bottled gas* Propane refills available. Superior Propane (tel: 726 1780) will assist with problems

*Showers* The YMCA (tel: 754 2960), situated a couple of miles from the harbour, is helpful to visitors and has excellent facilities including showers, for which a small charge is made

*Laundry/launderette* In the city

*Banks* In the city, with credit card facilities

*General shopping* Good

*Provisioning* Several large supermarkets in the south-western and eastern outskirts of the town

*Restaurants/hotels* A reasonable choice

*Medical services* Three large hospitals in the city, plus many doctors and dentists

## Communications

*Mailing address* C/o General Delivery, Main Postal Station 'C', 354 Water Street, St John's, Newfoundland, Canada AIC 5YI

*Post Office* In the city

*Telephones* Adjacent to the docks

*Bus service* Daily bus service to Port-aux-Bisques (14 hours) for the ferry to Sydney, Nova Scotia

*Taxis/car hire* Plentiful

*Air services* St John's airport has direct flights to the UK as well as links within Canada and the USA

*Springs*: 1.1 m/3 ft 7 in  *Flag*: British (Red Ensign)
*Neaps*: 0.9 m/2 ft 11 in  *Currency*: Bermudian dollar

*Tel/fax – Country code*: 1–441, *Area code*: none

| Charts | Admiralty | US |
| --- | --- | --- |
| General | 360 (1:300,000) | 26340 (1:200,000) |
| | 334 (1:75,000) | 26341 (1:50,000) |
| Approach | 868 (1:17,500) | 26342 (1:17,500) |
| Harbour | 1315 (1:7,500) | 26343 (1:5,000) |

## General

St George's is Bermuda's second town, considerably smaller than the capital, Hamilton. Distances are such that travel is easy between the two, and certainly storing before departure is best done in Hamilton. There is some interesting cruising to be had around Bermuda, with many isolated and attractive anchorages.

Buoyage follows the IALA B system as used in the USA.

## Approach

Brief details of the approaches to Bermuda will be found in Chapter 20.

St George's harbour is situated at the extreme eastern end of the island and is approached via a well buoyed channel, one branch of which leads north-west around the island towards Hamilton and the other through the Town Cut Channel into the harbour. A red and white pillar buoy [Fl(2) 6s] 2.3 miles east of the island marks the entrance to the channel. The powerful St David's Island light [F RG 63m 20M & Fl(2) 20s 65m 15M] lies about a mile to the south.

## Radio

Bermuda Harbour Radio monitors VHF channel 16 and also uses channel 27. All vessels must contact Bermuda Harbour Radio on VHF channel 16 before entering the buoyed channel, as should a cruise liner or other large vessel be departing a one-way traffic system will be in operation.

The narrow entrance to the Town Cut Channel at St George's, Bermuda. *Photo: Anne Hammick*

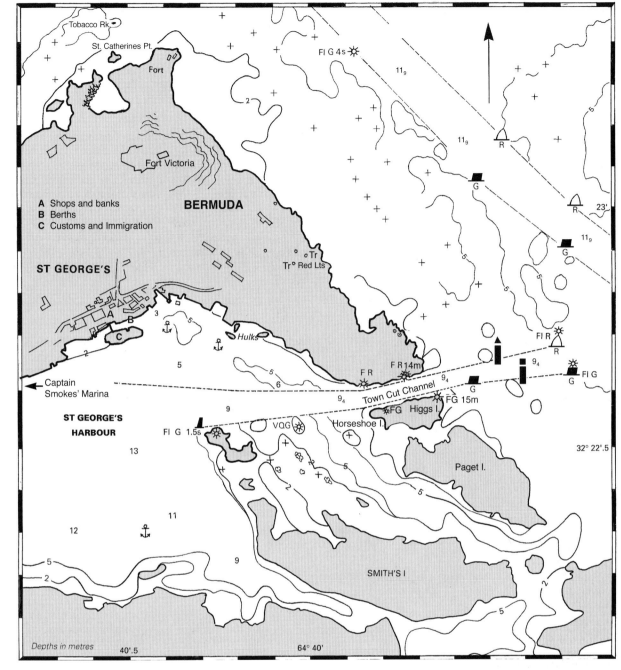

*Chart 76* St George's, Bermuda. Based on Admiralty Chart No 1315.

## Entrance

Although the Town Cut is narrow, entry with a reliable engine is not difficult. If faced with beating in under sail it might be wise to consider the alternative of a tow, which Bermuda Harbour Radio can arrange. In poor visibility, including heavy rain squalls, the Harbour Radio can monitor progress on radar. The Town Cut and its approaches are well lit, and in otherwise fair conditions entry after dark should not present problems.

Once through the Cut the harbour opens out, with good water to starboard. If entering after dark keep watch for anchored yachts, which may be unlit, and take care not to stray south out of the dredged channel.

## Anchorage and moorings

The main yacht anchorage is north of the dredged channel and east of Ordnance Island in depths of 2-5 m. Holding is good, but there are various old chains etc littering the bottom and a trip line may be advisable. Larger yachts will find greater depths in the southern part of the harbour, but it is a long dinghy ride ashore. Dinghies can be left at the steps inside Ordnance Island.

## Berthing and marinas

The only marina in St George's is Captain Smokes' at Godet & Young (tel: 297 1940, fax: 297 1813) on McCallans' Wharf. This occupies the western end of the 350 m wharf which runs from close west of Ordnance

Island. Otherwise, berthing alongside is on a strictly 'first come first served' basis, with yachts rafting on the northern side of Ordnance Island and at Somers Wharf and the eastern part of Hunters Wharf further west. Other wharves are reserved for shipping. None of the yacht berths are very deep, and as there is neither any charge nor any restriction on length of stay, space is seldom available. Berthing a yacht on any of the commercial quays is prohibited.

## Formalities

Fly the Q flag from offshore until clearance has been obtained. All yachts must call first at St George's, even if proceeding to Hamilton or elsewhere, securing at the Customs Berth at the eastern end of Ordnance Island immediately upon arrival. The office is manned 24 hours a day, monitoring channel 16 to be forewarned of arrivals. Only after the formalities have been completed may a yacht move out to anchor or continue to Hamilton. Two copies each of crew list and stores list will be required, plus ship's papers, passports and previous port clearance. A charge is made for clearance, currently of $15 per person.

In theory it is necessary to revisit the dock to obtain outward clearance, but in practice the skipper may be allowed to deal with the paperwork while the yacht remains at anchor – enquire on arrival.

## Facilities

*Boatyards/engineers* Meyer Industries Ltd (tel: 297 8078) north-east of the yacht anchorage can haul yachts up to 60 m (200 ft), also St George's Boatyard (tel: 297 0877, fax: 297 0878) in the western part of the harbour and Ballast Point Boatyard (tel: 297 1909)

*Electronics* Electronic Communications Ltd (tel: 295 2446) and Marine Communications (tel: 295 0558), both in Hamilton

*Sailmaker* Ocean Sails/Doyle (tel: 297 1008/9) have a full service sail loft. Triangle Rigging (tel: 297 2155) for rigging repairs

*Chandleries* St George's Boatyard, Captain Smokes' Marina and Dowling's Shell Marine Station (tel: 297 1914)

*Yacht and sailing clubs* The St George's Dinghy Club (tel: 297 1612) has waterside premises on the road leading to the Town Cut and is friendly towards visitors. The Royal Bermuda Yacht Club has impressive premises on Front Street in Hamilton

*Weather forecast* The Bermuda Yacht Reporting Service, located on Ordnance Island, displays a synoptic chart and forecast daily and, given some notice, will provide a departure weather briefing pack on request. Dedicated phone lines to the Bermuda Weather Service and a recorded marine forecast are also available

*Diesel* At St George's Boatyard, St David's Esso Marine (tel: 297 1996) or Dowling's Shell Marine Station (tel: 297 1914). Very large yachts may bunker at the Esso Station on the North Shore (tel: 297 1477) but it is unsuitable for the majority of yachts

*Water* At Captain Smokes' Marina and St George's Boatyard

*Electricity* At Captain Smokes' Marina and the marinas in Hamilton

*Bottled gas* At Captain Smokes' Marina or from Bermuda Gas & Utility (tel: 295 3111). Propane is in general use in Bermuda – butane, apart from Camping Gaz, is not obtainable

*Showers* At Captain Smokes' Marina and the St George's Dinghy Club. Water is a precious commodity in Bermuda and there may be a charge

*Laundry/launderette* Several in St George's and elsewhere

*Banks* Many, with credit card facilities

*General shopping* Good selection, particularly in Hamilton

*Provisioning* Wide choice of frozen foods, but more difficult for a yacht without refrigeration – see Chapter 20. Nearly all food must be imported, and is therefore expensive

*Restaurants/hotels* Many and various. Tourism plays a major part in Bermuda's economy

*Medical services* The King Edward VII Memorial Hospital at Paget, near Hamilton, plus many doctors and dentists

## Communications

*Mailing addresses* C/o St George's Post Office, St George's, Bermuda, or Captain Smokes' Marina, Godet & Young, PO Box GE 148, St George's, GE BX, Bermuda by prior arrangement

*Fax service* At Captain Smokes' Marina (fax: 297 1813)

*Post Office* In St George's

*Telephones* At Captain Smokes' Marina and in the town

*Bus service* Regular buses to Hamilton, Ireland Island at the west end of Bermuda and elsewhere

*Taxis* Easily available

*Car hire* No car hire – mopeds are available instead

*Air services* Daily air services to the USA, Canada and Europe

*Springs*: 1.6 m/5 ft 3 in
*Neaps*: 1.2 m/3 ft 11 in

*Flag*: Portugal
*Currency*: Portuguese escudo

*Tel/fax – Country code*: 351, *Area code*: (0) 92

| Charts | Admiralty | US |
|---|---|---|
| General | 1950 (1:1,000,000) | 51002 (1:750,000) |
| Approach | 1956 (1:175,000) | 51061 (1:250,000) |
| Harbour | 1940 (1:37,500) | 51062 (1:25,000) |
|  | 1940 (1:12,000) |  |

## General

Horta is the only town of any size on Faial, with a history reaching back to the mid-fifteenth century. The harbour is probably the best in the islands and has been a favourite with yachtsmen since Joshua Slocum visited in 1895 – he commented then on the friendliness and hospitality of the local people, and things have changed little.

No visit to Horta would be complete without a beer (or a coffee) in the Café Sport, run by the Azevedo family for three generations. Neither would it be wise to tempt the fates by neglecting to add a painting, or at least the yacht's name, to the thousands which cover the harbour and marina walls. Many famous yachts feature here.

## Approach

Approach and landfall on the Azores archipelago is covered in Chapter 21. However it should be repeated that the stated range of the light at Vale Formoso [LFl(2) 10s 113m 11M] near the western tip of the island is optimistic and may be nearer to five miles. The only other major light is at Pta da Ribeirinha [Fl(3) 18.5s 146m 28M] on the east coast north of Horta.

Faial has few offlying dangers and the coast may safely be closed to within half a mile or so. If approaching from south-east the Baixa do Sul (also known as Chapman's Rocks) with 7.0 m depths should be avoided if any sea is running. Horta lies near the south-east corner of the island, facing Pico across the Canal do Faial.

Lights and buoyage follow the European IALA A system.

Horta marina, looking north. The double row of buoys off the reception and fuel berth have since been removed.
*Photo: Anne Hammick*

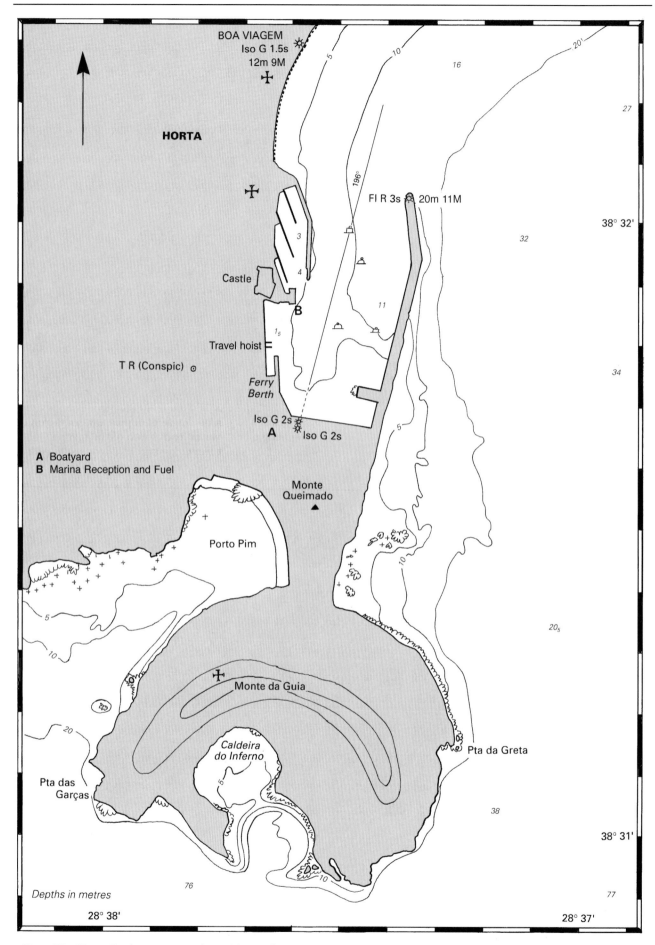

BOA VIAGEM
Iso G 1.5s
12m 9M

HORTA

FI R 3s 20m 11M

38° 32'

3

4

Castle

B

1₅

Travel hoist

T R (Conspic)

11

Ferry
Berth

Iso G 2s
Iso G 2s

34

A

A Boatyard
B Marina Reception and Fuel

Monte
Queimado

Porto Pim

5

10

20₅

Monte da Guia

Pta da Greta

20

Caldeira
do Inferno

5

Pta das
Garças

38

38° 31'

Depths in metres

76

10

77

28° 38'

28° 37'

*Chart* 77    Horta, Faial, Azores. Based on a plan in the *Atlantic Islands*.

**210    Horta, Faial, Azores**

## Radio

The port authorities operate on VHF channels 11 and 16 with the pilot service on channels 14 and 16. The marina staff (who speak English, French and Spanish as well as Portuguese) monitor VHF channels 11 and 16 from 0800–1230 and 1400–2000 daily. Mid-Atlantic Yacht Services uses channel 77 – office hours 0900–1300 and 1400–1700.

## Entrance

If approaching from westwards, Horta harbour will not be seen until the last headland is rounded, when a course can be steered directly for the breakwater head which has good depths close in. However avoid rounding it too tightly – the Pico ferry leaves at speed and tends to cut it fine. At night the breakwater light will probably be seen first, as the light of Boa Viagem tends to be overshadowed by town lights. The marina entrance is not lit, but in any case visiting yachts should secure to the reception/fuel berth on the western side of the entrance until assigned a berth.

There is at least one unlit steel ship's mooring buoy in the harbour, and if approaching the reception quay in darkness care must also be taken to avoid the yacht moorings laid opposite.

## Anchorage and moorings

Anchoring in the harbour is no longer allowed. Though yacht moorings exist they are all privately owned.

## Berthing and marinas

The Marina da Horta (tel: 22164/5/6, fax: 22523) opened in 1986 and is an object lesson in how such a facility should be maintained and run. The majority of yachts are allotted finger pontoons, with the larger ones rafting up inside the mole. Only the very largest yachts (over 30 m and with draught exceeding 4.0 m) berth in the outer harbour alongside the breakwater. However, with more than one thousand yachts passing through Horta annually the marina is frequently very crowded, and the possibility of building a second marina south of the castle is under discussion.

## Formalities

The Azores are an autonomous region of Portugal and therefore part of the EU. In theory this should mean fewer formalities for EU registered yachts arriving from another EU country, but in practice this represents such a small percentage of total arrivals that it is likely all yachts will be expected to follow the same clearance procedures for some time to come.

Fly the Q flag on arrival unless this is from another Azorean island. It is necessary to visit the *Policia Maritima* and *Alfandega* (customs) whose offices flank that of the berthing master on the reception quay. On departure both offices must again be visited, taking the receipted marina bill. Office hours are 0800–1230 and 1400–2000 and outward clearance remains valid for 24 hours.

## Facilities

The establishment of Mid-Atlantic Yacht Services (MAYS) (tel: 31616, fax: 31656, e-mail: mays@mail.telepac.pt) has vastly eased the situation for visiting yachtsmen needing to get work done. In addition to English, owners Duncan and Ruth Sweet speak French, German and Portuguese and have good contacts in mainland Portugal. MAYS, which is to be found opposite the root of the marina mole, is Azorean agent for over a dozen international manufacturers and can organise importation and fitting of most items. The company specialises in engineering, electronics, rigging and deck hardware, but amongst its other services will send and receive faxes and e-mail and handle cruisers' mail. As a bonus MAYS even run a free book swop.

*Boatyard* Capable of rough but serviceable repairs to steel, aluminium and wood, but no facilities for major fibreglass repairs. A 25 tonne travel lift has recently been purchased by the port authorities

*Engineers/electronics* Consult Mid-Atlantic Yacht Services

*Sail repairs* Ralf Holzerland (tel: 23194) will collect, repair and return sails

*Chandlery* Teófilo Garcia & Filhos Sa on the corner of Rua Vasco da Gama near the Café Sport, otherwise Mid-Atlantic Yacht Services

*Yacht club* The Clube Naval occupies the glass-fronted building on the water front south of the marina

*Weather forecast* A three day synoptic forecast is posted daily outside the marina office, plus a written forecast (Portuguese and English) outside the *Capitania do Porto* (near the Pico ferry berth)

*Diesel* From a pump at the marina reception quay, 0800–1200 and 1300–2000

*Petrol* By can from the diesel pump attendant or from filling stations in town

*Water* On the marina pontoons

*Electricity* On the pontoons (220 volt 50 Hz). Yachts must provide their own cable and plug, plus adapter if necessary

*Bottled gas* Camping Gaz readily available. Calor Gas and other non-standard cylinders can be refilled via the Shell shop south of the Café Sport. Mid-Atlantic Yacht Services will arrange this if required

*Showers* In the semi-circular building in the north-west corner of the marina area. A small charge is made

*Laundry/launderette* In the shower block (attendant service by machine, or DIY at large sinks), plus at least two others

*Banks* Several, with credit card facilities

*General shopping* Surprisingly good

*Provisioning* Several supermarkets, plus a small fruit and vegetable market at the northern end of the town with a fish market beyond

*Restaurants* A wide variety at very reasonable prices. Many accept Eurocheques or credit cards

*Hotels* Four star downwards

*Medical services* Hospital outside the town

## Communications

*Mailing addresses* C/o Café Sport, Rua Vasco da Gama, 9900 Horta, Faial, Azores, Portugal; Mid-Atlantic Yacht

Services, PT-9900 Horta, Faial, Azores, Portugal; or the Marina da Horta, Av Gago Coutinho e Sacadura Cabral 7, 9900 Horta, Faial, Azores, Portugal

*Fax service* At the Café Sport (fax: 31287), the marina office (fax: 22523), Mid-Atlantic Yacht Services (fax: 31656) and the post office

*Post Office* At the northern end of the town, open 0830–1830. Stamps can be bought at any shop displaying the green *correio* sign

*Telephones* At the main post office, Café Sport, marina bar and others

*Bus service* Circular route around the island. The tourist office will supply a timetable on request

*Taxis* Taxi rank outside the Estalagem de Santa Cruz

*Car hire* Choice of several (another thing which Mid-Atlantic Yacht Services will arrange)

*Ferry service* Several times daily to Pico, and also to the other islands of the 'central' group – details from the tourist office

*Air services* Daily flights to Lisbon and the other islands. All UK flights are routed via Lisbon

# 33 PONTA DELGADA,
## São Miguel, Azores

37°44'.5N 25°39'.5W  GMT-1

---

*Springs*: 1.7 m/5 ft 7 in      *Flag*: Portugal
*Neaps*: 1.3 m/4 ft 3 in       *Currency*: Portuguese escudo

---

*Tel/fax – Country code*: 351, *Area code*: (0) 96

---

| Charts | Admiralty | US |
|--------|-----------|-----|
| General | 1950 (1:1,000,000) | 51002 (1:75,000) |
| Approach | 1958 (1:150,000) | 51081 (1:250,000) |
| Harbour | 1958 (1:10,000) | 51082 (1:7,500) |

## General

Ponta Delgada is the largest town in the Azores, with a busy naval and commercial harbour. Other than Horta and Praia da Vitoria (Terceira) it is the only place which can be considered safe for yachts in almost all conditions, though strong winds from between east and south can send a heavy swell into the harbour. Ponta Delgada also offers the best shopping and provisioning in the Azores. The island of São Miguel is outstandingly beautiful, with spectacular lakes and hot springs, and well worth exploring.

Completion of a marina early in 1993 has increased the appeal of Ponta Delgada as a cruising stopover, in particular making it the obvious jumping off point for yachts bound for the Iberian peninsula.

## Approach

Much of São Miguel is high and often visible from many miles away. The coastline is largely steep-to, with few offlying dangers, but many of the headlands are fringed by rocks and all should be given at least 500 m clearance. If approaching from the west, Baixa da Negra lies about 0.5 miles south of the Airport Control Tower [Aero AlFlWG 10s 83m W28M/G23M] and should be given a wide berth. The island is relatively well lit, with powerful lights at Pta da Ferraria [Fl(3) 20s 106m 27M] at its western end and

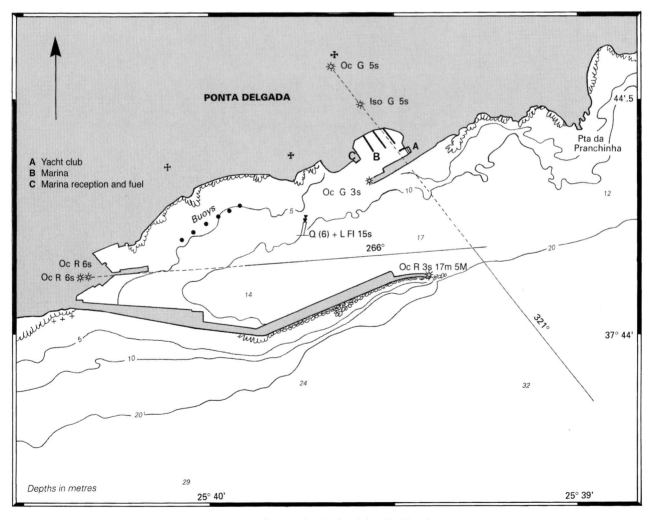

*Chart 78*   Ponta Delgada, São Miguel, Azores. Based on a plan in the *Atlantic Islands*.

---

**Ponta Delgada, São Miguel, Azores   213**

Pta do Arnel [Fl 5s 66m 25M] to the east. Santa Clara [LFl 5s 26m 15M] marks the headland to the west of Ponta Delgada.

## Radio

The port authorities operate on VHF channels 11 and 16 with the pilot service on channels 14 and 16. The marina monitors channel 16 from 0900–1800 daily.

## Entrance

Final approach and entrance is straightforward, though the grey stone breakwater may blend with the concrete esplanade if approaching on a bearing of less than 325°. A submerged rubble extension runs out from the end of the breakwater, which should therefore be given a minimum offing of 100 m. There are two sets of leading lights, both of them easily visible against the many shore lights behind, though if heading for the marina reception quay the second pair will not be used.

## Anchorage and moorings

There are a few mooring buoys, but most are privately owned - enquire at the Clube Naval. Otherwise it is possible to anchor at the west of the harbour in 8–10 m over sand, though this is not encouraged.

## Berthing and marinas

The marina - correctly the Marinaçores (tel: 27300, fax: 23390) - has already gained an excellent reputation. On arrival yachts should berth at the reception quay to visit the offices of the various officials and be assigned a berth. The marina office is open 0900–1800 daily. As in Horta, most visitors are directed to pontoon berths, with larger yachts rafting up inside the marina mole.

## Formalities

The Azores are an autonomous region of Portugal and therefore part of the EU. In theory this should mean fewer formalities for EU registered yachts arriving from another EU country, but in practice it is likely all yachts will be expected to follow the same clearance procedures for some time to come.

Fly the Q flag on arrival unless this is from another Azorean island. All officials now have offices in the marina area. The skipper should visit the *Policia Maritima* bearing ship's papers, passports and insurance documents, and will be advised of the other officials to be seen. On departure the office must again be visited, taking the receipted marina bill.

## Facilities

*Boatyards* Several yards where wooden fishing boats are built and steel repaired - enquire in the marina office. It is possible for yachts to be craned out on the hard-standing inside the marina mole

*Engineers/electronics* Enquire of the marina staff, who can also arrange refrigeration repairs. It may be worth contacting Mid-Atlantic Yacht Services in Horta (tel: 31616, fax: 31656) if parts have to be imported

*Yacht club* The Clube Naval de Ponta Delgada (tel: 23005, fax: 26383), which occupies most of the large building at the root of the marina mole, is particularly welcoming towards visiting yachtsmen. It has a pleasant bar and good restaurant

*Weather forecast* A forecast and synoptic chart is posted daily on the notice board in the marina. This normally covers the coming 48 hours, but a one-week forecast can be prepared on request

*Diesel* At the marina reception quay

*Petrol* From filling stations in the town

*Water* On marina pontoons. Hoses need special connectors (available in town if not already carried)

*Electricity* On the pontoons (220 volt 50 Hz). Again a locally available connector is needed, and yachts must provide their own cable and plug, plus adaptor if necessary

*Bottled gas* Camping Gaz readily available. Calor Gas and other non-standard cylinders can be refilled at the Shell depot on the main road to the airport

*Ice* In the marina complex, or from garages

*Showers* In the marina complex

*Laundry/launderette* In the town

*Banks* Several, with credit card facilities

*General shopping* Able to fill most needs

*Provisioning* Several supermarkets nearby, with a sizeable hypermarket a taxi-ride out of town. Also a good fruit and vegetable market with fish market attached

*Restaurants/hotels* Wide choice at all levels

*Medical services* A hospital near the harbour, plus several medical centres

## Communications

*Mailing addresses* C/o Marinaçores, Av Infante D Henrique, 9500 Ponta Delgada, Azores, Portugal, or the Clube Naval de Ponta Delgada, Av Infante D Henrique, Apartado 4, 9500 Ponta Delgada, Azores, Portugal

*Fax service* At the marina office (fax: 23390)

*Post Office* Open 0830–1830, but usually busy with long delays. Stamps can be bought at any shop displaying the green *correio* sign

*Telephones* At the marina office, the post office and elsewhere

*Bus service* Good network, with a reputation for running early. Timetable from the tourist office

*Taxis/car hire* No problem. Mopeds and cycles can also be hired

*Air services* Daily flights to Lisbon and the other islands. All UK flights are routed via Lisbon

# APPENDIX A - Suggestions for Further Reading

The following suggestions for further reading are indexed by chapter for easy reference. It is certainly not implied that every book under each heading need be consulted - all books (and authors) have their strengths and weaknesses, and in many cases parts of the subject matter overlap between one title and the next. Which books will be carried on board, and which read before departure and then left at home, must depend on the size of the yacht and the priorities of her skipper.

All should be available in bookshops, chandleries or through mail order catalogues, with the ISBN (International Standard Book Number) quoted where available. Where a book is available from both UK and US publishers note that the ISBN may differ.

Appropriate manufacturer's handbooks should also be carried, but for obvious reasons cannot be listed here.

## Preparations
(relevant to several chapters in Part I)

*Around the World Rally*, Jimmy Cornell (0-7136-3690-4) (ACN;SH)

*Blue Water Countdown*, Geoff Pack (1-85277-073-2) (YM)

*Cruising Under Sail, incorporating Voyaging Under Sail*, Eric Hiscock (0-7136-3564-9) (ACN; IM)

*Handbook of Offshore Cruising*, Jim Howard (0-7136-4044-8) (ACN; SH)

*Long-Distance Cruising*, Bobby Schenk (0-71530-245-0) (D&C)

*Ocean Cruising on a Budget*, Anne Hammick (0-7136-4069-3) (ACN; IM)

*Sell Up and Sail*, Bill & Laurel Cooper (0-7136-4786-8) (ACN;SH)

*The Voyager's Handbook*, Beth A Leonard (0-7136-4937-2) (ACN; IM)

## The philosophy of ocean cruising
*Sensible Cruising: The Thoreau Approach*, Don Casey & Lew Hackler (1-87742-288-5) (IM)

*The Self-Sufficient Sailor*, Lin & Larry Pardey (1-39303-269-8) (PB)

*There Be No Dragons*, Reese Palley (0-713-64713-2) (SH; ACN)

*Voyaging on a Small Income*, Annie Hill (1-85310-425-6) (WLB)

## The boat and her permanent fittings
*Seaworthiness: The Forgotten Factor*, C A Marchaj (0-7136-4347-1) (ACN)

*Desirable and Undesirable Characteristics of Offshore Yachts*, Technical Committee of the Cruising Club of America (0-39003-311-2) (WWN)

*The Capable Cruiser*, Lin & Larry Pardey (1-96440-362-4) (PB)

*Fibreglass Boats*, Hugo du Plessis (0-7136-4290-4) (ACN; IM)

*Surveying Small Craft*, Ian Nicolson (0-7136-3949-0) (ACN;SH)

*The Cruising Multihull*, Chris White (0-07069-868-6) (IM)

*Multihull Seamanship*, Dr Gavin LeSuer (1-89866-031-X) (FB)

*Multihull Voyaging*, Thomas Firth Jones (0-7136-4223-8) (AC; SH)

*Multihulls for Cruising and Racing*, Derek Harvey (0-7136-3562-2) (ACN)

*Spurr's Boatbook: Upgrading the Cruising Sailboat*, Daniel Spurr (1-87742-411-X) (IM)

*The Rigging Handbook*, Brian Toss (0-7136-4817-1) (ACN) (American title: *The Complete Rigger's Apprentice* (0-07064-840-9) (IM)

*Refrigeration for Pleasureboats*, Nigel Calder (0-87742-286-9) (IM)

*Boat Engines*, Dick Hewitt (1-89866-004-2) (FB)

*The Care and Repair of Small Marine Diesels*, Chris Thompson (0-7136-4588-1) (ACN;SH)

*Marine Diesel Engines*, Nigel Calder (1-85310-897-9) (WLB)

*Keep Your Marine Diesel Running*, Richard Thiel (0-87742-266-4) (IM)

*Boat Owner's Mechanical and Electrical Manual*, Nigel Calder (0-7136-4291-2) (ACN; IM)

*Boatowner's Wiring Manual*, Charles Wing (0-7136-4072-3) (ACN) (American title: *Boatowner's Illustrated Handbook of Wiring* (0-07071-092-9) (IM)

*Marine Electrical and Electronics Bible*, John C Payne (0-7136-4110-X) (ACN; SH)

*Boat Electrical Systems*, Dag Pike (0-71363-451-0) (ACN)

*The 12-Volt Bible for Boats*, Miner Brotherton (1-85310-254-7) (WLB; IM)

## Equipment for ocean and warm climate cruising
*Canvas Work*, Jeremy Howard-Williams (0-92448-660-0) (SH)

*Canvaswork and Sail Repair*, Don Casey (0-07013-391-3) (IM; ACN)

*Practical Sail Care and Repair*, Lisa Carr (1-85310-463-9) (WLB)

*Nicolson on Sails*, Ian Nicolson (0-7136-4468-0) (ACN; SH)

*Sails: The Way They Work and How to Make Them*, Derek Harvey (0-7136-4396-X) (ACN; SH)

*Independent Energy Guide*, Kevin Jeffrey (0-96441-120-2) (CLGP)

*Cruising in Tropical Waters and Coral*, Alan Lucas (0-540 07321-0) (ACN)

## Ocean navigation
*Celestial Navigation for Yachtsmen*, Mary Blewitt (0-71364-623-3) (ACN)

*Ocean Navigator*, Kenneth Wilkes, Revised by Pat Langley-Price & Philip Ouvry (0-7136-3924-5) (ACN)

*The Sextant Handbook*, Bruce Bauer (1-07005-219-0) (IM)

*Emergency Navigation*, David Burch (0-87742-260-5) (IM)

*Simple GPS Navigation*, Mik Chinery (1-898660-00-X) (FB)

*Simple Electronic Navigation*, Mik Chinery (0-90675-467-4) (FB)

*Using GPS*, Conrad Dixon (0-7136-3952-0) (ACN; SH)

### Radio and electronics

*A Guide to Small Boat Radio*, Mike Harris (0-7136-3436-7) (ACN)

*World Radio and TV Handbook*, Sennitt Andrew (0-82307-798-5) (WGP)

*Mariners Guide to Single Sideband*, Frederick Graves (0-91167-701-1) (SI)

*The Cruiser's Radio Guide*, Roger Krautkremer (no ISBN) (FSP)

*GMDSS for Small Craft*, Alan Clemmetset (1-89866-038-7) (FB)

### The crew

*All in the Same Boat*, Tom Neale (0-07046-434-0) (IM)

*The Cruising Woman's Advisor*, Diana B Jessie (1-07031-981-2) (IM)

*Cruising with Children*, Gwenda Cornell (0-7136-3561-4) (ACN; SH)

*The Hitch-Hiker's Guide to the Oceans*, Alison Muir Bennett (0-7136-4345-5) (ACN)

*Born to Sail - on Other People's Boats*, Jennifer P Stuart (0-9248-611-2) (SH)

### Provisioning

*The Care and Feeding of Sailing Crew*, Lin & Larry Pardey (1-39303-726-6) (PB)

*The Great Cruising Cookbook*, John C Payne (0-7136-4667-5) (SH; ACN)

*The Cruising Chef Cookbook*, Michael Greenwald (0-83066-864-0) (PCP)

*Sailing the Farm*, Ken Neumeyer (0-89815-051-5) (TSP)

### The mechanics of ocean cruising

*Living Afloat*, Clare Allcard (0-7136-4135-5) (ACN) (American title: *The Intricate Art of Living Afloat*) (0-39331-596-7) (WWN)

*Collins Gems: Guide to Flags* (0-00470-723-0) (HCP)

*Yachtsman's Ten Language Dictionary*, Barbara Webb & Michael Manton with the Cruising Association (0-7136-4087-1) (ACN)

### Safety when ocean cruising

*Oceanography and Seamanship*, William G Van Dorn (0-87033-434-4) (CMTP)

*The Weather Handbook*, Alan Watts (1-85310-409-4) (WLB)

*Weather at Sea*, David Houghton (0-90675-464-X) (FB)

*A Sailor's Guide to Wind, Waves and Tides*, Captain Alex Simpson (1-85310-571-6) (WLB)

*Heavy Weather Sailing*, K Adlard Coles, Revised by Peter Bruce (0-7136-3431-6) (ACN;IM)

*Storm Tactics Handbook*, Lin & Larry Pardey (1-83110-787-5) (WLB)

*Heavy Weather Cruising*, Tom Cunliffe (1-89866-027-1) (FB)

*Aground*, James E Minnoch (0-82860-098-8) (IM)

*First Aid at Sea*, Douglas Justins & Colin Berry (0-7136-4922-4) (ACN)

*Your Offshore Doctor*, Dr Michael H Beilan (1-7136-4695-0) (SH;ACN)

*Advanced First Aid Afloat*, Peter F Eastman (0-87033-465-4) (CMTP)

*The Ship's Captain's Medical Guide* (1-11550-684-5) (SOP)

*Where There Is No Doctor*, Werner David (0-94236-415-5) (HF)

*Bugs, Bites & Bowels*, Dr Jane Wilson Howarth (1-86011-045-2) (CB)

Books known to, and recommended by, the editors and their wide circle of cruising contacts are marked by a double asterisk. However, the omission of this symbol does not imply any criticism of a particular book - more probably the authors are simply unfamiliar with it.

All should be available in bookshops, chandleries or through mail order catalogues, with the ISBN (International Standard Book Number) quoted where available. Where a book is available from both UK and US publishers' note that the ISBN may differ.

## Atlantic Ocean and worldwide

*Ocean Passages for the World*, British Admiralty (NP 136) (HO) **

*World Cruising Routes*, Jimmy Cornell (0-7136-4838-4) (ACN; IM) **

*World Cruising Handbook*, Jimmy Cornell (0-7136-4419-2) (ACN; IM)

*Atlas of Pilot Charts, North Atlantic Ocean and Caribbean*, US Defense Mapping Agency (NIMA Pub 106)

*Atlantic Pilot Atlas*, James Clarke (0-7136-4554-7) (ACN; IM) **

*Street's Transatlantic Crossing Guide*, Donald M Street Jr (0-39303-329-5) (WWN)

## Atlantic coast of Europe and Africa

*The Cruising Association Handbook* (0-95037-426-1) (CA) **

*The Macmillan Nautical Almanac* (0-33367-096-6) **

*The Simpson-Lawrence Yachtsman's Almanac: North and West*, Michael Balmforth (1-87334-015-X) (CMP)

*The Yachtsman's Pilot to the Western Isles*, Martin Lawrence (0-85288-339-5) (ILNW)

*The Yachtsman's Pilot to Skye and North West Scotland*, Martin Lawrence (0-85288-364-4) (ILNW)

*The Yachtsman's Pilot to the West Coast of Scotland: Crinan to Canna*, Martin Lawrence (0-85288-250-5) (ILNW)

*The Yachtsman's Pilot to the West Coast of Scotland: Clyde to Colonsay*, Martin Lawrence (0-85288-189-4) (ILNW)

*West Highland Shores*, Maldwin Drummond (0-7136-5860-6) (ACN)

*CCC Sailing Directions: Outer Hebrides*, Clyde Cruising Club (0-90064-969-0) (CCC) **

*CCC Sailing Directions: Ardnamurchan to Cape Wrath*, Clyde Cruising Club (1-89978-625-2) (CCC) **

*CCC Sailing Directions: Kintyre to Ardnamurchan*, Clyde Cruising Club (1-89978-620-1) (CCC) **

*CCC Sailing Directions: Firth of Clyde, including the Solway Firth and Isle of Man*, Clyde Cruising Club (1-89978-615-5) (CCC) **

*East and North Coasts of Ireland Sailing Directions*, Irish Cruising Club (0-95017-176-X) (ICC) **

*South and West Coasts of Ireland Sailing Directions*, Irish Cruising Club (0-95017-175-1) (ICC) **

*Cruising Guide to Northwest England and Wales*, George Griffiths (0-85288-190-8) (ILNW)

*Lundy and Irish Sea Pilot*, David Taylor (0-85288-249-1) (ILNW)

*Bristol Channel and Severn Pilot*, David Cumberlidge (0-540-07422-5) (ACN)

*Isles of Scilly Pilot*, Robin Brandon (0-85288-149-5) (new edition by John & Fay Garey, due 1998/9) (ILNW)

*West Country Cruising*, Mark Fishwick (1-85277-101-1) (YM) **

*The Simpson-Lawrence Yachtsman's Almanac: South and East*, Michael Balmforth (1-87334-014-1) (CMP)

*The Shell Channel Pilot*, Tom Cunliffe (0-85288-386-2) (ILNW)

*North Brittany and Channel Islands Cruising*, Peter Cumberlidge (1-85277-069-4) (YM)

*Brittany and Channel Islands Cruising Guide*, David Jefferson (0-7136-3417-0) (ACN)

*North Brittany*, Nick Heath (0-85288-162-2) (ILNW) **

*Secret Anchorages of Brittany*, Peter Cumberlidge (1-85310-342-X) (WLB)

*North Biscay*, Nick Heath (0-85288-245-9) (ILNW) **

*South Biscay Pilot*, Robin Brandon (0-7136-3698-X) (ACN) **

*Atlantic Spain and Portugal*, Anne Hammick (0-85288-298-X) (ILNW) **

*The Macmillan Nautical Almanac: Iberian Supplement* (0-33372-768-1) **

*Cruising Guide to West Africa*, Steve Jones (0-95277-712-6) (RCCPF)

*South African Nautical Almanac*, Tom Morgan (0-94998-966-5) (via INLW)

## Islands in the Atlantic Ocean

*Atlantic Islands*, Anne Hammick (0-85288-267-X) (ILNW) **

*Madeira and Porto Santo Cruising Guide*, Gwenda Cornell (0-95174-864-5) (WCP)

*Canary Islands Cruising Guide*, Jimmy Cornell (0-95174-866-1) (WCP)

*Yachting Guide to Bermuda*, Edward Harris (0-92156-006-0) (BMMP)

*Azores Cruising Guide*, Gwenda Cornell (0-95174-862-9) (WCP)

*Faeroe, Iceland & Greenland*, RCC Pilotage Foundation (0-85288-268-8) (ILNW)

## Atlantic coast of South America

*South Atlantic South America*, Pete & Annie Hill (0-95277-710-X) (RCCPF)

## The Lesser Antilles

*Concise Guide to Caribbean Weather*, David Jones (0-96524-760-0) (NP) **

*Reed's Nautical Almanac: Caribbean Edition* (1-88466-616-7) (TRP)

*Passages South: A Gentleman's Guide*, Bruce Van Sant

(0-94442-831-2) (CGP) **

*A Cruising Guide to the Caribbean*, William T Stone & Anne M Hays (0-92448-657-0) (SH)

*Cruising Guide to Trinidad and Tobago*, Chris Doyle (0-94442-837-1) (CGP) **

*The Cruiser's Guide to Trinidad and Tobago*, Norma C Hoover & George B Gliksman (9-76805-438-7) (PPC)

*Venezuela*, Donald M Street Jr (0-39303-345-7) (WWN)

*Cruising Guide to Venezuela and Bonaire*, Chris Doyle (0-94442-838-X) (CGP) **

*Martinique to Trinidad*, Donald M Street Jr (0-39303-523-9) (WWN)

*The Lesser Antilles*, RCC Pilotage Foundation (0-85288-153-3) (ILNW)

*A Cruising Guide to the Leeward Islands*, Chris Doyle (0-94442-830-4) (CGP) **

*A Sailor's Guide to the Windward Islands*, Chris Doyle (0-94442-835-5) (CGP) **

*Yachtsman's Guide to the Windward Islands*, Julius M Wilensky (0-91875-201-0 ) (WC)

*Anguilla to Dominica*, Donald M Street Jr (0-39303-525-5) (WWN)

*VIP Cruising Guide - St Maarten to Antigua*, William J Eiman (0-96350-480-0) (VIP)

*Puerto Rico, the Passage Islands, the US and British Virgin Islands*, Donald M Street Jr (0-39303-305-8) (WWN)

*Virgin Anchorages*, Nancy & Simon Scott (0-94442-829-0) (CGP)

*Cruising Guide to the Virgin Islands*, Nancy & Simon Scott (0-94442-834-7) (CGP) **

*Yachtsman's Guide to the Virgin Islands*, Meredith Fields (0-93737-911-5) (TIP)

### The Bahamas

*The Exuma Guide*, Stephen Pavlidis (0-96395-667-2) (SWP) **

*Exumas: Explorer Charts*, Monty Lewis (no ISBN) (LO) **

*The Bahamas Cruising Guide*, Mathew Wilson (0-07052-693-1) (IM)

*Yachtsman's Guide to the Bahamas*, Meredith Fields (0-93737-921-2) (TIP)

*The Central and Southern Bahamas Guide*, Stephen Pavlidis (0-96395-669-8) (SWP)

*The Cruising Guide to Abaco*, Steve Dodge (no ISBN) (WSP) **

### US East Coast and Canada

*Reed's Nautical Almanac: North American East Coast* (1-88466-626-4) (TRP)

*Eldridge Tide and Pilot Book*, Marion Jewett White (1-88346-504-4) (ETP)

*Atlantic Coast*, Embassy Marine (0-93052-729-1) (EMP)

*Light List & Waypoint Guide: Maine to Texas*, John & Leslie Kettlewell (0-07034-301-2) (IM)

*Cruising Guide to the Florida Keys*, Frank Papy (0-96198-381-7) (CGP)

*Waterway Guide, Southern Edition* (0-91596-292-6) (IPC) **

*Intracoastal Waterway Facilities Guide*, Bob & Barbara Smith (0-96409-531-9) (self-published)

*The Intracoastal Waterway Chartbook*, John & Leslie Kettlewell (0-07034-300-4) (IM)

*The Intracoastal Waterway, Norfolk to Miami*, Jan & Bill Moeller (0-07042-986-3) (IM) **

*Florida's East Coast*, Embassy Marine (0-93052-747-X) (EMP)

*Cruising Guide to Eastern Florida*, Claiborne S Young (0-88289-992-9) (CGP)

*Cruising Guide to Coastal South Carolina and Georgia*, Claiborne S Young (0-89587-145-9) (CGP)

*Cruising Guide to Coastal North Carolina*, Claiborne S Young (0-89587-204-8) (CGP)

*Waterway Guide, Mid-Atlantic Edition* (0-91596-293-4) (IPC) **

*Guide to Cruising the Chesapeake Bay*, Chesapeake Bay Magazine (1-88472-601-1) (CBM)

*Cruising the Chesapeake: A Gunkholer's Guide*, William Shellenberger (0-07055-286-X) (IM)

*Chesapeake Bay Cruising Guide: Vol 1, Upper Bay*, Tom Neale (0-91875-222-1) (0-91875-222-1) (WC)

*A Cruising Guide to New Jersey Waters*, Donald M Launer (0-81352-238-2) (RUP)

*Waterway Guide, Northern Edition* (0-91596-291-8) (IPC)

*Long Island Sound*, Embassy Marine (0-93052-738-0) (EMP) **

*Cruising Guide to Narragansett Bay & the South Coast of Massachusetts*, Linda & Patrick Childress & Tink Martin (0-07016-304-9) (IM)

*Rhode Island, Maine and New Hampshire*, Embassy Marine (0-93052-739-9) (EMP) **

*Cruising Guide to Maine, Vol 1: Kittery to Rockland*, Don Johnson (0-91875-216-7) (WC)

*Cruising Guide to Maine, Vol 2: Rockport to Eastport*, Don Johnson (0-91875-218-3) (WC)

*Cruising Guide to the Maine Coast*, Hank & Jan Taft & Curtis Rindlaub (0-96492-461-7) (DPP) **

*Cruising Guide to the New England Coast*, Roger F Duncan, John P Ware & Wallace Fenn (0-39303-639-1) (WWN) **

*Coastal Guide to New England*, Stan Patey (0-07048-770-7) (IM)

*Where the Wind Blows: Marine Weather Canada*, Peter J Bowyer (1-50881-119-3) (BB) **

*Cruising Guide to the Bay of Fundy and the St John River*, Nicholas Tracy (0-07065-303-8) (IM) **

*Yachting Guide to the South Shore of Nova Scotia*, Arthur M Dechman (0-96944-160-6) (SSSP)

*Cruising Guide to the Nova Scotia Coast*, John McKelvy (0-96356-681-4) (PTP) **

*A Cruising Guide to Nova Scotia*, Peter Loveridge (0-07038-808-3) (IM) **

*The Cruising Guide to Newfoundland*, Sandy Weld (no ISBN) (PFP)

*Cruising Guide to the Labrador*, Sandy Weld (no ISBN) (PFP)

### Chart packs

*CGP Caribbean charts*:
  No 1, The Virgin Islands (St Thomas to Sombrero)
  No 2, The Northern Leewards (Anguilla to Antigua)
  No 3, The Southern Leewards (Guadeloupe to Martinique)
  No 4, The Windwards (St Lucia to Grenada)

*BBA chart kits*:
  No 2, Canada to Block Island
  No 3, New York to Nantucket

No 4, Chesapeake & Delaware
No 6, Norfolk to Jacksonville
No 7, Florida East Coast
No 9, The Bahamas
No 10, The Virgin Islands

*BBA Compact chart kits*:
  Cape Sable to Clearwater
  Cape Cod Canal to Cape Elizabeth
  Narragansett to Nantucket
  Long Island Sound
  Upper Chesapeake Bay
  Jacksonville to Miami

# APPENDIX C – Publishers

| | | | | |
|---|---|---|---|---|
| ACN | - Adlard Coles Nautical (UK) | | LO | - Lewis Offshore (US) |
| BB | - Breakwater Books (US) | | NP | - Nautorama Publishing (US) |
| BBA | - Better Boating Association (US) | | PB | - Pardey Books (US) |
| BMMP | - Bermuda Maritime Museum Press | | PCP | - Paradise Cay Publications (US) |
| CA | - Cruising Association (UK) | | PFP | - Puffin Press (US) |
| CB | - Cadogan Books (UK) | | PPC | - Paria Publishing Co (Trinidad) |
| CBM | - Chesapeake Bay Magazine (US) | | PTP | - Pilot Press (US) |
| CCC | - Clyde Cruising Club (UK) | | RCCPF | - RCC Pilotage Foundation (UK) |
| CGP | - Cruising Guide Publications (US) | | RUP | - Rutgers University Press (US) |
| CLGP | - Chelsea Green Publishing (US) | | SH | - Sheridan House (US) |
| CMP | - Clyde Marine Press (UK) | | SI | - Sea Inc (US) |
| CMTP | - Cornell Maritime Press (US) | | SOP | - Stationery Office Publications (UK) |
| D&C | - David & Charles (UK) | | SSSP | - South Shore Sailing Publishing (Can) |
| DPP | - Diamond Pass Publishing (US) | | SWP | - Seaworthy Publications (US) |
| EMP | - Embassy Marine Publishing (US) | | TIP | - Tropic Isle Publications (US) |
| ETP | - Eldridge Tide & Pilot Book (US) | | TSP | - Ten Speed Publications (US) |
| FB | - Fernhurst Books (UK) | | VIP | - Virgin Islands Plus Yacht Charters (US) |
| FSP | - Fantaseas Publications (US) | | WCP | - World Cruising Publications (UK) |
| HCP | - HarperCollins Publishers (UK) | | WGP | - Watson-Guptill Publications (US) |
| HF | - Hesperian Foundation (US) | | WLB | - Waterline Books (UK) |
| HO | - UK Hydrographic Office | | WSP | - White Sound Press (US) |
| ICC | - Irish Cruising Club (UK) | | WTC | - Wescott Cove Publishing (US) |
| ILNW | - Imray Laurie Norie & Wilson (UK) | | WWN | - WW Norton (US) |
| IM | - International Marine (US) | | YM | - Yachting Monthly (UK) |
| IPC | - Intertec Publishing Corp (US) | | | |

# APPENDIX D - Suppliers of Books and Charts

## United Kingdom

Imray Laurie Norie & Wilson Ltd, Wych House, The Broadway, St Ives, Huntingdon, Cambs PE17 4BT (tel: 01480 62114; fax: 01480 496109) (BA and Imray charts)
e-mail: ilnw@imray.com
website: http://www.imray.com

Kelvin Hughes Ltd, Royal Crescent Road, Southampton, Hants SO1 1FJ (tel: 01703 634911; fax: 01703 330014) (BA, US and Canadian and Imray charts)
website: http://www.kelvinhughes.co.uk

Reeds Nautical Bookshop, 19 Bridge Road, Hampton Court, Surrey KT8 9EU (tel: 0181 941 7878; fax: 0181 941 8787)
e-mail: tugsrus@abreed.demon.co.uk

Sea Chest Nautical Bookshop, Queen Anne's Battery Marina, Coxside, Plymouth, Devon PL4 0LP (tel: 01752 222012; fax: 01752 252679) (BA and Imray charts, new and secondhand books)

Simpson Lawrence Ltd, 218/228 Edmiston Drive, Glasgow G51 2YT, Scotland (tel: 0141 427 5331; fax: 0141 427 5419; sales hotline: 0141 300 9191)
e-mail: info@simpson-lawrence.co.uk
website: http://www:simpson-lawrence.com

Warsash Nautical Bookshop, 6 Dibles Road, Warsash, Southampton, Hants SO31 9HZ (tel: 01489 572384; fax: 01489 885756) (new and secondhand books)
e-mail: orders@nauticalbooks.co.uk
website: http://www.nauticalbooks.co.uk

Captain O M Watts, 7 Dover Street, London W1X 3PJ (tel: 0171 493 4633; fax: 0171 495 0755)

## USA / Canada

Armchair Sailor Seabooks, 543 Thames Street, Newport, RI 02840 (tel: 401 847 4252; fax: 401 847 1219) (BA, US and Canadian charts)
e-mail: armchair@seabooks.com
website: http://www.seabooks.com

Bluewater Books & Charts, 1481 SE 17th Street, Ft Lauderdale, FL 33316 (tel: 954 763 6533; fax: 954 522 2278)

Marine Press of Canada, 295 Mountain Street, Montreal, Canada (tel: 514 932 8342; fax 514 931 3711) (BA, US and Canadian charts)

Maryland Nautical Sales Inc, PO box 6309, 1400 E Clement Street, Baltimore, MD 21230 (tel: 410 752 4268; fax: 410 685 5068) (BA, US and Canadian charts)
e-mail: sales@mdnautical.com
website: http://www.mdnautical.com

McGill Maritime Services Inc, 369 Place d'Youville, Montreal PQ H2Y 2B7, Canada (tel: 514 849 1125; fax: 514 849 5804) (BA, US and Canadian charts)

The Nautical Mind, 249 Queen's Quay West, Toronto, Ontario M5J 2N5, Canada (tel: 416 203 1163; fax: 416 203 0729)
e-mail: books@nauticalmind.com

New York Nautical Instrument & Service Corp, 140 West Broadway, New York, NY 10013 (tel: 212 962 4522/3; fax: 212 406 8420) (BA, US and Canadian charts)
e-mail: sales@newyorknautical.com
website: http://www.newyorknautical.com

C Plath, 222 Severn Avenue, Annapolis, MD 21403-2569 (tel: 301 263 6700; fax: 301 268 8713) (US distributor for Imray-Iolaire charts)

Sheridan House Inc, 145 Palisade Street, Dobbs Ferry, NY 10522 (tel: 914 693 2410; fax: 914 693 0776)
e-mail: sheribks@aol.com
website: http://www.sheridanhouse.com

Tides End Ltd, Bellingham Chart Printers Division, PO Box 1728, Friday Harbor, WA 98250 (tel: 360 468 3900; fax: 360 468 3939) (US charts and reproductions)
e-mail: sales@tidesend.com
website: http://www.tidesend.com

Wescott Cove Publishing Co, PO Box 130, Stamford, CT 06904 (tel: 203 322 0998) (own range of yachtsmen's charts)

# APPENDIX E – Glossary of British and American Terms

In the same way that an American car has a hood, trunk and fenders while her English equivalent has a bonnet, boot and mudguards, many different sailing and related terms are used on either side of the Atlantic Ocean. In some cases a word may be common to both sides of the Atlantic, but with an alternative use limited to one side only. Others may be regional. Some of the following terms have nothing to do with sailing, but are included as they may be of help with the catering or other shopping.

| British | American |
|---|---|
| alien | extraterrestrial |
| anchor cable (chain and/ or rope) | anchor rode |
| aubergine | egg plant |
| barbecue | grill (noun or verb) |
| beacon | marker |
| bill (restaurant) | tab or check |
| biscuit | cookie |
| boomed staysail | club staysail |
| bottle screw | turnbuckle |
| burgee | pennant |
| can | jug |
| chips | fries, french fries |
| circular saw | skill saw |
| clinker (construction) | lapstrake |
| conical buoy | nun buoy |
| courgette | zucchini |
| cove line | railstripe |
| crisps | chips, potato chips |
| crosstrees | spreaders |
| deckhead | overhead |
| dodgers | weather cloths |
| dowel | plug |
| draught | draft |
| dustbin | trashcan |
| echo-sounder | fathometer or depth sounder |
| enter (at customs etc) | clear in |
| excess (insurance) | deductible |
| eyelet | grommet |
| fairlead | chock |
| fender | fendoff or bumper |
| finger berth | slip |
| first floor | second floor |
| fizzy drink | soda |
| foreigner | alien |
| fretsaw | coping saw |
| gas bottle (or cylinder) | tank or propane tank |
| gas | LPG or propane |
| grease nipple | zerk fitting |
| grill | broil |
| ground floor | first floor |
| guard rails | life lines |
| hatch boards | drop boards |
| inflammable | flammable |
| jam | jelly or preserve |
| jerry can | jerry jug |
| jig saw | sabre saw |
| jubilee clip | hose clip |
| junk rig | Chinese lug rig |
| kicking strap | boom vang |
| Kilner jar | Mason jar |
| lead (electrical) | cord |
| lee cloth | bunkboard |
| lifejacket | PFD (personal flotation device) |
| masonry wall (eg pier) | bulkhead |
| methylated spirits | denatured alcohol, stove alcohol |
| mince, minced beef | ground beef |
| mole wrench or mole grip | vise grip |
| nappies | diapers |
| off licence | liquor store |
| oilskins | foul weather gear |
| Panadol, paracetamol | Tylenol |
| paraffin | kerosene |
| petrol | gasoline (gas) |
| pick-up buoy | toggle |
| pipe wrench | alligator pliers |
| plug (electrical) | connector |
| polyester | Dacron |
| polystyrene | styrofoam |
| polythene | polyethylene |
| pontoon berth (individual) | slip |
| pontoon | dock |
| pontoons | floats |
| post | mail |
| pot (for lobster etc) | trap |
| public telephone | pay phone |
| pump handle screwdriver | yankee screwdriver |
| pumpkin (vegetable) | squash |
| pushpit | stern pulpit |
| range | distance |
| registration papers (yacht's) | documentation |
| return (ticket) | round trip |
| reverse charge call | collect call |
| rigging screw | turnbuckle |
| rowlock | oar lock |
| rubbing strake | rubrail |
| rubbish (biodegradable) | garbage |
| rubbish (non-biodegradable) | trash |
| rucksack | backpack |
| safety line (harness) | life line |
| scone | biscuit |
| shifting spanner | crescent wrench |
| shock cord | bungey cord |
| skin fitting | thru hull |
| skip (for rubbish) | dumpster |
| slip | slipway |

| British | American |
|---|---|
| slipped (of a yacht) | hauled |
| slippery (surface) | slick |
| socket (electrical) | outlet |
| soya granules | TVP (texturised vegetable protein) |
| spanner | wrench |
| split pin/ring | cotter key/pin/ring |
| sprayhood | dodger |
| squash (orange etc) | cordial |
| standpipe | public water supply |
| stilson wrench | pipe wrench |
| stopping | surfacing putty or trowel cement |
| swage | swedge |
| sweetcorn, maize | corn |
| sweets | candy |
| Talurite | Nicopress |
| tap | faucet |
| Terylene | Dacron |
| torch | flashlight |
| transit | range |
| treacle | molasses |
| Very pistol | flare gun |
| video (player) | VCR |
| visitor's berth | transient berth |
| water biscuit | cracker or saltine |
| water tower | standpipe |
| white spirit, turps substitute | mineral spirits |
| yacht | sailboat |

| American | British |
|---|---|
| alien | foreigner |
| alligator pliers | pipe wrench |
| anchor rode | anchor cable (chain and/or rope) |
| backpack | rucksack |
| biscuit | scone |
| boom vang | kicking strap |
| broil | grill |
| bulkhead | masonry wall (eg pier) |
| bumper | fender |
| bungey cord | shock cord |
| bunkboard | lee cloth |
| candy | sweets |
| check (restaurant) | bill |
| Chinese lug rig | junk rig |
| chips, potato chips | crisps |
| chock | fairlead |
| club staysail | boomed staysail |
| collect call | reverse charge call |
| connector (electrical) | plug |
| cookie | biscuit |
| coping saw | fretsaw |
| cord (electrical) | lead |
| cordial | squash (orange etc) |
| corn | sweetcorn, maize |
| cotter key/pin/ring | split pin/ring |
| cracker or saltine | water biscuit |
| crescent wrench | shifting spanner |
| Dacron | Terylene, polyester |
| deductible (insurance) | excess |
| denatured alcohol | methylated spirits |
| depth sounder | echo-sounder |
| diapers | nappies |
| distance | range |
| dock | pontoon |
| documentation | registration papers (yacht's) |
| dodger | sprayhood |
| draft | draught |
| drop boards | hatch boards |
| dumpster | skip (for rubbish) |
| egg plant | aubergine |
| enter (at customs etc) | clear in |
| fathometer | echo-sounder |
| faucet | tap |
| fendoff | fender |
| first floor | ground floor |
| flammable | inflammable |
| flare gun | Very pistol |
| flashlight | torch |
| floats | pontoons |
| foul weather gear | oilskins |
| fries, french fries | chips |
| garbage | biodegradable rubbish |
| gasoline (gas) | petrol |
| grill (noun or verb) | barbecue |
| grommet | eyelet |
| ground beef | mince, minced beef |
| hauled (of a yacht) | slipped |
| hose clip | jubilee clip |
| jelly or preserve | jam |
| jerry jug | jerry can |
| jug | can |
| kerosene | paraffin |
| lapstrake (construction) | clinker |
| life line (harness) | safety line |
| life lines | guard rails |
| liquor store | off licence |
| liquor | spirits or fortified wine |
| LPG | gas |
| mail | post |
| marker | beacon |
| Mason jar | Kilner jar |
| mineral spirits | white spirit, turps substitute |
| molasses | treacle |
| Nicopress | Talurite |
| nun buoy | conical buoy |
| oar lock | rowlock |
| outlet (electrical) | socket |
| overhead | deckhead |
| pay phone | public telephone |
| pennant | burgee |
| PFD (personal flotation device) | lifejacket |
| pipe wrench | stilson wrench |
| plug | dowel |
| polyethylene | polythene |
| propane tank | gas bottle (or cylinder) |
| propane | gas |
| railstripe | cove line |
| range | transit |
| rip-rap | underwater rubble (around breakwaters etc) |
| round trip (ticket) | return |
| rubrail | rubbing strake |

| | | | |
|---|---|---|---|
| sabre saw | jig saw | turnbuckle | bottle screw or rigging screw |
| sailboat | yacht | TVP (texturised vegetable protein) | soya granules |
| second floor | first floor | Tylenol | Panadol, paracetamol |
| skill saw | circular saw | VCR | video (player) |
| slick | slippery (surface) | vise grip | mole wrench or mole grip |
| slip | finger or pontoon berth (individual) | weather cloths | dodgers |
| slipway | slip | wrench | spanner |
| soda | fizzy drink | yankee screwdriver | pump handle screwdriver |
| spreaders | crosstrees | yawl boat | push boat (alongside) |
| squash (vegetable) | pumpkin | zerk fitting | grease nipple |
| standpipe | water tower | zucchini | courgette |
| stern pulpit | pushpit | | |
| stove alcohol | methylated spirits | | |
| styrofoam | polystyrene | | |
| surfacing putty | stopping | | |
| swedge | swage | | |
| tab (restaurant) | bill | | |
| tank or propane tank | gas bottle (or cylinder) | | |
| T-bone collision | port and starboard collision | | |
| thru hull | skin fitting | | |
| toggle | pick-up buoy | | |
| transient berth | visitor's berth | | |
| trap | pot (for lobster etc) | | |
| trash | non-biodegradable rubbish | | |
| trashcan | dustbin | | |
| trowel cement | stopping | | |

## Weights and measures

The following are intended as reminders only – full conversion tables will be found in most almanacs and some cruising guides. Liquid measures are assumed to be of water.

| *British* | *American* | *Metric* |
|---|---|---|
| (Long) ton = 2240 lb | (Short) ton = 2000 lb | Tonne = 2204 lb |
| Gallon = 160 fl oz | Gallon = 128 fl oz | |
| Pint = 20 fl oz | Pint = 16 fl oz | |
| | Cup = 8 fl oz | |

# APPENDIX F - The Beaufort Wind Scale

UK shipping forecasts give wind speeds in terms of the Beaufort Scale. Note that the table below gives equivalent wind speeds in knots rather than statute miles per hour.

| Beaufort number | Descriptive term | Mean wind speed knots | Mean wind speed m/sec | Probable mean wave height | | Likely sea conditions |
|---|---|---|---|---|---|---|
| 0 | Calm | 0-1 | 0-0.2 | – | – | Flat glassy calm |
| 1 | Light air | 1-3 | 0.3-1.5 | 0.1 m | 4 in | Low glassy ripples |
| 2 | Light breeze | 4-6 | 1.6-3.3 | 0.2 m | 8 in | Small waves without crests |
| 3 | Gentle breeze | 7-10 | 3.4-5.4 | 0.6 m | 2 ft | Small waves, crests beginning to break |
| 4 | Moderate breeze | 11-16 | 5.5-7.9 | 1 m | 3 ft | Longer waves, many with white crests |
| 5 | Fresh breeze | 17-21 | 8.0-10.7 | 2 m | 6 ft | Moderate cresting waves, some spray |
| 6 | Strong breeze | 22-27 | 10.8-13.8 | 3 m | 10 ft | Large waves with breaking crests |
| 7 | Near gale | 28-33 | 13.9-17.1 | 4 m | 13 ft | Large waves with some blown spume |
| 8 | Gale | 34-40 | 17.2-20.7 | 5.5 m | 18 ft | Very large waves with foam blown off crests |
| 9 | Strong gale | 41-47 | 20.8-24.4 | 7 m | 23 ft | High waves, visibility affected by spray |
| 10 | Storm | 48-55 | 24.5-28.4 | 9 m | 30 ft | Very high waves with overhanging crests |
| 11 | Violent storm | 56-63 | 28.5-32.6 | 11.5 m | 38 ft | Very high waves, sea white with foam |
| 12 | Hurricane | 64+ | 32.7+ | 14 m+ | 46 ft+ | Giant waves, air full of foam and spray |

# APPENDIX G - Weather Forecasts

Details of some ocean weather forecasts were given in Chapter 10. This Appendix provides selected information about weather forecasts that are available on the margins of the North Atlantic. As well as being of assistance whilst cruising in an area, they will often be useful during a passage, particularly in the early or latter parts of it.

A very large number of forecasts are available and comprehensive information is beyond this book. Complete details are given in *Admiralty List of Radio Signals, Volume 3, Parts 1 and 2*. These two books cover the whole world, but unfortunately both volumes are needed for an Atlantic crossing. It is emphasised that this Appendix is not intended to be a substitute for them, but rather to give brief details of some of the more useful English language forecasts for the voyaging yachtsman. It should be borne in mind that the information is as of February 1998 and details may change.

All times given are Universal Time, the modern equivalent of GMT; frequencies, unless otherwise indicated, are in kHz and are SSB. Those given for Weatherfax transmissions are the carrier frequency. Receivers (other than those dedicated solely to Weatherfax) normally need to be tuned to a frequency offset from this to receive the signals.

## Europe

### British Meteorological Office Shipping Forecast
*Times*: 0048, 0535, 1201, 1754 (but 1 hour earlier when Daylight Saving Time is in force, ie these times are 'clock' times)
*Frequency*: 198 Mode A3E (AM)
The chart shows the areas covered. The forecast starts with a list of areas for which gale warnings are in force. There is then a general synopsis followed by the forecast for each area for the next 24 hours. This takes the form: wind direction; wind speed in Beaufort notation; weather (eg fair, rain, showers etc); visibility (good >5 miles, moderate 2–5 miles, poor 1/2–2–1 mile, fog < 1/2 mile). The terms *imminent*, *soon* and *later* refer to < 6 hours, 6–12 hours and > 12 hours respectively. At 0048 and 0535 the area forecasts are followed by reports of actual conditions at various points on the coast of the British Isles.

This is a long established, accurate weather forecast that will meet most needs until the areas covered by Radio France Internationale (see Chapter 10) are reached.

### Gibraltar
*Times*: Throughout the day at frequent intervals, but particularly at 0730, 0830, 1130
*Frequency*: 1458 Mode A3E (AM)
Forecast for the area within 50 miles of Gibraltar. It is particularly useful for those transiting the Straits.

### Azores (Horta)
*Times*: 0935, 2135
*Frequency*: 2657
Forecast in Portuguese and English for the area within 50 miles of the Azores.

### Madeira
*Times*: 0905, 2105
*Frequency*: 2657
Forecast in Portuguese and English for the area within 50 miles of Madeira.

### Northwood (UK) Weatherfax
*Times*: Schedule 0230, 1530
    Surface analysis: 0400, 1545
    Forecast: 0320, 0650, 0950, 1210, 1500, 1800, 2120, 2320
*Frequencies*: 3652, 4307, 6425.5, 8331.5
Other information is transmitted at other times. The schedule gives details.
The area covered goes south to 32°N and west to 44°W.

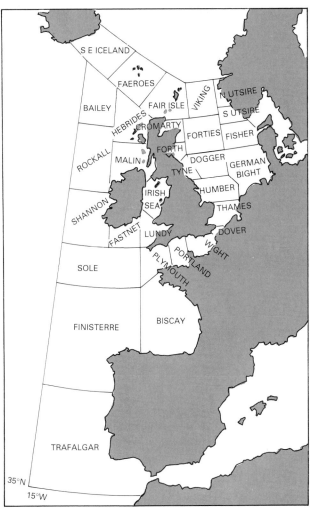

*Chart 79*    BBC weather forecast areas.

The information given at each forecast time varies, but over the 24-hour period forecasts for 1, 2, 3, 4 and 5 days are given. The Fleet Weather and Oceanographic Centre produces this forecast.

### Offenbach (Germany) Weatherfax
*Times*: Schedule: 1111
    Surface analysis: 0430, 0525, 1050, 1600, 2200
    Surface analysis (extended area): 0745, 1810
    24-hr forecast: 0512, 0730, 1832
    48-hr forecast: 0808, 0845
    72-hr forecast: 0821, 1900
    96-hr forecast: 0834
Additional information is transmitted at other times. The schedule gives details.
Frequencies: 3855, 7880, 13882.5
The extended area covers most of the North Atlantic of interest to voyaging yachtsmen, including much of the tradewind crossing, whilst the remaining transmissions cover the eastern half of the ocean.

## The Caribbean

Within the Caribbean, many VHF stations give local forecasts, as do local radio stations. These will give very frequent updates if there is a hurricane in the vicinity. Additionally, many of the popular cruising ports have a local VHF 'cruisers' net'. These usually operate in the mornings, generally at some time between 0700 and 0900, and normally include a weather forecast, either for the local area or, more often, for the whole Caribbean. The Caribbean SSB Weather Net (see Chapter 10) is also useful.

### Trinidad (North Post)
*Times*: 1250, 1850
*Frequencies*: 2735, 3165
Forecast for Trinidad, Tobago and the Eastern Antilles.

### Radio Trinidad
*Times*: 1030, 1200, 1500, 1630, 2000, 2350 (Sundays: 1045, 1200, 1630, 2345)
*Frequency*: 730 Mode A3E (AM)
Forecast for the Lesser Antilles.

### San Juan (Puerto Rico)
*Times*: 0305, 1505
*Frequency*: 2670 kHz
Forecast by the US Coast Guard for the eastern Caribbean, Puerto Rico and Virgin Island waters.

### Nassau
*Times*: On the odd hours (0100, 0300 etc)
*Frequency*: 2522
Forecast for the Bahamas and adjacent waters.

### Radio Bahamas
*Times*: 0815, 1315, 1845
*Frequencies*: 810, 1240, 1540 All Mode A3E (AM)
Forecast for the Bahamas.

### Bermuda Harbour Radio
*Times*: 1235, 2035
*Frequency*: 2582
Bermudan waters and the US offshore waters forecasts.

## United States

In addition to the High Seas Forecast mentioned in Chapter 10, American weather broadcasts can generally be divided into three types. The *inshore waters* or *local* forecast (sometimes called, confusingly, the coastal waters forecast) covers the area within VHF range of the shore. It is broadcast continuously in all areas on one of the US weather frequencies (WX1 - 162.55 MHz, WX2 - 162.4 MHz and WX3 - 162.475 MHz). The forecast varies in content and usually includes weather statistics and a land forecast, as well as marine information. Listening on one of these three channels when within VHF range of mainland USA, Bermuda, the Virgin Islands and Puerto Rico will give the appropriate forecast.

The *coastal waters* forecast covers the area from the coast out to the 1000 fathom line – approximately 100-150 miles. This zone is divided into numbered areas, from 1 and 2 at the Gulf of Maine and Nova Scotia down to 11, between Florida and Cuba. The forecast for these areas may be transmitted with the continuous VHF inshore forecast or can be obtained from one of the HF broadcasts detailed below.

The *offshore waters* forecast covers from the 1000 fathom line out to about 65°W and is split into two areas north and south of 32°N. The East Caribbean area covers most of the Lesser Antilles.

Coastal and offshore forecasts are transmitted by a large number of stations, and only a selection of them is given here. Forecasts for areas not of interest to the Atlantic voyager, eg Gulf of Mexico areas, are not mentioned, although they may be broadcast at the same times. Usually the transmission is by computer generated voice and this can, at first, be difficult to understand; a tape recorder will be useful. Much of the same information is also broadcast by radio telex. Most Weatherfax software packages for use with a PC can decode these. Full details, including times and frequencies, are not included here but are given in *Admiralty List of Radio Signals, Volume 3*.

### Whisky Oscar Mike (Pennsuco, Florida)
*Times*: 1300, 2300
*Frequencies*: 4363, 8722, 13092, 17241, 22738
Offshore forecast (south) and East Caribbean

### November Mike November (US Coast Guard Portsmouth, Virginia)
Different frequencies are in use at different times, as follows:

| Frequency | Time |
|---|---|
| 4426 | 0400, 0530, 1000 |
| 6501 | 0400, 0530, 1000, 1130, 1600, 2200, 2330 |
| 8764 | 0400, 0530, 1000, 1130, 1600, 1730, 2200, 2330 |
| 13089 | 1130, 1600, 1730, 2200, 2330 |
| 17314 | 1730 |

Selected forecasts (including the High Seas Forecast) are transmitted at these times on a complex schedule, details of which are given during the broadcasts. The most useful times to listen to initially are 0400, 1000, 1600, 2200.

### Whisky Oscar Oscar (Ocean Gate, New Jersey)
*Times*: 1200, 2200
*Frequencies*: 4387, 8749
Coastal and offshore (north) forecast

### November Mike Foxtrot (Boston)
*Times*: 0440, 1040, 1640, 2240
*Frequency*: 2670
Coastal and offshore (north) forecast

### Boston (Marshfield) Weatherfax
The schedule is complicated, but very comprehensive information for the whole north Atlantic can be obtained.

*Times*:  Schedule part 1: 0243, 1903
Schedule part 2: 0254, 1914
Surface Analysis (east): 0325, 0402, 0925, 1002, 1525, 1723, 2125, 2202
Surface Analysis (west): 0338, 0415, 0938, 1015, 1538, 1736, 2138, 2215
24-hr forecast: 0815, 2015
24-hr wind/wave forecast: 0825, 2025
48-hr forecast: 0855, 2055

Other information, much of it useful, is transmitted at other times. The schedule gives details.
*Frequencies*: 6340.5, 9108, 12750

## Canada

Continuous VHF forecasts, similar to those in the USA, are given. These will be on either WX5 – 161.650 MHz or WX6 – 161.775. These are the ship receive frequencies of International channels 21 and 83.

### Yarmouth
*Times*: 0540, 1040, 1625, 1730, 2348
*Frequency*: 2749
Offshore forecasts for Southern Nova Scotia and Maine waters.

### Halifax
*Times*: 0603, 1203, 1803, 2310
*Frequency*: 2749
Offshore forecast for Nova Scotia waters.

### St John s
*Times*: 0007, 1637
*Frequency*: 2598
Offshore forecast for Newfoundland waters.

# INDEX

**Page numbers in bold refer to illustrations**